A Linguistic History

A Linguistic History of Arabic

JONATHAN OWENS

OXFORD
UNIVERSITY PRESS

OXFORD
UNIVERSITY PRESS

Great Clarendon Street, Oxford OX2 6DP

Oxford University Press is a department of the University of Oxford.
It furthers the University's objective of excellence in research, scholarship,
and education by publishing worldwide in

Oxford New York

Auckland Cape Town Dar es Salaam Hong Kong Karachi
Kuala Lumpur Madrid Melbourne Mexico City Nairobi
New Delhi Shanghai Taipei Toronto

With offices in

Argentina Austria Brazil Chile Czech Republic France Greece
Guatemala Hungary Italy Japan Poland Portugal Singapore
South Korea Switzerland Thailand Turkey Ukraine Vietnam

Oxford is a registered trade mark of Oxford University Press
in the UK and in certain other countries

Published in the United States
by Oxford University Press Inc., New York

© Jonathan Owens 2006

The moral rights of the author have been asserted
Database right Oxford University Press (maker)

First published 2006
First published in paperback 2009

All rights reserved. No part of this publication may be reproduced,
stored in a retrieval system, or transmitted, in any form or by any means,
without the prior permission in writing of Oxford University Press,
or as expressly permitted by law, or under terms agreed with the appropriate
reprographics rights organization. Enquiries concerning reproduction
outside the scope of the above should be sent to the Rights Department,
Oxford University Press, at the address above

You must not circulate this book in any other binding or cover
and you must impose the same condition on any acquirer

British Library Cataloguing in Publication Data
Data available

Library of Congress Cataloguing in Publication Data
Data available

Typeset by SPI Publisher Services, Pondicherry, India
Printed in Great Britain
on acid-free paper by MPG Books Group, Bodmin and King's Lynn

ISBN 978–0–19–929082–6 (Hbk.)   978–0–19–956330–2 (Pbk.)

1 3 5 7 9 10 8 6 4 2

Acknowledgements and Dedication

THE challenge of developing a critical, coherent interpretation of Arabic linguistic history first confronted me when I began teaching a three-semester course on the subject at Bayreuth University, a course which through the (I would like to imagine) enthusiastic participation of students constantly presented new issues and perspectives.

A number of individuals contributed to the working and reworking of this book. Two anonymous readers provided stimulating criticism to the entire work, while Orin Gensler set out various challenging objections to Ch. 4, and for Ch. 6 Janet Watson gave helpful and pertinent criticisms and suggestions for new solutions. I would like especially to acknowledge the contribution of my colleague Pierre Larcher for the incisive critical insights he has provided in innumerable discussions, beginning many years ago in Benghazi.

The research on Nigerian Arabic, cited frequently in this book, has been supported for many years through the generosity of the Deutsche Forschungsgemeinschaft (German Research Council). In Nigeria, Dr Jidda Hassan of Maiduguri University provided many native insights into his language, while the university administration has generously supported and encouraged my continuing work there.

Not least I would like to acknowledge the invaluable support given me at Bayreuth University over many years by Klaus Wolf of the computer center as well as Dr Brigitte John for providing me with map templates.

The correspondence with John Davey of OUP was prompt, invigorating, critical, and encouraging.

Finally I would like to thank the publishers Harrassowitz Verlag for allowing me to reproduce portions of 'Al-Idghaam al-Kabiyr and the History of Arabic', which appeared in W. Arnold and Bobzin, H. (eds.) (2002). *Sprich doch mit deinen Knechten Aramäisch, wir verstehen es. Festschrift for Otto Jastrow* (Wiesbaden: Harrassowitz), 503–20, the Oxford University Press for allowing reproduction of large portions of 'Case and Proto-Arabic', *Bulletin of the School of Oriental and African Studies* 61: 51–73 and 217–27, as well as John Benjamins for allowing reprint from *Diachronica* 22 of parts of the article 'Pre-Diaspora Arabic: Dialects, Statistics and Historical Reconstruction'.

I dedicate the book to the memory of my brother Christopher.

Contents

Abbreviations and Symbols	x
Maps	xi

1.	Introduction: A Language and Its Secrets	1
	1.1. Proto-Arabic, Basic Terms	2
	1.2. The Early Sources	5
	1.3. The Role of the Modern Dialects in Interpreting Arabic Language History	8
	1.4. Scope of Work	13
	1.5. Language Change and Language Transmission	15
	1.6. A Critical Look at Some Truisms in Arabic Historical Linguistics	20
	1.7. Summary of Chapters	30
2.	Old Arabic, Neo-Arabic and Comparative Linguistics	34
	2.1. A Method vs. a Logical Matrix	34
	2.2. Stages in Arabic	38
	2.3. Arabic and the Dialects	43
	2.4. Neo-Arabic and the Neo-German school	47
	2.5. The Past is the Present: A Modern Logical Matrix	74
	2.6. The Arabic Tradition	75
	2.7. Conclusion	77
3.	Case and Proto-Arabic	79
	3.1. Introduction	80
	3.2. Case in the Afroasiatic Phylum	80
	3.3. Classical Arabic	85
	3.4. The Modern Dialects	101
	3.5. Case and Caseless Arabic	114
4.	Al-Idgham al-Kabiyr and Case Endings	119
	4.1. *Sharḥ Ṭayyibat al-Nashr:* A Fifteenth-Century Treatise on Koranic Variants	123
	4.2. Linguistic Attributes of 'Major Assimilation'	125
	4.3. Interpretive Summary	129

viii Contents

5. Pre-Diasporic Arabic in the Diaspora: A Statistical Approach to
   Arabic Language History 137
   5.1. Introduction 137
   5.2. Dialects, Procedure, Initial Results 142
   5.3. Statistical Results and their Meaning 151
   5.4. Interpretations 157
   5.5. The Interpretation of Arabic Linguistic History 166
   5.6. Statistics, Reconstruction, Hypothesis Testing 168
   5.7. Three Caveats 172
   5.8. Problems in Coding 173

6. Nigerian Arabic and Reconstruction of the Imperfect Verb 184
   6.1. The Basic Imperfect Verb 184
   6.2. Historical Significance 189
   6.3. Epenthesis 193
   6.4. The Old Arabic Evidence 194
   6.5. The Reconstructions and the Classical Arabic Verbal
        Mode Endings 195

7. *Imala* 197
   7.1. *Imala* in Old Arabic 197
   7.2. *Imala* in the Modern Dialects 212
   7.3. Reconstruction 220

8. Suffix Pronouns and Reconstruction 230
   8.1. Pausal and Context Forms and Case Endings 230
   8.2. Suffix Pronouns and Case Endings 234
   8.3. Pronominal Suffixes, Case Endings and Epenthetic Vowels
        in Dialects 235
   8.4. Syllable Structure 237
   8.5. A Data Survey 237
   8.6. Unproblematic Cases, Some Easy Generalizations 239
   8.7. More Difficult Cases 245
   8.8. Case Traces? 255
   8.9. Harris Birkeland and Old Arabic Object Pronoun
        Reconstruction 259

9. Summary and Epilogue 266
   9.1. Reconstruction and Continuity with Old Arabic 266
   9.2. Epilogue 267

Appendix 1. List and short summary of dialects included in study	271
Appendix 2. List of features used in comparison, Chapter 5, with brief exemplification	276
Appendix 3. Imala *in Zamaxshari*	281
Appendix 4. Table of suffix pronouns used in reconstructions in Chapter 8	283
References	285
Index	301

Abbreviations and Symbols

*	Pre-diasporic reconstructed form
**	Proto-Arabic form
#	Word boundary
~	Variant forms
1	First person
2	Second person
3	Third person
ABS	Absolutive
ACC	Accusative
C	Consonant
CA	Classical Arabic
CB	Christian Baghdadi
ELA	Eastern Libyan Arabic
F	Feminine
G	Guttural consonant
GEN	Genitive
H	Short high vowel, [i] or [u]
IN	Intrusive 'in' suffix in participal constructions
IND	Indicative
JB	Jewish Baghdadi
M	Masculine
MB	Muslim Baghdadi
N	Noun
NA	Neo-Arabic
NOM	Nominative
OA	Old Arabic
PL	Plural
Q	QurʔAan; Koranic citation
SA	Standard Arabic
SG	Singular
V	Vowel
WSA	Western Sudanic Arabic

Maps

1. Sample points, Middle Eastern dialects — 139
2. North African sample points — 140
3. Western Sudanic Arabic — 141
4. Reconstruction based on modern dialects of pre-diasporic *-in in participal forms — 162

1

Introduction: A Language and Its Secrets

Arabic has always been a puzzle to those who delve into its intricacies. A good number of medieval Arabic grammar studies include the word 'secret' or 'secrets' in their title, that of the twelfth-century grammarian Al-Anbari, for instance, ʔAsraar al-ʕArabiyya, 'The Secrets of Arabic', or Ibn Jinni's (d. 1002), Sirr Ṣinaaʕat al-ʔiʕraab, 'The Secret of the Craft of Grammar (or Inflection)'. Others unlock its secrets, such as Sakkaki's Miftaaħ al-ʕUluwm, 'The Key to the Sciences', and some, like the early tenth-century grammarian Ibn Al-Sarraj's Al-Uṣuwl fiy l-Naħw, 'The Foundations of Grammar' describe the core of the language. Secrets abound no less so today than 1,000 years ago when Ibn Al-Sarraj was active. Indeed, as the modern linguistic sciences expand, so too do the questions contemporary scholars ask of the language.

It is a source of endless fascination, however, that many issues which press on us today were equally addressed by the founders and early practitioners of Arabic grammar as well. Through their genius arose a core of linguistic thinking which was, in its theoretical underpinnings, significant in its own right, but which also produced a descriptive corpus of great detail. This corpus entices with its own secrets, one of which I seek to look into in this book. One key in this instance comes from the nineteenth century in the form of the comparative method, the secret, the form of Arabic spoken during and before the Arabic-Islamic diaspora of the early Islamic era. To unravel it, it is not only the early sources of Arabic, or Old Arabic as I term the collective early sources, which are relevant, but also the vast fabric of contemporary spoken Arabic, the Arabic dialects which have a central role to play. Bringing the two sources together in a cooperative, rather than dichotomous, antagonistic fashion, as has been a tradition in Western Arabic studies, yields new insights into the history of Arabic.

1.1. Proto-Arabic, Basic Terms

The study of Arabic language history in the Western scholarly tradition does not want for terminology. Old Arabic (*Altarabisch*), Neo- or New Arabic (*Neuarabisch*), proto-Neo-Arabic, proto-peripheral Arabic, poetic koine (*Dichtersprache*), and Middle Arabic are but some of the terms encountered. To provide an initial orientation it is useful to outline my own basic vocabulary used in describing historical varieties of Arabic. Note that I characterize a number of the following terms in a way different from their current use in many Arabicist circles.

1. *Proto-Arabic*. The fundamental object of any historical linguistics is the reconstruction of a proto-language. This is a well-known and established concept which will be familiar to most readers, and which is not dependent as a concept or as a method of application on the circumstances of any individual language or language family. The initial goal of a historical treatment of Arabic should be the reconstruction of a proto-language. Curiously, among the many terms in the Western Arabicist tradition, proto-Arabic is one relatively rarely encountered, though for present purposes it is the key object of study.

2. *Pre-diasporic Arabic*. Pre-diasporic Arabic plays an important role in this work. It is derived as follows. Beginning with the Arabic-Islamic expansion of the seventh century, Arabs and Arabic spread with great speed throughout the Middle East and North Africa. Indicative dates are, for instance, Fusṭaṭ (Cairo) founded in 643, Aswan already reached by 641, Andalusia (Spain) entered in 711, and Uzbekistan by 710. Arabic was suddenly spoken across a latitude stretching from the western tip of Europe to the western border of China. Migrations into these regions continued, to differing degrees of intensity in different regions at different periods, up to about the seventeenth century. With a large-scale Arabicization of the western Sahara (Mauritania, sixteenth century) and large, but not dominant influxes of Arab speakers into the western Sudanic region (fourteenth–sixteenth centuries) and into Cilicia in south central Turkey (seventeenth century), this expansion roughly reached its current borders (see Appendix 1 for region-by-region summaries). Comparing the linguistic results of this expansion, for instance Uzbekistan Arabic and the Arabic of the Lake Chad area, it stands to reason that features common to the two, particularly features which are in some sense rare or unusual, are explained not by chance independent development but by common origin. Given the great distance, both in time and geography between the two exemplified areas, this origin must be found at a time and place when the ancestral populations

were still together. This is pre-diasporic times, the Arabic associated with it, pre-diasporic Arabic.

Pre-diasporic Arabic is chronologically situated. However, the exact limits of its extent are at this point approximate. As an endpoint, I propose 790. This in fact is a date well after the initial Arab-Islamic expansion. The significance of this date is that it is when Sibawaih (d. 177/793, Islamic/Christian calendar) was active as a linguist. To the extent that any results of reconstruction based on contemporary dialects are comparable to Old Arabic sources, Sibawaih is the best point of comparison, since he is the very earliest source (or, problematically, the variant Koranic reading tradition, which is a generation before Sibawaih). Thus, Sibawaih is taken as an eyewitness to the pre-diasporic varieties. This is, admittedly, a convenient fiction. Sibawaih himself, so far as is known, never traveled personally in the Arabian peninsula and therefore was never eyewitness to the pre-diasporic homeland of Arabic. He was a native Persian speaker active in Basra who knew about varieties of Arabic from individuals in the Basran diaspora. Nonetheless, nearly all tribal (e.g. Qays, Banu Waaʔil, Tamimi) and areal (e.g. Hijaz, Medina) designations found in Sibawaih are situated in the Arabian peninsula, which allows the fiction to be associated with pre-diasporic regions.

For the starting date one can use the initial Arab-Islamic expansion, which began around 630. Kufa and Basra, for instance, were the first Islamic cities founded in southern Iraq, in 16/636 and 17/638 respectively. Of course, an Arab expansion into the lands bordering the Arabian peninsula had begun well before Islamic times (Retsö 2003). However, as the summary in the previous paragraph makes clear, it is only in Islamic times that the expansion moved well outside of this area.

I therefore propose the period 630–790 as the era of pre-diasporic Arabic. This is a *terminus ad quem*. A form reconstructed to this era in all likelihood existed before as well. Further reconstruction is thereby implied, as will be elaborated on below in this section. Eventually, moreover, it will be desirable to relate results of linguistic reconstructions such as undertaken here, more closely to population movements, as discussed at greater length in 1.4 below.

Pre-diasporic Arabic is a variety based on the results of reconstruction of modern dialects. Not all such reconstruction of course leads to pre-diasporic Arabic. A great deal of historical linguistic development occurred locally in the post-diaspora era. What can be reconstructed as pre-diasporic can only be established on a case-by-case consideration of data. While pre-diasporic Arabic is a reconstructed variety, it is not necessarily a unitary variety. To the contrary, it will often lead to the postulation of multiple pre-diasporic forms. In Ch. 8, for instance, the 2MPL object suffix is reconstructed as *-*kum*

∼ *-kun ∼ *-ku in the pre-diasporic period. This is not unexpected. Pre-diasporic Arabic, reconstructed to a period between 630 and 790, is roughly of the same chronological period as are the multifarious forms discussed in the Old Arabic literature (see next terminological point and sect. 1.2 below). A reconstructed pre-diasporic Arabic expands and complements the observations found in this literature.

Methodologically, pre-diasporic Arabic does, however, add an interpretive level between proto-Arabic and later varieties. In the model proposed here, proto-Arabic derives from reconstruction based on Old Arabic sources, as defined in the next point, and a reconstructed pre-diasporic Arabic, as described here.

In the current work the main focus is on pre-diasporic Arabic. This follows from the methodological incorporation of contemporary dialects into Arabic language history. This will be elaborated upon in sect. 1.3 below and elsewhere. However, at this point in our research I do not think it possible to neatly differentiate pre-diasporic from proto-Arabic on a priori grounds. A reconstructed pre-diasporic form could turn out to be a proto-Arabic form as well.

I would note here that some chapters concentrate explicitly on a reconstruction of pre-diasporic Arabic, Ch. 5 in its entirety and for the most part Chs. 2 and 6 as well. Chapter 7 offers a reconstruction both of pre-diasporic Arabic, and the deeper level of proto-Arabic, as do Chs. 3 and 4, though the latter treats only Old Arabic sources. Chapter 8 also presents both pre-diasporic and proto-Arabic reconstructions, though the weight there is on the former.

3. *Old Arabic.* Various reasons for the reticence to develop a proto-Arabic in the Western tradition will be suggested in the next chapter. Here I would mention just one: the early Arabic sources are so rich and detailed that they pre-empt a need to think in developmental terms, which the reconstruction of a proto-language entails. Arabic emerges fully existent at the hands of a sophisticated Arabic tradition in the eighth century. I term the complex of early written sources Old Arabic.[1] Those utilized in this work are described in 1.2 below. This terminology is at variance with the reigning Arabicist

---

[1] Another application of the term 'Old Arabic' is found in Macdonald (2000: 49 ff.), where it refers to the language in the few epigraphic traces in which it is attested. He contrasts Old Arabic with a sister branch of North Arabian, Ancient North Arabian (2000: 41), which is a group of diverse but closely related languages also attested epigraphically. One feature distinguishing Old Arabic from Ancient North Arabian is that in the former the definite article is ʔl while in the latter it is h-. In this article, Macdonald does not discuss where his 'Old Arabic' is to be situated relative to Classical Arabic or other linguistic constructs, other than to note that it is distinct from it (2000: 30).

tradition, which conceives of Old Arabic as a historical linguistic stage, as will be elaborated in Ch. 2.

4. *Classical Arabic, Modern Standard Arabic.* From among these early sources emerged a most enigmatic of chimeras, Classical Arabic. Whereas a characterization, even a definition of Classical Arabic is normally a sine qua non of scholarship on Arabic language history, I consciously avoid giving it any explicit content, even if I refer to the entity at various places in this work. The reason for this is that, as Corriente (1971, 1973, 1975, 1976; also Rabin 1955) emphasized, Classical Arabic is the endpoint of a development within the complex of varieties of Old Arabic. An adequate consideration of the forces which brought Classical Arabic into existence belongs within a broader study of historical Arabic sociolinguistics and this in turn requires a far more detailed reading of the early sources, Sibawaih, Farraʔ, the Koranic reading tradition, the early compilations of Arabic poetry, and so on, than is possible or necessary here. It will be necessary for the sake of practical orientation to refer in places to a set, normative variety of Arabic. For this I generally use either the so-called 'Standard Arabic' (or 'Modern Standard Arabic'), a largely standardized form of the Classical language which is taught in universities in the West, and which is close to the language of contemporary journalism in the Arabic world.

5. *Dialect.* A final term I use with considerable hesitation and with a touch of misgiving, and this is 'dialect'. Problems accruing to the use of this term in Old Arabic will be elaborated on in sect. 1.3 below. As far as contemporary Arabic goes, I much prefer the designation, spoken Arabic. A modern dialect, after all, is nothing more than the Arabic mother tongue. However, the well-known circumstance of diglossia renders a simple equation of mother tongue and dialect impossible. Contemporary spoken Arabic itself is a mixture of a native dialect and the Standard Arabic which is learned in schools and used in much of the Arabic media. T. F. Mitchell (1986) aptly termed this variety Educated Spoken Arabic.

I argue that contemporary Arabic is an essential part of proto-Arabic reconstruction. However, for this purpose it is not any part of spoken Arabic which is relevant, but rather that part of it which is learned as the mother tongue. In keeping with the Arabicist tradition, I term this the dialect.

1.2. The Early Sources

Arabic is blessed by a relatively large quantity of early material, in terms of the history of Western scholarship, perhaps too much. The plenitude of early material I suspect detracted from the need to incorporate later sources into a systematic history of Arabic, a point I elaborate on in the next chapter.

Although direct, contemporary evidence pertaining to Old Arabic exists as early as the fourth century AD, the material is relatively rare and incomplete until the late eighth century. The very earliest monolingual materials are six epigraphic inscriptions found from near Aleppo in northern Syria into southern Jordan. The earliest of these is the Nemara inscription of 328, located southeast of Damascus in Syria (Bellamy 1985). While they are interesting pieces of evidence, the material is so exiguous and hard to interpret that they can hardly be said to constitute an independent source for the interpretation of early Arabic (see sect. 1.6.2 below).

It is only in the Islamic era that early sources of Arabic begin to abound. Assuming standard interpretations of the history of the Koranic text, the so-called *muṣḥaf*, there was a written document by 652 at the latest (the Uthmanic codex). However, this consisted of only the barest consonantal skeleton with no short vowels marked, and even no diacritical points to distinguish consonants. An initial 't' and 'n', for instance, are formally indistinguishable. Moreover, extant Korans from this period do not exist, at best excerpts from early ones (see Puin 1996 on early Koranic fragments).

It was not until the eighth century that complete Koranic renditions (*Qiraaʔaat*), with all consonants and vowels spelled out, became available in the tradition of Koranic readers. Even these, however, are not fully systematized and written down until the tenth century by Ibn Mujahid (d. 324/936), and so it is not until this date that fixed, complete versions of the *Qurʔaan* are in general accessible to us. Ibn Mujahid, moreover, set out not one fixed version, but rather seven, each associated with an eponymous reader (*qaariʔ*, pl. *qurraaʔ*) who flourished in the eighth century. Other scholars (e.g. Jazari) compiled versions with ten and fourteen recognized readers (see Ch. 4 for details). A further uncertainty in using the *Qiraaʔaat* is that it is not always clear to what extent the *Qiraaʔaat* are based on an oral recitation tradition or on a 'philological' interpretation based on interpreting pronunciation from a written text (Larcher 2005a: 253). Despite these open questions, I regard the *Qiraaʔaat* as an important early source for interpreting Old Arabic.

The establishment of fixed versions of the *Qurʔaan* beginning in the second half of the eighth century was complemented by, and part of, an even more significant development, namely the codification of Arabic grammar. This began, and in a sense culminated, in one of the great landmarks of linguistic history, the *al-Kitaab* ('The Book') of the grammarian Sibawaih (d. 177/793). In nearly 1,000 densely written pages, phonetic nooks and syntactic crannies are explored in minute detail.² Sibawaih's importance in an interpretation of language history will be apparent at many places in this book. A second great contribution to early Arabic linguistic thought was the work of the Koranic commentator Farraʔ (d. 207/822). In over 1,000 pages, Farraʔ commented on many linguistic aspects of the QurʔAan in a work bearing the title 'The Meanings of the QurʔAan'.

These two works set the stage for a spate of philological activity on grammar and lexicography by other linguists, a number of whom will be introduced in subsequent chapters. Since, quite obviously, these earliest grammarians had no preconceived model of a standard variety of Arabic, there is found especially in their work a great number of observations on various grammatical and phonological constructions and vocabulary. These earliest sources themselves at times report on such an early diversity that even in the Classical era the comparative method needs to be applied to reconstruct a plausible source (see e.g. Ch. 7 on *imala*).

With an increasing standardization later grammarians, beginning around the early fourth/tenth centuries, had little new to offer as far as variational data goes, except for those with a penchant for gathering anecdotes and observations from earlier sources (e.g. the tireless fifteenth-century grammarian Suyuṭi). I leave these later sources largely untouched, as by and large they repeat the variational observations of the earliest grammarians.³

There are two further early sources with which I do not deal. One is so-called Middle Arabic, discussed in greater detail in the next chapter (sect. 2.3.3). Middle Arabic texts begin to be relatively numerous in the tenth century. As I, along with many other scholars today (see summary in Larcher 2001), view these as having a literary Arabic as their basis, with various dialectal intrusions, it is very difficult to integrate them casually into a consideration of Arabic language history. The time will probably come when use will be made

---

² Contrary to popular belief among some Arabicists (e.g. Mol 2003: 15), Koranic Arabic was not the most important variety serving as a basis for Sibawaih's analysis. This follows alone from the fact that the linguistic form of the QurʔAan was itself during Sibawaih's lifetime still in the process of being fixed according to the various parameters of the QiraaʔAat tradition. An adequate linguistic summary of what sources were used by Sibawaih is so inextricably tied to his linguistic methodology that it is an issue which, as an independent variable, needs to be treated in a separate work. To give one concrete indication of the relative unimportance of the Koranic text for Sibawaih's grammar, in the fifteen pages devoted to ʔimaala (= *imala*), discussed in detail in Ch. 7 below (see particularly Table 7.1), the QurʔAan and the Koranic readers are hardly mentioned.

³ Correlating later with earlier works in this regard is a separate study in and of itself; see e.g. Ch. 7 n. 13. In App. 3 I give one indication for how my assumption is substantiated on the basis of a comparison between Sibawaih's treatment of *imala* and that of Zamaxshari, who lived three and a half centuries after Sibawaih.

of them, but before that happens the Middle Arabic texts themselves will need greater scrutiny and analysis.

The other is early Arabic poetry (pre-Islamic, early Islamic). There are considerable difficulties in gauging the authenticity and status of this œuvre (Blachère 1980: ch. 2 is a good summary of issues, complemented by Zwettler 1978 for the orality factor). Not least is the fact that the collection and systematization of the pre-Islamic and early Islamic poetry was part and parcel of the same intellectual milieu that saw the systematization of grammar and the canonization of Koranic variants, namely the eighth and ninth centuries. In fact, most of today's collections can be traced most directly back to scholars living in the generation after Sibawaih, such as Aṣmaʕi (d. 213/828). A late eighth-century filter is again in place, which veils a direct insight into the more ancient eras. Nonetheless, or perhaps because of this fact, the language of the early poetry is quite uniform and is frequently referred to as a poetic koine.[4] Some scholars equate Classical Arabic with the language of this poetry (Brockelmann 1908: 23; Fück 1950; Bellamy 1985). It may be said that the language of poetry represents one register or variety coexisting with others of its era.[5]

1.3. The Role of the Modern Dialects in Interpreting Arabic Language History

The modern dialects have an indispensable role in an account of Arabic language history. This follows from the logic of the comparative method. Ideally the comparative method yields two basic units, a proto-language and its daughters. The daughters are connected to the proto-language by a set of linguistic rules, sometimes called 'laws'. An adequate historical account of a language should describe the rules by which a proto-language develops into its daughter varieties. In Arabic, the contemporary dialects are daughter varieties. The question is, whose daughters are they?

---

[4] For a contemporary linguistic audience (see Kerswill 2002) the term 'koine' in this context is not a particularly happy one, as the poetic koine does not demonstrably show characteristics of simplification or filtering out of alternative variants (though this is often assumed by scholars, Blachère 1980: 180). It does have a structural unity, though it is not clear that this arose in a process of koinization.

[5] The phrase 'others of its era' should be seen as much as a caveat as a descriptive statement. Against Brockelmann's implication (1908: 24), poetic texts are attested from no earlier a period than are what he terms 'tribal dialects' (*Dialekte der Stämme*). Brockelmann describes the poetic language (*Dichtersprache*) as if it were attested from pre-Islamic times, information on what he terms 'dialects' from a later period. This dichotomization is simply false, as Blachère soberly observes. The problem of dating early texts chronologically with any precision is one which runs throughout the Islamic sciences (see e.g. Gilliot 1990/1999, Rippin 1983/1999 on Koranic exegesis).

As I will argue throughout this book, there is little serious application of the comparative method in an account of the historical development of contemporary spoken Arabic. I think three reasons play a role in this failure, all of which have more to do with the sociopolitical status of the modern dialects and the history of their treatment in the West than with linguistic methodology.

The first concerns the relationship between Classical Arabic and the modern dialects, in particular the fact that the modern dialects have no official legitimization in the Arabic world. To set the two on an equivalent basis, which is what a dispassionate comparativist account must do, could be interpreted as calling into question the asymmetric diglossic relationship (Ferguson 1959a) between the high Classical (or Modern Standard) variety and the low dialect.

A second reason I believe is simply one of convenience. The Classical language offers a ready-made starting point for the summary of the history of Arabic. Fück's prestigious *Arabiya*, discussed in the next chapter (sect. 2.3.2), offers a history of Arabic (subtitle, *Untersuchungen zur arabischen Sprach- und Stil geschichte* [my emphasis]) which starts with the literary language and makes little serious attempt to incorporate dialect material (however defined, see Spitaler's review of 1953). While the title speaks both of language and stylistic history, it is in fact the latter which takes up the lion's share of the work.

A third reason combines two perspectives. The oldest detailed accounts of Classical Arabic are undeniably older, by a range of some 1,000 years, than any detailed accounts of the modern dialects. Coupled with this is an assumed greater complexity of the Classical language relative to the dialects (see e.g. Ferguson 1959b: 1.6.6 for further details). Linking these two perspectives, it is a relatively easy step to interpret the modern dialects as the simplified or even bastardized offspring of an older, more perfect Classical variety (Mahdi 1984: 37).[6]

Taking these three perspectives critically and beginning with the first, while comparing the dialects with the Classical language on an equal footing would be relatively uncontroversial among many linguists, the comparison might be misunderstood for cultural reasons. It may well be assumed for instance that a declaration of linguistic equivalence (as it were)

---

[6] Mahdi admonishes us to study the dialects in order that the negative influences (sicknesses, ʔamraaḍ) of the dialect on the standard language (fuṣḥaa) be eradicated. That is, one studies the dialects not to shed light on the Arabic language as a whole, but rather to purify the standard. Where Chejne's (1969) 'The Arabic Language' mentions the dialects it is often in a derogatory context (e.g. 84), though the discussion of language policy in the final chapters is balanced.

is tantamount to a statement of cultural and political equality between the dialects and the Classical language. Logically, however, linguistic reconstruction is independent of cultural and political considerations.

Considering the second point, convenience is no substitute for consistent application of a well-tested methodology.[7] Just why few serious attempts have been made to reconstruct proto-Arabic is ultimately a question for the historian of Arabic and Semitic studies. One reason, I suspect, is the (understandable) preference among philologists for the written word (Classical Arabic) over the spoken (dialects). What is not written is not fully legitimate. Linguistically orientated comparative studies of Arabic, and more generally oriental and Islamic studies, for the first half of the twentieth century have tended to be dominated by philologists.[8] In more recent years, since about 1960, there has been a remarkable growth in interest in modern dialectal and sociolinguistic aspects of Arabic (see e.g. part 2, 1987 of the journal *Al-ʕArabiyya*). These, however, have been largely restricted to descriptive and so-called theoretical linguistics, to the exclusion of comparative perspectives.

Turning to the third point, it is clear that the relative time of diachronic reconstruction is what comparativists work with, rather than the absolute time of the Gregorian calendar. In terms of absolute time the earliest, extensive sources of Classical Arabic date from the seventh or eighth centuries. These are far younger than the earliest sources for Akkadian, dating from about 2500 BC. No Semiticists, however, would argue that Akkadian therefore must be assumed to represent the earliest state of the Semitic languages. What is criterial is the relative time-scale which develops from the application of the comparative method. Here it emerges, inter alia, that the younger (in absolute terms) Arabic language contains an older inventory of phonological elements (e.g. a complete set of differentiated emphatic correspondences, Moscati et al. 1980: 24) than does the older Akkadian. Relative to the ur-Semitic phonological inventory one can say that Arabic is 'older' (in the sense that it has preserved older traits) than is Akkadian. An analogous argument applies in principle to any comparison between the modern dialects and the Classical language: a priori (i.e. prior to the application of the comparative method and/or internal reconstruction) one does not know whether a given trait in a

---

[7] One of the few explicit attempts is Cowan (1960) who concentrates exclusively on phonology.

[8] I think this prejudice is betrayed, for instance, in Brockelmann's (1908/1982: 6) contention that Akkadian is the oldest independent Semitic language. It is undeniably the oldest one attested in writing. There is, however, no way of proving that it is older than proto-Arabic or proto-Ethiopic (as opposed to an undifferentiated proto-west Semitic such as Brockelmann assumes). On comparative grounds, Diakonoff (1988: 24) assumes a dialectal differentiation of Semitic as early as 4000–5000 BC, which would give adequate time for a differentiated ancestor of Arabic to have arisen, parallel to Akkadian.

dialect is 'older' (in relative terms), 'younger' or 'equivalent' to a comparable trait in the Classical language.

Because it is so important, it is relevant here to consider three further aspects of the term 'Arabic dialect'.

First, there is the issue of what constitutes information on an Arabic dialect. In the contemporary era, I believe it fairly uncontroversial that the dialect is simply the L1 of native speakers. These native varieties may be differentiated by classical dialectological methods, using bundles of isoglosses to define dialect areas. As may be gleaned from the previous discussion, it is far more difficult to agree on what constitutes a 'dialect' in the classical era. A basic problem in my view is that from the perspective of the on-site observers in the late eighth and early ninth centuries, linguists such as Sibawaih and Farraʔ, the dialect-Classical Arabic distinction did not exist as it came to be understood by later linguists, such as Sarraj (d. 316/928) in the early tenth or by modern (or fairly modern) observers such as Brockelmann or Fischer. Thus, a feature which by modern, or even by tenth-century standards such as the 2FSG object suffix -ʃi, as in inna-ʃi 'that-you.F' is clearly 'dialectal' was not conceived of as such by Sibawaih (II: 322; see sect. 8.7.4 below; Owens 2004). This point is a very large issue which can only be sketched here. The issue of Arabic historical sociolinguistics has yet to be dealt with systematically. Without having the space to argue the point in detail, the position taken here is that methodologically it is necessary to distinguish between linguistic and sociolinguistic aspects of Arabic for purposes of interpreting Arabic linguistic history. Linguistically I put all linguistic material, whether that which became canonized in the classical language (the fuṣħaa), or that which may popularly be understood as dialectal, potentially[9] on a par for purposes of reconstructing the language history. Sociolinguistically all varieties are not equal, as many recent studies have shown. Sociolinguistic prestige should not, however, imply precedence in interpreting language history. As a terminological point, for reasons given in the next paragraph, I use the term 'varieties' of Old Arabic, rather than 'dialect' of Old Arabic when speaking of variants attested in old sources.

Secondly, it is not possible to put material from Old Arabic on a par with modern ones for basic descriptive reasons. As far as old varieties go, while tantalizing bits and pieces of odd material from a variety of sources exist (e.g. in Sibawaih, the Koranic reading tradition), there is nowhere near enough to construct an old dialectology in the sense of having a relatively complete

---

[9] This caveat is important. A demonstrable innovation found in a modern dialect cannot be used to reconstruct proto-Arabic.

phonological and morphological account of discrete dialects.[10] This is one reason I prefer the term 'varieties' of Old Arabic.

To illustrate this point an example from Rabin (1951) may be adduced. Rabin's is the most detailed attempt to describe an Old Arabic dialect, which he terms 'ancient West Arabian'. It is clear, however, that his description, admirable though it is, is not a comparative dialectology in a modern sense, nor can it be as the sources for such an undertaking are simply not available. What Rabin did was to sift through many Old Arabic sources, covering the region from Medina into Yemen, and identify local variants distinct from Classical Arabic. In Yemen, Medina, ʔAzd, Bakr, and Qays there is information about the variant ʕanṭa for 'give' (30, CA ʔaʕṭaa), among Hudhail (east of Mecca) and Taghlib (Iraq) about the weakening of an initial hamza (glottal stop) to /w/ or /y/ (82), in the Hijaz about the disappearance of the glottal stop (131). There is not a single feature, however, which is systematically described in the old literature in the form of a modern isogloss. The critical perspective here is the same as the general one for application of the comparative method: just as an historical linguistics requires at least the attempt to apply the comparative method, so too does a dialectology require systematic application of dialectological sampling methods. I should emphasize that these critical remarks are not directed against the remarkable observational achievements of the Arabic grammarians but rather at the unstated assumption among some contemporary Arabicists that an old dialectology is possible.

By contrast, there is today, fortunately, a relative surfeit of information on modern dialects. This has important methodological consequences in the present study. I begin the comparative study with contemporary dialects and work my way backwards, rather than going in the reverse direction, because in the contemporary varieties systematic sets of data can be compared across all domains of grammar.

Thirdly, as already noted, the term 'dialect' in the Arabic tradition of Arabic countries often carries a pejorative connotation due to the modern opposition between 'dialect' vs. 'Standard Arabic'. Only the latter is the 'real' Arabic so far as official recognition in Arabic countries goes, and similarly to speak of Old Arabic 'dialects' is to suggest the same secondary status of a variety opposed to the authentic 'Classical Arabic'. That is, 'dialect' in these terms is not so much a spatial linguistic designation as a sociopolitical one, and a

---

[10] This point is routinely ignored by Arabicists. Diem (1978: 138) for instance states that there are no modern dialects which roughly correlate with an old Arabic dialect. This claim, however, makes the dubious assumption that we have a detailed enough account of old Arabic dialectology to entertain the idea of finding detailed correlations.

negative one at that. This aspect of the term 'Arabic dialect' falls outside the scope of the present book.

1.4. Scope of Work

The book falls within the broad domain of historical linguistics. The essential element in historical linguistics is an application of the comparative method, without which historical linguistics as we know it would not exist. This is one of the great advances in the history of language studies, in theory allowing one to trace a branching differentiation of languages or dialects back to a common ancestor. This is effected via reconstructing unitary proto-forms from differentiated daughter varieties, via rules of change. To take a simple example from the current work, all varieties of Arabic (aside from Creole and pidgin varieties) minimally mark the first person singular of the perfect verb with -t.

(1) Cairene   Iraqi *qultu*   Najdi   Nigerian Arabic
     katab-t   katab-tu   kitab-t   katab ~ katab-t-x

Nigerian Arabic, and west Sudanic Arabic in general, has an unusual variation in this respect. The -*t* appears only before a suffix (to simplify matters). Even where the -*t* does not appear, however, its presence is felt by the stress attraction, explicable if it is assumed that -*t* is present in an underlying representation, hence the contrast, *'katab* 'he wrote' vs. *ka'tab* 'I wrote'. Clearly the 'loss' of the final -*t* in certain contexts in Nigerian Arabic is an innovation in Arabic. This is apparent in two ways: all other varieties maintain a -*t*, and a specific historical rule can be ascertained 'explaining' the lack of -*t* in Nigerian Arabic. Looking at the matter in a reverse order is unnecessarily complicated and unrealistic: if the Nigerian Arabic situation were the original, one would have to explain how a -*t* came to appear in all contexts in all other varieties of Arabic. On this basis a *-*t* (or *-*tu*) can be reconstructed for the 1SG perfect suffix. This proto-form is carried forward in most dialects, but in Nigerian Arabic it splits according to morpho-phonological context.

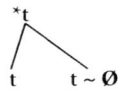

$$\begin{array}{c} {}^{*}t \\ \diagup \diagdown \\ t \quad t \sim \emptyset \end{array}$$

Roughly and glossing over many details (see (1) in sect. 5.2.4), the rule for the split is that -$t \rightarrow \emptyset$ before # (see Ch. 6 n. 2 for discussion).

(2) $t \rightarrow \emptyset$ ____ #

It can be seen that via the comparative method contemporary variation can often be explained as arising from a more uniform proto-variety. Chapters 7 and parts of 8 in particular exemplify this perspective of the comparative method in greater detail.

However, in recent years limits to the application of the comparative method have been pointed out or re-emphasized.[11] Some components of grammar probably do not lend themselves to an application of the method to any considerable time depth (Owens 1996), while effects of intensive language contact will often make an application of the method impossible (Durie and Ross 1996). In the present data as well, phenomena will be highlighted both in contemporary dialects and in the Old Arabic sources which do not necessarily yield unambiguous proto-forms, or which clearly point to the existence of a high degree of variation at the pre-diasporic level and perhaps at the proto-Arabic level as well. Chapters 2–6 and parts of 8 illustrate this perspective.

Moving to the fringes of a linguistic treatment of Arabic, it is a truism that the history of a language is intimately bound up with the history of the peoples who speak it. In some circles of scholarship this truism yields an important source of historical data. Particularly in societies lacking long-term written records, the comparative method applied to contemporary populations has been used as a tool to reconstruct population movements. The relation between language and population movement, for instance, was an important debate in Bantu history in the 1960s and early 1970s (see Guthrie 1962; Greenberg 1972). Where written records exist, the use of language as a mirror for certain historical events has tended to be neglected. This is certainly the case with Arabic. This is also unfortunate. There is, comparatively speaking, a wealth of written sources describing the distribution and spread of Arabic tribes, beginning in pre-Islamic times (Blachère 1980: i; Retsö 2003 for summaries) and continuing into the diaspora (e.g. Donner 1981).

Already in the pre-Islamic era movements from the southwest Arabian peninsula towards the northeast and into Jordan, Syria, and the Euphrates are reported. Arabs had also settled in the Sinai (de Jong 2000: 13). A major division was between the south and west Arabian tribes, sometimes eponymously identified as Qaḥṭaan, and the north and east Arabian groupings of ʕAdnaan (also identified as Rabiyʕa and Muḍar). As Retsö (2003: 24–102) shows, tribal affiliation in Islamic times became notoriously fickle, the subject of contemporary political vicissitudes. It would therefore be naive to expect

---

[11] Just as the comparative method was developed in greatest detail in nineteenth-century Germany, so too was there an early reaction against too rigorous an application of the method, in the work of dialectologists and Schuchardt, who emphasized the effects of contact on language change.

anything like a one-to-one relation between dialect and tribe. In contemporary times, there is relatively little linguistic import attached to the identically named Banu Hassan of Mauritania and Beneesan (< Banu Hassan) of Borno in Nigeria, even if it is plausible that both had a common ancestral origin in the Nile valley. An association between pre-Islamic Arabic dialectology and pre-Islamic tribal affiliation is an even riskier proposition. Names of groups change in different ways from the dialects they speak. Nonetheless, leaving all caveats aside, it may be suggested that if a comparative linguistic history of Arabic working from pre-Islamic times up to the present is attempted, the question can also be addressed of the extent to which the historically attested tribal migrations correlate with historical linguistic reconstructions. The current situation with Arabic comparative linguistic history, characterized as it is by a few simple dichotomies (see below, sect. 1.6.7 and Ch. 2), can only be improved on. I would suggest here that a far more detailed and systematic linguistic reconstruction of Arabic will eventually allow one to countenance closer correlations with historical movements and events documented in written sources.

In short, scholars are further along in summarizing and interpreting the written historical sources than the linguistic. I therefore concentrate exclusively on the latter, emphasizing the direct and systematic links that can be drawn between contemporary spoken Arabic and Old Arabic sources.

1.5. Language Change and Language Transmission

The relation between language and history sketched in the previous section is closely related to another theme which has gained or regained the attention of linguists in recent years, namely the conditions under which language is transmitted from generation to generation. This issue figured prominently as an assumption in the work of Thomason and Kaufman (1988), who assume the unmarked situation to be a complete transmission of a 'language' from one generation to another.

This question is obviously central to an understanding of the history of Arabic, since it is a language which, in the course of its spread over a large geographical expanse, has acquired many speakers via shift. At the outset I will make clear that this is also a question, as with the general theme of the relation between history and language sketched in the previous section, which will not be dealt with in this book. There are two main reasons for this, both of which derive from the observation that an automatic link between language change and the way language is transmitted has not been established. One reason is linguistic, the other extra-linguistic.

Beginning with the first, there have been no attempts to establish constants of change for languages as a whole. To be sure, there have been suggestions for specific subcomponents of language, most notably lexical change in the well-known theory of lexicostatistics developed by Morris Swadesh. As the articles in the two volumes of Renfrew et al. (2000) indicate, however, there is no consensus as to whether lexicostatistics is at all possible, some rejecting it outright (e.g. Matisoff 2000), while others (e.g. Ehret 2000) claim validity for it. Outside of the lexicon, beyond the banal observation that languages or parts thereof may simplify, become more complex, or remain relatively unchanged for relatively long periods of time, no predictive universals are available which can even roughly indicate for a given period of time, what sort of changes a language will be expected to undergo.[12]

As regards to extra-linguistic factors constitutive of the concept of transmission, there are many involved. The number of speakers, degree of multilinguality, prestige relations among languages/speakers of the languages in contact, and the nature of the social relations among the speakers of the various languages, are but some of the relevant variables. Given enough information on these variables, in some cases it is indeed possible to reconstruct plausible developmental frameworks, as will be illustrated below. Generally, however, such information is incomplete, at best, and even when it is relatively complete automatic predictions do not follow.

In linguistic studies the relation between transmission and language change has been documented on a case-by-case basis, usually beginning with the linguistic effects themselves, and moving from them to the social. This perspective was given explicit expression in the work of Thomason and Kaufman (1988), who studied well-documented, or fairly well-documented instances of language change and linked them to the broad sociolinguistic factors which could support the type of change documented. While this work hints that robust historical correlations may be recoverable, it offers few specific links of the type: given sociolinguistic configuration c, expect linguistic change l.

The problem may be sketched on the basis of Arabic, beginning at an extreme which indeed confirms a Lamarkian component of language, namely the formation of a creole. The historical study of creole languages shows that in most instances, extremes of social change are a prerequisite for creole formation. Multilingual populations are thrown together, have limited access

---

[12] Even if, as Matras (2000: 582) puts it, 'intelligent guesses' can often be made about what grammatical changes might occur, given a certain degree of sociolinguistic information about the nature of the contact community'. Kusters (2003) using in part data from varieties of Arabic, suggests broad correlations between linguistic change and social factors.

to a dominant lingua franca whose speakers, in any case, are of a higher and largely inaccessible social status, and from this mix evolves a lingua franca of the dominated multilingual population, the creole. A number of careful sociohistorical studies, beginning with Chaudenson (1979), have documented this relationship, and have shown that altering certain variables, for instance increasing the number of speakers of the dominant language, will affect the creolization outcome.

Arabic is among the languages with a contemporary creole variety, and the history of its formation in the southern Sudan of the nineteenth century exhibits classic elements of creole formation. The language itself, mutually unintelligible with Arabic, is simplified relative to any variety of Arabic (see sect. 1.6.4), and this simplification occurred in an environment of great social upheaval.[13] The resulting creole Arabic which evolved was a symbol of a social class midway between the dominant northern Egyptian/Sudanese and Europeans on the one hand, and dominated tribal societies on the other (Owens 1997).

At one extreme, therefore, the extra-linguistic components of transmission clearly and radically impinge on the form of language which is transmitted, or which evolves. Creole Arabic, however, is a small chapter in the history of Arabic, which hardly is transferrable to other periods of its history (see Owens 1989, 2001b; Fischer 1995; Holes 1995: 19–24, vs. Versteegh 1984a). Interpretive problems emerge when one looks at Arabic more broadly and when a further attempt is made to establish either language or socio-historical setting as an independent variable to determine universals of language change. I make this point with a simple example. In Arabic dialects are basically found three paradigms of suffix pronominal marking. The most complete paradigm is defined by the intersection of the features, person, number (SG vs. PL) and gender (M vs. F), as in Nigerian Arabic (3a). This gives ten contrastive forms. In a number of dialects (the current example is Cairene), gender is neutralized in the plural, reducing the forms to eight (3b). In some North African dialects (e.g. Djidjelli, Tunis, Susa) and in Maltese the gender contrast is also neutralized in the 2SG, reducing the forms to seven (3c). I have chosen the suffix pronouns as illustrative forms in order to distinguish all of these varieties of Arabic from Creole Arabic, which has lost suffixes altogether (see (5) in sect. 1.6.4).

---

[13] The works by Collins (1962, 1971, 1983) can be recommended as historical descriptions of the tumultuous years of the southern Sudan up to independence. McWhorter (e.g. 1998, 2001) has re-emphasized the role of simplification in creole genesis.

		(3a) Nigerian Arabic		(3b) Cairene		(3c) Susa (Tunisia)	
		SG	PL	SG	PL	SG	PL
1		'i	-na	-i	-na	-i	-na
2	M	-ak	-ku	-ak	-kum	-ək	-kum
	F	-ki	-kan	-ik	Ø	Ø	Ø
3	M	-a	-hum	-u	hum	-u	-hum
	F	-ha	-hin	-ha	Ø	-ha	Ø

Using this data as a model, two questions can be posed. The first is, given the linguistic data, what can be deduced about the broad social forces which supported the increasing morphological paradigm simplification. One common answer has been to adduce urbanization. Other important urban areas in the Middle East such as Damascus and Jerusalem, have structural paradigms identical to Cairene. However, this urbanization explanation hardly works for Maltese, nor for many North African dialects with paradigms such as (3c). Furthermore, there are many rural areas (e.g. Anatolian dialects of southern Turkey, Soukhne in eastern Syria) as well as Arabian peninsular dialects (e.g. Hofuf, see App. 4) with (3b). To anticipate the second perspective which will be elaborated on in the next paragraph, a quick response to these observations is often to invoke shift via contact. Already, however, this introduces two independent extra-linguistic variables, urbanization and contact, whose interaction, for a precise historical account, is difficult to gauge. When is one dominant and when the other, and when and under what conditions are both necessary to produce simplification? Only when such questions are seriously addressed and answered can the factors themselves be given plausible explanatory status.

The second question is the inverse of the first: given social configurations, what linguistic outcomes are expected? This perspective is, for the linguist, a more difficult one, as social configurations, as noted above, are made up of a great many variables whose relative influence on language are often imponderable. The difficulty in relating this perspective to change in the Arabic language is compounded by the fact that very frequently essential social, demographic, and political data are sparse or lacking altogether. Using paradigms (3a) and (3c) as illustrative fulcrums, one may begin with the observation that historically the ancestral populations of both Nigerian Arabs and many of the North African Arabs share a common origin in Upper Egypt (see Owens 2003 for arguments). This ancestral population began moving out of Upper Egypt into North Africa in the eleventh century, and into the Sudan and the Lake Chad area in the fourteenth. Minimally, therefore, one might expect a common socio-demographic origin to be reflected in linguistic forms. Clearly, however, there is none. Nigerian Arabic maintains a maximally contrastive paradigm, whereas Susa, illustrative of much of North Africa, is maximally reductive. Note that it is not at all self-evident why Nigerian Arabic should have maintained the contrasts. Arab society in this region has absorbed a large number of non-Arabic speakers (shift to Arabic via contact). Indeed, it is very plausible to assume that the Nigerian Arabic reflex of *ṭ > ɗ, an emphatic, voiced, dental implosive, is due to contact with Fulfulde speakers (and perhaps other languages), who have /ɗ/. Of course, one would want to examine the social structure of the community to determine what factors favor 'normal' transmission. For the moment, however, such ethno-historical information is lacking.

The data and issues sketched in this section, problematic though they are, are nonetheless relatively well documented. To invoke the role of transmission as a global factor in explaining change in the history of Arabic, beginning in pre-diasporic times and moving to the present, is to add variables which, at this stage in the study of the history of Arabic, are simply too numerous to deal with within a macro-analysis of language history.[14] Beyond the many imponderables noted here has to be added the further key variable of linguistic reconstruction itself. What form of Arabic should be taken as an initial input? Obviously it is an argument of this book that proto-Arabic itself is not a pre-given entity, but rather one which needs to be argued for using, inter alia, the comparative method.

To summarize this section, I do not believe that at this point linguistic and extra-linguistic data on Arabic are sufficiently well understood to reconstruct the role of transmission in Arabic language history. Relevant parameters which can ameliorate this situation are known. As pointed out in the previous section, to a degree contemporary linguistic data can be correlated with historical texts; contemporary micro-linguistic studies, inevitably focusing on the variable of variation, can be used to extrapolate back into earlier eras of language history (to this end see sect. 2.4.1.1), linguistic concepts such as saliency or transparency can be applied at least as diagnostic heuristics. These measures, however, are elements of an agenda for future research, not pre-existing instruments which can be used without qualification to question the arguments of the current work.

---

[14] One reader points out that transmission as an independent factor has been neglected in the current book: 'a serious neglect of the transmission of the language. There is almost nothing in the book on the effects of this transmission on the language structure...' The purpose of the current section is to clarify the reason for this neglect.

1.6. A Critical Look at Some Truisms in Arabic Historical Linguistics

In the following eight chapters I will develop my interpretation of certain problems in Arabic historical linguistics. Within the large complex of issues which make up Arabic historical linguistics, I believe there have developed a set of truisms whose theoretical or descriptive basis is taken for granted. I would like to take this opportunity to comment critically on a number of statements and perspectives often encountered in works on Arabic historical linguistics. Some, though not all, of these points are developed in greater detail in the following chapters. Since scholars often have these truisms at their disposal in their approach to interpreting the history of Arabic, I think it relevant to mention even positions not directly germane to the issues in this book, since I suspect they are part of the background noise, as it were, which accompanies analysis of Arabic language history.

1.6.1. *Mistaking a part for the whole*

Differences between so-called Old Arabic and Neo-Arabic are often established on the basis of partial differences only. This point will be illustrated and commented on in detail in Ch. 2.

1.6.2. *The future can be used to reconstruct the past, but it cannot dictate what is found there: Classical Arabic cannot be used to determine what predecessor varieties were*

This is a subtle point, not necessarily explicitly articulated in interpretations of Arabic history, but often present nonetheless. Again, criticisms of this approach will be found in Ch. 2 (see sect. 2.2.1). To confirm that this perspective is indeed prominent among Western Arabicists, reference may be made to Bellamy 1985. In this work, Bellamy gives a new reading of the famous Namaarah inscription. This is the oldest surviving inscription of Arabic (AD 328) and was written in Nabataean script. Of course, it is unvoweled, and the interpretation of many consonants is problematic. Bellamy's interpretation varies in a number of points from that of Dussaud, who interpreted and translated the text many years before Bellamy. Bellamy 'worked on the assumption that the language is Standard Arabic' and indeed finds this assumption confirmed: 'the language of the epitaph is the same language that we encounter in pre-Islamic poetry' (1985: 46).

The hidden assumptions behind this mode of argumentation are fraught with comparative dangers of considerable proportion. I will mention two here. First, Bellamy explores only one assumption, that the text is in Standard Arabic. This should be in and of itself unacceptable even for the most conservative of Arabicists. The construct Standard Arabic assumes, inter alia, a social milieu which, so far as we know, did not exist in 328. Beyond this, a dispassionate comparative analysis—should one assume on a priori grounds that a certain variety underlies the variety—needs to explore other assumptions, for instance that a certain Arabic dialect isn't equally commensurate with Bellamy's interpretation, or that using a certain dialect as a basis of interpretation doesn't also yield plausible results.

Second, and more importantly, it simply is impossible to claim that the language of the text is the same as that of poetry. The lack of short vowels alone means that important comparative issues are opaque (see sect. 2.4.1). There is for example no basis for assuming case or nunation (see sect. 3.4.1), and even the interpretation of the hamza (orthographically an alif) is problematic. A simple comparison I think renders the pitfalls clear. Following Larcher (2005a), the orthography of the pre-Islamic inscriptions may be compared to the unvoweled, unpointed *maṣaaḥif* or *Koranic* manuscripts (see Ch. 4). In these we know from the reading traditions that there are many ways in which individual words can be rendered and many of these do not correspond to the language of poetry.[15] A bare consonantal text leaves many interpretations open. Reading the pre-Islamic inscripts as reflexes of poetic Arabic is but one possibility out of many.

1.6.3. *Reconstruction on the basis of a* terminus ad quem *is convenient, but it is not comparative reconstruction*

This is related to the previous point. Whereas in the previous procedure the future is projected as a whole backwards into the past, in this one a protoform is assumed (but not demonstrated), and given this form attested variants are derived as a logical development from this proto-form. Reconstruction, however, proceeds in the opposite direction, from attested forms to reconstruction of the proto-form.

A case in point is the excellent and challenging work of Birkeland (1940). His is probably the most historically orientated work in a comparative linguistic sense found among Western Arabicists of the first half of the twentieth century. Birkeland (1940: 21–31) bases his interpretation to a significant part on the work of Sibawaih. An example can be cited here which will

---

[15] For instance, *imala* (see Ch. 7) plays no significant role in poetry, while the *hamza*, missing in some of the *Qiraaʔaat*, is represented in poetry.

be of relevance in Ch. 8. Sibawaih (II. 307 ff.) describes in greater or lesser detail four different realizations of the pronunciation of words before pause, or 'pausal form' as it is known in Arabic studies. These are *rawm*, *ʔiʃmaam*, *tadˤʕiyf* and *sukuwn*. Very briefly, *sukuwn* is simply pronunciation without a final vowel. *tadˤʕiyf* is the pronunciation of a final consonant geminate, so instead of the personal name, *xaalid*, one has the pronunciation *xaalidd*. *Rawm* and *ʔiʃmaam* are given greater attention by Sibawaih, and their realization appears more subtle than the previous two pausal variants. *ʔiʃmaam*, Sibawaih says, applies only to the vowel -u, *al-kitaab-ụ* 'the book'. It apparently has the realization of a voiceless or whispered vowel, as he reports that a blind person could not ascertain *ʔiʃmaam*, since it is realized only visually by lip-rounding (see sect. 7.1.3 for more comprehensive phonetic interpretation of this term). The phonetic quality of *rawm* is not spelled out in great detail by Sibawaih, though it appears to be a weakening of the pronunciation of the final -u and -i. It does not apply to final -a.

Birkeland assumes that the four realizations reflect differing stages in the loss of originally present short final vowels. His main source of evidence for this assumption comes from poetic renditions in which a final short vowel can be pronounced long (see sect. 8.1). Given this assumption, he reconstructs stages leading to the complete loss of a short final vowel in pausal position, termed *sukuwn*. The stages are as follows, illustrating each with the stereotyped example, *kaatib* 'writer, writing'. The suffixes -a, -u, -i mark accusative, nominative, and genitive, respectively.

(4) Development of pausal forms in Old Arabic, according to Birkeland

    a. Final short vowels, -u, -a, -i all present, *kaatib-u, kaatib-a, kaatib-i*

    b. Development of *rawm*, giving full final -a, and reduced -u, -i. *kaatib-a, kaatib-u/i*

    c. Development of *ʔiʃmaam*, leading to -a, -i, with -u represented only by voiceless realization: *kaatib-a, kaatib-i, kaatib-ụ*

    d. Development of doubling of final consonant (*tadˤʕiyf*) as compensation for loss of final vowels: *kaatibb*

    e. All final vowels lost = *sukuwn*: *kaatib*

The logical problem involved in this summary is that there is no evidence from Old Arabic sources which unequivocally confirms the original maintenance of short final vowels in pausal position. As Birkeland himself notes, pausal pronunciation of short vowels is equally attested in the earliest poetic recitation literature (see Sibawaih II: 325, ch. 507, see discussion in sect. 8.1). It is only reconstruction which can sanction one proto-form or another. It is thus equally plausible to assume the pausal forms (*sukuwn*) as original ones, and derive the full-vowel pronunciation as a later development. This is the position argued for here (see Ch. 3, 4).

Regarding Birkeland's five stages, it should first be noted that Sibawaih was simply describing variants which he heard. All five 'stages' are for Sibawaih synchronic variants, a point Birkeland (1940: 31) in fact concedes. What Birkeland did was to construct a plausible scenario by which they could be interpreted as historically successive. Beginning with the assumption that all vowels were originally present, Birkeland works his way down the scale, eliminating the vowels one by one. Logical problems are apparent, however. Stages 4b and 4c essentially eliminate final -u, -i. Stage 4d, doubling of the final consonant is interpreted as compensation for this loss. However, this explanation makes sense only if 4b and 4c were already accompanied by a final consonant doubling, which needs to be able to detect the presence of the final vowels. No evidence for this exists, however.

Interesting and often brilliant and challenging though Birkeland's interpretations are, they ultimately lack a comparative basis. Implicitly, Birkeland assumes and reconstructs an idealized Classical Arabic, sometimes termed the ʕArabiya, as the proto-form from which Old Arabic pausal phenomenon derives and deviates. This requires Birkeland turning Sibawaih's synchronic observations into historical stages. Since in most cases Birkeland offers no independent justification of these stages, they are open to other interpretations (see Ch. 8, especially sect. 8.9).

1.6.4. *The quick-fix syndrome*

The basic dichotomy of Old and New Arabic has frequently been associated with the assumption that as Arabic became widespread among a new population of speakers, radical changes occurred in it. This idea is found in Fück (1950) and Brockelmann (1908), among others, and is most radically expressed in Versteegh's (1984a) bold creolization hypothesis, whereby the modern dialects passed through a stage of creolization or pidginization. None of these authors, however, give a detailed account of what significant set of language changes occurred marking the transition from Old to New.

As an indication that Old Arabic and the modern dialects have a great deal in common, in the following three paradigms of singular object pronouns are given, attached to or modifying the word 'house'. The first column in (5) is Classical Arabic (in nominative case), the second the set of pronominal object suffixes as reconstructed on the basis of the modern dialects (see Ch. 8), and the third Creole Arabic, namely East African Nubi (Wellens 2003: 52).

(5) Nubi and varieties of Arabic

Classical Arabic	reconstructed Pre-diasporic	Nubi	
1 bayt-iy	beet-i*	be ta'yi	'my house'
2M bayt-u-ka	beet-ka* or beet-k*	be 'taki	'your(.M) house'
2F bayt-u-ki	beet-ki*		etc.
3M bayt-u-hu	beet-hu*	be 'to (< ta uwo 'of him')	
3F bayt-u-haa	beet-ha*		

Whereas the reconstruction based on the modern dialects yields forms nearly identical to Standard Arabic, the Nubi forms are entirely different and hardly could lead to the postulation of a paradigm similar to Standard Arabic. Were radical restructuring instrumental in a purported transition from Old to Neo-Arabic, one would expect a development along the lines of what occurred in Nubi: the suffix forms were lost altogether, and the M–F contrast was lost. Even if a loss of case endings occurred in the modern dialects (which I question), it would hardly constitute a case for radical change.

1.6.5. Dialects are mistakes, not languages

This point was mentioned in 1.3 and need not be elaborated upon. Its assumption, however, is lethal for a comparative linguistics.

1.6.6. The allegedly most complex variety has historical priority

This argument is related to the previous one, though developed particularly in Western thinking on Arabic language history. Ferguson in his classic article on Arabic diglossia (1959a) represents this line of thinking. Operating under the assumption that dialects are offshoots of Classical Arabic, Ferguson attempts to indicate ways in which dialects, the L(ow) variety, are simpler both phonologically and morphologically than is the H(igh) classical language. Leaving aside Ferguson's assumptions about the development of Arabic, on a strictly typological basis the observation can be shown to be false. Ferguson, like the majority of Arabicists (see sect. 1.6.1 above) cements his point by comparing Classical Arabic to selected Arabic dialects. Classical Arabic has interdentals, for instance, which Cairene Arabic lacks.

However, as soon as one compares Classical Arabic with the totality of contemporary Arabic dialects it is clear that the dialects are in many respects considerably more complex than Classical Arabic. Two examples from phonology and two from morphology make this clear.

Phonology. In fact, Ferguson is very circumspect about offering generalizations about differences between H and L phonology, giving no broad substantive differences. Discussing grammatical structure (i.e. syntax and morphology, 1959a: 333), Ferguson does suggest that an L variety will be simpler than the H. Extending the idea of simplification to phonology, as far as Classical Arabic and the dialects go, there are clear instances where the dialects are more complicated, for instance in having more of certain types of phonemes or of having more syllable structure rules.

Classical Arabic has four emphatic (phonemic) consonants which in Standard Arabic are conventionally represented as ṣ, ṭ, ḍ, and ḏ̣. Allophonic variants are excluded from the count.[16] Nigerian Arabic has lost ḏ̣ due its loss of interdental fricatives, but it has in addition to ṣ, ṭ, and ḍ phonemic ḷ, ṛ, and ṃ as well.

(6) gallab 'he galloped'
     gaḷḷab 'he got angry'
     karra 'he tore'
     kaṛṛa 'he dragged'
     amm 'uncle'
     aṃṃ 'mother'

Nigerian Arabic with six phonemic emphatics is thus more complex than is Classical Arabic. Many other dialects are like Nigerian Arabic in having a larger set of emphatics than does Classical Arabic.

Nigerian Arabic, again like many other dialects, has a rule which inserts an /a/after a guttural consonant ([ʔ, h, x, q], e.g. *ahamar* 'red' < *ʔaḥmar. This rule is lacking in Classical Arabic.

---

[16] In the Koranic reading tradition in particular one finds allophonic variants of certain consonants, especially emphatic [ṛ] and [ḷ]. These are clearly systematized in the later reading tradition, for instance in Dani's (d. 444/1053) *Taysiyr* (51–3), where the emphatic allophones occur before an /a/ or /u/, as in *al-ṣalaah* 'prayer' (Warsh variant, where after an emphatic consonant the [l] must occur), and *ḥaðar-a (al-mawt)* 'precaution' (against death). These are termed *mufaxxama* or *muɣallaṭa* variants. Ferguson's argument (1956) that emphatic ḷ is a phoneme of what he terms Classical Arabic holds (if at all) only for what he termed modern Classical Arabic. He does not investigate the issue in the Old Arabic literature. It can be suspected that the existence of allophonic emphatics in the Old Arabic literature probably masks the existence of these same sounds as contrastive phonemes. Using the arguments developed elsewhere in this book, one could certainly reconstruct emphatic [ḷ] and [ṛ] phonemes into pre-diasporic Arabic, an exercise which, however, I will not undertake here. It should be noted that dialects too, have further emphatic allophones. In Nigerian Arabic, for instance, [ḅ], [ṇ], and other sounds emphaticize in the neighborhood of other emphatics, as in *ṛabaḍ* 'he tied' or *ṛabanna* 'we tied' (with ḍ assimilation) so that as far as the current comparison with Old Arabic goes, the dialects, in terms of simple number, will have more emphatic variants than Old Arabic.

Morphology. Old Arabic has a single common form for the 1SG independent pronoun, *ʔanaa* 'I'. In certain Tihama (coastal) Yemeni dialects, on the other hand, the first person singular independent pronoun distinguishes a M and F form (Behnstedt 1985: 31):

(7) *ana* I.M
    ani I.F.

Old Arabic has a single prefix which can be prefixed before the imperfect verb, namely the future marker *sa-:*

(8) *yaktubu,* 'he writes'
    sa-yaktubu 'he will write'.

Taking a very brief survey of Arabic dialects, in Cairene Arabic there are a number of pre-verbal tense/aspect prefixes.

(9) *yiktib* 'he should write'
    bi-yiktib 'he writes'
    ħa-yiktib 'he will write'

That Egyptian Arabic is simpler than Old Arabic in its modal suffix system is irrelevant to the present observation,[17] which is that on a typological comparison, the Egyptian Arabic tense/aspect system of prefixes is more complicated than that of Old Arabic. When one considers other dialects the situation becomes even more complex. Western Libyan Arabic has a prefix *bi-* which marks future,

(10) *bi-yimʃi* 'he will go'.

In Nigeria Arabic the distribution of the prefix *b-* is complicated by an interaction of phonological and syntactic factors. The prefix *b-* rarely occurs before a consonant-initial prefix, hence, the contrast:

(11) *tu-ktub* 'you write'
     b-u-ktub 'he writes'.

In what I have termed 'non-control contexts', the prefix *b-* is disallowed under all circumstances.[18]

(12) *gul iktub* 'I said, he should write'

---

[17] Old Arabic has a three-way system of contrast, indicative, subjunctive, jussive, *yaktub-u, yaktub-a, yaktub.* Egyptian has an undifferentiated C-final form, *yiktib.*

[18] Non-control in the sense that the agent has no volition in the matter, the action being controlled by a person or entity of higher authority.

From this brief, very far from exhaustive exemplification of the realization of pre-verbal tense/aspect/mode markers in Arabic dialects it is clear that a holistic, pan-dialectal description of the formal properties of these markers alone is considerably more complicated than that of Old Arabic. Ferguson's suggestion that 'the grammatical structure of any given L variety is simpler than that of its corresponding H' simply does not withstand even a casual perusal of the literature on modern dialect phonology and morphology (see also Belnap and Gee 1994: 146, on simplification of the classical language).

I would caution that the observations here do not automatically lead to a historical account of their origin or their priority of origin. In fact, Ferguson's does not either. He simply assumed that the dialects were 'younger' and a prioristically linked this assumption to the weakly illustrated assertion that dialects developed in the direction of simplification.

1.6.7. *Beware of simple dichotomies; a nice label is not necessarily a nice concept*

There are four or five dichotomies which are invoked to characterize varieties of Arabic, expressed variously in dialectal, sociolectal, structural, or historical terms. The most pernicious in my view is the Old Arabic–Neo-Arabic split, which is the subject of the next chapter. Others include bedouin–sedentary, urban–rural, eastern Arabic vs. western Arabic,[19] and synthetic vs. analytic (see sect. 3.4.3). Each of these labels deserves separate critical attention, which is outside the scope of this book (see sects. 3.5.3, and 1.6.6 above on the question of complication, simplification, and analyticity). I would, however, make three brief critical points.

First, in the contemporary world it is relatively rare to find neat dichotomies such as an urban–rural split, and when they are found they are geographically limited. Arabic is spoken from Borno in northeastern Nigeria to the Red Sea, for instance, and one is hard put to identify an urban vs. a rural variety in the entire region, a distance equivalent to that from the Mississippi River of the US to the east coast. A bedouin lifestyle in Iraq will be associated with a very different dialect from a bedouin lifestyle in Chad or Cameroon.

---

[19] Cowan's (1960: 4) division of Arabic dialects into western and eastern dialects for purposes of proto-Arabic reconstruction is a good example of how an essentially good idea can be undermined by a prioristic dichotomies. My own work follows Cowan in allowing the dialects in principle an equal say in proto-Arabic reconstruction along with Old Arabic sources. As many examples in this book show, however, much historical phenomena in Arabic is reconstructible directly to pre-diasporic Arabic. Mandating an intermediary historical stage based on the east–west difference runs the risk of obscuring deeper historical relationships, which antedate dialect divisions as they developed in the post-diasporic era.

Secondly, once the dichotomies are in place, they tend to become hinges upon which more is hung than they can hold. I have argued this point recently in relation to the east–west dialect dichotomy (Owens 2003). The east–west dialect split divides the Arabic dialectal world roughly at a boundary in western Egypt or eastern Libya.[20] One of the main traits sanctioning the division is the expression of the 1PL imperfect verb.

(13a) *nu-ktub* : eastern 'we write'

(13b) *nu-ktub-u*: western 'we write'

All of North Africa, as well as Andalusia has (13b), while all of Asiatic Arabic has (13a). The problem comes with Egypt, which has both (13a) and (13b). To 'explain' the status of (13b) in many Egyptian dialects, scholars have traditionally resorted to a historical explanation: since North African Arabic has (13b), any Egyptian dialects with (13b) must have been influenced by migrations from North Africa (Woidich 1993: 354; Versteegh 1997: 162; Behnstedt 1998: 87). The problem with this explanation, however, is that no such plausible migrations are attested, particularly when the following consideration is brought into the equation. Western (13b) is also found throughout Chadian Arabic, so any migration that brought (13b) to Egypt must have been early enough, around 1500, for the form to be able also to spread into Chad.

A comprehensive consideration of the problem, considering both comparative linguistic and written historical sources leads to the conclusion that (13b) in fact originated in Egypt and spread to North Africa from there.

The overall problem illustrated here is that what was originally a simple dialectological label took on the status of historical linguistic explanation: 'North African' or 'western' Arabic is North African not only in a dialectological sense, but without justification becomes North African in a historical linguistic one as well.

Thirdly, I think these labels have become so widespread that they convey a false sense of security to an understanding of Arabic. Classify a dialect as bedouin or sedentary and one's work is done. Even if these labels are useful— and as I have suggested, their usefulness is limited—they have nothing to say about many aspects of Arabic language history, for instance the development of mixed Arabic and creole Arabic, the maintenance, spread or loss of originally rural varieties in urban centers today (see Amara 2005; Miller 2005), language maintenance in the face of a widespread incorporation of non-Arab speakers into a population (attested in many parts of the

---

[20] In fact, even as a dialectological concept the division is problematic, though this point may be ignored for the sake of argument.

western Sudanic region), not to mention many of the historical issues dealt with in this book.

1.6.8. *Peripheral dialects are not on an a priori basis irrelevant to language interpretation*

This is assumed in Fischer (1995). In comparative linguistics, as well as historical cultural studies, it is a standard precept that innovations move in waves and that it follows from this that older variants will frequently be found in peripheral areas, as innovations take hold in the center (see Holes 1991 for one application of this approach). In Chs. 3, 5, 6, and 7, features will be discussed which are found in dialects outside the Arabian peninsula, certainly peripheral by any traditional sense of the term, which point to forms which must be reconstructed in pre-diasporic Arabic.

1.6.9. *A truism which is indeed true: languages can be surprisingly conservative in many respects*

Consider the following two verb paradigms, one from Nigeria, the other from Iraq.

(14)   Iraqi   Nigerian Arabic (imperfect)[21]
   SG
   1   a-qbur 'I bury'   a-ktub 'I write', etc.
   2M   ta-qbur   ta-ktub
   2F   ta-qbur-i   ta-ktub-i
   3M   i-qbur   i-ktub
   3F   ta-qbur   ta-ktub
   PL
   1   ni-qbur   na-ktub
   2M   ta-qbur-aa   ta-ktub-u
   2F   ta-qbur-aa   ta-ktub-an
   3M   i-qbur-uu   i-ktub-u
   3F   i-qbur-aa   i-ktub-an

To those not familiar with comparative Semitics, I think if one were to say that the paradigms represent an Iraqi variety and a variety of Nigerian Arabic, the reader would probably try to locate the Iraqi variety in a modern Arabic dialect. In fact, whereas the Nigerian Arabic paradigm comes from the year 2005, the Iraqi paradigm is not a variety of Arabic at all, but rather is

---

[21] This illustrates the paradigm in what was termed the 'non-control' context (see (11), (12) above and n. 18). In this context the prefix b- does not occur.

Akkadian, from approximately 2500 BC. Nonetheless, the paradigms are virtually identical in all respects: they have the same dimensions of morphological contrast, the morphemes are nearly of identical form, and their sequence is the same, with a pre-verb stem prefix plus a suffix in the plural and second person feminine singular. Of course, there is a major difference in the meaning of the paradigms: in Akkadian the paradigm realizes a past tense (preterite) whereas in Nigerian Arabic it is an imperfect. Nonetheless, given the 4,500 years intervening between the two, it may safely be said that they have the same origin, and that as far as the form goes, they have not changed.[22] Measured against such remarkable paradigm stability—there is nowhere in language history where members of the same family can be compared over such a long period of time as with the Semitic family—the thrust of the present work that differences between Old Arabic and the modern dialects are relatively minor is rendered added plausibility.

1.7. Summary of Chapters

This book developed out of a series of articles which I had planned on the history of Arabic. Three of the chapters (3, 4, 5) have appeared in slightly different versions already. I decided to gather the remaining treatments together and shape them into a more cohesive form, reckoning that a representation in one place would facilitate an overall development of argumentation. Nonetheless, the original format of individual articles will probably peek through in places, in an unedited repetition or in a rapid shift in subject between chapters.

The remainder of the book consists of eight chapters. In Ch. 2, the basic concepts of Old Arabic and Neo-Arabic will be scrutinized, first in terms of a historical overview of their genesis in Western Arabicist thinking, secondly in terms of their validity in the context of comparative historical linguistics. It will be argued that sets of linguistic features characterizing the Old vs. New dichotomy are of questionable value in comparative historical terms. The intellectual historical background complements the comparative historical, it will be suggested, as the very concept of Old vs. Neo-Arabic was introduced before comparative historical linguistics became established in the West as a rigorous discipline.

---

[22] Rössler (1950) argues that the preterite paradigm of Akkadian shifted to the imperfect of Arabic and NW Semitic languages. This represents a shift in meaning, not in form. A slightly less ambitious comparison, in which form and meaning coincide, would be that between Ugaritic (c.1300 BC) and Nigerian Arabic, where the so-called prefix conjugation in each is an imperfect.

Chapters 3 and 4 consider in detail the status of short case vowels in Old Arabic. These have been the criterion par excellence taken to symbolize the dichotomy between Old and Neo-Arabic, Neo-Arabic being identified as the variety which has lost the vowels. It will be argued on the basis of old sources, the Arabic grammarians and the Koranic reading tradition, that a good argument can be made for there having been two varieties of proto-Arabic, one with short case vowels, one without. It is suggested that the variety without is the older.

The remaining chapters change the perspective from a primary focus on Old Arabic, first to one in which the modern dialects are the main center of attention, and then to one in which Old Arabic and the modern dialects are given equal weight. This, it was suggested above, is a prerequisite for any history of Arabic based on the comparative method, since a proto-form has to be able to 'explain' the development of its daughters. A mere labeling of elements as 'old' and 'new' explains nothing.

In Ch. 5 I argue for the importance of post-diasporic Arabic in interpreting Arabic language history. This is the spoken Arabic which spread in the wake of Arab-Islamic expansion which began in the seventh century. Four varieties of Arabic outside of the Arabic peninsula are compared. Two are large dialect areas, Mesopotamian and western Sudanic Arabic, while two are single varieties, Shukriyya Arabic of the Sudan and Uzbekistan Arabic. It is argued on the basis of a statistical treatment of forty-nine phonological and morphological features that similarities between far-flung varieties, western Sudanic and Uzbekistan for instance, are indicative of pre-diasporic unities. That is, post-diasporic varieties allow reconstruction of pre-diasporic linguistic features. This same perspective is followed in Ch 6, where the development of the basic imperfect verb is reconstructed on the basis of contemporary dialectal data.

Whereas Chs. 5 and 6 concentrate mainly on modern dialects, establishing that they are a legitimate mechanism for reading the linguistic history of the past even with minimal help from older sources, in Chs. 7 and 8, and to a degree in Ch. 6, I relate forms found in the contemporary dialects to their realizations in Old Arabic. Chapter 7 is a detailed treatment of the phenomenon of ʔimaala (= imala), the conditioned variant [ie] of the long vowel [aa]. It will be seen that there are striking identities, both phonetic and phonological, in the realization of ʔimaala in Sibawaih's description from the late eighth century and three modern dialects, as well as in Andalusian Arabic. These similarities are used to work out a comparative linguistic history of the phenomenon. Finally, Ch. 8 begins with a reconstruction of pronominal object suffixes solely on the basis of a sample of forty-nine modern dialects. The results of this reconstruction are then correlated with the descriptive material found in Old Arabic. It is first shown that the reconstruction, contrary to claims by some, yields no evidence for traces of old case suffixes. Second, it is argued that the reconstructions based on the contemporary dialects in all cases are readily interpretable as continuations of or developments from forms attested in the Old Arabic literature.

The overall thrust of the final four chapters is to greatly narrow the comparative linguistic difference between the modern dialects and Old Arabic as it has been popularly represented. In general the argument works in two directions. On the one hand, many features which have popularly been ascribed to the modern dialects to the exclusion of Old Arabic are shown to have analogues, often identical realizations, in the Old Arabic literature. On the other hand, even features which are not attested in the Old Arabic literature can be reconstructed into pre-diasporic Arabic, which, as seen in sect. 1.1 above, is chronologically coincidental with Old Arabic. The Arabic of the pre-diasporic era, both Old Arabic in the sense of sect. 1.1 above and pre-diasporic Arabic, again in the sense of sect. 1.1, emerges as a richer, more variable object than the Old Arabic–Neo-Arabic dichotomy implies.

I think it appropriate to end this introductory chapter with a caveat. A major aim of the book is to reorientate thinking about the history of Arabic. Linguistic history is written in small steps, incremented via individual case histories. I have chosen a number which I believe are at one and the same time central to the Arabic language and indicative of phenomena which are not explicable within reigning conceptions of Arabic language history. Conclusions which follow from these are based on the interpretation of many individual features, comprised often of circumstantial evidence. The history of a language so large, so long attested in such a rich array of sources as is Arabic is not readily reducible to a simple interpretation. From this it follows that this book is not a comprehensive history of the Arabic language. It offers one perspective for a historical account.

Furthermore, I deliberately eschew discussion of certain questions of general nature, for instance the status of a pre-Islamic koine or early Arabic diglossia or the social, political, and ideological underpinnings of the emergence of a standard Classical Arabic in the eighth, ninth and tenth centuries. This is not because the issues are not important, but rather that I think that these sociolinguistic questions can best be answered after other linguistic issues have been worked out in greater detail and to a degree independently of them.

One implication of the approach advocated here is that our understanding of Arabic language history is set for a period of uncertainty. Atomization precedes synthesis. Analyses which may be equally plausible, but mutually contradictory should be welcomed as pointing towards areas of future research.

2

Old Arabic, Neo-Arabic, and Comparative Linguistics

2.1. A Method vs. a Logical Matrix

The linguistic history of Arabic is challenging in two special ways which makes it rare, in one respect almost unique, among the world's languages. These challenges have had both positive, and I will argue, negative consequences for understanding the history of the language.

First and foremost, on the positive side Arabic is one of the few languages in the world for which a detailed linguistic description exists which is as old as the oldest literary and religious texts of the language. This literature goes back to the eighth century and it details not only minute facets of phonology, morphology and syntax, but also gives interesting data on different linguistic variants. The modern linguist thus meets not only linguistic forms, but also descriptions and interpretations of these forms as developed by the Arabic linguists themselves.

Second, and as it turned out negatively, the linguistic history of Arabic began to be described in the West in the first half of the nineteenth century. In and of itself of course this is neither good nor bad. However, the linguistic history of Arabic began at the same time as the general interest and development of historical linguistics and dialectology itself. Both these disciplines as independent intellectual fields of endeavor were essentially born in the nineteenth century. The family tree model of Indo-European (Stammbaum-Theorie), for instance, was first published by August Schleicher in 1853, one year before Fleischer (see sect. 2.2.2 below) introduced the idea of a 'holistic Arabic'. Historical linguistics during this period developed its own methodological rigor, culminating two decades later in the work of the neogrammarians Osthoff and Brugmann (see Jankowsky 2001). The idea of a proto-language linked to daughter languages via general rules of change, particularly phonological change, was made ever more precise as new information from newly described Indo-European languages became available. During this same era, dialectology established that non-normative forms of speech were as legitimate an object of study as a standard language (see e.g. Knoop 1982). An understanding of historical linguistics and dialectology grew coterminously with the definition of historical relations among the Indo-European languages, or the study of geographical variation within individual languages. The problem with Arabic, as will be seen, is that the historical relation among varieties of Arabic was basically fixed by the mid-nineteenth century, and thereafter impervious, if not oblivious, to reinterpretation, up to the present day.[1]

The notion of language history in linguistics[2] did lead in the nineteenth century to the postulation of language families other than Indo-European, including the Semitic family (Hecker 1982: 6). Language families assume a genetic relationship among all members, classically represented in a family tree model. Genetic relationship is confirmed especially via application of the comparative method, which above all uses retentions and shared innovations to establish subfamilies (Harrison 2003: 232–9).[3] It is assumed in this book that a historical linguistic treatment of a language or group of languages

---

[1] This remark deserves a chapter in itself rather than a footnote, though takes the subject too far afield for inclusion in the main text. In another domain of Arabic linguistics outside comparative grammar, European Arabicist scholarship was also largely cut off from newer developments in general linguistics. In its interpretation of the Arabic grammatical tradition, which today is recognized for its theoretical coherency (see e.g. the collection of articles in Auroux et al. 2001), European scholars at the turn of the nineteenth century were disparaging of it. The basis of their criticism was an implicit assumption of European cultural superiority founded in the universalistic claims of classical Greek learning. The Arabic grammatical tradition was particularistic and not based on logical principles. Merx (1891: 16) reprimands the Arabic grammarians because 'ils ignoraient le fait que la grammaire repose sur la logique'. Weil (1915: 383), anachronistically from today's perspective, dismissed the Arabic tradition because its strength lay *'nur in der Entwicklung der grammatischen Theorie'* (my italics). Weil further maintained that it was only the European tradition which was interested in language in general ('Sprache im allgemeinen', 385). This basically antagonistic attitude towards the Arabic linguistic tradition again contrasts dramatically with the then contemporary Indo-Europeanists. The great, early figures in American linguistics for instance were often comparative Indo-Europeanists as well. Two significant examples are Dwight Whitney and Leonard Bloomfield, both of whom were well versed, inter alia, in the classical Sanskrit linguistic tradition. Bloomfield, one of the founders of modern structural linguistics, in particular, openly expressed his debt to this tradition in formulating his own ideas of language structure (see Rogers 1987). The general point developed in this footnote, which complements the argument of the current chapter, is that the early Western Arabicist tradition was relatively distant from developments in general linguistics.

[2] Of course, the idea that languages can be in some way genetically related is much older (cf. e.g. the tenth-century Hebrew grammarian, Ibn Qureysh on Hebrew, Aramaic, and Arabic, Hirschfeld 1926). Language history as a linguistic idea requires a methodological incorporation into language structure, and this was systematized essentially in the nineteenth century when comparative linguistics was developed. The focus of this intellectual activity was Germany (see e.g. Jankowsky 2001; Einhauser 2001). Not infrequently one and the same university (e.g. Leipzig) witnessed the presence of both Semiticists/Arabicists and Indo-European scholars.

[3] The postulation of genetic relationship in chronological terms was an idea far ahead of a methodology to work out comparative details, i.e. the comparative method. Ibn Qureysh, cited in

requires both a clear statement of genetic relationship and at least the attempt to apply the comparative method.[4]

The idea of language history provides a powerful metaphor, which can assume a life independent of the comparative method on which it is based. Given a corpus of texts from different periods, very often clear 'developments' can be discerned: Modern English derives from Middle English which derives from Old English; New Egyptian from Middle from Old Egyptian. From a comparatively well-documented language such as English it is known that language periodization proceeds fitfully, as it were. There are periods when a language undergoes relatively little change from generation to generation, and others when a change can be rapid. In the period AD 800–2000, which covers approximately the same chronological time span as that discussed in this chapter for Arabic, English has changed considerably, from Old English via Middle English to Modern English. By contrast, a related Germanic language, Icelandic, has changed little in the same period.[5] Language history is thus different from simple chronology. A language stage, as characterized by a set of linguistic features, may last for a short period of chronological time, or for a long period. Till today, of course, the factors, both linguistic and extra-linguistic, influencing linguistic stability, are the object of study, as sketched in sect. 1.5.

For linguistic study, an optimal situation is when a language is attested over a continuous span of time, in a script that is fairly close to its spoken form. Lacking a body of older texts, minimally two stages can be reconstructed, the contemporary and at least one earlier stage, based on reconstruction via the comparative method and/or internal reconstruction. The history of most language families in Africa, Asia, and the Americas is reconstructed on this basis.

The sequence old/new or old/middle/new (or modern) can assume the status of an expectation rather than an empirical object to be established via

---

n. 2, for instance, correctly ascertained the genetic relationship between three Semitic languages, Aramaic, Hebrew, and Arabic. However this did not lead to a historical linguistics in any recognizable form. Without a comparative methodology, no historical linguistics is possible.

[4] Complemented by other methodologies as possible, e.g. internal reconstruction and mass comparison. Of course, as has now been shown, the comparative method does not work for many languages (Durie and Ross 1996) and may not be applicable to all domains of language (Owens 1996). Before its relevance can be dismissed, however, the comparative method must first be applied.

[5] Glendening summarizes Icelandic thus: 'Icelandic today is much as it was when Iceland was first colonized, mainly from Norway, in and after A.D. 874. It has in large measure marked time for a thousand years' (1961: p. v). Similarly, Kusters (2003: 204) writes, 'Icelandic inflection, for the greatest part, has remained the same as in Old Norse, except for the following changes: (1) The levelling of 1st and 3rd singular in the subjunctive and in the past tense, (2) the reduction of most subjunctive plural suffixes to the indicative forms, (3) the erosion of the middle voice distinctions.'

the comparative method. Once it is assumed that languages develop, the old/
(middle)/new motif follows logically. One stage must be older than another.
However, in comparative linguistic terms, this is what may be termed a
pre-theoretical logical matrix in that it may be expected to exist for any
language, but so long as the stages lack specific linguistic content it has no
substance. The logical matrix remains untested until it is filled in by plausible
substance. It may happen, for instance, that over a long period of time little
or no linguistic periodization is possible.

I would suggest that an untested logical matrix was applied to Arabic early
in the European study of the language in the nineteenth century and that this
reading of Arabic linguistic history has continued to inform its conceptualization into the present.[6] As early as the mid-nineteenth century European
scholars dichotomized Arabic into Old Arabic and Neo-Arabic. The latter are
the modern Arabic dialects.[7]

The dichotomization of Arabic into Old and New is faulty on two counts,
however. First, it mistakes chronology for linguistic history. Secondly, once it
was in place, it provided a framework for defining different linguistic stages of
Arabic on the basis of partial differences only (see sects. 1.6.1, 1.6.7).

These points will be argued in five parts in this chapter. Arabic has in a
sense two histories, one the literary language, one the 'holistic' language (see

---

[6] As evidenced in the fact that textbook-like works on Arabic (e.g. Versteegh 1997: 47, 93) routinely assume the Old–New dichotomy without discussion. Holes (1995: 30–1) speaks of Old Arabic and Middle Arabic, with a direct line of development to the modern dialects. Ferrando (2001: 137), while giving a good overview of different ideas surrounding the Old–New dichotomy, particularly the question, as it has been formulated, of whether Neo-Arabic has its roots in a period when Old Arabic also existed (e.g. Spitaler 1953; see 2.4.2 below). The legitimacy of the distinction as a grounded linguistic concept, however, is not questioned.

The pervasiveness of the Old–New dichotomy in the Western Arabicist tradition can be discerned in a survey of representative national writers. Besides those cited in the previous paragraph (Versteegh for Holland, Ferrando for Spain, Holes for England), one can note Fleisch (1974:13) or Cohen (1972) for France, while the German, Israeli (e.g. Blau), and American (e.g. Ferguson) contributions are treated in greater detail in the present chapter. Indeed, the distinction is so entrenched in the Western tradition that Cuvalay (1997: 6) writes, 'No matter how they describe the pre-Islamic situation, all theories of the development of the MA [modern Arabic] dialects acknowledge the occurrence of large-scale linguistic changes as a result of the spread of Arabic beyond the Arabian peninsula, which started with the Islamic conquests in the 7th century A.D.' The problem from the perspective of the current work is that the consensus (ʔijmaaʕ!) which Cuvalay describes does not have a comparative historical linguistic basis.

[7] Moreover, as Pierre Larcher (p.c. June 2004) points out, European Arabicists of the nineteenth century were strongly influenced by models of development in European languages. 'On ne peut rien comprendre du l'orientalisme européen, si on oublie que jusqu'au date récente les orientalistes ont tous fait du latin et du grec.' The logical matrix was also inspired by models from European languages. Goldziher (1877 1994: 20) held that 'The correct standpoint concerning the so-called colloquial language is that it represents a later level in the development of the Arabic language, just as Latin preceded the Romance languages.'

2.2.2). In sect. 2.2.1, I begin the discussion of periodization of Arabic on the basis of the literary language. The literary language is attested, inter alia, in the detailed linguistic texts of the Arabic grammarians. A closer look at these texts will reveal how difficult it is to achieve a periodization of the language even on the basis of the closed corpus of written descriptions. At the end of sect. 2.2, and in sect. 2.3, I examine the attempt by Arabicists to incorporate the spoken dialects into a holistic conceptualization of the language, beginning about 1850 and ending in 1950. In sect. 2.4, the most serious attempt to define the two stages, Old Arabic and Neo-Arabic, in linguistic terms is examined in detail. Data both from the modern dialects and the detailed descriptions of the Arabic grammatical tradition will indicate that most criteria proposed for distinguishing Old from Neo-Arabic are faulty, due in part to the failure adequately to consider all the sources. In sects. 2.5 and 2.6, I briefly consider two further logical matrices which have been invoked to understand Arabic language history. In sect. 2.5, a case is considered where the modern diglossic relation between Standard Arabic and dialect is projected into the Old Arabic era. In sect. 2.6, I indicate that the notion of linguistic history in the Arabic tradition itself was only weakly and unsystematically developed. Section 2.7 is the concluding discussion.

2.2. Stages in Arabic

Two different strands can be discerned in the Old/New dichotomy, one internal to what I will term 'literary Arabic', the other to what the nineteenth-century German scholar Fleischer (see sect. 2.2.2 below) conceived of as a holistic Arabic (*Gesammtarabisch*).

2.2.1. Literary Arabic

I begin with the first, as it is the simpler of the two. Literary Arabic is defined by a norm developed in the course of the eighth and ninth centuries on the basis of a fixed canon of texts, namely the *Quran*, pre- and early Islamic poetry and the early ʔaadaab or belles lettres literature, for example the writings of Ibn al-Muqaffaʕ (d. 139/756). The first two sources, the *Quran* and pre- and early Islamic poetry were themselves subject to a process of commentary, evaluation, and editing by Koranic commentators (e.g. Ibn Mujahid, d. 324/936) and Arabic grammarians, the best known of these being Farraʔ (d. 207/822) and Sibawaih (d. 177/793) respectively, so that these grammatical sources became a further element in the establishment of a literary norm.

It is the following four elements which Fischer (1982b: 37–45) defined as the sources for Classical Arabic.

(1) Sources for Classical Arabic
   Quran
   poetry
   early ʔaadaab literature[8]
   grammatical treatises

Using the Classical period as a pivot, Fischer on the one hand defines a post-classical era, the literary language of, approximately, 900–1100, characterized mainly by stylistic and lexicographic differences with the classical era. On the other, he identifies a pre-classical Arabic, the period before the classical. While Fischer recognizes the non-discrete nature of the periodization—elements of one period may also appear in another—the system creates a neat triadic division comparable to the old, middle, new linearization matrix, in which language periodization replicates chronology.

Already here, however, there appear fundamental problems which are peculiar to the nature of the Arabic sources which the system serves to elucidate by its classification. Writing about the classical period, Fischer (1982b: 44) notes that Sibawaih's grammar marked the culmination of the development of a standard Classical Arabic ('markiert den Abschluss der Ausbildung einer klassisch-arabischen Standardsprache').[9] At the same time, for the characterization of pre-classical Arabic Fischer, rather than define the variety in terms of linguistic attributes, refers the reader to Nöldeke's (1897) grammar of Classical Arabic. Nöldeke's grammar is replete with unclassical-looking forms. It happens, however, that one of Nöldeke's important sources for his grammar is none other than Sibawaih. Nöldeke for instance (1897: 14) notes the 3MSG object pronoun-(u)h, e.g. *lam ʔaḍrib-uh* 'I didn't hit him' instead of-*hu*, *ʔaḍrib-hu*, is an alternative form discussed in Sibawaih II: 313 (see discussion in sect. 8.9). Sibawaih cannot at one and the same time be the culmination of the classical period and a key source for the pre-classical

---

[8] It should be noted that the ʔaadaab literature was not a part of the linguistic data treated by the early grammarians. They used examples from the QurʔAan, from early poetry, from linguistic informants, and from their own constructed examples. A problem with the ʔaadaab literature is that much, if not all of it, is available only in later versions, which quite possibly—in some cases with certainty—were edited according to later stylistic norms (see Bosworth 1989; Latham 1990 for general discussion). Of course, a pre-Classical—Classical—post-Classical historical chain can be worked out for individual constructions. Larcher, for instance (2003: 189) argues that conditional sentences show a progressive simplification of verb forms in the condition and result clauses from what he terms pre-Classical Arabic (QurʔAan, poetry) to Classical to post-Classical Arabic.

[9] Fischer properly allows for a historical development even in the era of what is termed here Old Arabic. See sect. 2.5 for a further type of modern matrix.

as well.¹⁰ The same objection applies to the other sources used by Nöldeke. He cites, for instance, various exceptional constructions found in the different Koranic readings. The Koranic readings, however, are equally attested, at the very earliest, only in the eighth century, i.e. in Fischer's Classical era (see Ch. 4). Though Nöldeke did not use him as a source, it can be noted that the same 3MSG object suffix variant is discussed by Farraʔ (I. 223, 388), who observes that both bedouins (Arabs) and the Koranic readers ʕAaṣim (d. 118/736) and ʔAʕmash (d. 148/765)¹¹ use the-uh (or-Vh) variant in certain contexts.

In fact, Nöldeke himself was not attempting to define stages in the language history of Arabic. Rather (1897: 1), he was interested in exceptions to the rules of Classical Arabic as he understood it. In contrast to Fischer, Nöldeke does not commit himself on the question, whether the many exceptions to Classical Arabic which he noted are chronologically or comparatively prior to Classical Arabic. This indeed is a far-reaching question requiring application of the comparative method to each individual feature. Lacking this, the question needs to be left open whether the non-classical feature is older, contemporary with, e.g. a 'non-standard' form which did not get classicized, or newer than, Classical Arabic (i.e. innovation).

With this last observation the basis of a pre-classical literary Arabic as characterized by Fischer is taken away, at least pending closer comparative work. There are no large corpora of chronologically pre-Classical Arabic. All sources cited in (1) above derive from the eighth century, so chronologically all lie in what Fischer terms the classical period.

2.2.2. Holistic Arabic

A pre-Classical Arabic is therefore a logically possible entity, though not one which has been established on comparative linguistic terms. The problem of applying logical matrices to Arabic becomes much greater when the spoken language is added to the mix.

The stage for this was set at least one hundred and fifty years ago. The German Arabicist Fleischer suggested that a 'holistic language' (*Gesammtsprache*, i.e. 'holistic Arabic') could offer an all-inclusive linguistic umbrella to varieties of Arabic which could be very different from one another

---

¹⁰ Unless one assumes that one can identify, disentangle, and reconstruct Sibawaih's classical references from 'pre-Classical', something which Fischer does not undertake. Sibawaih himself did not think in terms of historical stages, but rather was an acute observer of the Arabic around him. The data he provides is synchronic.

¹¹ A Kufan Koranic reader, included among the fourteen readers; see Gilliot 1990: 160. He is cited very frequently by Farraʔ.

(1854/1968: 155).¹² This holistic Arabic could be divided into three stages, Old Arabic, Middle Arabic, and Neo-Arabic (*Altarabisch, Mittelarabisch, Neuarabisch*). Importantly, these three stages are definitional constructs. It would appear that Fleischer conceived of them in chronological terms. The first two stages, Old Arabic and Middle Arabic, basically correspond to Fischer's Classical Arabic and post-Classical Arabic respectively. Old Arabic is the language of the *Qurʔaan*, of poetry, and of the Arabic grammarians (Fleischer 1854: 154), while Middle Arabic is the literary language which emerged in the early Islamic era in the lands outside the Arabian peninsula (ibid.: 155). Neo-Arabic is not characterized explicitly, though clearly Fleischer understood this variety as the contemporary Arabic dialect.

The key element of the current exposition is that the logical matrix of Old Arabic, Middle Arabic, Neo-Arabic is imposed by fiat, rather than established on the basis of comparative linguistic practice.

My current critical introduction has a stringently linguistic basis. Understanding the motivation and causes underlying Fleischer's initiative, is an enterprise well outside the scope of the present book. This belongs properly to the history of Arabic studies in the West. It may be noted, however, that Fleischer's model is in part an attempt to incorporate the modern dialects into the total fabric of Arabic. He notes, for instance, that Neo-Arabic enjoys a serious status neither among Arab nor among many Western scholars (1885: 154).¹³ Citing work by the Finnish Arabicist Wallin on Najdi dialects, he suggests that Arabic peninsular dialects may be closer to Old Arabic than is commonly thought, perhaps being a direct descendant of these (1885: 157).¹⁴ In 1854, Arabic dialectology was very much in its infancy, and it may be, at the risk of being generous, that Fleischer was using the term 'Neo-Arabic' as a heuristic, a place-holder for the incorporation of the spoken dialects into Arabic studies, whose precise linguistic status was yet to be determined.¹⁵

---

¹² Fleischer's ideas appear in the introduction to an article on Arabic lexicography which was originally published in 1854, republished in 1885 in a collection of his articles, the latter work being reprinted in original format in 1968. Page references are therefore to the 1885 collection.

¹³ Unfortunately, a suspicion as justified today as it was 150 years ago. A standard work on the Semitic languages, Moscati et al. (1980: 14) essentially stops Semitic language history with Classical Arabic, modern dialects contributing nothing to it.

¹⁴ Fleischer does not explain where he sees Wallin's texts as closer to the Classical language than urban dialects. Wallin's texts are from Najdi Arabic, songs and poetry written in Arabic script and transcribed as Wallin says he heard them. Wallin notes, however, that the recitations do not necessarily follow the usual phonology of the dialect, the typical *tʃ* for instance being rendered in his texts as *k*, and *dz* as *q* (*ṣidiq* for *ṣididz*) (1851: 10, 1852: 218).

¹⁵ Fleischer himself described an opposition between a proper bedouin language, which was also the basis of Koranic Arabic and of the standard 'Arabiyya, and a debased, urban variety developed by non-Muslims (1847: 155). This discussion takes place in the context of a summary of a text which falls

However, the fact remains that this early matrix is not linguistically based. Moreover, in citing Wallin's work on Saudi Arabian dialects, Fleischer allows other, non-linguistic parameters to intrude into his interpretations. He suggests that urban Neo-Arabic (*städtisches Neuarabisch*) is further removed from Old Arabic than are the Arabian dialects. From this observation it is clear that the Old Arabic – Neo-Arabic dichotomy is to be understood as a historical linguistic development which, presumably, may show greater or lesser degree of innovation in Neo-Arabic. No comparative linguistic basis for this assumption is provided, however. Moreover, a further non-linguistic parameter, the urban–bedouin division obtrudes effortlessly into Fleischer's thinking, anticipating the imposition of other logical matrices onto an interpretation of Arabic linguistic history (see sect. 1.6.7).

Moreover, a brief look at Wallin's work shows that Wallin himself judged his bedouin Najdi dialect according to its conformity or lack thereof to Classical Arabic. *Laa taḍiiʕ* 'don't let get lost' appears in the text, 'rather than the grammatical *laa taḍiʕ*' (1851: 8), i.e. Wallin 'corrects' the Najdi negative imperative to the Classical jussive form. The Najdi basic verb *raad* 'want' is noted to occur rather than the grammatical [i.e. Classical Arabic] *ʔaraad* (1851: 4). *ʔabuu-k* 'your father', with fixed stem *ʔabuu*, is noted to appear instead of *ʔabaak* (in an accusative context) because 'the old case endings are not respected by the contemporary Arabs'. It may be Wallin was using reference to Classical Arabic as an orientation to the reader. However, its constant citation imparts to Wallin's commentary a normative character which can easily be understood as a historical development from the classical language to the modern dialect. In a work on Arabic phonology (1855: 7) Wallin offers a strictly descriptive summary of both Classical Arabic and the dialects, though does refer to an *imala* form (see Ch. 7) in the 'oldest language' (*älteste Sprache*), which he contrasts with the language of the modern bedouin. 'Old', and by implication here 'new' appears to be strictly chronological. In a further work (1858: 673–5) Wallin in a rather confused fashion explicitly summarizes the extent to which 'the old grammatical forms' (*die alten grammatischen Formen*) are maintained among bedouins.[16] Here a direct linear development from Classical Arabic to the dialect is stated.

---

within Blau's genre of Middle Arabic, i.e. one marked by deviations from the ʕArabiyya. Fleischer thus appears to be responsible for introducing a number of key, if problematic concepts including Old vs. Middle and Neo-Arabic, and bedouin (pure) vs. urban (debased).

[16] Wallin (1858: 674) notes for instance that the case endings are not used according to the rules of Classical Arabic. He goes on to say that the case endings can, however, be heard among some bedouin tribes ('man hört sie jedoch bei einigen Bediuinenstämmen'). What he terms case endings, however, are in fact epenthetic vowels, as will be seen in sect. 8.3; see also Ch. 3 n. 31.

With these examples of Fischer and Fleischer, the groundwork is laid for exemplifying the two main strands of Western interpretations of Arabic linguistic history. The first strand is an adherence to a strict chronological historical line. Neo-Arabic is not new because it is characterized by certain innovations relative to Old Arabic, but simply because the dialects are chronologically younger than Old Arabic. The second is an assumption that Classical Arabic as defined by the sources in (1) above is the historical standard for all further varieties of Arabic, be they literary varieties or the development of modern dialects. Both assumptions present fundamental impediments to a linguistic history of Arabic.

2.3. Arabic and the Dialects

In this section I introduce further interpretations of the history of Arabic. All of them assume an Old–New dichotomy, while one, as with Fleischer above, adds a middle variety as well. I should note that in this section I exemplify important types of interpretation without embedding them in a broader Arabicist intellectual history.

2.3.1. *Brockelmann: Old to New without discussion*

Carl Brockelmann is one of the most respected scholars in the history of Semitic studies, his *Grundriß*, published in 1908 and 1913 (vols. i, ii), to this day being a fundamental reference work in the field. In the *Grundriß* Brockelmann, while extensively cataloguing the Neo-Arabic reflexes of grammatical categories, is virtually silent about their historical status, other than their post-Classical Arabic emergence. The term 'Neo-Arabic' (*Neuarabisch*) does not appear until p. 45, and then as an exemplification of a form. Neo-Arabic is assumed, not defined or demonstrated. Earlier he notes that spoken dialects are very poorly attested in the research literature before the nineteenth century (1908: 25).

Brockelmann's silence on the emergence of Neo-Arabic is very much in keeping with the classificatory character of the *Grundriß*, the extensive listing of forms from the various Semitic languages being its great strength. In the introduction he explicitly states that for him reconstruction is a purely formal exercise, reconstructed entities having no correlate in a real language (1908: 4–5, 35). Furthermore, the Semitic languages are so similar to one another, that a geographically-based classification of the languages, presumably rather than one based on shared innovation, is the best approach to summarizing them (1908: 6). This approach coincides with his observation that the Semitic languages have experienced a great deal of close contact, speakers of one Semitic language often shifting to another. The remark, though interesting, remains an isolated aside, and in no way presages an interest in the effects of language contact on language change.

In short, by 1908 the dichotomy Old–New Arabic is confirmed as an organizational principle not in need of a comparative linguistic basis. Discussion of the comparative linguistic development of his Neo-Arabic out of Old Arabic is therefore entirely absent from Brockelmann.

2.3.2. Fück: Old to New, pre-diaspora to post-diaspora

A book of considerable influence in Arabic linguistic studies was Fück's *Arabiyüa* (1950). It is a work of great erudition, but one which is based mainly on non-linguistic literary sources. Nonetheless, it offers an explanation of the change in Arabic from Old to New. According to Fück the intensive contact between Arabs and non-Arabs in the first century of the Islamic conquests led to a massive grammatical simplification. At the same time there developed a class-based difference between an Arab upper class and a non-Arab lower and middle class (1950: 5–7).

Fück's full linguistic analysis is hard to follow here. On the one hand he suggests that massive simplification was in play. His evidence for this, however, is exiguous, and his analyses questionable. Relying, as noted, on literary sources (especially Jahiḏ's *al-Bayaan wa al-Tabyiyn* from the mid-ninth century), he quotes the following as an example of the extreme pidginization of the language (5):

(2) *ʃariik-aat-naa fi hawaaz-ha wa ʃariik-aat-na fi madaaʔin-ha wa kamaa ta-jii ta-kuun*[17]

Lit. Our partners in its Ahwaz and our partners in its Madaʔin and as they come, so they are = The ordered animals were delivered by our business partners in this circumstance.

Admittedly without a considerable degree of contextualization, the meaning would be quite opaque. Grammatically, however, the sentence shows a high

---

[17] As in Fück, who used a Cairo edition of Jahiḏ. In my Beirut edition (p. 90) is found *madaayin-ha* and *tajiiʔ*. Jahiḏ gives the correct form, as *ʃurakaaʔunaa b-il-ʔahwaaz wa l-madaaʔin yabʕaθ-uwna ʔilayna bi-haðihi l-dawaabb fa-naħnu nabiyʕuhaa ʕalaa wujuuhihaa* 'our partners in Ahwaz and Madaʔin send us these pack animals and we sell them as they are'.

Note that Fück leaves off the case endings in his transliteration (given in (2), though in my edition of Jahiḏ at least, no short vowels are indicated, so Jahiḏ's intent is impossible to gauge. Fück thus 'reconstructs' the lack of case endings here according to his conception of how this bad Arabic looked, not according to a linguistically grounded methodology.

degree of linguistic competence in Arabic, far too great to present it as an instance of pidginization. In particular, the morphology is completely correct, allowing for *fariik-aat* instead of *furakaaʔ*, and complex. Besides their correct personal prefixes, the two weak verbs occur in their correct conjugation, and the noun *fariik* has two suffixes, plural *-aat* followed by a pronominal suffix. A universal mark of pidginization is a lack of morphological structure, as indeed has been attested in Arabic itself (Thomason and El-Gibali 1986; see Owens 1997: 132, on a short tenth- century text; Smart 1990 on Gulf Pidgin Arabic). Contrary to pidginization, it appears that one is dealing here with a relatively sophisticated L2 variety, though of course the data is presented to us through the filter of Jahiḏ's stereotypes, not meticulously recorded texts.

On the other hand, Fück identifies a class-based variety, non-native Arab lower and middle classes in the early Islamic empire striving assiduously to learn the Classical Arabic of the Arab upper class. They basically succeeded, failing only to learn the case endings. This caseless variety then became the basis for Arabic urban dialects.

This presentation is rather confusing and as a linguistic explanation for the transition from Old to Neo-Arabic, unsatisfying. On the one hand in the course of the diaspora an abysmal pidgin developed, but at the same time a form of Arabic normal except for the loss of case endings. Given Fück's reliance on written sources, little better can be expected. Both summaries are correct in their own way, at least true to the sources, allowing for a better characterization of L2 varieties as indicated in the discussion around (2) above. Fück himself admits that 'the specifics of this development as a consequence of the lack of contemporary material are virtually unknown' (1950: 5). Ultimately, as with Fleischer 100 years before him, Fück's historical linguistics rests on a logical matrix of Old vs. New, with only the barest of linguistic substance to justify the dichotomy.

Before moving to the next model, it is worthwhile pausing to summarize the opinion of two linguists who, if indeed not directly influenced by Fück, developed ideas which are prominent in his work.

The first is the well-known koine hypothesis of Ferguson (1959b). Ferguson argued that in the early Islamic military camps a simplification or koinization of Arabic occurred which heralded in the modern dialects. In Fück's version (1950: 5) the military camps and early Islamic cities such as Kufa and Fustat (Cairo) saw the development of a common bedouin variety, which served as the basis of what became known as Classical Arabic. Ferguson took this same social milieu to be the breeding ground for a common variety of Arabic koine, simplified according to fourteen different parameters. In a sense, Ferguson's treatment is the first, and till today one of the few attempts to extensively define the transition from Old to Neo-Arabic according to linguistic parameters.¹⁸ In this sense Ferguson's work falls outside the critical paradigm developed in this first section. While I will not comment on his individual features in this work, it may be noted that they are subject to the same critical perspective as that developed in sect. 2.4 below.

The second is Versteegh's pidginization hypothesis (1984a), in which pidginization is held responsible for the simplification of Arabic dialects. In a recent work (2004) Versteegh appears to have changed his ideas somewhat, emphasizing second language learning rather than radical pidginization as the source of the old to new shift.

2.3.3. Blau: Old to Middle to New

The progression Old to Middle to New was met above in Fleischer's interpretation, in which Middle Arabic essentially has the value of Fischer's 'Post-Classical'. Fleischer assumes, but does not demonstrate the transition from Middle Arabic to Neo-Arabic. A very different interpretation of Middle Arabic was offered by Joshua Blau (1966, 1981, 1988, 2002). Based on extensive and careful textual analysis, Blau showed that there were many documents, personal and business letters, for instance, and many Christian and Jewish Arabic sources, written in what he termed Middle Arabic. While written in a basically Classical matrix, they exhibited many elements of modern Arabic dialects. The earliest is dated to the late seventh century. They become numerous, however, only in the tenth century. On the basis of his documentation, Blau suggested that Middle Arabic was the missing link in the transition from Old to Neo-Arabic, emerging in the early Islamic era as the result of contact between Arabic and non-Arabic speakers (1981). Blau's thesis can be viewed as an empirical application of the logical matrix. It is logical in the sense that given Old and New, something must be Middle as well. It is empirical in that his Middle is defined by a corpus of texts.

Subsequent work indicated that Blau's Middle Arabic could be given an interpretation other than a sequential, historical one. It emerged that both very early documents and very late ones (e.g. Doss 1995, on a seventeenth-century text), showed the same sort of deviations from a standard norm. Essentially, these deviations can be interpreted, according to perspective, as interference from the dialect in a learned Standard Arabic (e.g. *hada* for *haða* 'this.M', in *1001 Nights*, Mahdi 1984: 75), or as learning errors of a type all who

---

¹⁸ See Kaye 1976 for an early criticism. Abboud-Haggar 2003: 83–4 has a good summary of proposed koinization features, based on Ferguson (1959b), Cohen (1972), and Versteegh (1984a). Despite implicit misgivings (2005: 24), Behnstedt and Woidich (2005: 11–18) recently reaffirmed the non-comparativist approach in defining a purported old/new contrast.

have studied Standard Arabic as a second language will be familiar with; for instance, *lam taquwliy-na* 'you.F did not say', instead of *taquwl-iy*, with the suffix-*na* wrongly maintained in the jussive verbal form (Blau 1966: 269). In either case, Middle Arabic in these texts arises from a mixture of Standard Arabic and a spoken dialect and is adventitious upon these varieties (see Larcher 2001; Versteegh 2005 for summaries and overviews). Indeed, Blau himself has tended to move Middle Arabic from the historical to the stylistic realm (1982), no longer viewing Middle Arabic as a variety independent of Classical Arabic/Arabic dialects.[19] In his latest work (2002: 14) he writes that 'Middle Arabic is the language of mediaeval Arabic texts in which classical, post-classical, and often also Neo-Arabic and pseudo-correct elements alternate quite freely.' It is primarily a style, not a historical stage.

2.4. Neo-Arabic and the Neo-German school

After well over a hundred years of logical classification, an attempt was finally made to give linguistic content to the Old Arabic – New Arabic dichotomy. In ch. 3 of the *Handbuch der arabischen Dialekte* a number of phonological and morphological contrasts between the two are summarized.[20] This summary follows in the tradition of Ferguson (1959*b*, see sect. 2.3.1 above) and Cohen (1972), though the dialects rather than emerging in a sociolinguistic object, the koine, ostensibly have the status of a comparative linguistic end product, Neo-Arabic. I will devote the bulk of this chapter to a critical review of this summary, as the very idea of Old vs. Neo-Arabic stands or falls as a linguistic concept on the nature of the linguistic developments which are represented within it.

In all, Fischer and Jastrow discuss about twenty features. Rather than review each in turn, I criticize the entire concept by grouping the features into four types. A detailed discussion of representatives of each type will serve to characterize the efficacy or lack thereof of the features. The features may be characterized by the following four parameters.

---

[19] Holes (1995: 31) writes, 'it is possible to discern a clear line of development from the earliest written Arabic ephemera (c.AD 800) through medieval Middle Arabic texts to the modern colloquials'. To my knowledge, there is no detailed published work which has demonstrated such an assumed development; as noted here, the current consensus is rather to view Middle Arabic as a stylistic by-product. Against what can be termed the linear view of Middle Arabic development, Versteegh (2005: 16) warns us not to '[r]egard them [Middle Arabic texts] as true reflections of the vernacular speech of the writers, but as "the tip of the iceberg" giving us a glimpse of what had taken place in the spoken speech'. There is in any case a general consensus that a great deal more analysis remains to be carried out on Middle Arabic texts, which will shed further light on the two positions.

[20] A shorter summary of the features is also found in Fischer's chapter 'Das Neuarabische und seine Dialekte' in the *Grundriss* (1982*c*). The *Handbuch* remains a standard reference work for Arabic dialectology.

1. The contrast characterizes some, but not all modern dialects.
2. The contrast characterizes some, but not all varieties of Old Arabic.
3. The data are incomplete.
4. The contrast is valid, so far as our information goes.

I begin with the first. The most common, and most difficult problem in my view is that what is presented as an Old Arabic – Neo-Arabic dichotomy in fact pertains only to some of the modern Arabic dialects. Others are identical between Old Arabic and the modern dialects. In fact, it takes but one counter-example to disqualify a feature as an example for the holistic dichotomy Old Arabic–Neo-Arabic.

A case in point is a very fundamental element of phonology, the structure of syllables. In Old Arabic syllables with short vowels are CV and CVC (or CVCC, which can be ignored here). According to Fischer and Jastrow (1980: 40, sect. 3.3), 'In Neo-Arabic the relations are quite different: short vowels in open syllables are reduced to a large degree.' Here they contrast Old Arabic *katabat* vs. Damascene *katbet* 'she wrote'. Damascene, along with many dialects in the Levant, reduce the unstressed vowel in an open syllable in the structure *'CVCVC-VC →'CVCC-VC. They go on to point out that short high vowels are even more susceptible to deletion than are low ones.

Fischer and Jastrow, however, are not contrasting Old Arabic with Damascene Arabic or Levantine Arabic, but with Neo-Arabic, i.e. with all modern Arabic dialects. In these terms their generalization is false. The case of short [i] and [u] will be discussed in detail in the next section. Here it suffices to point out that descriptively one can range modern dialects along a long scale according to the behavior of short vowels or even short vowels in open syllables. I use the makeshift phonological parameters of open syllable in stressed, pre-stress, and post-stress position as classifying parameters. At the one extreme are dialects such as highland Yemeni (Behnstedt 1985: 53–4; Werbeck 2001: 59, *'firiħat* 'she was happy', *yiʕayyinu* 'they look', *yiʕaaliguh* 'he treats him'), and the Baħariyya oasis (Behnstedt and Woidich 1985: 64–8, 1988: 325, *'libisit* 'she wore', *tinaam* 'you sleep') where all short vowels are 'kept' in all contexts. Simplifying considerably (see Ch. 6 for detail), in western Sudanic Arabic (Chad, Cameroon, northeast Nigeria) nearly all vowels are kept in all contexts, post-stress high vowels in open syllables sometimes (depending, inter alia, on the consonantal context) being deleted (*ri'jaal* 'men', *'simiʔ* 'he heard', *simiʔ-o* → *'simʔ-o* 'they heard', but *'fihim-o* 'they understood'). Within noun and verb stems, Najdi Arabic keeps all short vowels in stressed or pre-stress position, deleting only those in post-stress open syllables, *ji'luus* 'sitting', *ri'jaal* 'men'. Vowels in post-stress open syllables are categorically deleted, 'sirig 'he was robbed' vs. 'sirig-aw → 'sirg-aw 'they.M were robbed' (Ingham 1994a: 27, 33). In various northern qultu dialects of Iraq, Syria, and Anatolia, high vowels in open syllables are always deleted, r'jeel 'men' (Sasse 1971: 92 on Mardin in Anatolia), unless they follow CC-, in which case they are maintained (yəktəb-uun 'they write'). The low vowel is deleted only under certain conditions. In the reflexive (muṭaawiʕ) prefix of verbs stems V and VI, for example, it is deleted tqaatal 'fight with' < *taqaatal). In pre-stress open syllables in nouns and adjectives /a/ may be raised, məkeetib 'office'<makaatib). In most other positions a low vowel is retained, 'katabat 'she wrote'. Moving to the extreme of deletion, in some North African dialects any short vowel in an open syllable will be deleted. This gives rise to stem alternations where the short vowel essentially has the function of a place-holder to prevent the build-up of too many consonants, k'təb 'he wrote vs. 'kətb-ət "she wrote" (Caubet 1993: 31; see sects. 2.4.1 and 5.8.3 below).

These observations can be summarized on the following grid, using as parameters occurrence of /a/ in an open syllable, high vowel in pre-stress open syllable and high vowel in post-stress open syllable. For purposes of presenting a simplified account, I do not include the Mardin forms like yəktəbuun, as this would entail expanding the conditions of occurrence where deletion does or does not occur, nor a rule which raises an /a/ to an /i/ in an open syllable in some dialects.

In Table 2.1, a '+' indicates that the vowel is maintained in the relevant position, a '−' that it is deleted.

What is developed here in very rudimentary form is the idea that modern dialects can be ranged along an implicational scale in regards to the three syllable structure parameters. Phonologically, maintenance of a short high vowel in a post-stress open syllable implies maintenance of all short high vowels in all positions. If an /a/ is maintained variably (see below), then

TABLE 2.1. Basic vowel deletion in Arabic dialects

	/a/ in open syllable	pre-stress high V	post-stress high V
Highland Yemen	+	+	+
Baḥariyya	+	+	+
Western Sudanic Arabic	+	+	+/−
Najdi	+	+	−
Mardin	+/−	−	−
Central Morocco	−	−	−

a high vowel will not be maintained in pre-post-stress open syllable position, and so on.

Between Mardin and Central Morocco it may be expected that intermediate cases can be found. The '+/−' for /a/ in Mardin hides a somewhat complicated situation, as illustrated briefly above. A fuller representation would need to break down both the high and low vowel open syllable contexts into a number of finer categories. All in all, however, it is clear from this short representation that the modern dialects cannot be subsumed under a single rubric such as Neo-Arabic as far as short high vowels in open syllables go. At very best (see below sect. 2.4.1.2, Old Arabic, and sect. 2.4.2), a contrast between 'Old Arabic' and dialects can be drawn only for some dialects. Moreover, as will be seen, assuming that dialects at a certain point on the implicational scale are closer to Old Arabic than are others is problematic.

Similar instances where Fischer and Jastrow allow a part to speak for the whole include the following.

- The 2FSG object suffix underwent the change in Neo-Arabic *-ki* → *ik*. Many dialects, however, maintain invariable *-ki* (sect. 42, 1980: 3.4.3, most qultu dialects of Mesopotamia, Uzbekistan, western Sudanic Arabic; see sect. 8.7.4 below).
- Many Old Arabic words have *a*, changing to *i* in Neo-Arabic, e.g. *man* → *min/miin* 'who?', or *anta* → *inta* 'you.MSG' (ibid. 44, sect. 3.6). However, *man* is found in many dialects[21] as well (Eastern Libya, some Yemeni dialects, Horan, Bahariyya oasis in Egypt) as is *anta* (Tihama in Yemen, some Omani dialects).
- Fischer and Jastrow themselves note that the ten standard verb forms (basic stem, 9 derived stems) are essentially identical to their Old Arabic ones (ibid. 46–7, sect. 3.8), i.e. do not form a basis for identifying two separate entities.

---

[21] The question of what constitutes 'many', and what the status of 'many' is, is one of a number of central issues which deserve separate treatment. Many can mean many speakers in absolute terms (10,000, 100,000, 1,000,000, millions, hundreds of millions?), and it may mean in many dialects. What the latter implies is difficult to say, unless the notion of dialect is given explicit definition, both in geographical (discussed in Ch. 5) and historical terms. Such a definition has never been undertaken in Arabic, historical dialectology in particular all but non-existent (there are significant recent exceptions, particularly regarding dialects in the Arabian peninsula, e.g. Holes 1991; Watson 1992). The forms cited as exceptional to Fischer and Jastrow's *a* → *i* generalization are from geographically separated regions, so are prima facie candidates for separate geographical dialects. Whether they have a particularly close shared dialect history requires careful comparative work. In any case, the 'exceptions' are well enough established among the contemporary Arabic dialects to remove *a* → *i* from the sets of rules defining a difference between Old and Neo-Arabic.

2.4.1. i vs. u, *An interpretive case study*

The question of short vowels provides a rich source of interpretive material. I will discuss one aspect of Fischer and Jastrow's proposed OA–NA contrast in greater detail in order to illustrate the range of sources which can be brought to bear on the issue of relations between Old Arabic sources and modern dialects. They observe (ibid. 43, sect. 3.5) that the opposition between *i-u*, the short high vowels, is only weakly represented in Neo-Arabic. This is undoubtedly correct, and as they observe in many dialects there is no contrast whatsoever, the two falling together in a common /ə/ whose phonetic realization is determined by consonantal context. For Moroccan Arabic, for instance, Heath (2002: 4–10) distinguishes three broad dialect areas. In the southern or Saharan dialect Old [i], [u], [a] merge in [ə]. However, the short vowels may be maintained in open syllables. For the northern type Heath does not attempt a generalization relating to all vowels in all positions, though he does speak of extensive loss of short vowels, all his examples being short vowels in open syllables. The central type, which is also the basis of a broad Moroccan koine, is similar to the northern type, except it appears that in many positions an old short vowel is simply lost altogether, as in *n-ktəb* 'I write' (southern *nə-ktəb*). In many grammars of North African dialects there is only one short vowel, represented in most grammars as /ə/, whose value is determined by phonetic context. This is the case for instance with Caubet (1993: 23) for Moroccan Arabic,[22] and Marçais (1956) for *Djidjelli* (Algeria) has only /ə/, whose value is again phonologically determined. Indeed, phonologically a case might even be made that the short vowel in some dialects is always determined by phonological rule, which would eliminate it from the grammar altogether at the abstract level (e.g. Owens 1980).

There are two fundamental problems in Fischer and Jastrow's formulation of the short vowel situation, however. First as in the other features discussed above, [i] and [u] in fact are maintained in various modern dialects. Secondly, Fischer and Jastrow imply that [i] and [u] were a stable opposition in Old Arabic. This does not stand up under close examination of the old sources, however. Both these objections will be exemplified in greater detail here. In 2.4.1.1, I discuss modern sources, including the results detailing a case study conducted in Nigerian Arabic. In sect. 2.4.1.2, I turn to the old sources.

Before proceeding to this discussion it may be helpful to sketch the basic issue with the following developmental trees. Example (3a) represents Fischer

---

[22] Except that she recognizes two short vowels /ə/and /u/, which, however, apparently are not phonemically contrastive. She says /u/ is rare.

and Jastrow's proposal. Short vowels are stable and/or contrastive in Old Arabic, while in Neo-Arabic they have changed in such a way that their stability and contrastive value is reduced.

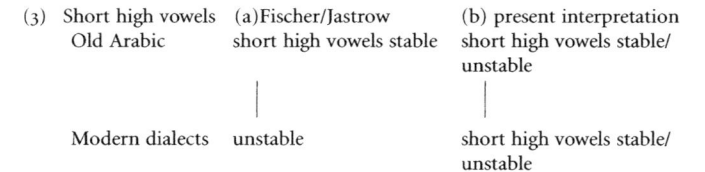

(3) Short high vowels   (a) Fischer/Jastrow   (b) present interpretation
     Old Arabic   short high vowels stable   short high vowels stable/
                                                    unstable
                                | |
     Modern dialects   unstable   short high vowels stable/
                                                    unstable

(Old Arabic ≠ Neo-Arabic   Old Arabic ≅ Neo-Arabic (≅ approximates to))

In comparative terms, Fischer and Jastrow describe an innovation which distinguishes Old Arabic from Neo-Arabic. The question I pose here is whether in fact an innovation has taken place which distinguishes Old Arabic from all varieties of Neo-Arabic. If not, as in (3b), this feature must be removed from the proposed set of factors constitutive of the differentiation between Old and Neo-Arabic.

2.4.1.1. *Modern short high vowels* While there are dialects, some of them very large, which exhibit rather dramatic short vowel loss, there are also many which exhibit short vowel retention to one degree or another. There are dialects with a phonemic contrast between the three, albeit only in closed syllables. For eastern Libyan Arabic Mitchell (1960: 379) cites the contrast, *ħigg* 'young camel', *ħugg* 'look!', *ħagg* 'he looked', and Fischer and Jastrow (1980: 53–4) themselves note that there are dialects which retain all three vowels, for instance some dialects in Syria, Lebanon, and Yemen.

In many other dialects a free variation of sorts is reported for the occurrence of i/u in closed syllables. In the North Yemen language atlas there are a number of entries where the same lexeme shows both [i] and [u] dialectal variants. For instance, the word for 'frog' with various consonantal difference is based on a stem like *ḏifdaʕah* or *difdaxah* (CVfdVC2-ah). In five of the variants the initial vowel is high [i] while in seven of them it is [u] (and two [a]), e.g. *ḏifdaʕah* vs. *ḏufʕayd-ah* or *dufduxah* (Behnstedt 1985: 203). In Shukriyya Arabic in the Sudan [i] vs. [u] are lexically specified by Reichmuth (1983: 59), *hidim* 'clothes' vs. *kufur* 'unbelievers'. They are not phonemically contrastive. In Uzbekistan Arabic different dialects may show a different vowel in the same lexeme, *miħitt* 'he puts' (Jogari, vs. *miħutt*, Arabkhona which is also in the Jogari dialect area), *jifir* 'well' (Jogari) vs. *jufur* (Djeinau, Zimmermann 2002: 16). In many areas it therefore appears that [i] and [u] may be in a broadly-based dialectal free variation (some localities having one vowel in a lexeme, others the other), while in other areas [i] and [u] are non-contrastive phonemically, but complementary on a lexically defined basis.

It will thus be instructive to look in greater detail at the behavior of [i] and [u] in one Arabic dialect where the two vowels in both open and closed syllables are very healthy. This will serve as one basis of comparison with the situation in Old Arabic in sect. 2.4.1.2. The dialect illustrated is Nigerian Arabic. While there are no phonemic contrasts between i-u, in closed syllables,[23] the two vowels have to be given phonemic status because it is not predictable in which form a high vowel will occur, for instance in the imperfect verbs, *bi-tumm* 'he finishes' vs. *bi-limm* 'he gathers'. However, the situation is far from clear-cut in that there is a large amount of lexical variation, idiolectal, sociolectal, and dialectal. In general, given an [i] or an [u] in a word, one will always find a lect where the same word will appear with the other vowel.

(4) *himirre* ~ *humurre* 'donkeys'
    bitimm ~ *butumm* 'he finishes'

To illustrate the situation in greater detail, I note the results of a brief survey I carried out more than ten years ago. I drew up a list of i/u alternating words, like those in (5), and elicited the form with the short high vowel. This may be a singular noun, a plural noun, a perfect verb, or an imperfect verb. In (5) the high vowel morphological forms elicited in the survey are given, along with their non-high vowel counterpart. I use the /i/variant as standard illustrative form only.

(5) high vowel   non-high vowel
    kitif 'shoulder'   *kataafe* 'shoulders' [i] in SG noun
    himirre 'donkeys'   *humaar* 'donkey' [i] in PL noun
    dirdir 'wall'   *daraadir* 'wall' [i] in SG noun, noun is
                               loanword[24]
    kibir 'he grew up'   *bikubar* ~ *bikubur* 'he grows up' [i] in
                               perfect verb

---

[23] In the examples below it will be seen that one vowel occurs in a closed syllable, while the other does not. In general in Nigerian Arabic vowel harmony obtains, so that an [i] or a [u] in one syllable will imply the same vowel in another. I assume that it is the vowel in the closed syllable which determines the vowel quality, though this is a theoretical question which does not need to be answered in this exposition. For the very closely related Ndjamena Arabic, Pommerol (1999: 15) gives the minimal pair *jurr* 'pull' vs. *jirr* 'fermented millet'. In Nigerian Arabic the latter is *jiir*.

[24] Loanwords are adopted to the arbitrary alternation in the same way native words are. It may be observed that Nigerian Arabs carry over the alternation into their L2 Hausa, for instance the word for 'all' may appear as both *duk* or *dik*. The first is standard Hausa.

bilizz 'he pushes'	*lazza* 'he pushed' [i] in imperfect verb, doubled verb
bijilis 'he sits'	*jalas* 'he sat' imperfect verb, normal triliteral verb
bijibduuha 'they pull it.F'	*jabadooha* 'they pulled it.F' imperfect verb, normal triliteral with object suffix

For the test, forty-six Nigerian Arabs were orally asked to fill in an answer. Twenty-four were from Maiduguri, twenty-two from various villages.[25] A total of twenty-eight pairs were elicited. Theoretically, 1,288 answers should have been elicited. In practice the number was considerably lower because, particularly in villages, the test method was not always understood, and could not be completed for each test person. Moreover, for an answer which required a plural noun, other plural forms were given than those with [i] or [u]. For instance, besides *himirre/humurre* as a possible test answer for the plural of *himaar* 'donkey', *hamiir* is another and was given by three respondents. *qazaal* 'gazelle, antelope' had ten responses of *qizlaan* as plural, while a plural for *naar* 'fire' was hard to elicit at all. In all there were 762 answer tokens with either [i] or [u].

The test was carried out by setting up a fill-in frame, of the following type,

(6) *kan daraadir katiiraat, keef taguula le waahid* ——
 'If "walls" are many, how do you say it for one? —— (wall SG)
 The expected answer is '*dirdir*' (or *durdur*).
 humma jabadooha hine amis haw gade kula humma dugut ——
 hine = *bijibduuha* (or *bujubduuha*)
 'They pulled it.F here yesterday and again now they —— (are pulling it) here.

After a few trial runs with non-test items, and running separate trials for nominal and verbal frames, the sharper respondents had no problem filling in the oral blanks. There were 18 nouns elicited, 10 verbs. The answers were noted by me on an answer sheet prepared for the questionnaire. The sessions were not recorded.

The words were chosen based on the observational experience that these (in fact, many others) could appear with either [i] or [u] in the same lexeme. For present purposes the test results confirmed this basic observation. In all, there

---

[25] The villages are Tuba, Kinyande, Warabasa, Mbewa, Ambuda, Kirenawa, Magonari, Dala Axadari, Mule Shuwari, Wayatanga, Kace (Dole), Mitene (Dole), Lagaje (Dole), Abbari (Mallis). The first ten locations can be found in Owens (1998*a*: 91). For these last four, neighboring villages from the aforementioned map are given in brackets.

are 407 [i] tokens, 355 [u]. In addition, 72 tokens of [ə] were recorded, which I will not consider in detail.[26] Looking more closely at the breakdown of the forms, only two words returned no variation at all as far as the high vowel quality goes (see Table 2.2). Otherwise, all other lexemes have both [i] and [u] in their responses. In general, there is much less variation among individual verb forms than among nouns. The 5 verbs and 5 nouns with the least i/u variation are as follows. No summarizing statistical tests such as regression analysis were run, though it appears by inspection that significant influencing factors could be the following. Phonologically velars favor [u], alveolars [i]. Individual lexemes will tend towards [i] or [u], as the list shows. Only one noun has close to a 50 per cent split, *kirkimme* 'protrusion' (i/u = 8/10). Otherwise, the difference nearly always lies at a 2 : 1 ratio or higher. Finally, as far as individual lexical patterns go, the fiʕil verb form favors [i]. However, among nouns, no pattern-based generalizations are evident. In the list in Table 2.1, there are 4 fiʕille plurals, 2 i-dominant, 2 u-dominant.

None of these factors is categorical. The plural *lisinne* 'tongues', for instance, composed entirely of alveolar consonants, in the Maiduguri sample returns 12 *lisinne*, but 6 *lusunne*. The imperfect *bikubar* (or *bukubur*) returned in the perfect 13 *kibir* vs. 16 *kubur*.

TABLE 2.2. i/u variation in Nigerian Arabic, selected lexemes

	[i]		[u]	
Verb	No.	%	No.	%
limis 'he touched'	35	100	0	
bilizz 'he pushes'	40	97.5	1	
simin 'get fat'	27	91	2	
bugulub 'gallop'	2		32	96
bijibduuha 'they pull her'	38	92.5	3	
Noun				
rukubbe 'knees'	0		10	100
dirdir 'wall of house'	36	97	1	
ininne 'reins'	24	80	3	
lijimme 'halters'	32	88	4	
rugubbe 'necks'	2		12	86

[26] Four lexemes account for 54 of the 72 [ə] tokens. Three of these are [r] contexts, *bərʃ* 'mat', *kərkəmme* 'protrusion', *rəgəbbe* 'necks', and one is an emphatic context, *ḑənne* 'ears' (SG. *ḑaan*).

TABLE 2.3. Villages vs. Maiduguri

	Maiduguri	Villages
[i]	281	222
[u]	126	133

Note: df = 1 chi sq = 3.5, p < .06

Turning briefly to the dialect and sociolectal distribution of the forms, the following points are relevant.

Comparing Maiduguri vs. villages, there is a tendency for the city to favor [i], villages [u]. The breakdown is shown in Table 2.3.

For some lexemes the differences can be quite marked. The plural of *kaab* (or *kaʔab*) 'elbow', for instance, is 18 : 1 in favor of *kuʔubbe* in villages, but 7 : 6 in favor of *kiʔibbe* in Maiduguri.[27]

Within Maiduguri all but one respondent can be grouped by the parameter of neighborhood. Three neighborhoods are represented by at least four respondents each: Gambaru, Gwange, and Dikkeceri. The results are in Table 2.4, this time including the realization [ə]. Gambaru tends to be populated by Arabs from the western part of the Nigerian Arabic dialect region, Gwange and Dikkeceri from those from the east (which I have

TABLE 2.4. i/u in three Maiduguri neighborhoods

	i	u	ə
Gambaru	168	65	17
Gwange	72	37	13
Dikkeceri	14	15	2

Note: df = 4, chi sq = 9, p < .06

---

[27] Looking more closely at the Maiduguri data, the respondents came mainly from three different neighborhoods in the city, Gambaru, Gwange, and Dikkeceri. As shown in Owens (1998a), neighborhood is an important grouping variable in understanding the variation in Maiduguri Arabic. Comparing these three neighborhoods, there is a tendency for Gambaru to favor [i]. Gwange and Dikkeceri to favor [u] (without the [ə] variant, chi sq. = 7.1, df. = 1, p < .027). In general, Gwange and Dikkeceri are heavily populated by immigrants from what I term Bagirmi Arabic, which is an eastern and southern dialect, whereas Gambaru is more populated by a western and northern dialect. In my sample, nearly all Gambaru respondents are from this area. A closer look at the [i] vs. [u] forms might thus show a dialectal difference, carried over into Maiduguri (as indeed is the case for many other features). However, in the village sample there are too few villages, in fact only one, from the Bagirmi area to test this idea.

called the Bagirmi area). However, the difficulty in drawing linkages based on home area, or ancestry as I term it, is seen in a comparison with the same variable in naturally occurring data (recorded texts). In texts, which include in part the speakers in the present sample, it is in fact the Gambaru area with a higher proportion of [u], Gwange with higher [i] (Owens 1998a: 143).

The villages themselves tend to have balanced representations of i/u (though in most villages only one person was asked). The most extreme differences are 14 [i] vs. 7 [u] (Mitene) and 13 [i] vs. 6 [u] (Kinyande). In natural data, summarized in Owens (ibid.) i/u values in a sample of twenty-two villages gave an almost even split of the two sounds. In three villages more than one person was questioned, Magonari with 4, Mule Shuwari with 3, and Dala Axderi with 2. In Magonari, 4 individuals were questioned (i/u) 1: 5/7, 2: 8/3, 3: 5/8, 4: 11/5, the individual differences balancing into a 29/23 split. In Mule Shuwari and Dala Axderi on the other hand, the [i] value predominated considerably, 22/12 in Dala, 34/12 in Mule. This difference is suggestive, as Mule and Dala are neighboring villages directly south of Maiduguri on the Dambua road, while Magonari is east of Maiduguri, close to the administrative center of Mafa (= Muba). On the admittedly inadequate basis of three cases, one is tempted to speak of predominantly [i] villages vs. [u] villages, perhaps even [i] regions vs. [u] regions. This suggestion is put forward in light of the argument advanced in this chapter, namely that the [i] ~ [u] variation attested here essentially continues an alternation attested in the pre-diasporic era. To understand how such alternation could be maintained over such a long period, in such a broad geographical area, more detailed socio-dialectal studies such as that sketched here are needed.

This survey is indicative of a broad maintenance of short i/u variation in both nouns and verbs. The important overall point is that both [i] and [u] despite their non-contrastive status are firmly embedded in Nigerian Arabic, and their presence in a given lexeme in a given speaker cannot be reduced to categorical grammatical or sociolinguistic rule.

2.4.1.2. *Short high vowels in Old Arabic sources*   Turning to the situation in Classical Arabic, there are various indices which point to an analogous situation as in the modern dialects. That is, Fischer and Jastrow's characterization of the opposition [i] vs. [u] as weakly developed ('schwache Ausbildung der Opposition *i : u*', 1980: 43, sect. 3.5) applies to a large degree to Old Arabic as well. This becomes clear when evidence of four different types is considered.

1. *Old Arabic.* The first issue relates to distributional aspects of [i] and [u] in Old Arabic where it may be observed that there are relatively few

morphological patterns where short i/u are phonemically contrastive. In fact, such positions are limited to the initial syllable of words, and to the case endings –i 'genitive', -u 'nominative' (see (17) below on this). Thus, one has contrasts such as:

(7) *misk* 'a sweet scent'
musk 'avariciousness'
mask 'skin' (Quṭrub, 26; Kisaʔi (Brockelmann 1898), 45)

(8) *zijaaj* 'arrowheads'
zujaaj 'glass'
zajaaj 'type of clove' (Quṭrub, 19).

In a very few triliteral perfect verbs [i] and [u] are contrastive.

(9) *xalaqa* 'create'
xaliqa 'become soft, cooked'
xaluqa 'become worn' (lbn Manḏur, *Lisaan*, 10: 85–90)

Even for this last contrast in (9), however, [i] may vary freely with [u] (Kofler 1940–2: viii. 60). Moreover, Chouémi (1966: 82), in a study of the verb in Koranic Arabic, does not find a clear semantic distinction based on front and back short high vowels in this verb form. His conclusion about the tri-valued second stem vowel is 'En ce qui concerne les types de cette forme, nous pensons qu'il n'existe en réalité que deux types: *faʕala* et *faʕila*, *faʕula* n'étant qu'une variante de *faʕila*.' In the current interpretation this is to be understood that in Koranic Arabic the stem vowel exhibited a contrast between low [a] and high [i/u] only. The phonetic front-back short high vowel distinction was not well-enough profiled or not salient enough to support a robust semantic contrast. It can also be noted that in his summary of the meaning of verb stems, Sibawaih (II: 246–58) does not cite any minimal pairs based on the [u]–[i] contrast. He does contrast high and low vowels, as in *ħazina* 'become sad' vs. *ħazana* 'sadden'. Two of the earliest sources, therefore, fail to confirm the three-valued contrast in (9).

In other positions both [i] and [u] occur, but they are defined by morphological patterns where they have no independent phonemic (i.e. contrastive) status. To anticipate a further issue, in most positions [i] and [u] are contrastive with /a/ but not with each other.

(10) *muʕallim* 'teacher'
muʕallam 'taught'

(11) *taṣarruf-an* 'behavior.ACC'
taṣarrafa 'he behaved'

(12) ʔaḥruf 'letters'
    ʔaḥmar 'red.M'

In other cases, as with Nigerian Arabic, [i], [u] may be lexically specific, without being phonemically contrastive.

(13) ʔaktubu 'I write'
    ʔarjiʕu 'I return'[28]

In traditional phonological terms, therefore, the contrastive value of [i], [u] is functionally limited.

Phonotactically, sequences of *i...u* never occur within lexical stems and even across morpheme boundaries there is a tendency to avoid this sequence. Thus the 3.MSG object pronoun-*hu* and 3.MPL object pronoun-*hum* often (in the Classical sources both variants are attested) have the allomorphs -*hi/-him* after an /i/(or palatal /y/).[29]

(14) min bayt-i-hi < bayt-i-hu
    from house-GEN.his
    'from his house'
    yuʔaddi-hi
    return-it.M
    'who pays it back' (Q 3: 75; Ibn Mujahid, 131)
    quluwb-i-him
    hearts-GEN-their.M
    '(over) their hearts' (Q 2:7; Ibn Mujahid, 108)

The sequence *u...i* is restricted to passive verbs, *fuʕila* 'it was done' (see (16) below).

2. *Old Arabic sources, Sibawaih, Farraʔ.* Turning to Classical sources, there is both direct and indirect evidence for the 'weak' status of contrastive i/u. In this section I rely on the fundamental work of Sibawaih and Farraʔ.

Sibawaih is the greatest of Arabic linguists, his *Kitaab* in nearly 1,000 pages treating many points of Arabic in great detail. In the second volume (Derenbourg edition) in particular, phonetic and phonology are discussed in many places, including the status of short vowels (see also sect. 2.4.2 below).

---

[28] Of course, in the imperfect verb the non-contrastive value of the root vowel is further indicated by the tendency towards neutralization of vocalic contrast around guttural consonants in favor of the harmonic [a] value, *yaqraʔu* 'he reads' etc. (Zamaxshari, 278).

[29] Cf. also the Banu Waaʔil variant of the 2MPL -kim after /i/, *bi-kim* 'with you.MPL', Sibawaih II: 321. 23.

Sibawaih notes that in some dialects (especially Tamimi, i.e. Najd, eastern Arabic), both [i] and [u] are subject to deletion in open syllables.

(15) ʕalima → ʕalma 'he knew' (II: 399.2)
karuma → karma 'he is honored' (II: 277.22)
munṭaliq-un → munṭalq-un 'leaving'

Interestingly, this applies to the passive verb as well,

(16) ʕuṣira → ʕuṣra 'be pressed'.

In general, in his inimitable explanatory style, Sibawaih notes that the a-i/u or i/u-a sequence is avoided for articulatory ease, the reduction of [i] or [u] serving to avoid having to move the tongue quickly from a low to high or high to low position. The u-i sequence (16) is considered by Sibawaih to be very marked, and he notes that the passive verb is the only sequence in the language where u-i is found within a lexeme (II: 278.6).

There are two important points in this context. First, as in the modern dialects, the open syllable is a position particularly conducive to vowel reduction. Second, i/u fall within a common class of 'short high vowels' both in general subject to deletion in open syllables. In this respect they are collectively opposed to the low vowel /a/, which, although subject to deletion as well (see (20)), is so only when four or more open syllables in sequence are in play. This confirms the observation above that the primary short vowel opposition runs along the low–high axis, a pattern that will be seen in the following as well. Contrastive [i]–[u] on the other hand is of much weaker functionality.

The weakly articulated contrast between [i] and [u] is further in evidence in the case endings-u 'nominative', -i 'genitive'. I will deal with case vowels extensively elsewhere in Chs. 3 and 4, using both the grammatical and the Koranic traditions as the basis of my argumentation. What is relevant for present purposes is that Sibawaih recognized a realization of nominative-u and genitive-i before an object suffix, i.e. not in pausal position, in which the vowel contrast was neutralized. This is termed *ixtilaas*, and is characterized by a very rapid, indistinguishable vocalic quality (*yusriʕuwn al-lafẓ*).

(17) min maʔman-ə-ka
'from your haven'
yaḍrib-ə-haa
'he hits her' (II: 324.19)

It is noteworthy that Sibawaih goes out of his way to indicate that a short vowel is still audible before the suffix (see further sect. 2.4.2 and n. 38).

This treatment of the nominative and genitive endings is also attested in the Koranic reading tradition, and in fact is associated with the tradition of the Basran, Abu ʕAmr ibn ʕAlaaʔ (= Abu Amr, Ibn Mujahid, 156; see sects. 4.2, 4.3) where it is given the general designation of *taxfiyf* 'making light'. Notably, Sibawaih also cites Abu Amr on this point (II: 324.18).

From this discussion it is clear that Sibawaih described varieties of Arabic in which the phonemic functionality of [i] and [u] was severely curtailed. Indeed, this extended to the two vowels in their prime morphological guise, where even their case marking function could be neutralized. In some cases Sibawaih identifies the variety with a dialect region, eastern Arabia, while in others, as in the discussion of *ixtilaas*, he appears to present the phenomena as widespread variants. In any case, the lack of a well-profiled contrastive function of short [i] and [u] was very well established in Old Arabic.

Comparable examples can be found in the second great early grammarian, Farraʔ, one of the eponymous founders of the so-called Kufan school of linguistics. In his *Maʕaaniy*, for instance, he notes in various places free lexical alternation between [i] and [u], as in ʕijl ~ ʕujl 'calf' (I: 382, also I: 227, 328, II: 122, 189, 236, etc.). Analogous to (16) above, he observes that Q 11: 28 has two alternatives:

(18a) ʔa nulzimu-kumuw-haa

(18b) ʔa nulzim-kumuw-haa
'Shall we compel you (to accept) it'

In (18b) the indicative mode ending /u/ is simply 'deleted'. He offers the general observation that 'they find a [u] after an [i] or a [i] after a [u] or a [u] after a [u] or [i] after a [i] marked' (II: 12). It is clear from his examples that Farraʔ limits his observations to sequences of two short high vowels in sequences of two or more open syllables, offering as further examples, *rusul-un* → *rusl-un* 'prophets', *yaħzunuhum* → *yaħzunhum* '(the terror) will bring them (no) grief' (Q 21: 103), *yuxabbirunaa* → *yuxabbir-naa* 'he informs us'. That is, in a sequence CVCHCV, where H = a short high vowel, the vowel may be 'deleted' (in Farraʔ's terminology, see also his II: 137, 160).

3. *Didactic manuals*. Indirect evidence for the weakly established contrastive value of [i] vs. [u] can be ascertained by the existence of a book such as Qutrub's (d. 206/821) *Muθallaθaat*. This is a short treatise in which lists of lexically contrastive examples are given, one each containing [i], [u], [a]. Examples (7, 8) above are taken from this book. It is notable here that the majority of the examples, 44 out of 63, are of vowels in word-initial CVCC

closed syllable position. The remainder are of initial CVCaa(C)a (as in (9) above). Here it may be noteworthy that twelve of these latter examples have a sonorant at C2.[30]

This short treatise falls into a ninth-century genre in which certain morphological and phonological patterns were summarized in single works, often in verse form. Sijistani is a longer work giving the contrast (or lack thereof) between verbs in the *faʕala* and *ʔafʕala* forms,[31] while Farraʔ deals extensively with gender in his *Muðakkar wa l-Muʔannaθ*. This genre is also attested later; Farrukhi (Al-Farruxi), for instance, in a later work (sixth–twelfth century), where minimal pairs of *ḍ* vs. *ð̣* are illustrated. What is particular about these books is that they appear to be aimed at an audience which is not familiar with these contrasts. All three of these examples are of features which in the modern dialects are dialectially restricted or which have completely disappeared, for instance the contrast of *ḍ* vs. *ð̣* (see sect. 2.4.5 below). Vollers (1906: 15), commenting on Koranic variation between *ð̣* and *ḍ*, had already perceived that this contrast was weakly established from its very first orthographic appearance.

A genre which explicitly dealt with language errors was the *laḥn al-ʕawaamm*, common speech errors of the educated (see Pellat 1960/1986; Molan 1978; Larcher 2001: 593). The first work of this type was, reputedly, very early, that of Kisaʔi (d. 183/798 or 189/804; Brockelmann 1898; see Fück 1950: 50 for discussion of attribution). The title, in fact, is something of a misnomer, at least as far as Kisaʔi's work goes. First, it is relatively rare that the actual error is pointed out. On p. 33, for instance, sets of correct forms are given with the pattern *faʕuwl*, *habuwṭ* 'falling', *ṣaʕuwd* 'rising', etc. One can only suppose that speakers incorrectly use *fuʕuwl* in these words. Many of the 'errors' are in fact of a highly literary or learned type. In the first two pages, for instance, the first twelve errors noted are all words from the Quran, *ḥaraṣta* 'you desired' (12: 103, not *ḥariṣta?*). For present purposes what is interesting is that a great number of the errors, thirty-nine in all,[32] concern the short vowels i, u, a. On p. 45, *misk/musk/mask*, also cited in Quṭrub, is given. Of these cases, thirty-one deal with the contrast between *a-i* or *a-u*, which as seen above is phonemically of far greater functional importance than *i-u*. Examples include *maḥlab* 'seed of mahlab plant' vs. *miḥlab* 'milk bucket' (38) and *judud*

---

[30] i.e. a pattern reminiscent of the so-called 'bukura' syndrome, which inserts a vowel before a sonorant (Sibawaih II: 309). The vocalic contrast is not explained by this observation, however.

[31] Shahin (2004: 9) lists five ninth- century titles in addition to Sijistani dealing with the difference between form I and IV verbs.

[32] Included in these thirty-nine are either references to general patterns, such as *faʕuwl* noted above, or individual words, like *ḥaraṣta*.

'new.PL' vs. *judad* 'ancestors' (p. 41). Further, of the eight i-u contrasts, seven occur in closed syllables, e.g. *ṣufr* 'brass' vs. *ṣifr* 'nothingness' (43). As with Sibawaih and Farraʔ (see sect. 2.4.1.2, above), the important contrast is low [a] vs. high [i/u]. Direct [i] vs. [u] contrasts are limited, both in number and in terms of position in a syllable.

In both these short works the contrastive distribution of i/u in Old Arabic is seen to be limited and the inclusion of short vowels in this didactic genre points to an early or original lack of salience of the contrast. This last observation leaves unresolved the question whether Quṭrub's *Muθallaθaat* reflects the breakdown of a 3-vowel contrast, or the attempt by grammarians to take one variety which had the contrast and impose it throughout the language-speaking community. The first perspective would certainly be the one favored by proponents of the Old/New dichotomy. Here, didactic books would be needed to instruct the rapidly expanding Arabic-speaking public about correct Arabic. Beyond the objection that it is impossible to answer the question of who the works were intended for, more fundamentally the works stem from the very period when Old Arabic is purported to be all-dominant. There simply are no detailed descriptions of Arabic before the generation of Kisaʔi, so any assumption about what previous generations spoke is conjecture needing comparative linguistic support.

This basic chronological observation in my view serves to support the second perspective, that the didactic genre above all reflects the imposition of a norm on the basis of one or more varieties out of a number available. In this variety, short i/u are phonemically contrastive in certain positions. It can also be assumed, however, that there were other varieties where i/u were not phonemically contrastive, similar to the situation in contemporary Nigerian Arabic and various other modern dialects.

4. *An example from the* Lisaan al-ʕArab. A rich source for lexical information comes from the Arabic lexicographers. Ibn Manḏur's *Lisaan al-ʕArab*, written in the thirteenth century (Ibn Manḏur, d. 711/1311), represents a detailed culmination of this tradition, its sixteen volumes including 80,000 root-based entries (Haywood 1965: 81). Although late in chronological terms, the lexicographical tradition as embodied by Ibn Manḏur was one where, as it were, little got lost. Arabic lexicographers of later generations assiduously recorded and summarized what their predecessors had done before them.

The entries are encyclopedic in scope, but wanting in organization, so they make for difficult reading. Typically a longer entry will contain quotes from poetry, ḥadith, the *Quran*, and detailed grammatical discussion. The relevance of lexicography to the current discussion can be shown on the basis of one entry, ḥ b b (vol. I: 289–96).³³ The entry is nearly eight pages long, small print and double columned, and by my count contains twenty-nine separate lemmas. However, it is not always easy to say where one lemma begins and another ends. Roughly it is divided into three parts. The first concerns the meaning 'love', or as it is defined at the beginning of the entry, ḥubb, naqiyḍ al-buxḍ 'love, the opposite of hate'. This meaning runs for approximately four pages, whereupon a second general meaning al-ḥabb: al-zarʕ ṣaxiyran kaana ʔaw kabiyran, 'seed, large or small' begins. After two pages other isolated meanings continue the entry until its end.

The problem for the present issue begins at the very beginning of the lemma, where as an alternative to ḥubb, a verbal noun which introduces the entry, ḥibb is given as a free variant. The [i] alternative appears to be the lesser-known one, since as soon as it is given, it is legitimitized as it were by a poetic quotation.

In any case this is reminiscent of the i/u variation discussed in detail in sect. 2.4.1.1 for Nigerian Arabic. Furthermore, it is explicitly pointed out that the verb ḥabba is unusual (ʃaaðð) in that in form I its imperfect form only has a variant with the vowel [i], yaḥibbu 'he loves', the only transitive doubled verb of this type. Here again short high vowel quality must be explicitly noted (see also Kisaʔi's Laḥn, 33, for related remarks).³⁴

By the same token, within this entry [i] and [u] are clearly contrastive, at least in the apparently more common version of ḥubb 'love', which can be opposed, a page later, in a rather long discussion to ḥibb 'friend, companion', a word backed up by a number of ḥadith references. One of six plurals of ḥibb in the sense of companion is ḥubb. This last is a fuʕul plural, < ḥubub, with the second vowel assimilated between two identical consonants (e.g. as in the passive of doubled verbs). Wright (1896–8/1977: 202) notes that fuʕul plural forms have an alternative fuʕl, rusul ~ rusl 'prophets' (see (19) above), including CVCC forms like laðiyð, luðð 'pleasant.PL'.

This [i]/[u] vocalic contrast is ostensibly backed up by other entries, for instance on p. 295 al-ḥubb, 'a large pot', a word said to be derived from Persian (Faarsi) ḥunb. However, the further discussion of the meaning 'seed' (p. 293) gives cause for caution here. The first entry for 'seed' is ḥabb 'seeds' (collective), SG. ḥabba 'one seed'. Citing the linguists/lexicographers Azhari, Jawhari, and Kisaʔi, ḥibba is identified variously as a desert plant seed or an undomesticated plant seed, opposed to ḥabb, applied, according to Jawhari,

---

³³ ḥbb (Arabic script, bbḥ) is in volume i because the sequence follows the order R(adical)3, R1, R2, i.e. the entry comes under 'b'.
³⁴ Transitive doubled verbs are said to expect [u].

a predecessor of Ibn Manḏur in lexicography (d. 398/1007, author of the *Ṣaḥaaḥ*), only for domesticated food plant seeds (e.g. wheat, barley). The singulative *ḥabba* is used for all meanings, both domesticated and wild plant seeds. However, one source, Abu Hanifa, is cited as using *ḥibba* for any plant, i.e. = *ḥabb*. Putting all these sources together, *ḥibba* and *ḥabb*, depending on which source one uses, are in free variation in the general sense of 'seed'.

Summarizing over many details, the discussion gives the following meanings.

(19) *ḥubb* 'love; large pot; friends'
ḥibb 'love; friend'
ḥabb 'seed, seed of a domestic food plant'
ḥibba 'seed, seed of a wild plant'

In some meanings the short vowels are contrastive, whereas in others they are not. This is if the entries are considered in their entirety. Based on the citations for Ibn Manḏur's sources, the non-contrastive meanings are often variants from different sources: *ḥibb* 'love' comes from a line of poetry and *ḥibb* in the sense of 'friend' from a ḥadith, *ḥibba* the 'seed' interpretation of Abu Hanifa. In both cases a lexical free variation effect is analogous to the i ∼ u variation in Nigerian Arabic; the variation is free when enough sources are considered.

Looking at the matter from the other angle, a seemingly solid [i] vs. [u] minimal pair, for instance *ḥubb* 'large pot' vs. *ḥibb* 'friend' could arise simply through the compilation efforts of the lexicographers. *ḥubb* 'large jar' a Persian loanword[35] could derive from a different speech community from that of *ḥibb* 'friend', attested particularly in the ḥadith literature. Finally, the contrast *ḥibb* 'friend' *ḥubb* 'friends' at the abstract morphological level is non-contrastive (*ḥibb* vs. *ḥubub*). A similar point pertains to (8) above. In his Koranic commentary to Q 24: 35 Farraʔ notes that while the general reading (*ijtamaʕ al-qurraaʔ*) is *zujaaj* 'glass', both *zijaaj* and *zajaaj* for this meaning are possible (*qad yuqaal*) (II: 252). In the Koranic context, 'glass' is *zujaaj* ∼ *zijaaj* ∼ *zajaaj*, the short vowels in non-contrastive free variation. In the larger lexicographical context the three forms also form contrastive meanings.[36]

---

[35] This word is not included among Persian loanwords in Arabic in the extensive study of Asbaghi (1988). In Gulf Arabic, a large earthenware waterpot is in fact *ḥibb* (not *ḥubb* apparently, Qafisheh 1997: 116, Holes 2001: 100).

[36] The entry in the *Lisaan* for *zjj* (ii: 285–8) creates new problems. Ibn Manḏur for the zVjaaj form gives *zijaaj* = 'arrowheads, old she camels, long-necked bottles', *zajaaj* 'long-necked bottles', *zujaaj* 'long-necked bottles'. *Zajaaj* in Quṭrub's sense of cloves does not appear, nor in the modern Wehr or the *Muḥiyṭ al-Muḥiyṭ* of the nineteenth-century lexicographer Bustani (1997: 267). For the latter,

What cannot be gauged is whether the contrastive meanings are associated with a single speech community, or whether they represent a pan-dialectal amalgam whose contrastiveness derives from the lexicographers' compilation.

Looking at a more or less arbitrary sample of ten roots from volume I, usually a given root shows a single high vowel value for those positions where theoretically a phonemic contrast can occur. For instance, *juzʔ* 'part' (45), always has [u], never [i], though theoretically an [i] could occur here. *ħizb* 'group of people' (308), on the other hand, always has [i]. Of the ten roots, five have only [u] (*kubb* 'cluster', (695), *kufʔ* 'equal, similar' (138), *ruħb* 'breadth' (413), and *ʕujb* 'surprise' (580) and three have only [i] (*ħizb* as above, *ʕibʔ* 'load' (117), and *sibb* 'veil, screen, rope' (456). Two show variation. *ʃirb* ~ *ʃarb* ~ *ʃurb* 'drinking' (487) appear to be free variant forms of the verbal noun (as in Farraʔ II: 282), like *ħubb* ~ *ħibb* above. *Xibb* 'rottenness, rough sea' (342) is like the total entry for *ħibb*: some forms are in free variation, *xabba* ~ *xibba* ~ *xubba* 'dirt path', while others are contrastive, *xubb* 'a rag' vs. *xibb* (as above, 'rough sea, rottenness'). This brief survey would indicate that for the majority of roots [i] and [u] are lexically determined, but phonemically non-contrastive. In a minority, basically free variation between [u] and [i] reigns, with some meanings showing contrast via the different high vowels.

Addressing the problem from the perspective of the rich Arabic lexicographical tradition, the phonemic status of [i] and [u] is again seen to be problematic. Even in those few positions where the two are potentially contrastive, there is indexical evidence which relativizes the importance of the phonemic contrast. Overall the amalgam of forms found in Arabic dictionaries is very much analogous to the amalgam of forms one can collect from the modern dialects. Phonemic contrasts (cf. eastern Libyan Arabic) can be found, but they are rare; lexically specified but phonemically non-contrastive roots are found (e.g. Shukriyya), and a degree of free variation is attested (cf. Nigerian Arabic).

The discussion of the functional status of [i] vs. [u] in the original Old Arabic offered in this section has been detailed, though hardly exhaustive of the old sources. To the extent that the phonemic contrast existed, it is, as in

---

'glass' is indifferently *zajaaj* ~ *zujaaj* ~ *zijaaj*. Curiously, Ibn Manḍhur mentions *zujaaj* in the sense of 'glass' only elliptically, in a definition: *zajjaaj*: 'a manufacturer of glass (*zujaaj*)'. Similarly, Quṭrub's form *musk* (7) is not found in the *Lisaan*, the editor of the *Muθallaθaat* Al-Zawi noting (26 n. 1) that he did not find the form in any dictionary. Such citations possibly retricted to Quṭrub suggests that some of the forms he collected were restricted to very small communities. While ancient scholars, not unlike their modern counterparts, had few qualms about maligning their opponents, it may be noted that Quṭrub's late contemporary Ibn Sikkit suggested that Quṭrub falsified his data (Versteegh 1983: 170).

the modern dialects, largely limited to closed syllables. There are ample examples of deletion of the short high vowels in open syllables, again a phenomenon attested in the modern dialects. Viewing the dialects in their entirety, it is hard to view the functionally restricted modern dialectal realization of short high vowels as qualitatively different from that attested in the oldest Arabic sources.

2.4.2. *Old Arabic itself is not unitary*

Returning to the list at the beginning of sect. 2.4, the second problem, the diverse character of Old Arabic, may be illustrated with an example taken from the syllable structure rules discussed above. Fischer and Jastrow (1980: 40 sect. 3.3) note that Old Arabic allowed extended sequences of short open syllables, as in *li-ḥarakati-ka* 'for your.M movement'. As noted above, there are modern dialects which also permit similar sequences, e.g. *katabata* 'she wrote it.M' in Nigerian Arabic or *'bagarateh* 'his cow' (Highland Yemen, Behnstedt 1985: 63). If four is the upper limit in the dialects, as opposed to five in Old Arabic it is because there are no morphological patterns in the dialects supporting more than a sequence of four open syllables. However, even in Old Arabic long sequences of short open syllables were subject to reduction. Examples pertaining to short high vowels in open syllables have already been introduced in sect. 2.4.1.2, above. In fact, sequences of short vowels in general tended to be avoided. Discussing rules of assimilation (*ʔidɣaam*), Sibawaih notes that in Hijazi Arabic, at a word juncture when five open syllables result from the juxtaposition of two words, then under various conditions the final vowel of the first word will be deleted. Example (20) illustrates a typical case.

(20) *jaʕala laka → jaʕal laka* (II: 455)

Sibawaih states that sequences of five open syllables are 'heavy', as I understand the term, 'marked', requiring deletion of a vowel. In the Koranic reading tradition, the so-called *ʔal-ʔidɣaam al-kabiyr* 'major assimilation' describes such 'deletion' (if indeed it was deletion, see Ch. 4) in detail.

Sibawaih notes that within words constraints on sequences of short vowels can be equally severe. Discussing the alternative forms of the object suffix pronouns-*kum* ~ -*kumuw* and-*hum* ~ -*humuw*, he notes that the -C final variant is preferable when the suffix -*kumuw* would produce a sequence of four open syllables, thus (21a) rather than (21b), with the hyphen representing a syllable boundary.

(21a) *ru-su-lu-kum* 'your.MPL prophets', = 3 open syllables

(21b) *ru-su-lu-ku-muw* = 4 open syllables

Here Sibawaih invokes the generalization that 'obviously in their [Arabs'] speech there is no noun with four open syllables' (... ʔa laa taraa ʔannahu laysa fi kalaamihim ism ʕalaa ʔarbaʕat ʔaħruf mutaħarrik, II: 319. 19).

The problem here is not to formulate the situation such that processes attested in the modern dialects, in this case short vowel deletion in open syllables, were already adumbrated or anticipated in Old Arabic. This mode of reasoning is quite old. Nöldeke, a great scholar of literary Arabic, for instance, notes examples of deletion of a case or mode vowel such as illustrated in sect. 2.4.1.2, above (1897: 10). His explanation, however, is to attribute such forms to Arabs who had settled outside the Arabian peninsula, or to note that they often occur in scatological verse. Neither observation carries comparative linguistic weight, however.[37] Why scatological verse should be more prone to deletion of a case vowel is not elaborated upon. As far as the debased form of ex-peninsula varieties go, Nöldeke's thinking is based on an a prioristic judgment. He nowhere offers sociolinguistic arguments for the proposition that they should be more apt to loose case endings than Arabic in the peninsula itself. Nöldeke's assumption may be that Arabic in the Arabian peninsula was or is inherently more conservative than diaspora varieties. There is a simple counter-example to this assumption, however. Holes (1991) shows that affrication of /k/ to [tʃ] or [ts] began in Central Arabia and spread outwards from there (see sect. 8.7.1). I would add here, with purposeful irony, that Nöldeke had no misgivings using as one of his chief sources for Old Arabic, Sibawaih, a man whose native language was not Arabic, who himself was settled in Basra, one of the earliest Arab-Islamic diasporic cities, who never so far as we know set foot in the Arabian peninsula, and who was dependent for his information on the very clientele who Nöldeke sees as speaking caseless Arabic.

As a general criticism, Nöldeke's explanation begs the question of what the old language was. A similar problem of logic was already met above in sect. 2.2. Pre-classical Arabic was established using the same source as that for Classical Arabic, namely Sibawaih. But if the sources are the same, then other methods, e.g. the comparative method, have to be applied to determine what parts of Sibawaih are pre-, post-, or simply 'Classical'. Similarly here.

---

[37] As seen in e.g. (18), Sibawaih's *ixtilaas* variant must have been widespread, as he offers a standard, constructed example *yaḍrib-u-ka* → *yaḍrib-ə-ka*. The vowel-deletion variant is exemplified only in poetry, though is treated in the same chapter, indeed in the very next sentence after the *ixtilaas* variant is noted. In some sense they belong to a common category in Sibawaih's pantheon of Arabic variants. It could be that complete deletion was not as unusual as Nöldeke assumes; see in this respect Abu Amr's Koranic recitation practice in sect. 4.3.

If avoidance of sequences of short open syllables is part of Old Arabic, and a similar avoidance is found in some of the modern dialects, then this is not a feature that can be used to differentiate the two presumed varieties. It simply characterizes both. Of course, it can be shown that vowel reduction has gone much further in some modern dialects (see Table 2.1), but this is properly a part of the history of those dialects which evince such behavior, not 'Neo-Arabic' in general.

At this point it may be useful to illustrate the discussion with further developmental trees. In (22) vowel reduction is illustrated on the basis of the 3F.SG. verb form *katabat* 'she wrote'.

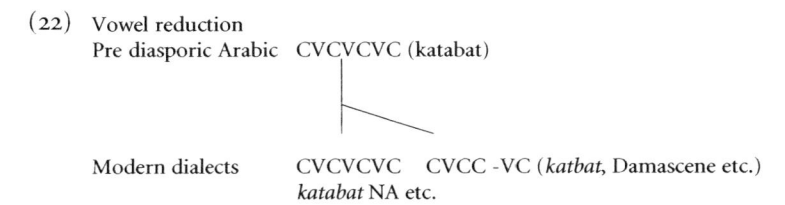

(22) Vowel reduction
      Pre diasporic Arabic   CVCVCVC (katabat)

      Modern dialects   CVCVCVC   CVCC -VC (*katbat*, Damascene etc.)
                             katabat NA etc.

This shows that some modern dialects continue the given pre-diasporic Arabic verbal paradigm, while others have innovated, reducing the unstressed vowel in the open syllable. It is clear that there is no linguistic basis here for differentiating 'Old' from 'Neo-' Arabic, since no innovation occurred in many modern dialects.

A related strategy in this regard is to observe that Neo-Arabic in fact is identical to a certain feature in Old Arabic, but to explain this as an attribute of an Old Arabic dialect, not of Old Arabic.[38] Fischer and Jastrow (1980: 44)

---

[38] As seen in sect. 1.3, the problem of Old Arabic 'dialects' is a vexed one. As those who have worked on old 'dialects' have observed (e.g. Kofler 1940: 64), there is no term for 'dialect' in the older literature, which is hardly surprising since there was no systematic dialectology. The closest one has is perhaps *luɣa*, and in some cases, e.g. *luɣat al-ḥijaaz* etc. 'dialect of the Hijaz', 'dialect' is an appropriate translation. *luɣa* can equally refer to a 'variant' without further association (idiolect, sociolect, etc.), however.

The treatment of Old Arabic 'dialects' in the Western literature is, like so many themes, a topic in itself. Kofler (1940-2), who is often cited as an authoritative work—and is significant—is a curious summary of many different Arabic linguists and authors whose systematicity is difficult to discern. In his discussion of case, for instance (1942: 26-30), Kofler notes that Sibawaih (II: 325, Derenbourg edn.) cites poetic license forms (see (6b) in Ch. 7 for an example) where expected case suffixes are lacking altogether. He classifies this as dialectal. Strictly speaking, however, here his reference derives from a poetic citation. This is all Kofler has to say in his entire work about Sibawaih's treatment of case. However, in the same chapter (506) and on the very page before Kofler's remark on Sibawaih's poetic license (II: 324), Sibawaih has his discussion of *ʔiʃbaaʕ* and *ixtilaas/tamṭiyṭ* (see sect. 8.1) as case realizations, as summarized around e.g. (18) above. Kofler did not comment on this at all. Perhaps Kofler did not consider the latter forms as dialectal. However, there is nothing in Sibawaih's language which allows one to distinguish an evaluative difference between what Sibawaih discusses on II: 324

observe that modern dialects generally have *i* as the preformative vowel of the imperfect verb

(23) t-i-ktib, n-i-ktib 'you write, we write', etc.

This is not to be understood as an innovation, but as a continuation of an old dialectal form which deviated from Classical Arabic (see Versteegh 1997: 42; Larcher 2004; Larcher 2006, citing Farraʔ). For what it is worth the observation is valid. However, if the modern dialects continue old forms, wherever they are to be situated in Old Arabic (see below), there is no basis for introducing them into a discussion which purports to differentiate Old from Neo-Arabic. Lacking further comparative analysis, they simply can be said to characterize both. This is illustrated in (24).[39]

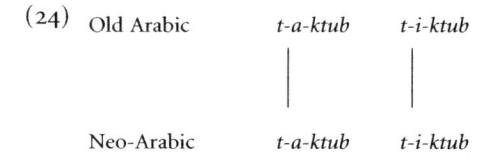

(24) Old Arabic   t-a-ktub   t-i-ktub
                         | |
      Neo-Arabic   t-a-ktub   t-i-ktub

2.4.3. Lack of information

A third aspect of Fischer and Jastrow's summary is a problem which is still very much with us today, namely that generalizations are formed on the basis of the data available. It is only in the 1980s that more intensive research in Yemen for instance (cf. especially Behnstedt 1985, 1987: 5) turned up 'old' features thought lost in the dialects, the glottal stop (*jaaʔat* 'she came'), a contrast between reflexes of the emphatics *$\d$ > $\d$ (ʔaxḏar 'green') and $\d$ > θ (ʕaθm 'bone') or the word *maa* for 'what?' for instance. Even so Fischer and

---

from II: 325. ʔiʃbaaʕ, for instance, is implicitly recognized as a variant, when Sibawaih identifies its practitioners 'as for those who use ʔiʃbaaʕ (ʔammaa allaðiyn yuʃbiʕuwna . . .). Regarding the complete "loss" of the case suffix, Sibawaih identifies the issue as, 'and it is possible that they "delete" a nominative or genitive in poetry' (wa qad yajuwz ʔan yusakkituw l-ħarf al-marfuwʕ wa l-majruwr fiy l-ʃiʕr..., II: 324. 21–325. 1). In fact, it would appear that the first case is closer to a 'lectal' form of some sort, being identified with an unnamed group of people. The complete loss of a case vowel, on the other hand, is more in the nature of a stylistic variant (qad yajuwz). Holes's (1995: 41 n. 15) characterization of Kofler as having 'classified' old Arabic dialects assumes very rudimentary standards for a systematic classification. In any case, the discussion in this footnote is but a small indication of the exegetical problems involved in interpreting the many language variants cited in the old literature in terms of simple 'modern' categories.

[39] Similarly Fischer and Jastrow's feature 3.7.2 (1980: 45). In modern dialects doubled verbs have the same person inflections as do weak final verbs, *radd-ayt* or *radd-eet* 'I returned', like *ban-eet* 'I built'. In Old Arabic, doubled verbs have a normal inflection, with vowel epenthesis, *radad-tu* 'I returned'. The texts require considerable discussion, but I would suggest that the citations *taqaṣṣaṣ-tu* → *taqaṣṣay-tu* (e.g. Sibawaih II: 442, Farraʔ I: 217) are, in fact, an Old Arabic reflex of -*ayt*.

Jastrow's summary basically left off the entire Sudanic dialect region (inter alia, Carbou 1913; Lethem 1920; Trimingham 1946; Kaye 1976 being available), a consideration of which adds to my category three criticisms. I think a point will soon be reached where no 'new' old features are found, though the general tendency resulting from empirical research since 1980 has been to reduce further the set of features Fischer and Jastrow used to set Old Arabic off from Neo-Arabic.

2.4.4. *Valid differences*

This leads to point 4 in the list in 2.4, which is crucial for those wishing to see the dichotomy of Old Arabic/Neo-Arabic as a linguistically grounded one. In fact, there are a few instances in Fischer and Jastrow's list which survive the criticisms of points 1–3. I can identify four, represented as historical developments.

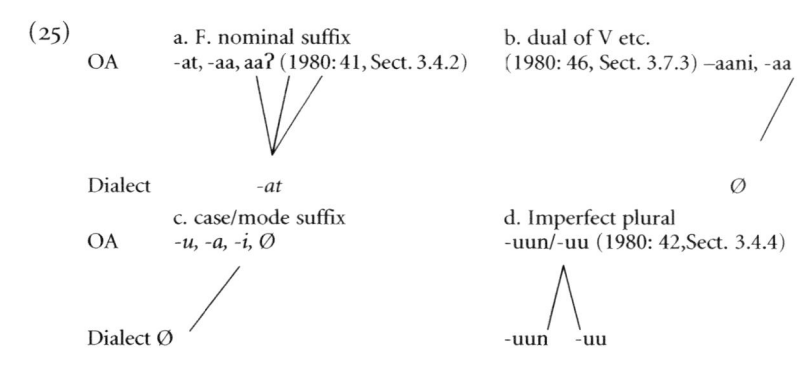

(25)
       a. F. nominal suffix   b. dual of V etc.
OA   -at, -aa, aa? (1980: 41, Sect. 3.4.2)   (1980: 46, Sect. 3.7.3) –aani, -aa

Dialect   -at   Ø
       c. case/mode suffix   d. Imperfect plural
OA   -u, -a, -i, Ø   -uun/-uu (1980: 42, Sect. 3.4.4)

Dialect Ø   -uun -uu

Before discussing these in greater detail, the general question may be raised whether four quite heterogeneous features are adequate for defining so broad and allegedly fundamental a difference as that between Old and Neo-Arabic.

Turning to the features themselves, I will discuss only one of these in detail, (25b). In my analysis (25b, c) are of a common developmental type, and therefore consideration of one serves for both. I therefore discuss (25b) only. A fuller consideration of (25a) requires considerable background in the analysis of final vowels and pausal phenomena, and this in turn requires detailed discussion (and criticism) of the work of Birkeland. I discuss aspects of this work in Ch. 8 below. Example (25d) I leave without discussion.

Example (25b) represents the loss of the dual. Nearly all modern dialects continue a dual form in nouns. Classical Arabic, however, has a morphological dual in verbs, pronouns, demonstratives, and relative pronouns as well, and these are not attested in the dialects. On this point, Fischer and

Jastrow's own exposition is illuminating (1980: 46). They note that among Semitic languages, Arabic is unique in having a fully 'developed' system of dual marking, encompassing all nominal and verbal categories. They explicitly argue that (25b) is not a simplification in the modern dialects, but (it appears) a retention of the original proto-Semitic situation, where the dual, if indeed it is reconstructible to proto-Semitic (see Retsö 1995), is restricted to the noun. This point is an important one for my interpretation of Arabic language history. It shows that even if consistent differences between Old Arabic, however defined, and the dialects are discernible—and it has been seen here that there are in fact very few important ones—it does not automatically follow that the reflexes borne by the modern dialects are necessarily innovations. The modern dialect dual could in fact be 'older' in comparative linguistic terms than is the dual in Old Arabic, whose spread to verbal and other categories is to be seen as innovative. The situation can be sketched as in (26).

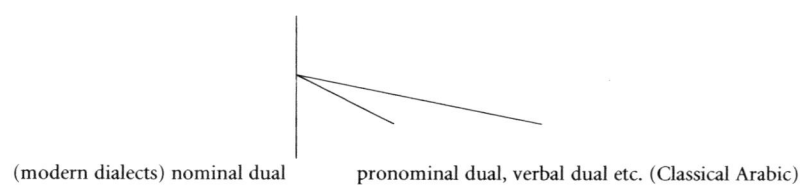

(26) (26) nominal dual (proto-Arabic)

(modern dialects) nominal dual   pronominal dual, verbal dual etc. (Classical Arabic)

In terms of our tree developments, in this case the comparative method returns an interpretation 'upside down' as it were from chronology. I would note that I argue (see Chs. 3, 4 below) that the same interpretation applies to (25c). The 'caseless' modern dialects in fact continue an older Semitic and Afroasiatic feature. Note according to these two interpretations, the number of differences between Neo-Arabic and a reconstructible proto-Arabic are reduced by 50 per cent.

Aside from interpretive problems, the four features in (25) do not represent a grammatically coherent development in the direction of the dialects, in that they come somewhat haphazardly from different domains of grammar. Furthermore, the citation of a difference which consistently distinguishes Old from so-called Neo-Arabic does not automatically make Neo-Arabic younger in a comparative sense, as argued in the previous paragraph.

In a later work (1995), Fischer attempted to work out the relations between Old Arabic and Neo-Arabic in a more systematic and principled way. Rather than derive the modern dialects directly from Old Arabic, as in the 1980 model, Fischer establishes an intermediate category which he terms proto-Neo-Arabic, and exemplifies the construct with the independent pronoun series, perfect verb suffixes, and various question words. Here he uses categories reminiscent of Brockelmann. Brockelmann (1908: 24) distinguished between a poetic koine (*Dichtersprache*), in which he saw the origins of Classical Arabic, and tribal dialects in the northern Arabian region, from which it appears he derives the modern dialects. As mentioned above, Brockelmann does not treat his Old/New dichotomy in a comparative linguistic manner, so one can only interpret how he saw the precise development. Brockelmann does regret the fact that there are hardly examples of Arabic dialects (*Vulgararabisch*) from the Middle Ages, so one can suspect that he saw a development: Old Arabic dialects → Arabic dialects in Middle Ages → modern dialects, though this is speculation.[40] In any case, Old Arabic had dialects on the one hand and a classical Arabic on the other, which were two quite different entities for him.

Fischer, however, develops a linguistically more sophisticated system than the earlier work, as he is committed to recognizing explicit developmental states from Old Arabic to the modern dialects. Moreover, the proto-Neo-Arabic stage is given a degree of ambiguous leeway, in recognition of the fact that various 'typical' modern dialectal forms in fact would appear to have an old heritage. The third person F singular suffix, for instance is given as either *-at* or *-it*. In (27) I give Fischer's (1995: 81) paradigms for OA (his terminology) and proto-Neo-Arabic perfect verb paradigm, to serve as the basis of discussion.

(27) OA   Proto Neo-Arabic
      SG
      1 *katab-tu*   *katab-tu, katab-t*
      2 M *katab-ta*   *katab-t*
        F *katab-ti*   *katab-tii*
      3 M *kataba*   *katab*
        F *katab-at*   *katab-at, katab-it*
      PL
      1 *katab- naa*   *katab-naa*
      2 M *katab-tum*   *katab-tum, katab-tuu*

---

[40] Conveniently, Brockelmann finds evidence for Old Arabic dialects only from Suyuṭi, a grammarian who also is late (d. 1505). It may be suggested that Brockelmann's logically formed developmental matrices (Old—(Middle?)—New) conveniently prevented him from using Sibawaih's 'dialectal' material (or other, e.g. the reading tradition) in his comparative grammar, which would have complicated his data considerably.

	F	katab-tunna	katab-tin
3	M	katab-uu	katab-uu
	F	katab-na	katab-an

What is above all striking is how similar OA and proto-Neo-Arabic are. In fact, the differences are even exaggerated. Looking at more Arabic dialects, for instance, 2MSG -*ta* (or in Yemen -*ka* in some highland regions), as noted by Fischer, is attested in about fifteen locations in north and central Yemen, and T. Prochazka (1988: 27) leaves open the possibility that it is attested in Saudi Arabian Tihama as well. Similarly -*nah* 3FPL and -*tunnah* 2FPL is attested in Ghaamid, (southern Hijaz, T. Prochazka 1988: 27). In the 3MSG. the 'proto-Neo-Arabic' form in fact is identical to the pausal form of Old Arabic. This is, as I have noted above, an issue requiring separate treatment, but in this context it does reduce on a prima facie basis the difference between Old and proto-Neo-Arabic.

Looking at the Old Arabic sources, it will be seen in sect. 8.9 that the 3FPL suffixes -*tunna* and -*na* are problematic representations in Old Arabic, given standard interpretations of the notion of pausal position. It will be suggested there, that Fischer's proto-Neo-Arabic -*an* or -*in* is also plausible as a pre-diasporic form, which takes the form into the Old Arabic era.

Even without considering the points raised in the previous two paragraphs, on the basis of (27) alone there is no linguistic ground for differentiating Old Arabic and proto-Neo-Arabic, as the two are largely identical. The linguist's Occam's razor does not allow a distinction between Old Arabic and proto-Neo-Arabic to be made. The critical conclusion here melds with that reached above: were the concepts Old Arabic and Neo-Arabic not inherited baggage from the nineteenth century, they would not be recognized as independent entities in contemporary Arabic linguistics.

2.5. The Past is the Present: A Modern Logical Matrix

The Old–New dichotomy is not the only model in which Arabic language history is understood via interpertations other than those provided by the comparative method. A further approach to reading the formative years of Arabic language history, the eighth and ninth centuries, is to project the present-day Arabic realities back onto this early period. This approach was encountered in a different context among the truisms in Ch. 1 (sect. 1.6.2). If today Arabic is marked by a diglossic, high–low, Standard Arabic–dialect dichotomy, the same difference is discerned in the past as well. In this interpretation, Sibawaih's task for instance is seen as describing a 'high form of

Arabic' (Al-Nassir 1993: 116). Sibawaih was, apparently, aware of 'a colloquial form of the language', but fundamentally concerned only with the high variety. This approach obviates the need for posing the difficult question of defining the diverse elements constitutive of Sibawaih's and other early grammarians' thinking: Sibawaih's task is seen as applying available rules to a predefined language corpus.[41] Like other logical matrices, however, it defines away the problem of understanding Arabic language history by ignoring three key elements. First, the relative linguistic complexity of Arabic in Sibawaih's day is ignored. Second, the sociolinguistic context in which Sibawaih was working is taken to be equivalent to that found in Arabic countries today. Thirdly, it is silent about the comparative historical relation between modern native varieties of Arabic and older ones.

2.6. The Arabic Tradition

Before moving to the conclusion I think it appropriate to mention briefly the analytic basis of the Arabic grammatical tradition, upon which a good part of this chapter draws. In general a historical perspective is missing in it. The term *ʔaṣl* 'source, root, underlying form', which is important in Arabic morphological theory (Owens 2000, see Baalbaki 2008: 98 ff.) usually refers to a logical source, akin to deep structure in earlier forms of generative grammar. Thus the verb *qaala* 'he said', is said to have the ʔaṣl *qawala*, with the form *qaala* derived via general rule converting an *aWV* sequence to *aa*. There is no claim that *qawala* is historically anterior to *qaala*, however.

The grammarians were certainly aware of the notion of change. However, the issue was treated within the framework of a logical matrix rather than by a systematic methodology. This may be exemplified through a discussion by the late grammarian Suyuṭi (d. 1504). Suyuṭi's *al-Iqtiraaħ* is a synoptic attempt to distill principles of Arabic linguistic theory as it had developed in the previous seven centuries (see Suleiman 1999). It is relevant to cite Suyuṭi in this context, despite his late date, because he brings together nearly all threads of previous Arabic theory in one work. Discussing the origin of language (31–5), Suyuṭi adduces the example of non-declined nouns like *ʔayna* 'where' and *kam* 'how many'. Nouns in Standard Arabic usually are inflected as

---

[41] Early Arabic language history is frequently dispatched in a few summarizing sentences. Hoffiz (1995: 15) for instance, states as a matter of fact that since pre-Islamic times, 'the Arabic Language has existed in two forms, Literary Arabic... and the colloquial dialects of Arabic'. That this is a projection of later circumstances onto pre-Islamic times is apparent. There is, strictly speaking, no written, literary œuvre attested from the pre-Islamic period itself, only interpretations of the oral literature which, as seen in Ch.1, sect. 1.2, derives largely from the ninth century.

nominative, accusative, and genitive, theoretically *kam-un, kam-an, kam-in* respectively. *kam*, however, has no inflection, being invariably *kam*.

In Arabic grammatical theory each word class has certain unmarked properties, and one of those of nouns is case inflection. Should a subclass of nouns lack this property, a reason for this lack needs to be found, in order to maintain balance in the system (Versteegh 1977). One of the reasons for the lack of inflection in *kam* was said to be because of its frequent use (*kaθrat al-istiʕmaal*). This was a general explanatory device applied elsewhere as well to certain frequently-occurring word forms which failed to show an expected property (e.g. *lam yaku* 'it was not' for *lam yakun*). In the case of *kam* the discussion went beyond this explanation to speculation whether 'frequent use' did not imply that *kam* in fact originally had a full inflection, *kam-un*, etc. Frequent use then reduced it. Suyuṭi allows this as a possibility. The explanation he prefers, however, following the solution of the ninth-century grammarian ʔAxfash, is that at its very origin, Arabs had realized that *kam* and other such words would be frequently used, and they therefore did away with the case endings on these words even before they could be used.

The logical matrix is evident here in two ways. First, the very supposition that *kam* had case endings is derived from the observation that in the unmarked instance, nouns have case endings: nouns have case endings, *kam* is a noun, therefore *kam* can be assumed once to have had case. No linguistic evidence supporting the assumption of a former case ending presence is adduced, however. Second, Suyuṭi's preferred solution equally rests on logical deduction: the Arabs in their wisdom (*ħikma*) suppressed case endings knowing they would have become redundant under the frequent use clause. The formulation is rather in the form of a grammatical constraint: certain word classes, in certain grammatical positions will lack case endings. From both perspectives there is no linguistic sense, from a contemporary perspective, that a change *kam-un* (etc.)→*kam* can be countenanced in Suyuṭi's account (see Bohas and Guillaume 1984; Larcher 2005b, for further discussion).

At the risk of sounding polemical, it is no criticism of the Arabic tradition to say that a historical linguistic perspective was lacking in their theory. According to the definition of historical linguistics adopted here, historical linguistics exists only when the comparative method is systematically applied, and this method did not exist until the nineteenth century. The genius of the Arabic tradition lay elsewhere, in the realm of formal synchronic grammar (Owens 1988), and probably without a highly developed theoretical interest I think it inconceivable that such a rich source of data, only a small part of which is treated here, could have been gathered and systematized. Indeed,

I think the descriptive and theoretical achievement of the Arabic grammarians is enhanced when compared to the inconsistent and unsystematic attempts of modern Western scholars to develop a coherent account of Arabic language history against the backdrop of a badly applied comparative linguistics.

2.7. Conclusion

The conclusion is a sobering one. Put simply, after over one hundred and fifty years of Western research on the language, there is no meaningful comparative linguistic history of Arabic. The distinction Old Arabic–Neo-Arabic was postulated on the basis of a logical matrix, not one grounded in comparative linguistic theory. The Western Arabicist tradition has either accepted the distinction as the working basis for Arabic language history without reflection (e.g. Brockelmann) or has allowed often incisive and pointed comparative linguistic observations (as frequently in Fischer and Jastrow 1980; Fischer 1995) to be pressed into the Old Arabic–Neo-Arabic mold in which it does not fit.[42]

Clearly the problem today does not lie in the lack of data. The last forty years have given us a wealth of dialectal data, which, as seen above, can be correlated with data from the Old Arabic era, and also can be used to expand upon our knowledge of proto-Arabic.

It is clear that in the present exposition modern Arabic dialects are given a much more important role in the interpretation of Arabic linguistic history than is usually the case. In part, this is simply a rectification of past practice. As seen, Arabic dialects have largely been excluded from this sub discipline by fiat. Arabic linguistic history, however, is no more coterminous with a history of Arabic dialects than it is with a history of the Classical language. Fleischer's goal of a holistic Arabic is as cogent today as it was 150 years ago. It will be reached, however, only with the basis of a grounded linguistic methodology, and this involves, inter alia, a principled exposition of relations between modern sources and whatever old ones that are available. In the broad scenario described here, Arabic is better conceptualized not as a simple linear dichotomous

---

[42] There are of course dissenting voices in this paradigm. Vollers (1906) was essentially shouted down, first by the then contemporary Arab tradition (according to Vollers's account in his introduction of the presentation of his thesis in Algiers, 1906: 3), and later by his German colleagues (e.g. Nöldeke 1910). Rabin states simply that, 'The modern colloquial here [Yemen] continues the ancient dialect' (1960/1986: 564). Unfortunately, this statement is not backed up by more concrete exemplification, and it is not clear whether Rabin considers other dialects not to continue his ancient dialects, and if they don't, what criteria are set to distinguish the different cases. There is also the significant work of Birkeland (1940) on pausal forms which unusually for someone working in the Old/New paradigm applies principles of comparative linguistics. This is discussed in greater detail in sects. 8.1 and 8.9.

development, the Old vs. Neo split, but rather as a multiply-branching bush, whose stem represents the language 1,300 years ago. Parts of the bush maintain a structure barely distinguishable from its source—in linguistic terms parts in which an Old–New dichotomization is wholly irrelevant. Other parts of the bush are marked by striking differences, differences which distinguish them as much from other parts of the appendages as from the stem. It is a complex organism which resists a simple description in terms of a dichotomous structure.

In the following six chapters through case studies based both on Old Arabic and modern dialect sources I further exemplify the irrelevance of the Old–New dichotomy for understanding Arabic linguistic history and at the same time the need to approach the subject from a comparative linguistic perspective.

3

Case and Proto-Arabic

It is a fundamental precept of comparative and historical linguistics that genealogical affiliation can only be established on the basis of concrete linguistic features, the more central the feature the more important for classificatory purposes. While there is no absolute consensus about how a central linguistic feature can be identified, it can be taken as axiomatic that long-term reconstruction and classification rests most fundamentally on phonological and morphological criteria. Of these two, Hetzron (1976b) has argued that it is the morphological which is the most important because morphology represents the level of grammar that is both more complex and more arbitrary in the sense that the sound-meaning dyad has no natural basis. Precisely this arbitrariness ensures that morphological correspondences are relatively unlikely to be due to chance.

Though Hetzron's principles of genetic classification were surely colored by his experience in comparative Semitic and Afroasiatic, where there are striking morphological correspondences to be found between languages widely separated both geographically and diachronically (see example (14) in sect. 1.6.9 above), his principle of morphological precedence, as it can be dubbed, may be taken as a general working hypothesis. Unquestionably, morphological case belongs potentially to the basic morphological elements of a language. Whether morphological case belongs to the basic elements of a language family is, of course, a question requiring the application of the comparative method. In Niger-Congo, for example, case apparently does not belong to the proto-language,[1] whereas in Indo-European it is a key element of the proto-language (Antilla 1972: 366). In Afroasiatic, to which Arabic belongs, the status of case in the proto-language is, as yet, undecided. Nonetheless, the assumption of a case system within at least some branches of the language family, Semitic in particular (Moscati et al. 1980), has had consequences both for the

---

[1] In an overview of Niger-Congo languages edited by Bendor-Samuel of the ten or so Niger-Congo families, only the Ijoid languages appear to have some case marking (1990: 115). My colleagues at Bayreuth, Gudrun Miehe and Carl Hoffman, both with long experience in Niger-Congo, inform me that it is very unlikely that case belongs to the proto-language.

conceptualization of relations within Semitic and for the reconstruction of the proto-language for the entire family. Given the as yet uncertain status of morphological case at the phylum level, I believe a critical appraisal of its status at all genealogical levels to be appropriate. Within this perspective in this chapter, I seek to elucidate the interplay between case conceptualization and the reconstruction of one proto-variety, namely Arabic. Given the importance of Arabic within Semitic, conclusions reached regarding this language will have consequences for the subfamily and beyond, as I will attempt to show.

The chapter consists of five parts. In sect. 3.2, I briefly review the status of case in the various branches of Afroasiatic. Here it will be seen that a case system is not self-evidently a property of the entire phylum. In sect. 3.3, I turn to case in Classical Arabic, inter alia considering the descriptive work of Sibawaih, who as has been seen, was instrumental in defining the nature of Classical Arabic. Finally, in sects. 3.4 and 3.5, I consider the evidence for case in the modern Arabic dialects, addressing in particular the question of whether the dialects should be seen as being the offspring of a case-bearing variety, and if not whether caseless varieties are innovative or go back to a caseless form of proto-Semitic.

3.1. Introduction

Probably the most prominent difference between Old Arabic, however defined in the past literature, and modern dialects, the one at the head of the differentiating list (Fück 1950: 2, see sect. 2.3.2 above; Fischer 1982a: 83; Blau 1988: 2), is the case and mode inflectional system. It is thus time to turn to a detailed consideration of this phenomenon in the debate about the relationship between Old Arabic, proto-Arabic, and the modern dialects. I will concentrate exclusively on the central feature of Arabic case marking, short-vowel nominal inflection.

3.2. Case in the Afroasiatic Phylum

The phylic unity of Afroasiatic rests on striking correspondences found in all branches of the phylum within the verbal and pronominal systems. Personal markers (in pronouns and/or verbs), for instance, in -k 'second person' (SG and PL), -nV '1PL' (m in Chadic), $s \sim \int$ 'third person', a second and third person plural formed from the consonantal person marker + u + (nasal) (nasal lacking in Chadic) are found in all branches. Verb conjugations differentiated according to prefixing and suffixing classes (in various distributions) are found in three of the branches, Semitic, Cushitic, and Berber, while the other two, Egyptian (suffix only) and Chadic (prefix only) have conjugations with clear correspondences to one or the other (see e.g. Rössler 1950; Voigt 1987; Diakonoff 1988). It is therefore equally striking that only two of the five[2] branches, Semitic and Cushitic, have languages with morphological case systems. Even within these two branches there is a good deal of variation among individual languages, and the question of the extent to which Cushitic case corresponds to Semitic is far from clear. In sect. 3.2.1, I briefly summarize the situation for Cushitic, and in sect. 3.2.2, that for Semitic.

3.2.1. *Case in Cushitic*

While many of the Cushitic languages have case systems, it is by no means clear that they derive from a proto-Cushitic case system. Such a proposal has been put forward by Sasse (1984) where a proto-Cushitic case system with nominative opposed to accusative is postulated.[3]

Against this Tosco (1993, in the spirit of Castellino 1978: 40) has argued that the origin of many Cushitic nominative markers lies in a focus morpheme. Tosco's argument is based on both universal and formal considerations, the main features of which are as follows.

First of all he notes (as have a number of scholars before him) that the nominative-absolutive (roughly = accusative) distinction in Cushitic is typologically odd since it is the nominative which is the marked form by a number of criteria. It is the nominative noun, for example, which is morphologically marked (see (1) vs. (2)),[4] e.g. Oromo.

---

[2] I assume a very traditional Afroasiatic family tree, well aware that there are classificatory questions at all levels. I do not think, at this point, that such questions bear crucially on the present treatment of case, however.

Berber and Chadic do not have case. Since Egyptian orthography did not mark short vowels, whether or not ancient Egyptian had a case system is difficult to know. Even if Callender's (1975) attempt to reconstruct ancient Egyptian cases on the basis of the functional behavior of verbal forms is on the right track, his attribution of formal values to them (e.g. nominative -u, accusative -a) is speculative at best, at worst no more than the filling in of an Egyptian consonantal text with short vocalic values taken over from Classical Arabic. Petrácek (1988: 40) does not reconstruct a case system for ancient Egyptian.

[3] Sasse leaves open the possibility that other cases might be reconstructible. Diakonoff (1988: 60) proposes an 'abstract' proto-Afroasiatic case system, characterized above all, apparently, by its abstractness. Formally there was an opposition between $i \sim u$ vs. -$a \sim \emptyset$, though how this system worked functionally at the proto-Afroasiatic stage is not spelled out in detail. Diakonoff's reconstruction rests largely on data from Semitic and Cushitic, and hence is open to all the criticisms of postulating a proto-Cushitic case system contained in this section. Furthermore, his entire reconstruction of Afroasiatic case is based on the dubious assumption that the proto-language was an ergative one. His claim (1988: 59) that Oromo (and similarly, I suspect, his claims for Beja, Sidamo, and Ometo) is an ergative language (or has traces of an ergative system?) is mysterious (see Owens 1985).

[4] Greenberg (1978: 95, universal 38) notes that if there is a case system, the subject of the intransitive verb will be marked by the least marked case (also Croft 1990: 104).

(1) namičč-í   ní-dufe
    man-NOM   pre v-came
    'The man came'.

(2) namíččá   arke
    man (ABS) saw
    'He saw the man'.

The unmarked absolutive serves as the basis for further inflections, cf. genitive (*ka*) *namičč-áa* 'of the man'. Furthermore, the nominative has a more restricted distribution, limited only to the subject, and is far less frequent in texts. In these points the Cushitic nominative has close affinities to grammaticalized topics.

Reviewing the literature on Cushitic languages, Tosco further shows that a suffix *-i* throughout the branch, e.g. Highland East Cushitic (e.g. Sidamo *mín-i* 'house-i', Central Cushitic (Awngi *-kí*), is found which marks not only subjects but other topicalized constituents as well. Where *-i* has been grammaticalized as a subject marker other markers develop as topicalizers. An *-n* is particularly common in this function, as perhaps exhibited in the Harar Oromo.

(3) namíččá-n   arke
    man-topic   saw
    'I saw the *man*'.

Relating the Cushitic data to Semitic, it is furthermore noteworthy that Sasse's reconstruction, nominative *-*i*/-*u*, absolutive *-*a* does not self-evidently correspond to the three-valued Semitic system. In fact, as Tosco shows, the only widespread nominative-like (Tosco's topicalizer) inflection on full nouns is -*i*.[5] It is true that a 'nominative' *u* is found throughout Cushitic, though as part of the article or demonstrative, not as a nominal affix (e.g. Oromo *kuni* 'this-NOM', vs. *kana* 'this-ABS').[6] Moreover, Cushitic case marking is, unlike Semitic, overwhelmingly (Central Cushitic Awngi (Hetzron 1976a: 37) and Oromo are exceptional) phrase final. In Somali, for instance, where the nominative subject is generally shown by lowering a tone from H to L, one has in absolutive case, *nín* 'man' → NOM *nin*, but NOM *nín-ku* 'the man', where the

---

[5] In a number of Highland East Cushitic languages (Hudson 1976: 253 ff.) the nominative (or topic) form is phonologically determined relative to the absolute form: if the absolute ends in a front vowel or -*a* it is -*i*, if in -*o* it is -*u*.

[6] Paradoxically, the Semitic article/demonstrative system is neither particularly unified, nor do most of the Semitic languages (including Classical Arabic and most stages of Akkadian, Von Soden 1969: 47) show case differentiation in it (Moscati et al. 1980: 110).

determiner assumes the low tone, allowing *nín* to re-assume its unmarked absolutive form with high tone (Saeed 1987: 133). Any attempt to link this Cushitic data to Semitic case would have to account for significant structural mismatches. To these problems can be added that of the Cushitic genitive, which neither Sasse nor Tosco integrate into their models, both cognizant of the special problems accompanying the task.

To summarize this section, while it is certainly correct, paraphrasing and changing Sasse's (1984: 111) formulation slightly, to speak of certain Cushitic endings as bearing 'a striking resemblance to certain formatives... in other Afroasiatic branches', it does not appear possible, at this point at least, to link these directly to Semitic case markers. Even assuming a link to be possible, it would not automatically follow that it would be made in terms of case. Indeed, given that it is only the Semitic branch (following Tosco for Cushitic) which unequivocally has a proto-case system, it would not be surprising if such a system developed at the proto-stage Semitic out of markers of another type.

3.2.2. *Semitic case*

It is not my purpose here to review the literature on case in Semitic. The situation in Arabic will be reviewed in detail anyway in the next two sections. For present purposes two basic points need to be made.

First, although a three-valued case system (nominative -*u*, accusative -*a*, genitive -*i*) can be reconstructed for proto-Semitic, only a minority of well-attested Semitic languages have it. Moreover, assuming Moscati et al.'s tripartite classification of Semitic into Northeast, Northwest, and Southwest sub-branches, caseless languages (or dialects) are attested in each sub-branch. The earlier stages of Akkadian (Northeast) had it, though after 1000 BC the case system showed clear signs of breaking down.[7] Most of the Northwest Semitic languages did not have case (Hebrew, Aramaic, Phonecian), only Ugaritic[8]

---

[7] The outside observer may be slightly disquieted by Von Soden's observation (1969: 80) that even in Old Assyrian and Old Babylonian exceptions to the expected case-marking system occur. He attributes these to orthographic errors or to 'bad pronunciation' (?). A closer study of such 'errors' would be interesting.

[8] Even Semiticists are not unified about which Semitic languages demonstrably have case systems. Rabin (1969: 161) in a minority opinion, cautions that there is not enough data to reconstruct case syntax in Ugaritic and hence does not include Ugaritic among the attested case-bearing Semitic languages. He has a two-valued case system for Gəʕəz (as opposed to Weninger's 1993 one), but would apparently rather identify the Gəʕəz Ø 'nominative' etymologically with the Akkadian absolutive (i.e. lack of morphological case) than with Classical Arabic -*u* (1969: 196). Some modern Ethiopian Semitic languages (e.g. Amharic -*n*) have secondarily developed an object case, sometimes sensitive to definiteness features. Barth's (1898: 594) assumption that proto-Hebrew had case is based crucially on the *assumption* that proto-Semitic had case and only case (i.e. no parallel caseless variety, see sect. 3.5). Reading between the lines of his article, however, it is clear that one could no more justify

and Eblaitic (probably) possessing it. The situation with Ugaritic in this respect is not very satisfying, as the only direct evidence for case endings comes from the word-final symbol for the glottal stop. In Gordon's (1965) lexicon, these amount to barely ten noun lexemes from which the entire case system must be constructed. It is noteworthy that neither Rabin (1969, see n. 8 above) nor Petrácek (1988: 39) list Ugaritic among the case-bearing Semitic languages. Among the Southwest Semitic languages Classical Arabic has it, though Gəʕəz (in chronological terms attested some 350–500 years earlier) probably did not, at least not in a way which self-evidently corresponds with the three-valued proto-Semitic system. The modern Ethiopic Semitic languages do not have it (see n. 8), nor do the modern Arabic dialects. The modern South Arabian languages do not have it, while the situation for epigraphic South Arabic is unclear due to the script.

From a distributional perspective one can approach the problem in two ways. First, it can be assumed that the cases are original and lost in those varieties where not attested. This, of course, is the approach taken by most Semiticists (e.g. Moscati et al. 1980: 94), and could be said to be supported indirectly at least by the situation in Akkadian where the breakdown of a case system is diachronically attested. A second approach would be to view the caseless situation as original, the Akkadian and Classical Arabic system as innovative. This is problematic in view of the fact that Akkadian is the oldest of the languages in absolute terms, and that the case system in the two languages is in general terms comparable. It is unlikely that the two innovated in the same way independently of each other, and if they did not, a common origin pushes the case system back into the proto-stage. A third solution is that the proto-language had two systems (two dialects as it were), one with case, one without. I will be developing this perspective in the rest of this chapter. For the moment, it suffices to note that postulating a caseless variety at the proto-Semitic stage is supported by family-internal distributional facts, namely the broad range of Semitic languages which do not have case systems (to turn the argument introduced in the previous point on its head), and the arguments of the previous section, where it was seen that Semitic case, within Afroasiatic, is probably innovative.

---

the reconstruction of a case system from internal Biblical Hebrew sources than one can an Arabic case system from the modern Arabic dialects. There are no attempts to my knowledge to explain how the assumed proto-Semitic case system disappeared so completely throughout the family. Moscati (1958), for example, is not so much an attempt to justify the assumption of a family-wide proto-case system as to determine the length of the assumed endings. Given the significant counter-evidence that some Semitic languages/varieties never had a case system, it may minimally be expected that the assumed disappearence of case from these varieties be given a unified explanation.

Second, it can be noted that in the Semitic languages with a case system there are contexts where, in synchronic terms, the system is neutralized. In the Akkadian genitive relation, the possessed noun does not bear case (or appears in the so-called absolute form) before a nominal possessor, and before a pronominal possessor generally only when the possessed noun ends in a vowel (Von Soden 1969: 82 ff., 189 ff.).

(4) beel-Ø   biit-i-m
    master-Ø house GEN-M
    'master (Ø = "absolute" case) of the house'
    aʃʃas-su
    wife-his

In Classical Arabic the neutralization, at least in traditional accounts (see sects. 1.6.3, 3.3.2.3), occurs in pausal position. Besides raising questions of the functional centrality of case in Semitic (see sects. 3.3.1), the presence of these caseless contexts suggests that even those Semitic languages with morphological case systems possessed traces of the caseless variety. I will touch on further case-related comparative aspects of Semitic below (sects. 3.3.3, 3.4.2, 3.5).

Brief though the remarks in the present section are, they are consistent enough to underscore Petráček's conclusion (1988: 41, see also Rabin 1969: 191), based on comparative Afroasiatic data, that 'the robustly structured case system of Semitic can be regarded as a Semitic innovation' ('Die prägnant gebildete Struktur des Kasussytems im Semitischen (-*u*, -*i*, -*a*) dürfen wir als eine semitische Innovation ansehen.'). If this point is accepted, however, there emerges a further Semitic-internal issue, namely at what point Semitic itself developed a case system, and whether this development represented the ancestor of all Semitic languages or only some of them. In the rest of this chapter I will attempt to show that a detailed consideration of the issue for proto-Arabic will provide one important component in answering the question.

3.3. Classical Arabic

It should by now be becoming clear that the assumption that there is a clear distinction between those Semitic languages with case systems and those without, the latter possessing, in this respect, an older trait than the former, is perhaps not so unproblematic as represented in the textbooks (e.g. Moscati et al. 1980; Fischer 1982*a*). In this section I examine the status of case in Classical Arabic in greater detail, using two sources. In sect. 3.3.1, I summarize the work of Corriente, not adequately integrated into the debate about Old

Arabic, perhaps because his views about case in Old Arabic are somewhat iconoclastic and perhaps because Corriente himself did not follow his own ideas to a further logical conclusion. In sect. 3.3.2, I turn to the grammarian who, if not the founder of Classical Arabic, doubtlessly played a more pivotal role in explicitly defining its form than any other individual, namely the eighth-century grammarian Sibawaih, in order to gain a more precise insight into the nature of the Classical Arabic which he defined. This account will initiate the comparison between the Classical language and the modern dialects, a necessary step in the discussion of Blau's theory deriving the modern dialects from the Classical language.

A work which took a philological perspective a diachronic step deeper is Diem's (1973) study of case endings in the Arabic words found in the Aramaic inscriptions of the Arabs of Nabataea in southern Jordan, dating from about 100 BC.[9] Diem shows that Arabic personal names found in the inscriptions did not show traces of a living case system. If Diem's interpretation of the data is correct, it would mean that the *oldest* written evidence of Arabic is characterized by a linguistic trait, the lack of functional case endings, which is otherwise said to be a characteristic par excellence of *Neo*-Arabic (see sect. 3.2.2).

3.3.1. Corriente

In a series of articles (1971, 1973, 1975, 1976), Corriente argued that Classical Arabic stood at the end of a development, and that its crystalization in a more or less fixed form was due in large part to the efforts of the Arabic grammarians. Many of the points he makes relate to the case system. These include evidence of two main sorts, linguistic internal interpretations, and an examination of the philological record.

The first perspective is prominent in his 1971 article where Corriente showed that the functional yield of Classical Arabic cases—roughly those contexts where a difference of meaning can be effected by a change of case alone—is vanishingly low. While one may agree with Blau (1988: 268) that case systems generally have a high degree of redundancy, the point stands that Arabic case is functionally not deeply integrated into the grammar. The case forms, furthermore, are not well integrated into the morphology (1971: 47). They are marked by a lack of allomorphy, exceptionlessly tacked on to the end of the word, with little morpho-phonological interaction with either

---

[9] The Nabataean Arabs used Aramaic as their literary variety. Diem (1973: 237) writes: 'Es wurde zu zeigen versucht, dass das Nabatäisch-Arabische schon im ersten Jahrhundert v. Chr. das Kasussystem des Semitischen aufgegeben hat.' Whether this variety of Arabic ever had case becomes a question of historical reconstruction.

the stems they are suffixed to or the items which may be suffixed to them. To this can be added that fact that unlike many languages, they are not subject to variational rules based on animacy and/or definiteness. Moreover, as seen in the previous chapter (sect. 2.4.1.2, Old Arabic sources), the nominative/genitive contrast, -u/-i, may be phonologically neutralized in some varieties.

In his 1975 article Corriente cites deviations from the classical norms found in various verses of the *Kitab al-Aghani*, including an inflectionally invariable dual (1975: 52, cf. Rabin 1951: 173, also, of course, Qur?aan 20. 63), mixing up of cases (1975: 57), or their complete absence (1975: 60). Corriente's explanation for this phenomenon, as well as for the development of Middle Arabic out of Old Arabic, was to postulate a caseless form of Arabic formed in pre-Islamic times along the northwest Arabic borderland in Nabataea (1976: 88; expanding on Diem 1973). Associated with commercial centers, this variety of Arabic would have quickly acquired prestige status and in the aftermath of the early Islamic Arabic diaspora served as a model for the development of caseless Middle Arabic in urban contexts. Note that he does not break with Blau completely, in that he sees the caseless varieties arising out of the border contacts.

The present study agrees with Corriente on the need to recognize a caseless form of Arabic existing contemporaneously with case varieties. Where issue can be taken with his account is the readiness to postulate a simple link between one variety of Old Arabic (Nabataean Arabic) and the modern dialects. The difficulties in drawing such a simple linkage will become evident in the discussion in sects. 3.4 and 3.5, as well as elsewhere in this book. As a general introductory remark, however, it may be noted that integrating the modern dialects into the reconstruction of proto-Arabic will yield results which do not self-evidently replicate the linguistic entities defined by the Arabic grammarians, or by the epigraphic record (e.g. caseless Nabataean Arabic). This follows from the different methods and goals of the comparative method and of the Arabic grammarians to whom I turn presently, and from the very fragmentary nature of the epigraphic record. A full reconstruction of proto-Arabic requires independent and detailed definition of each of these components, before they are put together into a larger picture.

3.3.2. *Sibawaih*

Barring a full-scale study of all the material to be found in all grammatical treatises, the reasons for concentrating on Sibawaih in the first instance are self-evident. His *Kitaab* is, even by modern standards, a paragon of detail and completeness (if not necessarily of organization and clarity of style). More importantly, it is arguably the only comprehensive grammar where a large body of eyewitness observations of actual linguistic usage are systematically recorded. This is not to deny that interesting material is to be found in the later treatises. Nonetheless, later grammarians were dependent to a large degree on Sibawaih for the simple reason that the *Arabiyya* came to consist of a more or less closed set of data by the tenth century,[10] rendering observations on the contemporary spoken language superfluous (see below).

Turning to Sibawaih, there are two aspects of his work which may be kept in mind when interpreting his observations on Arabic. The first is that Sibawaih was confronted by a mass of variant forms which he evaluated in his own inimitable style, to which I turn presently. By and large, in the later grammars, those written after the end of the ninth century, the variant forms were either excluded altogether or treated in the more detailed grammars (e.g. Ibn Al-Sarraj; Ibn Yaʕish) in addenda to the general rules. If the rare, new material was added, it was nearly always by reference to forms recorded from personages/tribes contemporaneous with Sibawaih or before.[11]

The second point relates to what may be termed Sibawaih's attitude towards the linguistic data which he described. Carter (1973: 146; see Ditters 1990: 131 for criticisms) has contrasted Sibawaih's 'descriptivist' approach with the 'prescriptivism' of later grammarians. This contrast of styles, as noted in the previous paragraph, reflects a general reorientation in the definition of what sort of data is allowable in the definition of the *Arabiyya*. It is not clear, however, what is to be understood by descriptivism, whose characterization Carter does not elaborate on. Understanding Sibawaih on this point is important to defining his theoretical linguistic thinking, to comprehending the sort of raw linguistic data which his detailed observations make accessible to us, and to informing us of the motivations for and mechanisms by which grammars generally are developed. Baalbaki (1990: 18) has made the important point that the grammarians, confronted by a mass of linguistic data, were 'not content themselves with a purely descriptive exposition of linguistic material, but attempted to present this material within a *coherent* system' (my emphasis). Sibawaih, he observes, was the key figure in this process. In the next three subsections I discuss aspects of this system, with special reference to case-related problems.

---

[10] The work of the lexicographers, for which there are relatively few critical modern studies, may have to be excepted here. Unlike grammar, lexicography deals with an open-ended system. Adding a word to the lexicon rarely changes the lexicon in the way that adding a rule to the grammar potentially changes the entire grammar.

[11] In this respect the analogy with the history of Arabic linguistic thinking breaks down. There were conceptual breakthroughs after the tenth century, though in areas of thinking adjacent to the core areas of morphophonology and syntax, such as pragmatics and semantics.

Before beginning this exposition, however, it is relevant to mention that the very terminology of case marking among the grammarians may bear on the question of the existence of case in Old Arabic. The two oldest grammatical works, one (Sibawaih's) definitely from the end of the eighth century, the other equally old or only slightly younger, utilized case form as a central formal criteria for organizing their exposition of syntactic structures. Grammars and case-marking go hand in hand in the history of Arabic grammatical theory. Xalaf al-ʔAħmar's *Muqaddima fiy l-Naħw* is a short, practical grammar (see Owens 1990: ch. 9), whereas Sibawaih's *Kitaab* is one of the most detailed grammars of Arabic ever written. Sibawaih in particular goes to considerable pains at the very beginning of his grammar (I: 2.1 ff., see Baalbaki 1990) to functionally distinguish lexically determined from syntactically determined short vowels, the latter of course being the case markers. Sibawaih's terminology is thus:

(5a) Short vowel terminology in Sibawaih

lexical	morpho-syntactic	phonetic value
ḍamma	rafʕ	u
fatħa	naṣb	a
kasra	jarr	i

It appears that the 'discovery' of functionally-differentiated vowels was preceded by a time when the same terminology was used undifferentiated for vowels of both types. Such a system is still in evidence in Farraʔ's terminology (Owens 1990: 159; Talmon 2003).

(5b) Short vowel terminology in Farraʔ

lexical	morpho-syntactic	phonetic value
ḍamma ~ rafʕ	rafʕ	u
fatħa ~ naṣb	naṣb	a
kasra ~ xafḍ	xafḍ	i

In Farraʔ the morphosyntactic values also are used to describe the phonetic values of lexical vowels, so that the vowel in *ʔumm* 'mother' (I: 6) is described as *rafʕ*.[12] This supposition finds support in Versteegh's study on early Arabic

---

[12] That Farraʔ's terminology should be the 'older', though he lived a generation after Sibawaih (in absolute time!), may be explained by Talmon's theory (e.g. 1990, 2003) that Farraʔ represented an older grammatical tradition than did Sibawaih. I would tend to accept Farraʔ's explanation for the variant -*i* of *al-ħamd-i lillaahi* (I: 3) among some Bedouins, that the nominative is assimilated to the following -*i* of *li-* within the compound-like unit that has arisen due to 'frequency of use'. Nonetheless, the example illustrates (1) the convenience of not having a distinctive terminology for case vs. lexical vowels, and (2) the non-case functional value of final nominal vowels among at least some groups of speakers.

grammatical theory. He shows (1993b: 125) that the Koranic exegete Muḥammad al-Kalbi (d. 145/763), who lived a generation before Sibawaih, used the term ḍamm for a *u* vowel 'within a word', as an 'ending' (Versteegh does not specify what sort here), and for a nunated noun. *naṣb* is used for a lexical vowel *a*, an ending, and for nunation, and similarly for the other terms on the lists in (5).

Rather than consider the data in terms of their implications for an understanding of the development of Arabic linguistic theory, which has been one interest in such data to date, they may be interpreted in terms of the present question of the status of case endings in the history of the language. In these terms it appears that Sibawaih made explicit two aspects of vocalic variation, one lexically, the other morpho-syntactically determined, which existed in the language he described.

What may be asked here is whether the variation and imprecise distinction between lexical and morpho-syntactic vowels found in Farraʔ and other early linguists and commentators doesn't originate in the fact that there were actually varieties of Arabic which Farraʔ studied where vocalic variation at the end of words did not represent case endings, i.e. were caseless varieties of Arabic. Under such circumstances a consistently differentiating terminology would, of course, have been unnecessary. Farraʔ's 'imprecise' terminology would thus not reflect a less differentiated grammatical thinking than Sibawaih's, but rather its application to a different data base. This perspective is admittedly speculative, though the idea of relating early terminological problems to actual language forms, should be pursued further.[13]

3.3.2.1. *An example* The following example will serve both as an introduction to Sibawaih's treatment of case in Classical Arabic, and to the way in which he processed linguistic data. Starting from ch. 24 (I: 31 ff.) Sibawaih considers some fairly complex data in which he is concerned to define the case form of a topic and/or agent noun (see Khan 1988: 25 ff. for discussion). A basic contrast is shown in (6a) vs. (6b).

(6a) zayd-un   laqiy-tu   ʔax-aa-hu (I: 32.16)
      Zayd-NOM   met-I   brother-ACC-his
      'As for Zayd, I found his brother'.

(6b) zayd-an   laqiy-tu   ʔaxaa-hu (I: 32.20)
      Zayd-ACC
      'As for Zayd, I found his brother'.

---

[13] One thinks e.g. of the meaning of the designations for linguistic varieties/entities, *kalaam*, *luɣa*, *qawl* (Versteegh 1993b: 91, 99 ff.) in the development of the notion of an ʕArabiyya.

'Zayd' can equally appear in nominative or accusative form here. Were Sibawaih a simple descriptivist he would presumably have been content to note that a topic can appear in nominative or accusative form, in free variation. Such a statement appears to account for most of the topicalization structures which Sibawaih discusses in this and the following chapters. Such an approach is quite foreign to his methodology, however. For Sibawaih, no variation is simply 'free' because every variant which he catalogs implies its own conceptual interpretation. In the present example, both nominative and accusative cases are justified by a series of analogies with other, simpler structures and paraphrases with examples which allow a regularization of apparently anomalous structural elements.

At the beginning of ch. 31 (I: 31. 17 ff.) Sibawaih explains the following pairs of examples (where (7a) corresponds to (6a), (7b) to (6b)).

(7a) zayd-un   ḍarab-tu-hu
     Zayd-NOM   hit-I-him
     'As for Zayd, I hit him'.

(7b) zayd-an   ḍarab-tu-hu
     Zayd-ACC
     'Zayd, I hit him'

Example (7a) contains a nominative noun in the function of topic (mubtadaʔ), with the verb structurally set against the topic as its comment[14] (mabniyy ʕalaa l-mubtadaʔ, see Levin 1985). Here the nominative in Zayd is explained by the general property that topics are nominatively marked. In (7b) the problem is to explain the accusative in Zayd, which Sibawaih does by assuming an implicit verb (ʔiḍmaar al-fiʕl I: 32. 1) of the same value as the main verb which governs the accusative in Zayd (= (ḍarabtu) zaydan ḍarabtuhu).

Sibawaih then proceeds to more complex examples where the co-referential pronoun is detached from the verb, first where the direct object is marked by a preposition (zayd-un/an marartu bihi 'As for Zayd, I passed him'), then to the set in (6). Example (6a) is explained analogously to (7a), as a topic (nominative) + comment structure. That in (6b) is more problematic because in contrast to (7b) there does not appear to be a direct semantic link between the topicalized noun and the main verb. There is no obvious sense in which the action of 'hitting' can be directly related to the topic, Zayd. To

---

[14] The term 'comment' is a more appropriate translation of the later 'xabar'. Levin (1985: 302) translates Sibawaih's term as 'the part which makes the sentence complete'. For brevity's sake I use the shorter term 'comment'.

explain these structures Sibawaih invokes a new principle, namely that 'if the action falls on the object containing a co-referential pronoun it is as if the action falls on the object itself' (I: 32. 17). This semantic equivalence carries over to a morpho-syntactic one, where the topicalized noun assumes the same case form as the item it is linked with. In (6b), for instance, the co-referential pronoun *-hu* links *ʔaxaa-* to *zaydan*. Since *ʔaxaa-* is accusative, so too can *zayd* be.[15] This principle is invoked a number of times to explain ever more complex structures in the succeeding pages (particularly I: 42).

Examples such as these from Sibawaih can be repeated many times over. I will come back to them presently, noting only for the moment that what is important here is that an example cited by Sibawaih always has to be integrated into his linguistic thinking. Sibawaih cites (6a) with minimal comment because for Sibawaih its structure is clear. When he moves to (6b) he is confronted by a new structural state of affairs which requires new principles, new explanations. What happens, however, when he meets structures which he finds clearly wrong? In fact this happens relatively infrequently.[16] It is true, as Carter (1973) points out, that Sibawaih does have an evaluative vocabulary which allows him to rank the acceptability of one structure against another. When he uses it, however, it is usually to recommend a over b, without rejecting b altogether. In the present example, for instance, he says that the nominative (7a) is 'better' (I: 32.22). Clearly, however, he makes this judgment on the basis of the grammatical merits of each structure, i.e. in terms of the rules by which he evaluates them in the first place.

Nonetheless, it is important for present purposes to know if Sibawaih sets limits to the acceptable. One positive answer to this question can be illustrated in his discussion of pausal forms, which will be referred to further in sect. 3.2.3. Sibawaih (II: 309, ch. 495) notes that it may happen in -CC# final nouns (particularly with sonorants as the final C apparently) that in pausal position the genitive or nominative case markers are not deleted but rather by a process of what may be termed 'case epenthesis' form a final CVC syllable. Thus 'some Arabs' instead of saying *bakr(u)* or *bakr(i)* have *bakur#* 'Bakr-NOM', *bakir#* 'Bakr-GEN'. He adds, however, that this is possible only so long as the resulting structure meets acceptable word structure constraints.

---

[15] Sibawaih may not be entirely convinced of this explanation himself, for he adds two further (somewhat strained) examples where a noun is grammatically affected by a verb, without bearing a direct semantic relation to the action represented in it. Thus one might say, 'I honored him as you honored his brother' (I: 32. 17) where the honoring is equal in both actions, though in the first it is 'him' who is honored, whereas in the second it is not 'him' but his brother.

[16] Admittedly 'infrequently' is an impressionistic evaluation. It can in principle be fairly strictly measured, however, taking all the examples completely disallowed by Sibawaih divided by all his examples discussed. The percentage would be quite low.

ʕidl- 'equal', may undergo genitive case epenthesis, ʕidil#, but in the nominative this is impossible, *ʕidul, because 'they [bedouins] have no words of structure fiʕul' (II: 309. 20). Here the non-occurrence of particular forms is apparently confirmed not in terms of what Sibawaih observed or tested, but rather in terms of the violation of his own general rule.

What should by now be clear is that there is no pure data to be found in Sibawaih. Everything he observes and writes about is filtered through his own grammatical thinking. One salutary effect of this is that it was this very systematization of linguistic facts which helped him to produce a work of extraordinary detail. In examples (6)–(7) discussed above, Sibawaih starts with basic N-V-Obj structures, moves to N-V-prep-Obj structures, and finally to N-V-Obj-possessor pro structures, with each step tackling a slightly more complex case. His description is partly carried along and expanded by the very logic of his grammatical thinking.

This is not to say, however, that Sibawaih had no regard for the linguistic facts provided to him from his various sources. I think examples such as (6) and (7) can be understood in the following way. Sibawaih was presented with raw data, and this was that the topic noun varies freely between nominative and accusative case. He accepted both forms, but on terms of his own theoretical making. It was Sibawaih's achievement to integrate these 'facts' into a more or less coherent whole (the definitive interpretation of Sibawaih remains to be written), in this case through such concepts as 'topic', *mabniyy ʕalaa al-mubtadaʔ*, co-referentiality, and so on.

At the same time one has to assume that there are many elements of 'Arabic' which were outside the scope of Sibawaih's cognizance. Some of these, of course, are due to the mundane fact that Sibawaih was mortal, the amount of observations he could make finite. Other elements, however, would have escaped Sibawaih's notice because they could not be fitted into his linguistic thinking (Baalbaki 1990: 22). This is a necessary corollary of the system-drivenness of his methodology. As seen above, Sibawaih on principle rules out forms such as * ʕidul. It is therefore possible if such forms did exist that they would not have been observed by him. Caseless forms of Arabic could similarly have been outside his purview.

3.3.2.2. *Stable cases, free variation* While it is improper to speak of free variation of case within a Sibawaihian analytic framework, the fact remains that this effectively is what he documents in many instances. Looking beyond the topic construction, there are many examples of what amount to free variation in case form discussed in the *Kitaab*. In fact, the discussion above around (6)–(7) is typical of Sibawaih's exposition, intimately concerned to define the proper case forms. Full proof of this is a task beyond the confines of the present exposition. What can be offered here is a brief overview of the type of case variation Sibawaih dealt with, based on a review of the first 100 pages of the *Kitaab*, just under a quarter of book I. In these 100 pages, roughly the following topics are dealt with (initial pages of topics are given): general concepts (1), transitivity (10), negative in *laysa* and *maa* (18), left noun dislocation (*tanaazuʕ*, 28), extraposition (31–64) arranged according to type of predicate and predicational type, extraposition in inalienable-like constructions (64), governance of participles, verbal nouns, and adjectives (70), extension of function (*ittisaaʕ* and *iʃtiɣaal*, p. 90; Owens 1990: 251 ff.). In the following I will excerpt a representative example, summarizing Sibawaih's comment on each example.

(8a) maa ʕabdu llaahi ʔax-aa-ka ~ ʔax-uu-ka
'Abdullahi is not your brother'. (I: 21.20)
Usual = nominative, accusative = dialectal usage, *maa al-ħijaazi*

(8b) ḍarab-tu   wa   ḍaraba-niy   zayd-un ~ zayd-an
hit-I   and   hit-me   Zayd-NOM ~ ACC
'I hit (Zayd) and Zayd hit me'. (I: 28.18)

Nominative better because of proximity to second verb, which logically requires a nominative agent. Accusative also allowable.

(8c) ʔa   zayd-an ~ zayd-un   ʔanta   ḍaarib-u-hu
Q   Zayd-a   you   hit-NOM-him
'As for Zayd, are you going to ~ have you hit him'? (I: 45.30)

Accusative correlates with verb-like imperfect meaning of active participle, nominative with nominal-like perfective meaning. This example follows the much more detailed and complicated instances of extraposition with verbal predicates, as in (6), (7) above.

(8d) ʕabd-a ~ ʕabd-u llaahi   fa-ḍrib-hu
Abdallah-ACC ~ NOM   so-hit-him
'Abdallah, so just hit him'. (I: 58.12)

Accusative is preferred, since marked modal sentences (imperatives, conditionals, questions) imply a verbal predicate (which governs the accusative). Nonetheless, contexts can be found (as here) allowing nominative as well.

(8e) ḍuriba   ʕabdu llaahi   ðahr-u-hu ~ ðahr-a-hu
hit   Abdallah   back-NOM ~ ACC-his
'Abdullahi was hit on his back'. (I: 68.9)

Nominative, as *badal* or *tawkiyd*, accusative as nominal complement brought into direct governance of the verb, with implied preposition (ʕalaa ḏahrihi) like *daxaltu l-bayt-a* ~ *fiy l-bayt-i*.

(8f) ʕajib-tu   min   darbi   zayd-in   wa   ʕamr-in/an (I: 81.1)
     surprised-I from   hitting Zayd-GEN and   Amr-GEN ~ ACC
     'I was surprised by the beating of Zayd and Amr'. (I: 81.1)

Genitive in Amr by agreement with Zayd, accusative by virtue of an understood verb (ḏaraba) ʕamran.

(8g) ḏuriba   bihi   ḏarb-un   daʕiyf-un ~ ḏarb-an daʕiyf-an
     hit   by it   hitting-NOM   weak-NOM   ~ hitting-ACC
     'A weak blow was hit with it ~ It was hit a weak blow with'. (I: 97.2)

In passives without an expressed underlying direct object, the choice is free as to which of a range of further complements can be promoted to agent. In this case, either the verbal noun is promoted (NOM), or no complement is promoted (ACC).

As the brief expositions make clear, there is no single explanation for the observed variation. It may be due to dialect variation (8a), though more frequently ((8b), (8d)–(8g)) it is embedded within the logic of Sibawaih's own grammatical formulations. In some instances Sibawaih ranks the alternatives by some measure of relative appropriateness, while in others both variants are of equal value. In one case it may be objected that the example is not of free variation at all, since in (8c) the use of accusative or nominative in *zayd* presumably correlates with a difference in meaning. While the point of this section does not stand or fall on such examples, it is relevant here to draw a distinction between what Sibawaih said, and what one may read between the lines of his pronouncements. In particular, given his predilection (and task) of systematizing the language, one may at certain points (though certainly not in general) question whether what is systematized is really a part of the Arabic as spoken in the eighth century, as opposed to the language as idealized by Sibawaih and other grammarians, who probably were more ready than the population at large to concretize subtle distinctions among competing variants whose origin was not necessarily of a purely linguistic (as opposed to stylistic, sociolinguistic or dialectal) nature. In any case, taken as a whole, 'free variation' is an adequate characterization of the *product* of Sibawaih's observations in (6)–(8). This does not mean, of course, that the variation would be conceived of in such terms by Sibawaih himself. To the contrary, as the explanatory notes are intended to make clear, each variant for Sibawaih is associated with its own structural logic.

It does not appear that the variation in the case system points to an impending breakdown. Sibawaih is too specific about which forms are uniquely correct in many contexts, and too specific about the implications of choosing one variant or another to lend such speculation any weight. Taken as a whole, however, the variation does point to a system with an inner dynamic and flexibility, a variation which grew out of variegated historical developments. It could even have evolved out of a non-case system (see sect. 3.3.2.3).

It can be noted here, before moving on to the next point, that there is a clear structural tendency in the variation, namely that most case variation involves the accusative as one of the two alternatives. Expanding on this observation, it is fair to say that the accusative is the unmarked term relative to frequency of functional occurrence. The only positions which are unequivocally *not* accusative are objects of prepositions and possessors (= genitive), comments, topics when the comment is not a verb, and agents in VS (verbal) sentences (=nominative). Otherwise (the various objects, *tamyiyz, ḥaal*, even subjects after the ʔ*inna* class of complementizers) sentence constituents take accusative, or vary freely in accusative with another case form (as in examples above).

3.3.2.3. *Pausal and context forms*   Probably the greatest degree of variation (of any type) associated with a single functional position is that relating to pausal forms. Sibawaih devotes most of the twenty-eight pages between II: 302–30 to its explicit description, as well as various references to it in other parts of his work. It is clear that for Sibawaih pausal context is not simply a nominal stem minus the indefinite and case suffixes, but rather a position engendering phonological changes of various sorts.[17] A basic summary is found in Ch. 1, sect. 1. 6. 3. The topic is potentially important, because it has been assumed by many scholars (Nöldeke 1897: 10; Brockelmann 1908: 462; Birkeland 1952: 9; Fleisch 1974: 23; Blau 1981: 3; Diem 1991: 303) that the modern caseless dialects derive from the Classical Arabic pausal forms. Naively perhaps, it may be examined here whether in fact a one-to-one correlation may be discerned in Sibawaih's characterization of pausal forms and potential reflexes in the modern dialects. This question adumbrates a further one which will be examined in even greater detail below in sect. 3.4.1 and in Ch. 8, namely whether reflexes of old case endings can be found in the

---

[17] As with many of his concepts, Sibawaih does not define what he means by pause and context. The fact that he includes topics among the 'pausal' chapters which are not obviously descriptions of pausal phenomenon, e.g. the Assad and Tamimi realization of -*ʃi* for -*ki* 2FSG object suffix (ch. 504, see sect. 8.7.4), means that a closer look at these concepts in Sibawaih is appropriate.

modern dialects. In both instances the perspective is the same, namely to enquire into which ways the modern dialects can be shown to continue or develop from the language as described in the Old Arabic sources.

Concentrating here on those chapters which explicate pausal (*waqf*) forms,[18] it emerges that much of what Sibawaih describes for pausal phenomena is not immediately relatable to the modern dialects. The following typology, without answering definitively the question of the extent to which there is a direct link between pausal forms in Sibawaih and the modern dialects, at least defines where the problems lie. The typology consists of two main parameters. One relates to Sibawaih's description of a particular phenomenon as being a property of context or pausal position (or both), the other to the extent of distribution of the phenomenon, both in Sibawaih and in the modern dialects. I will illustrate these points here by means of an informal scale, at whose initial point no obvious connection between the dialects the Sibawaih's description exists and at whose end point a fairly plausible relation may be postulated.

On the one extreme there are many parts of Sibawaih's description which have no relevance to the current question because they have no obvious reflexes in the modern dialects. Perhaps the most obvious example of this sort is the fate of the case vowels themselves. In pausal position they don't simply disappear. Rather, the pausal position they occur at may take on four different values (ch. 494), as described briefly in Ch. 1. The important point is that since the case vowels do not occur in the modern dialects it is impossible to draw connections between Sibawaih's description and their reflexes in the modern dialects.

Moving up the scale, a second type pertains to word-final *-aa*, apparently when written with the *alif maqṣuwra*. Sibawaih notes (II: 314. 8) that although most Arabs pronounce it in pause as *-aa*, the Qays change it to *y*, as in *ḥublaa* → *ḥublay* 'pregnant' (see sect. 7.1). Among modern dialects, Blanc (1964: 50) notes that a final feminine *-a* irregularly undergoes ʔimaala in Jewish Baghdadi Arabic, *ḥeblee* 'pregnant' being among the lexical items where this happens. The *-aa* → *-ay/-ee* change is frequent neither for Sibawaih nor in the modern dialects. While there may be a connection between the Qays pausal form and the Baghdadi example, definitive proof is highly unlikely.

A third instance is where Sibawaih notes that 'some Arabs' employ case epenthesis in pausal position, e.g. *bakru#* → *bakur#* 'Bakr'. This case is more

---

[18] There are fourteen chapters in the page range cited above (ch. 490–504, 507) which deal exclusively or extensively with pausal forms. There is probably nowhere to be found a more detailed description of pausal phenomena in Classical Arabic than in Sibawaih.

interesting than the previous one in two directions. On the one hand for the Classical language, Sibawaih does not appear to place such severe restrictions on the Arabs who use the form. On the other for the modern dialects, as will be seen in sect. 3.4.2 below (18), under certain interpretations it can be related to fairly widespread contemporary phenomena. Very briefly, many modern dialects have a rule inserting an epenthetic vowel before a sonorant (e.g. *-r, -l*) consonant (see Ch. 6). Interestingly, all Sibawaih's examples, admittedly only seven in all, have a sonorant, *-r, -l,* or *-m* as the final consonant. Uncharacteristically, if sonority is indeed a conditioning factor, Sibawaih does not state a phonological environment respective of the final consonant, though he does explicitly note (II: 310. 5) that the process does not occur when a semi-vowel occurs as C_2 (e.g. *zayd, ʕawn*). Even if the sonority condition plays a role in Sibawaih, a difference exists with the modern dialects, where, as will be seen, the rule applies anywhere in a word, not only finally as in Sibawaih. Certainly the present example potentially represents a more general correspondence between the modern dialects and Sibawaih's treatment of pausal phenomena than the case discussed in the previous paragraph. The correspondence is not complete, however, so there will always be a risk in drawing definitive conclusions.

In a fourth set of cases correspondences can be drawn between modern dialects and a variety of pausal alternatives, or even with context forms. Sibawaih, for example (ch. 500) says that the pausal form of nominative and genitive nominals of the form *faaʕiy* may be *raami#, raamiy#,* or *raam#* 'has thrown'.[19] The modern dialects have *raami* here, or perhaps *raamiy,* the choice between the short *-i* or long *-iy* being one of phonological theory (see n. 27), but not the pausal *raam.* On the other hand, the definite context forms also have *-iy, al-raamiy,* so they could also have been a 'source' for the modern dialectal forms. In this case correspondences between some of Sibawaih's morphological alternatives and modern dialects are close to perfect, but still too ambiguous to decide on a definite correspondence. In this category, instances can be cited where it is Sibawaih's context form which provides the clearest link to the modern dialects. Such a case is found among the Tamim (II: 314. 14), who in the F. near demonstrative have *haaðih* in pause,[20] but *haaðiy* in context. In modern dialects *haaði(y)* 'this. F' is very common.

I think that the examples are representative of a general predicament, however, namely that in only rare cases can an unequivocal connection be

---

[19] Carter (1990) suggests that the last form is rare.
[20] Though later (II: 322. 15) Sibawaih reports from a reliable source that some Arabs have *haaðih* as a context form.

drawn between Sibawaih's description of pausal forms generally, i.e. not only those relating to the treatment of the final case vowel, and comparable forms in modern dialects. Even when such connections exist, it is rarely so that they would explain anything but a part of modern dialectal forms. Similarly, one would like to know why often only certain Arabs ('some of them', the Qays, Tamim, etc.) have forms analogous to the modern dialectal ones. Until these problems have been given more serious attention, I think it overly selective to argue that the modern dialects arose from pausal forms, when the main piece of evidence supporting this position in Sibawaih would appear to be that only one of four alternative ways of pronouncing case vowels in pausal position is by deleting the vowel altogether.

Besides interpretive problems of the above kind, there is a more unequivocal argument against assuming that Classical Arabic pausal forms were the forerunners of the dialectal caseless forms. According to Sibawaih, pausal forms should occur only before pause. He mentions at various points in his discussion that the peculiarities which he describes for them do not apply to forms in connected speech (*waṣl*, e.g. II: 302. 8, 306. 5, 313. 18). Dealing as we are with written texts there is no way to measure where precisely pauses were placed in the Classical language, at least not in non-poetic style, which certainly must be assumed to be the purported model of the modern dialect ancestor. To get an idea about how frequent pauses actually are in spoken language I used a corpus of texts which I collected from the spoken Arabic of NE Nigeria. The texts are transcribed with a basic phonetic alphabet, and pauses are explicitly marked, wherever they occur. Since this material is computerized it is an easy matter to get a basic statistic about how many pauses there are in each text. Table 1 gives basic information from five texts about the number of pauses relative to the total number of words.[21]

TABLE 3.1.

Text no.	Number of words	Number of pauses	word/pause ratio
1	2,460	598	4.11
2	6,287	956	6.57
3	5,329	1,264	4.21
4	7,152	1,325	5.39
5	3,455	689	5.01
Average			5.09

[21] All five texts are informal conversations recorded between Nigerian Arabs.

The ratio of 5:1 means that on average, only one word in five occurs before a pause. Four words in five do not. Assuming this ratio to be generally representative of spoken Arabic, it is clear that most words do not occur in pausal contexts, and by extrapolation that in Classical Arabic the non-pausal forms in normal speech would have considerably outnumbered the pausal. To argue that the modern dialects grew out of the pausal forms of the Classical language is to say that forms which are a relatively small minority became the standard for the further development of the language. This I think is a priori problematic. A popular refinement on the pausal origin hypothesis is speculative. This would have it (e.g. Corriente 1976: 84; Blau 1988: 9) that under the influence of foreign language learners, even in the Classical language the pausal forms began to be used for the non-pausal. Strictly speaking the idea is unverifiable; Sibawaih gives no intimation of such a process, and there are no modern analogies, in Arabic at least, by which to be guided. Trying to reconstruct the presumed process, lack of motivation is a stumbling block. Judging by the complex morphology of modern Arabic dialects (see sect. 1.6.6), it appears that non-Arabs learned complex Arabic morphology and phonology and made it into their native language apparently with little problem. Why should they have had such a problem with the cases? Moreover, what was really dropped were short final vowels, among which were found the cases. Even in the unlikely situation that the cases were too difficult for non-Arabs to learn, conceptual difficulty can certainly not be invoked to explain the disappearance of, say the -a from ʔayna 'where'.

The hypothesis which I am developing avoids these mental gymnastics, since it is (roughly—see sect. 3.5 for more refined discussion) claimed that the dialects descend from a variety which never did have case endings.

Before moving on to the modern dialects, I would like to mention one well-known characterization of Sibawaih, which he treated, inter alia, among the pausal forms. This is the opposition between the high vowels *i, u* vs. the low vowel *a*, in particular the relative stability of the latter against the former. This was documented at some length in sect. 2.4.1.2. Thus the high vowels are deleted in open syllables in CaCi/uC-V forms, both nouns and verbs, e.g. *kabid-un* → *kabd-un* 'liver', *ʕaḍud-un* → *ʕaḍdun* 'upper arm' (II: 317. 17, 320. 6), *ʕalima* → *ʕalma* 'he knew', *ʕuṣira* → *ʕuṣra* 'it was squeezed' (II: 277. 22), vs. *jamal-un* (*jamlun). Similarly, as is well known, when indefinite, whereas the high vowel case markers, -*u* (NOM) and -*i* (GEN) are deleted in pause, the low vowel -*an* (ACC) is lengthened to -*aa*. It is precisely in this lack of symmetry where one might search for the origins of the Arabic case system (proceeding on the assumption that case in Semitic, where it exists, is innovative). This pausal alteration may represent an older state of affairs where an -*a(a)* suffix (as seen above, representing the unmarked case in Arabic) was opposed to a bare nominal stem (Ø). The nominative and genitive vowels may then have developed out of epenthetic vowels which were inserted in particular contexts.[22] One can cite for analogous morpho-syntactic dualities in related languages, the Gəʕəz opposition -*a*-Ø (genitive-Ø), or even the Berber construct-independent (unmarked, *u*-Ø) state contrasts.

Having developed the thesis that a caseless variety of Arabic is as old or older than one possessing case, on the basis of the comparative and philological record, it will be the main task of the second part of the chapter to bring evidence to bear on the question from the modern dialects. This will lead to the development of a general model defining the genesis of case in Arabic.

3.4. The Modern Dialects

In the previous three sections the status of case in proto-Arabic was examined in the light of comparative Afroasiatic, comparative Semitic, and the treatment of case among the earliest Arabic grammarians. The thesis was developed that a caseless variety of Arabic is prior to a case-based one.

Having considered the issue from the perspective of the past, it is now time to look to the present, to the modern dialects, to see what light they shed on the thesis. In particular, to claim that the modern dialects descend from a caseless ancestor implies that the relevant forms are so distributed that they

---

[22] This suggestion is speculative, and it should be emphasized is not crucial to the argument. Its overall plausibility may be heightened by the following (again speculative) considerations. Mauro Tosco (p.c.) points out that it is relatively unlikely for non-morphemic material to be reinterpreted with a morphemic value, as the present suggestion entails. To reply to this, it can be pointed out that the 3MSG object suffix variant -*u* found in many modern dialects is reconstructed later (sect. 8.7.6) as being precisely a former epenthetic vowel. Furthermore, there are situations where it is very common for non-morphemic material in one language to acquire morphemic value in another, namely via language contact. A standard example is Arabic *kitaab*, where non-morphemic *ki*- becomes in the Swahili loanword *ki-tabu* identified with the Swahili *ki*- noun class marker, hence pl. *vi-tabu*. The process is quite regular and is not restricted to this one class of nouns (see e.g. Krumm 1940: 52 ff.). It cannot be ruled out (though proof is equally elusive) that a similar process did not occur, introducing case into Arabic. The oldest mention of the 'Arabs' is from an Akkadian text of 853 BC. Actual contact between speakers of Akkadian and speakers of proto-Arabic very likely occurred. It could therefore also be that Akkadian speakers with a functional case system shifting into Arabic (or Arabic-Akkadian bilinguals) reinterpreted the original Arabic epenthetic vowels as case vowels. This process may have been helped if Arabic already had a suffix -*a* (perhaps adverbial, as in Hebrew). (See sect. 3.5 on coexistence of case and caseless varieties, and sect. 4.2 (13) for parallels between the distribution of case suffixes and epenthetic vowels.) Tropper (1999) suggests that proto-Semitic had a multifunctional absolute case -*a*, which fell together with the accusative -*a* in west Semitic. Taking this suggestion in another direction, one might interpret the -*a*-Ø contrast as originally one of an absolute marker vs. Ø, with the nominative/genitive contrast developing out of Ø, and in Classical Arabic the absolutive case developing into the accusative.

could not have descended from the Classical Arabic as described by Sibawaih. I will attempt to motivate this claim from two perspectives. In sect. 3.4.1, I summarize the distribution of elements which possibly point to traces of case, and in sect. 3.4.2, address aspects of the question of syllabic reorganization which is implied by the loss of the final short vowels.

3.4.1. Case traces?

Blau (1981: 167) identifies certain dialectal elements which he suggests are traces of a now defunct case system. It is appropriate to look at each in detail in order to determine to what extent it is necessary to derive them from old case markers. Blau considers three candidates. I summarize two cases here, while a third is treated only cursorily at this point, being the subject of detailed treatment in Ch. 8.

The first of these is a suffix *-an* appearing on a small set of forms in many dialects, e.g. *ɣaṣb-an* (*ɣaṣbin* in some dialects) in *ɣaṣb-an ʕann-u* 'he must (despite his wish to the contrary)', *taqriyb-an* 'almost'. This appears to go back to the adverbial usage of the accusative. However, these cases are so lexically restricted that no far-reaching conclusions can be drawn from them. Some may be borrowed from the standard language, and if they are relics of something old, it is hard to conclude from the isolated examples that they are survivals of a case system (see n. 22).

The second of these is a nominal suffix, again *-an* or *-in*, which appears in various dialects.[23] The suffix is dialectally more widespread than often assumed, occurring in Spanish Arabic (= *-an*, Corriente 1977: 122; Ferrando 2000), throughout the Sudanic Arabic dialects (= *-an*, Owens 1993a: 111, 140, 144; Reichmuth 1983: on Shukriyya in eastern Sudan), in Najdi (central and eastern Saudi Arabia) Arabic (= *-in*, Ingham 1994a: 47 ff.), Tihama Arabic in Yemen (= *-u*, *-un*, Behnstedt 1985: 60), in Uzbekistan/Afghanistan Arabic (= *-in* Ingham 1994b: 47; Fischer 1961 on Uzbekistan Arabic).[24] This suffix is formally similar to the Classical Arabic indefinite nominal suffix, which varies according to case as *-un*, *-an*, *-in*, nominative, accusative, genitive. For reasons given below, I term it the 'linker' *-n* in the dialects (see n. 28).

---

[23] Most of Blau's examples (1981: 191–200) fall in this category.

[24] Afghanistan Arabic is a nineteenth-century offshoot of Uzbekistan Arabic, and may thus be combined with it. The explanation for the appearance of a low vowel *-an* or high vowel *-in/-u(n)* is not self-evident. In Sudanic Arabic the *-an* form seems to be linked to the consistent low-vowel value of many formatives, verbal FPL suffixes *-an*, preformative vowels of verbs, definite article. In Najdi and Tihama Arabic, however, paradigms often occur with both high and low values, e.g. Najdi verbal FPL suffix appears as both *-in* and *-an* depending on verb class to which it is suffixed.

The formal similarity carries over in an interesting fashion to nouns ending in long vowels. For the dialects, I restrict my observations here to Nigerian Arabic, as detailed information on this point from other areas is lacking. In Old Arabic, nouns are customarily represented as ending in a long vowel when written with a final *-aa* or *-iy*, as in ʕaṣaa 'stick', *hudaa* 'guidance', and *qaaḍiy* 'judge'. When a pronominal suffix is added the length is apparent from the orthography.

(9) ʕaṣaa-ka 'your stick'
    qaaḍiy-hum 'their.M judge'

When the indefinite *-n* is added the final vowel is said to be shortened, though a final *-aa* is still written orthographically long.

(10) ʕaṣa-n 'a stick'
     qaaḍi-n 'a judge'

There are thus two kinds of suffix, those which preserve the length of the final vowel, or subject to interpretation (see n. 27 below), lengthen a length-neutral final vowel, and those which shorten a long vowel. The Old Arabic indefinite suffix represents the latter type.

In Nigerian Arabic the basic situation is identical, though for Nigerian Arabic, as well as for all other dialects I would represent a final vowel as length-neutral.[25] When a pronominal suffix is added a final vowel is lengthened. The difference in length is confirmed by the stress placement: a first heavy syllable (-VCC or -VVC) from the end of the word is stressed in this dialect, and when a suffix is added stress shifts to the lengthened syllable.

(11) lu'sunne 'tongues' vs. lusun'nee-hin 'their.F tongues'
     ga'naagi 'drums' vs. ganaa'gii-hum 'their.M drums'

The linker *-n* does not induce vowel lengthening, and so it does not draw stress.

(12) bagar   amay-aat[26]   lu'sunne-n   xuʃun
     cows   having. FPL   tongues-n   rough.PL
     'rough-tongued cows'
     raajil abu   ga'naagi-n   katiir-aat
     man   having drums-n   many.FPL
     'a man with many drums'

---

[25] In Nigerian Arabic, acoustically the final vowel in *lu'sunne* 'tongues' strikes me as identical to the /e/ of *be'her* 'river, lake'. No instrumental studies are available. When a suffix is added, the vowel is lengthened, *lusun'nee-ku* 'your.PL tongues', as is apparent in the stress shift.
[26] There are many variants of this associative marker, including *mahanaat* and *amanaat*, as well as *amayaat*.

The parallel in the received pronunciation of Arabic *qaaḍiy/qaaḍi-n* and the Nigerian Arab pronunciation of *ganaagii/ganaagi-n* is noteworthy. In the non-suffix form the final vowel in *qaaḍiy/ganaagi* is relatively tense. When the *-n* is added, it becomes laxer, [ɪ], [*qaaḍɪn*], [*ganaagɪn*].

The similarity between the Old Arabic indefinite suffix and Nigerian Arabic linker is as follows. In both Old Arabic and Nigerian Arabic (and all other Arabic dialects), pronominal suffixes induce vowel length on a final vowel. The indefinite/linker *-n* induces a shorter, laxer pronunciation of the final vowel in the two varieties.[27]

Despite the formal similarities between the two suffixes, and although in most studies it is referred to as an indefinite marker or by the terminology of the Arabic grammarians, *tanwiyn*, and is usually assumed to derive from an old case marker (Blau 1981; Holes 1990: 43; Diem 1991), close inspection shows that it has quite different grammatical properties and a related, but in detail different linguistic history. Differences relate both to form and function. First, the entire *-Vn* sequence is a single morpheme, appearing and disappearing as a unit. Second, the vowel has a single value, *-i*, *-u*, or *-a* according to dialect. This is not a commutable case system. Third, it is always optional. While it occurs only with indefinite nouns, it cannot be said to mark indefiniteness (as *-n* does in Classical Arabic) because indefiniteness is minimally indicated in most dialects by the lack of the definite article. Fourth, its primary function appears to mark an adnominal relationship between an indefinite noun + modifier.[28] This usage is attested consistently in all the dialects cited (though I have no text examples for the Tihama) and in fact is the only one common to all, as the following examples show.

(13a) Spanish Arabic (Corriente 1977: 121)
 muslim-iin-an   liṭaaf
 Muslim-PL-n   bad
 'bad Muslims'

---

[27] A topic which I touch on in this work though do not deal with systematically is the status of the length of final vowels in Old Arabic and the dialects. It is possible to view the vowel-final Old Arabic forms such as *qaaḍiy* and *hudaa* as length-neutral. In nouns a lexical final vowel is non-contrastive. The contrast short vs. long would emerge in this view only when a suffix is added, as in (9) vs. (10). The issue of final vowel length is bound up with questions of underlying vowel length which in turn implies taking a stance on issues of theoretical phonological import, which are too far removed from the purposes of this book for systematic treatment here.

[28] Following Croft's (1990: 118) comparative typological terminology, it can be termed a 'linker' or 'ligature'.

(13b) Sudanic Arabic, Shukriyya in E. Sudan (Reichmuth 1983: 190)
 ba-jii-k   wakt-an   gariib
 I-come-you   time-n   near
 'I'll come to you soon'

(13c) Najdi Arabic (Ingham 1994a: 49)
 kalmit-in   rimy-at
 word-n   thrown-F
 'a word thrown down'

(13d) Afghanistan Arabic (Ingham 1994b: 115)
 ħintit-in   ħamra
 wheat-n   red
 'red grains of wheat'

While the distribution of this suffix is not precisely the same in all dialects—in Spanish and Nigerian Arabic, for example, it may be suffixed only to a noun, in Najdi to noun and adjective—and its frequency of occurrence variable—it disappears from Spanish Arabic in later texts, for example, but in Najdi and Shukriyya Arabic it occurs frequently—its basic characteristics are common to all its dialectal occurrences. So-called nunation and mimation phenomena in Semitic language do not have enough in common functionally and semantically to allow Moscati et al. (1980: 96) to reconstruct a common proto-Semitic indefinite form. The present data suggests that yet another function, namely nominal linkage, has to be added to the various ones served by Semitic final -Vn nasal suffixes.

In a point which will be repeated in the following discussion, it is reasonable to reconstruct the nominal linker *-Vn into a form of Arabic immediately predating the variety described by Sibawaih, i.e. pre-diasporic Arabic in the terminology adopted here. This follows from the wide geographic distribution of a relatively uniform morpho-syntactic phenomenon. It appears in the earliest forms of Spanish Arabic, which means it was probably brought into Andalusia in the eighth century. Though Arabs first moved into the Sudanic area only after 1300, they derive basically from tribes which migrated into Egypt in the seventh and eighth centuries and were increasingly marginalized from the eighth century onwards and pushed ever further South (see sect. 5.2.2.2 and Owens 2003). Arabic in Afghanistan is relatively recent, dating from the nineteenth century, its speakers having immigrated from Uzbekistan, where they have lived since the eighth century (see sect. 5.2.2.3). There have been Arabs in central Saudi Arabia and parts of Yemen since pre-Islamic times. It thus appears that this common feature existed in one variety of Arabic no later than the time of the Arabic diaspora at the beginning of the

Islamic era. Within the context of the general discussion in this section, note that there is no necessity for deriving the -*Vn* forms from Classical Arabic case marker + indefinite marker.

Since my interpretation of the origin of these -*Vn* forms is at variance with Blau's, a digression comparing our views is in order. Blau (1969: 40) recognizes a possible explanation for the commonalities in terms of a single origin, though rejects it in favor of one based on independent parallel development. To be fair to Blau (1981, written originally in 1965), important sources on the distribution of the -*Vn* (Corriente 1977; Reichmuth 1983; Owens 1993*b*) were not available to him (though Carbou 1913 on Chadian Arabic is an older source) and so the current criticisms are based on a wider data base. In particular, Blau compared only three varieties, various Arabian peninsular varieties, Uzbekistan Arabic, and Jewish Middle Arabic. Nonetheless, on grounds of principle, doubts can be raised about Blau's a prioristic conclusion that 'It seems improbable that the dialects of Central Asia, at the beginning, shared in the linguistic development that affected the modern Bedouin dialects' (1969: 40). This is a good example of truisms pre-empting linguistic argumentation (see sect. 1.6.7). Chapter 5, moreover, argues that Uzbekistan Arabic is indeed a repository of traits attested elsewhere in the wide reaches of the Arabic-speaking world. Much more crucially, however, Hetzron's principle of morphological specificity coupled with diffusionist theory would inform us that the widespread attestation of a -*Vn* suffix in a comparable function at all extremes of the Arabic-speaking world (Andalusia, the Sudanic region, Uzbekistan, Afghanistan), and also in its very center (Arabian peninsula) renders the speculation that the form is innovative in each area virtually impossible. In passing I would note that only two of the groups using -*Vn*, Najdi (central Arabia) and the various Sudanic area speakers, are in some sense 'Bedouin', while three, Andalusia, Uzbekistan/Afgan, and Tihama, are not.

A third set of forms which has been assumed to represent case relics are the vowels which appear with, or have become part of certain pronominal object suffixes, namely the following.

(14) -*ak* 2MSG, -*ik* 2FSG, -*u*/-*a* 3MSG

Thus for Egyptian Arabic Birkeland (1952: 12, 19) sees the *a/i* in the second person forms as relics of the accusative and genitive suffixes, respectively, the -*u* a nominative. It will be seen in Ch. 8 that there is little to recommend in identifying case remnants in these morphemes.

It has been shown in this section, and it will be shown further in Ch. 8, that various forms which potentially are interpretable as relics of the Classical Arabic case system have other equally plausible or even better explanations.

3.4.2. *Epenthesis, final short vowels, stems*

The loss of the final vocalic case markers, according to proponents of this theory, had consequences for syllable structure (Fischer and Jastrow 1980: 40; Blau 1981: 3). Coupled with a tendency of short high vowels to be deleted in open syllables (see sects. 2.4.1.2 and 3.2.3), this led to a basic reorganization of syllable structure in Neo-Arabic in which the insertion of epenthetic vowels plays a significant role. This is because, like Classical Arabic, the majority of dialects have maintained a basic syllable structure constraint disallowing sequences of three consonants. Thus, assuming the Old → Neo-Arabic model for the moment, given a nominal form like **kalb-V-haa* (V = case) 'her dog', the loss of the case vowel in dialects leads to unacceptable *CC-ha* structures. As Fischer and Jastrow (1980: 41) point out, there are generally two solutions to this problem, both involving the insertion of an epenthetic vowel. In eastern Libyan Arabic, for example, the epenthetic vowel (underlined) comes between the first two consonants, *kali̱b-ha*, in Nigerian Arabic between the last two, *kalba̱-ha*. Note that the first solution is comparable to that used in the Classical language, e.g. *radd-tu* → *rada̱d-tu* 'I returned' (*Kitaab* II: ch. 560), while the second is also attested in Sibawaih in the imperative of these forms, *rudd + haa* → *rudd-a̱-haa* 'return her' (II: 163, see n. 31 below).

In this section I would like to make a general overview of the phenomena of epenthesis and stem structure, as it bears directly on the question of the presumed origin of the modern dialects from old pausal forms. This data will also be one basis of the discussion in Ch. 8, and in Ch. 6 will be the mainstay of a historical interpretation of the syllabic structure of the imperfect verb.

Two basic types of epenthesis can be distinguished in the dialects. The first, illustrated in the previous paragraph, is dependent on consonantal sequence. As mentioned, *CCC sequences are not allowed in most dialects,[29] the constraint being lifted in one of the two ways just illustrated. I will term this linear epenthesis, since it depends on the linear sequence of consonants, rather than on consonant quality (see below and Ch. 6).

(15) Linear epenthesis

(15a) CCC → CəCC (ə = epenthetic vowel; see below for quality), *galb-ha* → *gali̱b-ha*

(15b) CCC → CCəC *galb-ha* → *galb-a̱-ha* 'her heart'

---

[29] The significant exceptions, like many dialects of Morocco and Algeria, do not affect the present discussion, since in them the lifting of the *CCC constraint is either a secondary development or one which must also be included in the proto-language, as discussed further in Ch. 6 below. In many dialects a final pause, #, has the same status as a C, inducing the same epenthetic effect, e.g. Eastern Libya *kabʃ#* → *kabiʃ#*.

It should be noted here that in a few dialects, e.g. Najdi (Ingham 1994a: 17) a sequence of VVC-C word internally induces the same epenthesis effect, *beet-hum* → *beeti̱-hum* 'their house', i.e. CCC ~ VVCC → C/VVCəC.

In very general terms—here and elsewhere I am summarizing the variants in broad strokes—the (15a) solution is found, inter alia, in eastern Libyan Arabic,[30] rural Iraqi, Horan (northern Jordan), most Egyptian dialects south of Asyut, and the eastern Nile delta (Behnsted and Woidich 1985: 56), and in the Shukriyya dialect of the Sudan (Reichmuth 1983: 70). The (15b) solution is employed in most Egyptian dialects north of Asyut, Chadian and Nigerian Arabic, Najdi Arabic, and most Yemeni dialects.

The epenthetic vowel is usually a high vowel whose precise value, front, back or mid, is determined by consonantal context. In a few dialects, including WSA and Cairene, the value of the epenthetic vowel is determined by the nature of the following consonant formed by the pronominal suffix. There are three epenthetic vowel values, [i, u, a]. [u] occurs before a suffix with [u], [a] occurs before -ha and otherwise [i] occurs.[31]

(16) WSA and Cairene
galb-u-hum 'their.M heart' (Cairene has ʔ, ʔalbuhum, etc. here)
galb-u-ku
galb-a-ha
galb-i-hin
galb-i-ki
galb-i-na

In addition, it can be noted in passing, there are dialects which allow sequences of three consonants.

(17) *galb-kum* (Najdi, also Rosenhouse 1984: 72 in certain conditions in Galilee)

A second type of epenthesis is dependent on the quality of consonants. This is less widespread than the first type, though is still found in most parts of the Arabic-speaking world. Two main subtypes can be distinguished here. The first is what Blanc termed the '*gahawa* syndrome', the eponymous *gahawa*

---

[30] I think it likely that all modern North African dialects employ a variant of this solution.

[31] An identical rule with a part the epenthetic insertion contexts is attested in Sibawaih (II: 163, ch. 409). Discussing the imperative of doubled verbs which have a third person singular object suffix, Sibawaih notes that non-Hijazi speakers add a vowel between verb and stem. The vowel is harmonic with that of the pronominal suffix, so that one has *rudd-a-haa* 'return it.F' and *rudd-u-hu* 'return it.M'. That the vowel is epenthetic, not functional, is clear from the Hijazi alternative, *urdud-haa*, where the Hijazi segmentation (essentially (14a) above) does not require epenthesis before the object suffix.

'coffee' having the prototypical trait of inserting a low vowel in the following sequence. It may be termed guttural epenthesis.

Guttural epenthesis

(18a) $C_{gut}C \rightarrow C_{gut}aC$ (gutturals = h, ħ, ʕ, ʔ, x, ɣ, in some dialects (e.g. NA) q
(18b) *gahwa → gahawa 'coffee'

This is found, inter alia, in Najdi Arabic, Sudanic Arabic (see sect. 1.6.6), eastern Libyan Arabic, Egyptian Arabic around Asyut and south (Behnstedt and Woidich 1985: 45), and some rural Iraqi dialects (but not other Egyptian dialects, Hijazi, most Yemeni dialects, or most *qultu* dialects of Mesopotamia).

A different subtype of consonantal environment is provided by the sequence.

Sonorant epenthesis

(19a) $CC_{sonorant} \rightarrow C\partial C$ (sonorant = l, r, n, sometimes w, y, m)
(19b) bajri → bajəri 'I run' (Nigerian Arabic)

This has already been alluded to above in the discussion of pausal phenomena in Sibawaih, sect. 3.2.3 above. Here an epenthetic vowel is inserted before a sonorant. This is attested in different realizations, inter alia, in Najdi Arabic, much of Egypt south of Cairo (Behnstedt and Woidich 1985: 47 ff.), the Tihama region of Yemen (Behnstedt 1984: 49), Spanish Arabic (Corriente 1977: 72), and Chadian and Nigerian Arabic. Dialects such as eastern Libyan, Cairene and most of the Nile delta, highland Yemeni, the Arabic of Uzbekistan, and urban Baghdadi do not have it, or at least do not treat such clusters any differently from other consonant clusters.

What is interesting to note is that the epenthetic vowels often come in precisely the position where case vowels occur in Classical Arabic. In fact, taking a broad reading of Sibawaih, the occurrence of pre-suffixal epenthesis in Najdi Arabic mirrors in surprising fashion the distribution of case vowels. This results from the following two epenthetic rules, outlined above in (15b, 18).

(20) $VV/CCC \rightarrow VV/CC\partial C$, $CC_{sonorant} \rightarrow C\partial C$ (note that sonorant epenthesis takes precedence if the 2 rules conflict)
been-ham → beena-ham 'between them', rajl-ha → rajil-ha 'her husband' (examples from Ingham 1995).

The broad reading of Sibawaih identifies the sonorant epenthesis rule with the case epenthesis rule discussed in sects. 3.2.2 and 3.2.3.

Looking at nominal forms with a C-initial pronominal suffix, the contexts where linear epenthesis (14) will occur,[32] it happens that in this dialect the only forms where epenthesis does not occur are those with an *a* as the final stem vowel, e.g. *baʕad̥-hum* 'some of them'.[33] Generally speaking it appears that a reasonably long stretch of speech will contain a majority of forms with one typical epenthetic vowel or another before C-initial pronominal suffixes. To verify this, I counted all forms of noun + C-initial pronominal suffix in the six Rwala (northern Najdi) texts of Ingham (1995). There are a total of twenty-nine nouns with C-initial pronominal suffixes, twenty-one of these undergoing one of the two epenthesis rules,[34] only eight lacking them. In other words, this dialect of Arabic tends to mimic Classical Arabic in the distribution of noun stem final vowel before C-initial consonantal suffixes: where Classical Arabic has a case vowel, this dialect tends to have an epenthetic one. The relatively frequent occurrence of the *-in* linker further imparts a 'classical' flavor to this variety.

I am not, I should perhaps emphasize, intimating that the case vowels of Classical Arabic are in reality epenthetic vowels. Besides the clear functional contrast between the two, the parallel only works before C-initial object pronoun suffixes. Looking at a wider comparative context, however, it is not unreasonable to relate these dialectal epenthetic vowels to similar phenomena found in other Semitic languages, e.g. in Gəʕəz and Hebrew, where a connecting vowel may occur before pronominal suffixes (Weninger 1993: 13, 35 e.g. *ʕaṣm-ə-ya* 'my bone', Blau 1976: 67, *suusə-ka* 'your m horse'). While such vowels are often interpreted as relics of an old case system (Blau 1976: 67), the present interpretation would suggest that they are the 'relic' of an ur-Semitic epenthesis system. What is probably less disputable is that proto-Semitic had at least a system of linear epenthesis operating in the context CC# → CəC#. This alternation is attested in different branches of Semitic, cf. the Akkadian possessed noun, *uzun* 'ear' (Von Soden 1969: 18), the Aramaic and Hebrew segolates (Heb. *ʔozen* 'ear'), the Arabic dialects (eastern Libyan *wiðin* 'ear', see n. 33) as well as Classical Arabic (*lam yardud#*, and the case epenthesis discussed in sect. 3.2.1). Though admittedly a sketchy overview, the attested

---

[32] V-initial pronominal suffixes, such as 1sg -*i* do not create the context for epenthesis.

[33] Note that these are precisely sequences where a case vowel, should one occur, would appear in an open syllable in the context CVC-V$_{case}$-CVC, e.g *jabal-u-hum* 'their.M mountain'. In the Old Arabic examples from Sibawaih and Farraʔ illustrating either short high vowel deletion or a murmur vowel (*ixtilaas*) pronunciation, the deleted/murmured vowel (underlined in the following) is typically in a CV-CV-CV context (see examples in sect. 2.4.1.2, Old Arabic sources). In other words, insertion does not occur in Rwala in those contexts where deletion/murmur does characterize certain Old Arabic varieties.

[34] I included locative nouns like *been* 'between' in the count, but did not include active participles.

universality of epenthesis rules in Semitic, as opposed to the only sporadic appearance of case systems, lends greater credence to my suggestion above that the Classical Arabic case system grew *in part* at least out of epenthetic phenomena.

Returning to the major theme of this section, looking at the distribution of epenthetic rules among the dialects, one is led to the same conclusion as with the linker *-*Vn* discussed in sect. 3.4.1, namely that each of the epenthetic rules is represented in such a spread of modern dialects that their origin, in their diverse guises, must be at least as old as the *ʕArabiyya* described by Sibawaih, that is, eighth century or older. For instance, the common guttural epenthesis rule of Spanish, Nigerian, Tihama, and Najdi Arabic, but equally its lack in highland Yemen, Cairene, eastern Libyan, and urban Baghdadi points to both its presence and its lack, at the time of the original Islamic diaspora in the seventh/eighth centuries; similarly, with cluster and sonorant epenthesis. If this is the case, however, one does not have to seek the origin of the epenthetic rules as the result of syllabification changes associated with the loss of final vowels, including final case vowels, in Old Arabic. Rather, epenthesis can be reconstructed as part of pre-diasporic and proto-Arabic. I develop this point further in Chs. 6 and 8.

3.4.3. Dialects vs. linguistic features

As mentioned in sects. 1.6.7 and 2.3.3, Blau (1981, 1988) has developed a model for the development of Arabic, attractive for its linguistic simplicity and for its socio-historical plausibility. Pre-Islamic Old Arabic, spoken by Bedouin tribes, was transformed during the early Islamic period in an urban context where Arabs mixed with foreign learners of Arabic into a Middle Arabic. The linguistic reflex of this transformation was a shift from a synthetic-type language to an analytic type (Blau 2002: 16). It is important at this point to look at what is understood by these terms, concentrating on morphological and syntactic features.[35] Blau's inventory of features includes the following (1981: 3–4). I would note that the list replicates some of the features included in Fischer and Jastrow's account of Neo-Arabic features. For the sake of completeness, and because some of the features are new, I include Blau's entire list here. The following, moreover, extends my critique of dichotomous labeling (sect. 1.6.7), to another binary pair of terms, synthetic vs. analytic, which is well established in the Western Arabicist vocabulary. Also, in contrast to the critique of the Old/New dyad of Ch. 2 which is explicitly within the

---

[35] Blau includes phonological features as well, though it is hard to see how, intuitively the opposition analytic vs. synthetic is to be applied to them.

realm of historical linguistics, the current discussion being based on a purely structural dichotomy adds another critical dimension to the debate.

Leaving aside problems in the definition of syntheticity and analyticity (see Retsö 1994: 335; Cuvalay 1997: 19), the list is open to criticisms of two major types, both of which were dealt with in some detail in the previous chapter. On the one hand, some analytic features are in fact well attested in Old Arabic, in the sense that they are described in some detail in Sibawaih. The full agreement in VS sentences, for instance, is in evidence in Sibawaih's stock example ʔakaluw-niy il-baraaɣiyθ 'The lice ate me up' (e.g. I: 411). As Levin (1989) explains, Sibawaih does not condemn this as substandard usage, though Levin does suggest that it is a minority usage (1989: 60). In such a case it is hard to see the dialects as representing a radically new development. On the other hand, most of the other features establish a contrast only between Classical Arabic and some modern dialects. While Blau recognizes this, the methodological problems related to this have not been emphasized enough. Regarding the list in Table 3.2, some of the features such as the comparative expressed by 'more' (e.g. in Chadian Arabic) are quite rare among the dialects. The analytic genitive may be given special attention, since it is a favorite distinguishing point between the Old and Neo-Arabic (e.g Versteegh 1993a: 69). Here, discussion of this feature in terms of analyticity or simplification often misses at least three points. First, Classical Arabic does have an analytic genitive, namely in the form of the prepositions *li* 'for' and *min* 'from'. Classical grammarians even regarded *li* as the '*ʔaṣl*' of the direct genitive (Owens 1990: 14 ff.), though this is a theory-internal question bearing only indirectly on the linguistic function of the construction. Second, the so-called analytic genitive, marked by an independent morpheme is in nearly all dialects but an alternative to the direct genitive. The choice between the two is more a lexical, semantic, stylistic, and pragmatic matter than a question of historical replacement of one by the other (e.g. Owens 1993b: 65; 2002;

TABLE 3.2. Analytic vs. synthetic features, Blau

Synthetic	Analytic
Cases and moods	No cases
VS, partial verb agreement	VS, verb–subject agreement
ʔiḍaafa, direct genitive	Analytic genitive
Comparative adjective	Comparative expressed by 'more'
Dual	Decreasing use of dual
Internal passive	No internal passive
lam + imperfect	Negative only by *maa*

Eksell 1995: 66). Furthermore, S. Prochazka (2002: 153) reports that in Cilician Arabic in south-central Turkey only the synthetic is used. Third, in most dialects the analytic genitive can hardly be said to be a simplified form. To the contrary, it is usually marked by a morpheme agreeing in number and gender with the head noun, and hence is morphologically more 'complicated' than the Classical Arabic analytic genitive in *li*.

It is true that a few items on the list do distinguish Classical Arabic from the dialects. The dual in dialects is restricted exclusively to nouns, whereas in Classical Arabic it occurs on adjectives, pronouns, verbs, etc. as well. Whether they suffice to define broad varieties of languages in terms of syntheticity vs. analyticity is doubtful, however. Moreover, as seen in the previous chapter, the historical question of priority of the dual forms remains open.

Blau's list is more striking for a fatal methodological shortcoming, and this is that his dichotomization is no dichotomization at all, or at best only a dichotomization based on the a priori abstraction, Classical Arabic vs. dialect. But what is the basis for making this abstraction, if not the synthetic/analytic traits he assigns to each group? Blau has no way independently to identify the very entities he is trying to distinguish. It is clear from the foregoing discussion that no such general criteria are to be found. Some of the criteria, e.g. the analytic genitive, have little basis in fact. Others do not distinguish two groups in the way Blau would want. Nigerian Arabic and Classical Arabic, for example, share the property of having comparative adjectives, Najdi Arabic and Classical Arabic the property of having internal passives, etc. I return to this point presently. It may then be asked whether the few features which genuinely do distinguish two varieties of language are sufficient to justify drawing far-reaching conclusions about their development (see Ch. 2). The problem becomes more acute when one considers arguments such as the one advanced in the present chapter that what is probably the key feature in the synthetic–analytic contrast, case vs. non-case, is a dichotomy which can be reconstructed into proto-Arabic, and hence did not arise as an urban trait in pre- or post-Islamic times.

The conclusions reached in the previous chapter on the Old/New contrast is equally applicable to the analytic/synthetic one. It was seen in Ch. 2 that on close inspection the list of elements distinguishing Old and Neo-Arabic is perhaps useful as a typology of traits which *may* in any given instance distinguish the Classical language from the dialects, though the list as such does not justify the conceptions of Old and Neo-Arabic as historical concepts. Similarly here, Blau's synthetic/analytic list may define a structure contrast between some varieties of Old and some varieties of Neo-Arabic. There are far too many exceptions, however, to maintain the dyad as a useful analytic tool.

3.5. Case and Caseless Arabic

The suggestion that modern Arabic dialects are the descendent of a caseless variety is not entirely new. As early as Vollers[36] it was proposed that pre-diasporic caseless varieties of Arabic existed, and that these represent the ancestor(s) of the modern dialects (see Spitaler 1953; Diem 1973, 1991;[37] Retsö 1994; and Corriente 1975, 1976). All these scholars, however, assume that at some point in the prehistory of Arabic a unique case-variety ancestor existed. The present proposal is a qualitatively different interpretation of the development of Arabic, however, in arguing that there was a variety of proto-Arabic which never had morphological case in its history. Lately Zaborski (1995) and Retsö (1995) have argued, convincingly in my opinion, that there are various traits in the modern Arabic dialects, notably pronominal forms and the 'pseudo-dual', which preserve old Semitic or proto-Afroasiatic forms which are lacking in the Classical language. This latter work is important, for it creates a geometric figure out of what in comparative Semitics has too often been defined as a one-dimensional structure beginning with Akkadian and ending with Classical Arabic.[38] Adding the modern Arabic dialects creates a geometric structure with at least two dimensions in the sense that developments and/or archaisms from proto-Semitic may move directly from the proto-language to the modern dialects, bypassing Classical Arabic completely. This structure is atemporal in the sense that evidence from any point in it potentially gives insight into older stages of the family history. It has to be emphasized that privileging on a priori, non-linguistic grounds any variety (or varieties) for purposes of reconstruction will more likely than not distort the historical reality.

---

[36] His highly original work was published in 1906. It will be discussed in greater detail in the next chapter.

[37] Diem (1991) assumes that the modern dialects descend ultimately from a case variety, but that already in pre-diasporic times caseless varieties had emerged, to which the modern dialects are most closely related. This perspective is significant in that Diem recognizes that if this is the historical development, an alternative explanation to Blau's for the disappearance of the case endings must be provided. His alternative explanation for their disappearance is no more compelling than Blau's, however. Diem argues from a functional perspective that syntactic redundancy led to the case disappearance in pre-diasporic times. As Corriente (1971: 36, the originator of the dysfunctional case system debate) shows, there are *no* varieties of case Arabic (poetry, Qur?aan, MSA, etc.) where the case forms have a high functional load. However, if there *never* was a 'need' for the case system, it is a curious conclusion that its functional desuetude led to its disappearance, that a trait which the system always possessed should be the motive force behind its disappearance.

[38] In the standard introduction on the subject, Moscati et al., modern reflexes of the Semitic languages, including the modern Arabic dialects, are all but ignored for purposes of Semitic reconstructions.

Figure 3.1 is a working sketch of development of case in Arabic.

Old Arabic here refers to the oldest form of Arabic attested in descriptive detail, dated to the seventh/eighth centuries (see sect. 3.1). I suggest in a number of places in this book (sect. 2.4.1.2, Old Arabic sources; Ch. 4; sect. 8.1) that caseless varieties can be inferred in this period via interpretation of concepts such as *ixtilaas*. So-called Middle Arabic texts are perhaps characterized by interference from this variety (as early as the seventh century, Diem 1984: 268). It must be assumed on the comparative evidence adduced above that in the Old Arabic period caseless varieties existed.[39]

The designation of the original proto-Semitic nominal as C-Ø means that it does not possess case. Whether it had suffixes marking other relational phenomena, such as an *-a* (cf. *-a* as an adverbial marker, as in Hebrew and Classical Arabic, or *-a* as a genitive/object marker, as in Gəʕəz, or *-a* as absolutive as in n. 22) out of which the case system developed is an independent question. It is assumed that case marking in Semitic is a younger trait than nominals lacking case marking on the basis of the Afroasiatic evidence (sect. 3.2.1). Proto-Arabic had both the 'original' caseless nominals, and the case-marking of certain other Semitic languages (sect. 3.3.2). Proto-Arabic here is a reconstructed form which can be dated only in relative terms. The direct evidence that it has case appears only in the seventh and eighth centuries, particularly with Sibawaih's detailed grammar. At some point, the rightward pointing arrow in Fig. 3.1 is not meant as pointing to a specific date, the case-variety of the spoken language emerged with the caseless. The direct evidence that proto-Arabic does not have case, barring Diem's work (sect. 3.1.2) which defines a date of around 100 BC, comes from the modern dialects.

```
Proto-Semitic        Proto-Arabic    Old Arabic: 7th/8th century   modern dialects
C-Ø nominals →       C-Ø →           (C-Ø) →                       C
     ↘
     C-case →        C-case →        C-case
C-case = final case-marked nominals, C-Ø = no
```

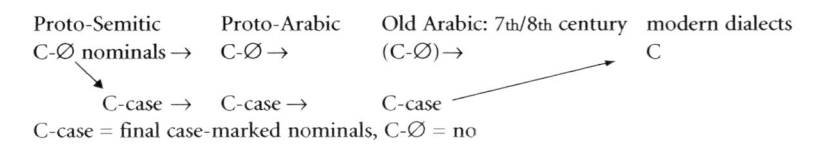

FIGURE 3.1. Proto-Arabic case

---

[39] It is logically possible, but on comparative grounds vanishingly unlikely, that at the time of the Arabic diaspora in the early Islamic period, case marking suddenly disappeared just before the expansion began. This would (1) contradict Blau's own hypothesis, since the case marking would have to have disappeared before large-scale mixture with non-Arabic populations took place and (2) would require that the different epenthesis rules, particularly (15a, b), immediately developed in the place of the vowelless forms. Postulating such a sequence of events could save case forms for all varieties of Old Arabic, though at the cost of suspending normal application of the comparative method.

Since caseless forms can be comparatively reconstructed at least as early as the seventh/eighth centuries, from the time of the Arabic diaspora, they are minimally as old as the case-Arabic described by Sibawaih, and hence can be projected into proto-Arabic as well.

Note that Fig. 3.1 represents one linguistic feature in two manifestations, case and non-case. It is not a model for the development of modern dialects as a whole. It is, it should be emphasized, no more than a rough working model for the development of Arabic. Only with the detailed analysis of bundles of traits will a generally valid picture emerge. Even then the model will fail to encode relevant aspects of the language development. In particular, it would be wrong, when one starts integrating further linguistic traits into the model, to expect automatically to find large bundles of features correlating with the case and caseless varieties respectively (see Table 3.2). It will be difficult, if not impossible, *linguistically* to reconstruct discrete entities, dialects, sociolects or whatever, where the magical speakers of Classical Arabic will be found; nor is it necessarily to be expected that the proto-Arabic split into case and caseless varieties will yield dialectal entities corresponding directly with the modern dialects.[40]

This I think follows from the nature of Classical Arabic, or more accurately, the nature of Sibawaih's linguistic thinking. The role of Sibawaih in defining Classical Arabic cannot, I believe, be overemphasized. But as seen above in sect. 3.3.2, Classical Arabic for Sibawaih is as much a way of thinking about language as it is a language. It is as broad and flexible, containing as many sometimes conflicting (see (6), (7)) linguistic features as Sibawaih's own linguistic rationalizations, his own linguistic theory, allow him to incorporate. It is thus in one sense inaccurate to speak of Classical Arabic as an entity defined by unique, mutually exclusive structures. It is, referring again to Baalbaki (1990), the means by which many entities were joined within a discrete, though flexible whole.

Before concluding this chapter I would like to expand on this point, since the suggestion that a language can simultaneously have both case and caseless

---

[40] Even reconstructing the history of a very few modern dialectal features is a much more intractable undertaking than most Arabicists would probably care to admit. For example, Diem (1991) argues that those modern dialects with the linker -*Vn* suffix (see (13)) tend to be those with the guttural epenthesis rule (18), on the basis of which correspondence Diem draws various diachronic conclusions. In fact, only two of the -*Vn* dialects, Najdi and Sudanic Arabic (though Shukriyya is not competely clear), are also *gahawa* (guttural epenthesis) dialects, whereas three of the -*Vn* dialects are not (Andalusian, Tihama, Afghanistan, according to Ingham's text 1994*b*: 115). From the reverse angle, eastern Libyan Arabic and some Upper Egyptian varieties around Asyut and Luxor have guttural epenthesis but no -*Vn*. Diem's use of cultural ('*bedouin*' dialects, *Nomaden*dialekte') concepts in the description of linguistic constructs, unfortunately a sanctioned practice in Arabic linguistics, serves to make sound reconstruction even harder.

varieties may strike many Semiticists as odd. However, the suggestion is plausible, if not indeed necessary, from two perspectives. First, if Diem (sect. 3.2 above, see n. 10) is correct that there existed caseless forms of Arabic as early as 100 BC, it necessarily follows that at least between 100 BC and AD 800, a period of almost a millennium, there coexisted case and caseless varieties of the language. Clearly, one cannot put an absolute duration on how long the coexistence occurred, though if it lasted for 900 years it must have been of an extremely stable sort.

Second, it is useful to look at modern dialectal and sociolectal analogies to determine whether diametrically opposed features can coexist. Of course many examples can be found, of which I will cite only two. Among modern dialects can be found quite striking differences coexisting along long geographical borders. Excellent examples of this are found in Behnstedt's atlas of Yemeni Arabic where, for instance, Tihama dialects lacking a morphological feminine plural and having the suffix -t as perfect subject marker in first and second person forms (katab-t 'I wrote', 1985: 116, 125) sit next to central Yemeni forms possessing the feminine plural and marking the subject with k (katab-k 'I wrote'). Equally striking is the sociolinguistic coexistence of different varieties side by side in the same urban settings. Arabic-speaking neighbors, in the city of Maiduguri in northeast Nigeria, for example, use essentially two systems of marking verbal mode. A minority, originally migrants from western Chad, have no verbal mode markers, so that, for example, *gaal yamʃi* means either 'he said that he was going' or 'he said to go'. More commonly indicative is marked by a *b-* prefix (familiar in many dialects), subjunctive by its lack, so that a morphological minimal pair exists between indicative *gaal bimʃi* 'he said that he was going' and subjunctive *gaal yamʃi* 'he said to go'. As might be expected, there is individual speaker variation, though there are no indications that one or the other variant is dying out (Owens 1995, 1998a).[41]

Looking at the postulation of two opposed coexisting linguistic features, case and caseless, in terms analogous to data which dialectologists of Arabic have been describing for years makes the coexistence of the two varieties over a very long period of time look less exotic and dramatic than it might be portrayed. Of course, at some point the case endings did die out, and it may

---

[41] Mauro Tosco (p.c.) has pointed out that the -*t*/-*k* variation in Yemen is of a qualitatively different sort from the presence/absence of a feature, which is what the case/caseless hypothesis assumes. The Nigerian Arabic indicative/subjunctive, however is precisely analogous (and many more such cases could be cited, the occurrence of -*Vn* in sect. 3.4.1 being another one), and the neutralization of M/F contrast in the plural in Yemen is similar. What the -*t*/-*k* variants do show is that perceptually prominent variation among central morphological categories may be subject to a stable variation which has endured well over 1,000 years.

well be that the acquisition of many new native speakers of Arabic in the period following the Islamic diaspora did play a role in tipping the advantage towards the caseless variety. Proving this in linguistic terms will be very difficult, however.[42] In any case, a look at the striking mixtures of linguistic features which one finds in today's modern dialects suggests that it is unlikely in former times that there was a neat correlation between say, dialects with cases, retention of FPL, retention of dual, etc. as opposed to those which lacked these features. It is more likely that these features, in their presence and absence, moved about somewhat independently of each other, as Rabin's (1951) study suggests. Indeed, Sibawaih's task can be seen partly as one of corraling these disparate elements into a single conceptual whole, with the case-variety given particular attention by him. In such a situation, however, for the average speaker of Arabic the disappearance of case endings did not necessarily imply anything other than the disappearance of case endings. A single linguistic feature was lost, not a complete dialect or variety, and certainly not the entire edifice of Old Arabic.

To conclude, in this chapter I have attempted to expand on the caseless hypothesis of proto-Arabic by arguing that evidence from all stages of the language history, from Afroasiatic, into Semitic, through the *Arabiyya*, down to the modern dialects (and back), have to be integrated in a full account, and that when this is done evidence for the hypothesis is quite strong. At the same time, it has been suggested that localizing the source of this caseless variety in one particular form of Old Arabic remains an open, perhaps impossible task. This chapter has further advanced the argument that a more active incorporation of evidence from the modern Arabic dialects into comparative Arabic language history will also contribute to an understanding of the larger Semitic and Afroasiatic families.

---

[42] It is commonly accepted, for example, that the Arabic culture of Chad and northeast Nigeria was strongly influenced by Fulani culture, and that it is likely that Fulani–Arab contact led in many instances to language shift to the advantage of Arabic (Braukämper 1993). Nonetheless, the Arabic of northeast Nigerian maintains many conservative traits, including a fully functioning FPL morphological paradigm and the -*Vn* linker suffix summarized in sect. 3.4.1. Intensive contact with foreigners alone does not imply simplification.

4

Al-Idgham al-Kabiyr and Case Endings

Observations about linguistic variants in Arabic are as old as the Arabic grammatical tradition itself, perhaps even older. Indeed, what most (though not all, see Wansbrough 1977) students of Arabic would regard as the oldest extensive Arabic document, namely the *QurɁaan*, exists not in one fixed form, but rather in a set of variant versions. In this chapter, I will continue with my interpretation of the form of Arabic as it existed in the seventh and eighth centuries by recourse to a discussion of these variant versions.

As seen in the previous chapter, in the Western Arabicist tradition, it has been a standard practice to contrast Classical Arabic or Old Arabic possessing case endings with the caseless modern dialects. In a historical perspective, as argued for in Ch. 3, it is not at all clear that a distinction between two varieties of Arabic, one with case, another without case, can be postulated as constituting successive varieties, the case-variety being the primeval variety which at some point evolved into a caseless one.

A brief look into the history of Western Arabic studies, however, reveals that a more nuanced and differentiated attitude to this question once held sway. In particular, at the turn of the twentieth century the German scholar Karl Vollers (1906: 165) proposed that the *QurɁaan* was originally composed in a variety without case endings. Vollers's argumentation on this point is embedded in a larger one in which he claimed that the *QurɁaan* was revealed in a west Arabian dialect differing in many respects from Classical Arabic. In what he regarded as the official version of the *QurɁaan*, this variety was later replaced by a more prestigious variety, associated basically with an eastern Arabian dialect.

Vollers's historical interpretation of the Koranic revelation and later remodeling according to classical norms, though bold, is, as has been pointed out in a number of places, difficult to verify, and his thesis is weakened by a number of factual errors regarding the status of the variant readings. In fact, it should be pointed out, Vollers, for whatever reason, did not base his argument on a detailed reading of the *Qiraaʔaat*, but rather drew on a range of sources including lexicography, grammar, and excerpts from the *Qiraaʔaat* themselves.

Despite any shortcomings, however, his linguistic interpretation of the state of Arabic in the early seventh century was remarkably prescient. Moreover, I will attempt to show, his assumption that there was a Koranic variant without case ending receives partial support from the Koranic reading tradition itself. I present this evidence here. The present chapter may be read in conjunction with Kahle's (1948) summary of a manuscript written perhaps by a fifth-century scholar named al-Maliki, in which various *ħadith* are cited, pointing directly and indirectly to the practice of reading the *Qurʔaan* without case endings.

The caseless variety of Koranic reading was associated with the tradition of the Basran Koranic reader and grammarian Abu ʕAmr ibn ʕAlaaʔ (henceforth, Abu Amr), one of the seven 'received' *Qurʔaan* readers canonized in Ibn Mujahid's (d. 324/936) *al-Sabʕ fiy l-Qiraaʔaat*. Abu Amr died in 770, and hence if the tradition associated with him is true, it would mean that a tradition with a caseless variety is as old as traditions with case endings. Recall that the original written Koranic text, the *mușħaf*, was unvoweled (and unpointed), and that it is precisely the *Qiraaʔaat* which give the permitted range of variants in rendering a complete oral interpretation of the text. Among the different reading versions, none of Ibn Mujahid's seven has any officially sanctioned precedence over any of the others (when or where the eponymous reader flourished is irrelevant), so should any of them be proven to sanction a caseless reading, the caseless reading is as 'old' as any other.[1]

This point is doubtlessly not lost on Koranic scholars, Arabicists, and Orientalists of a persuasion other than Vollers's. To accept Vollers's position would require a fundamental rethinking, inter alia, of the status of caseless vs. case forms of Arabic. Indeed, already in 1906 in the preface to his book, Vollers decried the intolerant scepticism to which he was subjected when he presented his thesis to Arab scholars in Algiers. For Western Arabicists, the criticisms of the distinguished Theodor Nöldeke (1910) were probably of greater importance.[2]

---

[1] In fact, after Ibn Mujahid further complete versions were summarized, and there developed a further subvariant, the 'non-canonical variants' (rough translation of *ʃawaaðð al-qiraaʔaat* 'exceptional readings', see Bergsträßer 1933: 15), which are well-known variants which did not fit into the 7, 10, 12, or 14 series. The linguistic and exegetical basis of these variants itself requires separate attention.

[2] In more recent times a few scholars have implicitly (Corriente 1971) or explicitly (Zwettler 1978: 119 ff.) taken a critical, though in my view ultimately inconclusive evaluation, of the Nöldeke tradition.

Al-Idgham al-Kabiyr and Case Endings 121

Certain criticisms by Nöldeke are correct. Vollers, for instance, opposes a received version against the *Qiraaʔaat*, which is a misinterpretation of the entire concept of the variant readings (see above).[3] This observation, however, hardly invalidates Vollers's thesis, and further criticisms by Nöldeke turn out to be surprisingly weak for a scholar of his stature. Nöldeke, while pointing to the existence of the *al-ʔidɣaam al-kabiyr*[4] tradition, never explored its significance for Vollers's thesis. This was the practice associated with Abu Amr (and perhaps Kisaʔi) of allowing inter-word assimilation according to various conditions, which will be discussed in greater detail in sect. 4.2 below. Nöldeke simply remarked that (as of 1910 of course) the works describing this Koranic reading tradition were not available (or lost). The existence of the tradition, even if only rumored or reported upon, without concrete exemplification, could have given Nöldeke cause for circumspection, rather than rejection of its significance. Furthermore, Nöldeke was aware that Sibawaih had written on inter-word assimilation,[5] even if Sibawaih never linked it to a particular Koranic tradition, so the question of the existence of the phenomenon in classical times would presumably not have been an issue for Nöldeke. Rather than assume an air of caution, however, Nöldeke displayed a zealousness in rejecting Vollers's thesis which carried him beyond the bounds of measured academic judgment.

Der Orientale neigt dazu, den feierlichen Vortrag heiliger Texte künstlich zu gestalten; das taten auch die Juden und die Syrer. Aber die wirkliche Sprache blickt doch überall durch. Und das läßt sich mit Sicherheit sagen: hätten der Prophet und seine gläubigen Zeitgenossen den Koran ohne I'rab gesprochen, so wäre die Tradition davon nicht spurlos untergegangen.   (1910: 2)

The Oriental is inclined to intone holy texts with artificial pomp. The [ancient] Jews and Syrians did the same. Nonetheless, the true language is perceptible behind the

---

[3] Though a misinterpretation all too prevalent in contemporary Arabic studies. Allen (1998: 51), intended as a standard textbook on Arabic literature, describes the process of 'establishing a single written version of them as the canonical source and declaring other versions non-canonical'. This ignores the entire Islamic *Qiraaʔaat* tradition, representing the situation roughly as Vollers assumed in 1906 with one received version opposed to various non-canonical ones. Nöldeke's criticisms of nearly one hundred years ago are as relevant here as they were in Vollers's time.

[4] *ʔidɣaam* = form IV verbal noun; alternatively a form VIII verbal noun is used for the designation, *iddiɣaam*.

[5] Even here Nöldeke errs in points of editorial detail and in points of substance. Nöldeke, for instance alludes to ch. 564 as Sibawaih's chapter on *ʔidɣaam*, though in the Derenbourg edition discussion of *ʔidɣaam* does not begin until ch. 565, and inter-word assimilation not until ch. 566. More seriously, Nöldeke appears to assume that Sibawaih discusses exactly the same linguistic conditions relating to *al-ʔidɣaam al-kabiyr* as did Abu Amr. Such an assumption is correct only, as will be argued, if Abu Amr's rendition basically lacks final short vowels. This, however, is an assumption which Nöldeke argued against.

façade. And one can therefore say with certainty, that if the Prophet and his companions had articulated the Qurʔaan without case endings, such a tradition would not have disappeared without a trace.

The problem here is that Nöldeke's conclusion (how could the tradition have disappeared?) is not supported by anything but Nöldeke's own (rhetorically embellished) belief in its correctness. I would draw attention to four points in Nöldeke's claim. First, Nöldeke would appear to assume that the Qiraaʔaat faithfully reproduced Muhammad's actual speech. Perhaps he is only responding to the logic of Vollers's own assumptions in this regard, though it is highly questionable that a tradition codified some 80–160 years after the death of the Prophet could have, or would have even attempted to, preserve Muhammad's own pronunciation with perfect accuracy (see Beck's series in *Orientalia*, beginning 1945 for an introduction to some of the relevant issues). This leads to the second point. If the reading tradition in fact represented decentralized, locally defined alternatives to Koranic recitation, then there should on an a priori basis be no contradiction in finding that one of these traditions had a caseless variety as its basis. Nöldeke's (and Vollers's) mistake was to associate this variety with the person of the Prophet.

Third, Nöldeke I believe misconstrues the symbolic importance of a caseless variety of Arabic in the reading tradition. I will argue below that the Abu Amr tradition, in fact, should be interpreted as representing such a variety, though nowhere in the Qiraaʔaat tradition (e.g. Mujahid, Jazari) is this variety represented as one lacking case (*Piʕraab*). The defining characteristic of the Abu Amr tradition, however, is not lack of case endings, but presence of assimilation. This is why the term *al-ʔidɣaam al-kabiyr* 'major assimilation' eventually (see n. 5) became associated with it (rather than, say *ʔilɣaaʔ al-ʔiʕraab*). Recalling that by tradition the reading practices are prior to the grammatical, the lack of stigmatization of the Abu Amr tradition – a stigmatization might have been expected given its caseless character – is due to its establishment before what may be termed the 'ideology of *Piʕraab*' became established in the Islamic tradition. In the early history of Islam, *Piʕraab* simply did not have the normative force which the grammarians later established for it (see Larcher 2006a; Larcher and Guillot 2005b).

Fourth, and finally, I would repeat the point alluded to above, that given Nöldeke's cognizance of the Abu Amr tradition, his appeal to argumentation *ex silentio*, i.e. lack of concrete texts implying non-existence of the tradition itself, was, in 1910, to say the least, dangerous.

To this point the discussion points perhaps to interesting ideological issues in the conceptualization of early Arabic, but thus far not to concrete linguistic ones, or at least, not ones for which concrete linguistic data has been applied. Clearly, therefore, the existence of a traditional work describing the functioning of *al-ʔidɣaam al-kabiyr* is of crucial importance in putting the discussion on a concrete linguistic footing.[6]

4.1. *Sharḥ Ṭayyibat al-Nashr:* A Fifteenth-Century Treatise on Koranic Variants

Such a document is provided by the *Sharḥ Ṭayyibat al-Nashr*, a work in the variant reading (*Qiraaʔaat*) tradition written by Ibn al-Jazariy (henceforth, Jazari) and commentated by a modern scholar, Ali Muḥammad al-Ḍabbaaʕ (henceforth, Ḍabbaʕ). Jazari died in 833/1429 in Damascus. The work is about 330 pages long, consisting of rhymed verse written by Jazari, with detailed explanation by Ḍabbaʕ. As is the nature of such texts, the meat of the explanation lies in the commentary (*sharḥ*). Here I should note one conditional caveat to the following analysis. It rests, namely, for the most part on Ḍabbaʕ's amplification of Jazari's text. While it may be assumed that Ḍabbaʕ's interpretation is correct and faithful to his sources, I have not confirmed all of them independently myself, on the basis of other medieval *Qiraaʔaat* texts.[7]

The editor Anis Mahra appropriately places the *Sharḥ Ṭayyibat al-Nashr* within the Koranic reading tradition. Jazari is said to have studied twelve different Koranic variants, and in the present work deals with ten different ones, as follows.[8] The first seven are identical with Ibn Mujahid's basic seven reading traditions, the last three additional, sanctioned traditions.

---

[6] Pretzl (1934: 293) implies that the *al-ʔidɣaam al-kabiyr* tradition is limited among Koranic readers, noting that Ibn Mujahid himself did not mention it. His information as of 1934 is probably correct. The editor of a standard and more recent edition of Ibn Mujahid's *al-Sabʕa fiy al-Qiraaʔaat*, Shawqi Ḍayf (1972), notes in his introduction to the *al-ʔidɣaam al-kabiyr* (p. 113) that he (Ḍayf) edited his chapter on this subject on the basis of non-consecutive pages which he found in the manuscript and ordered them before al-Baqara (second chapter of *Qurʔaan*), analogous to the practice in later works on the *Qiraaʔaat* (like Dani). It would therefore appear that *al-ʔidɣaam al-kabiyr* is a topic treated in Ibn Mujahid, whose work is the most important in the *Qiraaʔaat* literature.

[7] Ibn Mujahid summarizes different treatments of *ʔidɣaam* among the seven received schools, noting that Abu Amr (pp. 116–22) assimilated inter-word, basically under the conditions defined in the *Sharḥ Ṭayyibat al-Nashr*. His basic generalization relating to Abu Amr's treatment reads as follows: 'Abu Amr would delete the vowel of the first consonant (*ʔaskana l-ʔawwal*), and assimilate the first consonant in the second, if the consonants were both voweled, in different words and of the same pattern (*ʕalaa miθaal waaḥid*)'. Ibn Mujahid does not go into detail about what he means by 'of the same pattern'. Much of what Ibn Mujahid says about Abu Amr's treatment is found in Ḍabbaʕ's summary of *al-ʔidɣaam al-kabiyr*.

[8] See ʕAbd Allah (1984: 179–218) for information about the standard Koranic variants, exceptional variants, the relationship between the reading tradition and the written Koranic text, and various other basic points regarding the variant readings.

TABLE 4.1. Koranic readers

Reader	Place	Date of death
Nafiʿ	Medina	169/785
Ibn Kathir	Mecca	120/737
Abu ʾAmr	Basra	154/770
Ibn ʾAmir	Damascus	118/736
Ạsim	Kufa	127/745
Ḥamza	Kufa	156/772
KisaʾI	Kufa	189/804
Abu Jaʿfar	Medina	130/748
Yaʿqub	Basra	205/820
Bazzar	Baghdad	229/843

For the most part, the first 150 pages are taken up with general topics, for instance the treatment of the vocalization of the 3MSG object pronoun *hu* (66 ff., see sect. 8.9 below), length of vowels (71 ff.), deletion of *hamza* (77 ff.), *imala* (115 ff., see Ch. 7), r (*raaʔ muraqqaqa*, 133 ff., see sect. 1.6.6 above), l (*laam muraqqaqa* 139 ff.), pausal phenomena (141 ff., see sect. 1.6.3.) and final -y (148 ff.). Starting at p. 168 individual topics relating to each chapter are successively treated, beginning with *al-baqara*, except for the first chapter (*al-faatiħa*) treated earlier (48 ff.). The readers and the chain of transmission associated with each are summarized at the very beginning of the work.

Its overall structure appears to represent an orthodox treatment of variant reading issues. As with Ibn Mujahid, for instance, general issues are treated first (though they occupy more space than in Ibn Mujahid), and the linguistic issues themselves are basically identical. Jazari/Ḍabbaʕ's treatment of 3MSG -*hu* is comparable in substance to that of Ibn Mujahid (130–2), for instance.

Among the various topics, two types of assimilation are distinguished in the *Sharħ Ṭayyibat al-Nashr*, 'little' or 'minor' and 'big' or 'major'. Both types deal primarily with assimilation across word boundaries. Little assimilation (106–13), *al-ʔidɣaam al-ṣaɣiyr*, describes assimilation when a word ends in a consonant (prepositions, and particles such as *hal, qad*), while big, or 'major' assimilation *al-ʔidɣaam al-kabiyr*, bigger also in the detail with which it is treated (54–66), describes assimilation when a short final vowel is left off.[9] Major assimilation is the first topic treated in detail because, Ḍabbaʕ explains, it occurs at the very beginning of the *Qurʔaan* in:

[9] In practical terms a choice must be made, when describing assimilation, to speak of deleting a vowel, then applying assimilation (as in Mujahid), or to assume that no vowel is there to delete (the argument of the chapter). In the examples cited I represent final vowels simply because this mode of

(1) al-raħiym-i   malik-i → al-raħiym malik-i (1: 2)
    art-merciful -GEN   master-GEN
    'Most merciful, Master... (I: 3/4)[10]

Both types of assimilation pertain to complete assimilation, the pronunciation of two consonants (ħarfaan) as one. The different grades of assimilation treated by the grammarians (e.g. Sibawaih chs. 565–9) are thus not distinguished here.

Although major assimilation is given prominence in the Sharħ Ṭayyibat al-Nashr, in fact being one of the longest thematic sections in the book, it is not a widespread phenomenon among the readers. It is associated with the Basran reader Abu Amr via his interpreter, Suwsi. It may also be associated with the Kufan KisaɁi through his interpreter Duri (54).

The tradition relating to major assimilation is not a unitary one, though specific names are cited only inconsistently. DabbaʕS for example speaks of some of the followers of major assimilation (Ɂaṣħaab al-Ɂidɣaam) who assimilate in a certain (jussive) context, while others do not (56). Later he refers to the 'readers of assimilation' (ruwaat al-Ɂidɣaam). On the other hand, regarding the phrase al-raɁs-u ʃayban only Susi is said to assimilate (al-raɁsh ʃayban 'the head (glistening) of white hair' (19: 4) (58). It is also noted that certain readers outside the assimilation tradition assimilate certain Koranic excerpts (61–5), that Ḥamza, for example, assimilated t in four instances. In one comment (63) it is noted that among current practitioners of assimilation a phonetic realization is preferred where a slight, undifferentiated vocalic trace (a weakening quality, rawm, see Sibawaih II: 307, see sect. 1.6.3 above) is left between the assimilated sounds, whereas among the classical readers (al-qudamaaɁ) complete assimilation was preferred.

4.2. Linguistic Attributes of 'Major Assimilation'

Though dealing basically with similar phenomena, impressionistically, the linguistic treatment of the variant readings is more sophisticated in the Sharħ Ṭayyibat al-Nashr than in Ibn Mujahid's tenth-century prototype. This is in evidence in the treatment of major assimilation. The technical terminology is compatible with the sophisticated linguistic treatment of assimilation

---

representation will be familiar to the informed reader. Although there is a degree of inconsistency in the mode of representation, the reader should take the discussion in sect. 4.3 as representing the proposed analysis of the Abu Amr tradition.

[10] The Koranic citations in Jazari are not specified according to chapter and verse. Many are unique collocations, but some are not, and for these I have chosen an arbitrary passage from the QurɁaan which matches Jazari's citation.

(ʔidɣaam) in the standard grammars, and further technical terminology is introduced appropriate to its status in the Koranic variants. Thus, at the very beginning of his chapter three conditions are distinguished, that involving two identical consonants (mutamaaθalaan) such as the two *m*s in (1) above, two with the same place (muxraj) of articulation such as θ-ð, and two which are close in terms of place/manner of articulation, such as θ-t.

It is further in evidence in the interaction of major assimilation with general linguistic rules. This may be illustrated in the interpretation (57) of the fragment ʔaal(a) luwṭin 'Lot's people', which is noted to occur four times in the Qurʔaan (e.g. 27. 56, 54. 33). The practitioners of major assimilation (ʔaṣḥaab al-ʔidɣaam) are divided as to whether assimilation (→ ʔaal luwṭin) is applicable here. Those who do not accept it would appear to argue that the form ʔaal has undergone too many morpho-phonological changes (ʕilla, two prior to idɣaam) to allow a further one, namely major assimilation. The sequence of rules would be:

(2) ʔahl(a) (luwṭin)   Base form (ʔaṣl)
 → ʔaʔl(a) (luwṭin)   transformation (qalb) of h to ʔ
 → ʔaal(a) (luwṭin)   change (badal) of ʔaʔ to ʔaa
 → ʔaal (luwṭin)   major assimilation.

The interpretive problems surrounding this derivation fall squarely within mainstream Arabic phonological discourse.

Regarding the status of major assimilation it is stated that it is sanctioned to apply unless rules specifically forbid it from doing so, i.e. that assimilation is, within its tradition, the unmarked option. An important question is what, if any, the status of the 'underlying' final vowels is. In Jazari/Ḍabbaʕ no explicit mention is made of this point. Ibn Mujahid (116) specifically says that when two similar consonants (ʕalaa miθaal waaḥid) in two words meet, that the first should be made vowelless (ʔaskin al-ʔawwal) and then assimilated. He clearly takes the voweled forms as basic. From a procedural and pedagogical point of view, such a perspective is to be expected. Ibn Mujahid's work, however, was severely practical and compilatory, largely devoid of discussion of theoretical issues, even if his work assumes a basic knowledge of Arabic morpho-phonological practice. The fact that one can describe the starting point as having a final short high vowel does not necessarily mean that the vowels were underlying in the Abu Amr tradition, as I will discuss in sect. 4.3.

Conditions sanctioning the use of al-ʔidɣaam al-kabiyr are stated in phonological, morpho-phonological and lexical terms. Phonologically, for instance, final geminated consonants do not undergo major assimilation, as in al-ḥaqqu ka-man 'is the truth, like one...' (13: 19, see n. 15). Moreover, assimilation is not favored when the short vowel occurs after two consonants (of which the geminate condition is a special case). Thus the assimilation of the *n* of *naḥnu laka* → *naḥl laka* 'we for you' is singled out as exceptional because the *n* occurs after a consonant (i.e. *Cn*).

Morpho-phonologically assimilation is said not to apply[11] to the agentive pronoun -*tu*, as in *xalaqtu ṭiynan* 'I created from mud',[12] while a number of lexical exceptions are stated, illustrated inter alia in sect. 4.3 below.

With a few exceptions (see below) major assimilation describes inter-word assimilation governed by various phonological contexts. As noted above, in opposition to minor assimilation, all cases involve words which normally end in a short vowel. Note that the relevant distinguishing characteristic is simply a short vowel, not a morpho-phonological category such as inflectional vowel (*ʔiʕraab*) or fixed lexical vowel (*binaaʔ*). One thus finds examples such as (3) and (4) treated in the same paragraph, under the same conditions (assimilation of *l*, *r*, 58), though the first case involves the absence of a lexical vowel (-*a*), the latter of a genitive inflectional -*i*.

(3) *qaala   rabb-u-kum*   → *qaar rabbukum*
    said   God- NOM-your
    'he (Moses) said your God...' (26: 26)

(4) *ʔilaa   sabiyl-i   rabbi-ka*   → *ʔilaa sabiyr rabbika*
    to   way-GEN   God-your
    'on the way of your Lord' (16: 125)

The categories of consonants allowing major assimilation are dealt with sequentially (56–61), and will be summarized non-exhaustively here. By far the largest class concerns the progressive assimilation of *t/d*, which may be assimilated to a following: *s, ð, ḍ, ḍ, t, ʃ, θ, z, ṣ*, and *j* as in

(5) *yakaad-u   sanan   barqi-hi*   → *yakaas sanan...*
    be near-IND flash   lightning-his
    'the flash of his lightning nearly...' (24: 43)

and *l, r,* as in (4) above and in

(6) *ʔaṭhar-u lakum* → *ʔaṭhal lakum*
    '(they are) purer than you...' 11: 78.

Further consonant sequences allowing assimilation are *ḍ-ʃ, k-q* (see below), *ð-s/ṣ/j, j-t* and *b-m*. A number of these are (as (3) above) lexically restricted.

---

[11] The terminological opposite of *ʔidɣaam* is *ʔiðhaar*, where the 'original' consonants appear.
[12] Though even here, some readers assimilate the -*ta* (i.e. use -*t* alone) in one fragment (57).

b assimilates to *m*, for instance, only in the word *yuʕaððibu* 'he punishes' (e.g. 2: 284), as in *yuʕaððim man* 'he punishes whomever'. *n* may be assimilated in certain words.

Generally major assimilation occurs in contexts where the high vowels *i*, *u* occur (i.e. as in the non-*al-ʔidɣaam al-kabiyr* tradition). In sequences of *aal/ra+ l/r*, for example, assimilation is allowed only in the verb *qaala* (see (3) above); sequences of *Cda* do not allow assimilation of *d* unless explicitly sanctioned, and so on.

The unmarked direction of assimilation appears to be progressive (first consonant assimilating to second), which accounts for the opposite effects in (3) and (6) above. There are cases, however, of regressive assimilation (second to first), as in

(7) *xalaqaka* → *xalaq-qa*
 '(who) created you' (18: 37).

It would appear that the nature of the consonants plays a role here, with the unmarked case being progressive assimilation, unless certain sets of consonants occur where other precedence factors are operative (*q* over *k* for instance, in (7)), though the issue is not discussed explicitly, and there are too few examples to generalize.

In a few cases intra-word assimilation is treated within this category. This pertains particularly to the 2MSG object suffix -*ka*, illustrated in (7) above.

What is not mentioned at all is the issue which most directly concerns the purpose of this chapter, namely the argument that a Koranic reading tradition exists (the use of the present tense underlines the fact that the traditions never die) which uses a caseless form of Arabic. I believe the only reference to the morpho-phonological status of the final short vowels pertains to the agentive pronominal suffix -*t*, mentioned above. The case or mode status of the final vowels is not only irrelevant, as examples such as (2, 4 vs. 5) indicate; the absence of the final short vowels is treated as a basically phonological phenomena as well, hence the inclusion of both fixed and inflectional vowels e.g. (3, 6 vs. 7) within the same conceptual framework.

It is relevant to note here that Abu Amr's *al-ʔidɣaam al-kabiyr* was also reported to be even wider than any specific constraints related to assimilation. Ibn Mujahid (157) notes that he was said to use a 'weakened' (*taxfiyf*) pronunciation throughout the *Qurʔaan*, and that he assimilated in places where no one else did (wa al-qawl maa ʔaxbartuka bihi min ʔannahu kaan yuʔθir al-taxfiyf fi qiraaʔatihi kullihaa. Wa al-daliyl ʕalaa ʔiyθaarihi al-taxfiyf ʔannu kaan yudxim min al-ḥuruwf maa laa yakaad yudximuhu xayruhu). Furthermore, in a report attributed to al-Yazidi, he is said to have often deleted a short [i] or [u] completely at the end of the verb, before a suffix. The tradition to be sure is, not unusually, contradictory here. Other reports say only that he weakens a final vowel. It is clear, in any case, that in the Abu Amr tradition, more so even than elsewhere, a short final vowel was of negligible functional status.

4.3. Interpretive Summary

One point that emerges from the present discussion is the legitimacy of the *al-ʔidxaam al-kabiyr*, major assimilation tradition. Jazari/Dabbaʕ present the topic as an uncontroversial one and embed it in a linguistic discourse (e.g. (2) above) which clearly reflects a long association with Arabic grammar (see n. 6 for Ibn Mujahid). Nöldeke was premature to ignore its significance.

That said, there remain interpretive problems in embedding this particular tradition into an understanding of the form of Old Arabic in all its varieties, an understanding of which is a prerequisite for the reconstruction of proto-Arabic. I will begin by outlining positions which may be, or have been advocated by others and work my way towards what I think a plausible reading of the facts allows.

Before proceeding, I should note that I believe a fuller discussion of the Abu Amr tradition will require, inter alia, a representation of the problem in a contemporary phonological framework, perhaps more than one, to elucidate the question from different perspectives. Furthermore, assumptions concerning Old Arabic syllable structure and stress are relevant, the basis of which is not always readily discernible even in the more detailed grammatical texts. I would reiterate, in any case, that the major assimilation tradition is about phonology, morpho-phonological constraints playing only a limited role (see discussion above concerning the perfect verb suffix -*tu*), so that understanding the tradition requires a phonologically sound interpretation.

As noted above, the *al-ʔidxaam al-kabiyr* tradition is generally silent about the underlying status of the final short vowels, the absence of which is necessary to trigger assimilation. A literalist reading might argue that even in the tradition of major assimilation the short vowels are present in underlying structure in all instances and deleted in those cases where assimilation occurs. Such an interpretation requires two rules, one deleting the vowel (8a), the second assimilating the consonant (8b). I will represent the rules linearly, in the manner of the medieval Arabic grammarians. The subscript '$_a$' represents an assimilable consonant.

(8a) $C_{1a}\text{-}V_h \# C_{2a} \rightarrow C_{1a} \# C_{2a}$

(8b) $C_{1a}\#C_{2a} \rightarrow C_{2a}C_{2a}$

Example (8a) says that short high vowels are deleted word finally (ignoring limiting conditions described above), while (8b) is the assimilation rule proper (assuming assimilation only between the requisite consonants, the subscript 'a' marks assimilable consonants). The rules must apply sequentially. Logically (8b) cannot precede (8a), since (8a) creates the environment for assimilation to operate. Example (8a) is thus in a feeding relation to (8b), which can be represented '(8a) → (8b)'. What is linguistically odd about this is that (8a) applies only in those cases where (8b) does, that is, that it must anticipate (8b) before (8b) has operated. Within the Arabic morphophonological tradition where rules work sequentially such a formal representation is unusual (though perhaps not unique).

As discussed in sect. 4.2 above, the *al-ʔidɣaam al-kabiyr* tradition as described by Jazari/Dabbaʕ is embedded in a well-articulated Arabic phonological tradition of analysis. It is relevant, therefore, briefly to consider assimilation in this tradition. I use Sibawaih as the basis of discussion. Having lived but one generation after Abu Amr and having consulted him on linguistic issues, he can be assumed to have dealt with a variety of Arabic similar to that described by Abu Amr.

As I interpret Sibawaih's treatment of assimilation, rules of the type (8a) followed by (8b) do not exist. As might be expected, however, there are interpretive problems. Rules of the type (8b), assimilation across a word boundary, are described in considerable detail by Sibawaih (II: chs. 566–9). Though inter-word assimilation is normal in his description of assimilation, his examples assume a C-final word in the first position (i.e. *mabniy ʕalaa l-sukuwn*), such as *iðhab fiy* → *iðhaf fiy* 'go to' (461: 6) or *hal raʔayta* → *har raʔayta* 'did you see' (II: 461. 23).[13] Examples therefore are typically either imperative singular verb + N/V or particle + N/V. Such examples are accounted for by (8b), without the need for (8a).

One exception, involving V-final words, pertains to cases where the consonants on either side of the word boundary are the same. Here cross-word assimilation is allowed, as in

(9) *jaʕala #la-ka* → *jaʕal laka* 'he made for you' (II: 455.21).

Sibawaih sets preferences here, however, in particular allowing this only when the consonants are identical, and favoring it when the deletion of the vowel breaks up a long series of open syllables, in this case five (see sect. 2.4.2 (21)).

---

[13] It is relevant to note that Sibawaih's list of assimilation possibilities differs in detail from Jazari's. While Jazari, for example, allows assimilation of $l + r$ (e.g. (6) above), Sibawaih does not (II: 461. 6).

He also gives a few examples of deletion even where the deleted vowel is a case ending, as in

(10) θawb-u bakrin → θawb bakrin 'Bakr's cloth' (II: 457.18).

Whether cases such as these count as assimilation (as I have provisionally termed it) is debatable, however, as a geminate consonant necessarily arises as soon as the two identical consonants are juxtaposed.[14] Formally, they are exhaustively accounted for by (8a), appropriately formulated to specify identical consonants, so there is no need to postulate the sequence (8a) followed by (8b).

Looking at the problem from the perspective of (8a), while elision of a short high vowel in an open syllable within a word is not unattested (e.g. Sibawaih II: 277, ʕalima → ʕalma 'learn'), such cases do not feed into a further assimilation rule such as (8b). As in (9), (10) sequences of two identical consonants on either side of the vowel will give rise to a geminate consonant, though as with (9), (10) there is no need to invoke an extra assimilation rule as the gemination arises as soon as the vowel deletes, as in (11).

(11) yaqtatil → yaqtitil → (yaqttil) → yaqittil[15] 'combat' (II: 459. 3)

For Sibawaih, then (8a) applies within words, and between words only when the two consonants are identical; (8b) applies across word boundaries, with an input in which two consonants abut on one another.

In Sibawaih, while (8a) and (8b) are needed as independent rules, there is no evidence that they should be construed in a feeding relation, with the output of (8a) feeding into the input of (8b). This being so, a rule of the type 8a → 8b would, in Classical Arabic phonology, be unique to the one Abu Amr reading tradition. The situation can be summarized as a scala, as in (12).[16]

(12a) C_1-V_h#C_1 → C_1C_1 (Sibawaih)

(12b) C_{1a}-V_h#C_{2a} → $C_{2a}C_{2a}$ (Abu Amr)

(12c) C # C → C C (?)

---

[14] As an alternative to assimilation, there is also always the possibility of keeping the consonants separate with a murmur vowel (ixfaaʔ).

[15] The change from yaqtatil to yaqtitil would appear to be interpreted by Sibawaih in terms of vowel assimilation. The vowel /i/ between the q and tt is an epenthetic one. The third stage is not stated explicitly by Sibawaih, though may be assumed (Orin Gensler, p.c.).

[16] I can dispense with one argument in favor of postulating (12a) (= (8a)) as prior to (12b) (= (8b)). This would run along the line of Nöldeke's explanation for the lack of tanwiyn in Arabic script, namely that the basis of the writing tradition are pausal forms. One could conceivably suggest that the basis of major assimilation as well is pausal forms, those without final short vowels. However, while this would account for the lack of the short vowels, it hardly could simultaneously account for the assimilation, which, logically, requires lack of pause.

Example (12a) is described by Sibawaih; (12b), implying (12a) as well, is the Abu Amr tradition, interpreted as in Ibn Mujahid with a final vowel underlyingly present. A further step would be (12c), with final high vowels present in no contexts. Example (12c) is identical to (8b), except that it is taken as the underlying form, not dependent on the deletion of a final short high vowel (i.e. (8a)). While (12c) is not described as a general case in the literature, so far as I know, it is a position open for reconstruction, as I will outline presently.

While proving the non-existence of 8a → 8b is logically impossible, a plausible alternative is readily available. Rather than assume the presence of final vowels which must be deleted, a counter-assumption is that in this variety there are no short high vowels present in the first place. This is represented in (12c) above. This formulation is implicit in the very existence of major assimilation, as the phenomenon itself is straightforwardly comprehensible as assimilation of CC sequences under close juncture. This interpretation has the important effect of bringing the phenomenon into line with Sibawaih's own description of cross-word assimilation: with the exception of identical consonants, Sibawaih allows such assimilation only where the first word ends in a consonant in the first place. Assuming C-final words as the basic input allows the al-ʔidxaam al-kabiyr to be interpreted within mainstream medieval Arabic phonological descriptions.

Three potential problems relating to the current analysis may be mentioned. First, my interpretation assumes a C-final input not only when assimilation occurs, but also when assimilation does not occur (see (14b) below).[17] I am aware that evidence against this position can be found even in the Abu Amr tradition. For example, Ibn Mujahid (p. 149) notes that Abu Amr would 'imalize' (aa → ie, see Ch. 7) in the context aar-i, where –i is a genitive ending (e.g. ðaati qarier-in 'affording rest', Q 23: 50). Using a literal reading of the Abu Amr tradition, one could limit the instances of inter-word assimilation to those described by (8a, b) (= (12a, b)) below.

Against a literalist reading, I would argue that the status of many grammatical elements in the Qiraaʔaat tradition still awaits detailed comparative treatment, and that in some instances reconstructed forms may be necessary, which are not attested directly in any single variant. In this regard, it is relevant to note that a general tendency in the Abu Amr tradition is for the neutralization of short high vowels, apparently in all contexts, not only those

---

[17] The two positions I have outlined either assume the underlying presence of the short vowels, which are deleted, or their non-existence. Other interpretations are imaginable. For instance, a position between the two would begin from the assumption of their non-presence, introducing them in contexts where C#C sequences would not be prohibited, i.e. the set of contexts defined by (12c).

discussed here under the rubric of major assimilation. For instance, he was said to use ʔiʃmaam (see sects. 7.1.3 below and 1.6.3), apparently even word internally. I represent ʔiʃmaam here as an epenthetic vowel, as in ʕan ʔasliħatəkum 'of your arms' (Q4: 102) and in yuʕalliməhum ('instruct them' Q2: 129, see discussion at sect. 2.4.1.2, Old Arabic sources). In general, as seen at the end of sect. 4.2, Ibn Mujahid (157) reports that the Abu Amr tradition is known for the 'weakening' (taxfiyf) of various elements (especially short vowels and the glottal stop). How far this generalization goes is a matter of interpretation, one logical endpoint, weakening in all contexts, being outlined in this chapter.

Second, it may be asked, if the al-ʔidxaam al-kabiyr tradition had as its base forms words without short vowels, why there should exist a distinction between major and minor assimilation. Minor assimilation, after all, explicitly has as base form C-final words. There are three considerations here.

First, it appears that minor assimilation was common to all variants, so it would have been confusing to assimilate a tradition practiced by only some of the readers, the al-ʔidxaam al-kabiyr, to the al-ʔidxaam al-saxiyr. In other words, even if the phonological phenomena were identical, the fact that the al-ʔidxaam al-kabiyr marked two traditions, assured it of a conceptually distinct status. Second, it may be assumed that V-final forms would have been taken as the standard, if only on a formal basis. Major assimilation lacks vowels present elsewhere in the reading tradition outside Abu Amr (and perhaps, Kisaʔi), hence the need for a special designation of this phenomenon.

Third, the possibility may be held open that there were, in fact, vowels appearing word finally in the Abu Amr tradition. This is the case in those instances where assimilation (8b) occurs. After his description of the contexts where assimilation is allowed, Jazari (61) notes that as an alternative to complete assimilation, one may instead pronounce a vowel-like element, either rawm 'labialization' or ʔiʃmaam 'rounding and fronting' (see sect. 1.6.3). An alternative to (3), for instance, would be something like

(13)　qaala rabb-u-kum → qaar^w rabbukum.[18]

rawm neutralizes morphological marking (in both Sibawaih and Abu Amr). In what way ʔiʃmaam does is an issue beyond the confines of this chapter.

Evaluating the status of these vowel-like qualities within both the reading and grammatical traditions, what I suggest is that they are epenthetic

---

[18] As noted above (end of sect. 4.1), rawm and ʔiʃmaam are favored by the post-classical generation (al-mutaʔaxxariyn), which introduces a further, diachronic variable into the interpretation of assimilation.

insertions in the C#C context, not weakenings of erstwhile case or lexical vowels. I would furthermore suggest that such insertions might occur in any C#C context, not only those where they alternate paradigmatically with assimilation. This would align the *al-ʔidɣaam al-kabiyr* tradition with the observations of Quṭrub, summarized below, and it would imply that even in the *al-ʔidɣaam al-kabiyr* tradition the status of word-final consonants would have been different from the *al-ʔidɣaam al-ṣaɣiyr*, where no epenthesis occurred.

Note that formally this suggestion is compatible with (8b) above. In the interpretation advocated here, for inter-word vowel deletion (8a) does not exist so far as the variety used by Abu Amr goes,[19] hence (8b) can operate directly. Such vowels as do occur word finally (other than those morphologically determined, like vocalized pronominal suffixes) are added by rule and thus, not having underlying status do not need to be deleted. Rather than (8) above, I would suggest instead that (14) describes the status of final vowels and inter-word assimilation in the *al-ʔidɣaam al-kabiyr* tradition.

(14a) $C_{1a}\#C_2 \rightarrow C_2\ C_2$ (= old (8b), with assimilation under appropriate conditions)

(14b) $C_{1a}\#C_2 \rightarrow C_1$ ə # C2 (ə = vowel-like element)[20]

A third objection is that apart from the short vowels, case is also represented in the two long-vowel suffix forms, *-uwna* NOM and *-iyna* ACC/GEN, as well as in the dual suffixes (see sect. 2.4.4 for discussion of these). These are also part of the Abu Amr tradition. At this point the inference from the current discussion is that the Abu Amr tradition has a case-marking system thus:

(15) Short vowels
-a accusative/adverbial vs. Ø or ə
Long vowels
-uwna nominative vs *-iyna* accusative/genitive.

Nouns fall into declensions, only one of which has the traditional Classical Arabic case contrast.

Of course, even in the *Qurʔaan* (Q20.63) there is one generally accepted instance of neutralization of the nominative/accusative contrast. Moreover, in Koranic rhyme a final *-uwna* can be equivalent to a final *-iyna* (Bell 1958: 69). Taking a leaf from Kahle (1948) and Wansbrough (1977), one might see in the

---

[19] Because there are no final vowels to delete. Example (8a) operates for Sibawaih, but only when the two consonants are identical.

[20] I would assume that in the Abu Amr tradition, the stricture on maintenance of the high vowel in *al-ḥaqqu ka-man* in reality is a condition inserting an epenthetic vowel in a CC #C sequence.

Abu Amr tradition the remnants of a once more widespread tradition, whose bare traces are still visible, but whose substance was superseded by a different interpretation of Arabic grammar. Scholarly inquiry along these lines leads to the heart of Arabic historical sociolinguistics.

I would argue that nearly one hundred years after the publication of Vollers's work, his suggestion that *al-ʔidɣaam al-kabiyr* tradition within Koranic variants has as its basis a caseless variety of Arabic is indeed a plausible approach to understanding this tradition. Indeed, against Vollers, I place this variety among the canonical variants themselves. The Koranic variants thus encompassed both varieties. Taken alone, students of the history of the Arabic language, to the extent that it is accepted at all, may not be particularly impressed by this conclusion. However, when it is linked to further, related phenomena, its significance is enhanced considerably.

First, it can be recalled that the early ninth-century linguist Quṭrub had suggested that the final short vowels were non-functional. Versteegh (1983) devotes a well-researched article to Quṭrub's position, which was opposed to that of linguists such as Sibawaih. Versteegh seeks to explain Quṭrub's views in philosophical terms. A simpler explanation is readily accessible, however. When Quṭrub spoke of the morphological inconsistency of short vowels, he was simply referring (in contemporary terminology) to their phonologically determined nature. He observed varieties of Arabic where the final short vowels had, as with the major assimilation tradition, no morphological value, but rather were phonologically determined.[21]

Second, there are various indications in the works of the earliest grammarians, Sibawaih and Farraʔ, that case did not play a role in varieties of Old Arabic in certain functionally restricted domains (see previous two chapters).

Third, as seen in the previous chapter, approaching modern Arabic dialectology as comparative historical grammar leads to the reconstruction of a caseless variety of proto-Arabic. In other words, reconstruction dovetails with the attestation of a caseless variety of Old Arabic, as evidenced in the *al-ʔidɣaam al-kabiyr* tradition. In this instance, philology recapitulates historical reconstruction based on comparative dialectology.

Before moving on to my concluding remarks, I would emphasize that the interpretation advocated here, while situated within a tradition first

---

[21] I am indebted to Ignacio Ferrando for calling my attention to this. The interpretation of Quṭrub runs up against severe difficulties due to the fact that on this issue we have his ideas at second hand only, from Zajjaji (*Iyḍaaḥ*: 70–1). In favor of Versteegh's account is the fact that Quṭrub appears to base his arguments against the systematicity of the case (*ʔiʕraab*) on case-marked forms. In favor of my interpretation is Quṭrub's overall conclusion that the vowels at the end of words have a purely phonological character.

elaborated by Vollers, draws quite different conclusions and has different implications both for the interpretation of the history of Arabic and for the *Qiraaʔaat* tradition. For Vollers the coexistence of case and caseless forms of Arabic was interpreted as primarily a stylistic difference, high, literary (case) vs. low, vernacular (caseless), secondarily as a dialectal one, east (Najd = case) vs. west (Hijaz = caseless). Vollers was quite content to see the case variety as historically primary (169). His major, and most controversial conclusion was that the *Qurʔaan* was remodeled so that Mohammed's original caseless (Hijazi) revelatory style was refashioned in the name of literary correctness on a case-based (eastern) variety.[22]

My purposes are strictly linguistic and are based on the methodology of the comparative method. With Vollers, it is argued that case and caseless forms coexisted in the eighth century, but against Vollers, there is no decisive linguistic evidence to assume that the case forms are historically primary, even if the argument for a prestige differential is compelling. It follows from this that there is no contradiction in having coexisting Koranic variants, about which no conclusions can be drawn as to historical anteriority. Indeed, assuming that the reading traditions developed before a standardizing grammatical model became prevalent,[23] it is quite natural to expect that reading traditions should develop simultaneously around any varieties prevalent in the community.

Taken together with the previous chapter, the current interpretation of the *al-ʔidɣaam al-kabiyr* tradition provides further evidence that Old Arabic case was a weakly established category. This allows the question to be raised whether it is an original proto-category at all. My answer is that it is not.

---

[22] Though I believe it more fruitful to pursue the idea that the caseless variety is original. Orin Gensler (p.c.), while seeing the plausibility of postulating case and caseless varieties of Arabic into the proto-language, would still see the case variety as inherited from proto-Semitic, given the correspondence of the Arabic system with that of Akkadian and Ugaritic. He also points out that one might work on the basis of an intermediate number of cases in a proto-stage, *a* vs. *i/u* for instance, which is certainly a further line of investigation worth following.

[23] Versteegh's studies (1993b, 1999) have thus far revealed no elaborate, sophisticated pre-Sibawaihian grammatical works or schools. I would, in any case, speak of a unified normative tradition only in the tenth century (Owens 1990).

5

Pre-Diasporic Arabic in the Diaspora: A Statistical Approach to Arabic Language History

5.1. Introduction

The importance of the modern dialects for an understanding of the Arabic language was stressed in the introductory chapter and incorporated in various ways into historical linguistic interpretations in Chs. 2 and 3. Not to incorporate this information systematically into an account of Arabic linguistic history is to write half a history of the Arabic language. In this chapter I more explicitly develop the construct 'pre-diasporic Arabic', as explained in 1.1, an idea which relies on an examination of post-diasporic varieties.

Before proceeding, the role of dialectology in historical linguistics may be briefly commented upon. Dialectology as a linguistic tradition can be viewed as a counterfoil to historical linguistics. Dialectology requires a synchronic spatial or socio-spatial starting point. Wedding dialectology and historical linguistics is of course possible, though here intrudes a problem of what may be termed 'reification'. Tracing the development of a dialect, it might be assumed that a dialect is a complete, discrete entity, comparable say to a building, which moves relatively changeless through time. Under this assumption there is a temptation to start with whatever set of features one has used to define the dialect in question, and to assume that the same set of features will cohere through time, each changing in consonance with the others.

This may not be the case, however. Indeed, from a historical perspective one has to begin with the assumption that each component of language and each feature has its own history: lexis changes at a different rate from phonology, verbal morphology differently from nominal, and so on. The recognition of this is what lies behind Thomason and Kaufman's (1988) attempt at typologies of potential rates of change in different components of grammar.

The fact that dialects do not change in a coherent, uniform fashion leads to a methodological and practical quandary. To do justice to the historical linguistic reality of a single dialect, one needs first to trace the development of each feature which may potentially be included in a given dialect: in a given period of time, some features will change a little, others a lot, others not at all. It is, however, practically not possible to reconstruct the large numbers of individual features which are customarily used in defining a dialect, unless one has a great deal of time at one's disposal. Historical dialectology is not simply the history of a single dialect.

Fortunately, there are two factors which allow one to circumvent practical constraints, to a certain degree at least. The first is the advent of the computer, which allows the average linguist to create relatively large data bases with which complex data can be analyzed into manageable units quickly. The second is the reality of contemporary dialects for certain languages, Arabic in particular, and the historical inferences which may be drawn from them. Arabic is spoken as a native language by about 250 million in an unbroken land area stretching from Lake Chad to northern Iraq, from Mauritania to Yemen. Sprachinsels outside this area also are found. Its variety is legion.[1] The diaspora to these regions began in earnest with the first Islamic conquests, around 630. Once populations had moved in opposite directions, say into northern Iraq, southern Egypt, or Chad, contact between them was largely or wholly lost. These two factors can be used in historical interpretation.

Turning then to the present data, a relatively large number of linguistic features are coded in a statistics program. I use forty-nine, twenty-five phonological and twenty-four morphological. These features are chosen from dialects at opposing ends of the Arabic-speaking world, under the premiss that retentions in particular will be due to a common inheritance dating back to the original diaspora. Since this large-scale diaspora began about 630, an indirect insight into the Arabic of this early era can be achieved. In a nutshell, this is the program followed in this chapter.

The methodology used here has a number of ramifications, however, two of which can be made explicit in order to give a more comprehensive account of the issues involved. First, the comparison between two dialect regions will throw into relief what is understood by the very term 'Arabic dialect'. I have selected two widely separated dialect areas for detailed scrutiny, Mesopotamia (Map 1) and the western Sudanic area in Africa (Map 3). The populations of

---

[1] Moreover, in the past forty years spoken Arabic has increasingly come into contact with Standard Arabic, resulting in what Mitchell (1986) terms educated spoken Arabic (see Owens 2001a for sociolinguistic summary).

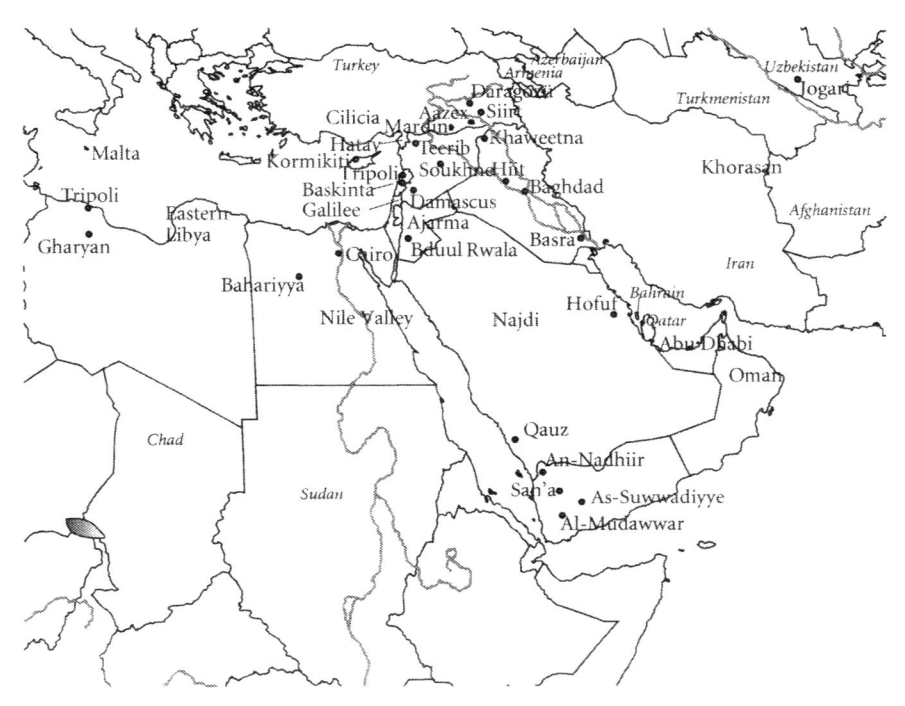

MAP 1. Sample points, Middle Eastern dialects

these two regions took separate paths of migration and would have remained out of contact with each other. It will emerge, however, that the two areas differ rather dramatically in terms of their dialect coherency, at least as measured by the features chosen here, and this coherency difference itself calls for historical reflection. Second, it will be suggested that the large-scale statistical comparison does at a certain point have to give way to the reconstruction of individual linguistic features as a way of reconstructing pre-diasporic Arabic. I single out two features for greater scrutiny in this respect, complementing the statistical approach with a close reading of the philological evidence.

Initially, therefore, two separate issues inform this chapter. One is dialectological, the other historical and comparative. It may in fact appear that I have contradicted myself, above arguing that the concept of 'dialect' conceived of as a coherent unit is antithetical to historical linguistic interpretation, but here suggesting that dialectal units are legitimate elements in historical linguistics. This apparent contradiction, however, will disappear once the statistical treatment gives the dialectal units internally differentiated

MAP 2. North African sample points

character. Ultimately, it will emerge that contemporary dialectology converges with reconstruction to yield a defensible historical interpretation about the nature of pre-diasporic Arabic.

Before moving on, I would note that there are two advantages in a statistical treatment. First, it keeps the researcher honest. I do not think it possible on an a priori basis to determine which linguistic variables are relevant to the problem of reconstruction. Dialectologists of Arabic often choose a few salient features to define very large dialect areas. Traditionally, for instance, North Africa is said to be marked by the presence of the feature for the 1PL imperfect verb, *n- -u*, as in *n-ukutb-u* 'we write', vs. *n-* in eastern dialects, *n-uktub* 'we write'. Even if such a characterization is useful for a dialectological classification, it does not follow that this one feature is criterial for defining the spread of Arabic into North Africa (see discussion in sect. 1.6.7). A relatively large data set is a reminder that many linguistic variables potentially are in play.

Second, as indicated above, larger dialect areas themselves are more or less homo/heterogeneous. Labels such as Mesopotamian Arabic and western Sudanic Arabic are abstractions. The use of statistics allows these abstractions

Sample points underlined: Mada
Cultural-historical regions in italics: *Bornu*

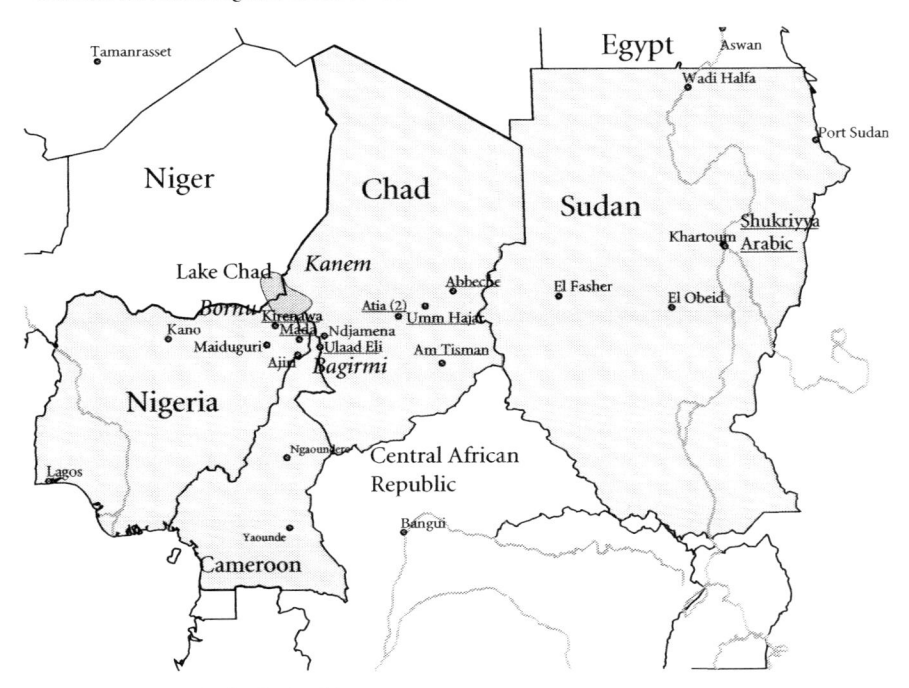

MAP 3. Western Sudanic Arabic

to be identified by their component parts. These component parts consist of (1) the different individual dialects and (2) the different variables chosen for comparison.

A set of linguistic data coded for numerical analysis is fraught with methodological and interpretive problems, including choice of linguistic variables, choice of dialects, interpretation of allo-variants, consideration of sociolinguistic variables, and assignment of numerical codes to individual cases. In the final analysis each linguistic variable has to be coded one way or another, and there may be no optimal formula for doing this. Therefore, I have attempted to elucidate the reasons behind my coding system, and to indicate some of the many interpretive problems in it.

The chapter is divided into eight parts. Section 5.2 introduces the data and dialects used; sect. 5.3 presents the basic statistics and initial interpretive results. Here it will be seen that the statistics help orientate a historical interpretation, but that a more precise interpretation requires the introduction of further types of data. This is done in sect. 5.4, where two specific features are discussed in greater detail and general conclusions relating to the interpretation of Arabic linguistic history are drawn on the basis of the overall data. Section 5.5 sums up the main points of the chapter. The rest of the chapter essentially has the status of an appendix in which the linguistic basis of the statistics are elucidated. In sect. 5.6 further applications of the data bank pertaining to questions of language contact and change are presented in a series of seven short hypotheses. In sects. 5.7 and 5.8 problems of methodology and coding are discussed. In Appendix 2 can be found a list of the variables and the coding of each is briefly illustrated.

5.2. Dialects, Procedure, Initial Results

The realization of forty-nine linguistic variables, all from phonology and morphology, have been compared between two dialect areas, Mesopotamia and the western Sudanic area, and in addition as a control, to Uzbekistan with Shukriyya Arabic (see sect. 5.2.2 and Maps 1, 3).

5.2.1. Linguistic variables

The variables are all basic elements in the grammar of the dialects, the realization of $ṭ$ or q, the realization (or lack thereof) of short vowels in open syllables (see sect. 2.4.1), the realization of the 1SG person suffix in perfect verbs, the realization of the (M)PL suffix in the imperfect verb, and so on. Even the most rudimentary dialect grammar describes these elements. Their centrality ensures that they may be used in a comparison of widely separated dialects. The features used are listed in Appendix 2, with an example of the realization of each value in a case. There are many methodological and theoretical issues connected with the choice of these variables, and their individual realizations in the different dialects. At a number of places various of these problems are addressed, and sects. 5.7 and 5.8 are devoted entirely to explaining how and why I have coded the material one way and not another. I do not pretend that the choices made here are the only ones possible or that they are the optimally perspicacious ones in each case. By explicitly alluding to the problems, I open the discussion up to others, who may want to view the material in a different way.

5.2.2. The dialects

Turning to the choice of dialect areas, four considerations are in play. First, as noted above, I compare two modern dialect areas which were settled in the course of the Arabic diaspora that accompanied the spread of Islam. Second, the areas lie in different directions, so that it is unlikely that there has been significant movement between these regions after the initial migrations out of Arabia. In general, common features should be due to common inheritance from the era of original expansion, or before. Third, areas are compared which, very roughly, are matched in size: these are Mesopotamia and the western Sudanic area. The Mesopotamian area is here limited to Iraq and the bordering area of southern Turkey (Anatolia). Iraq has an area of 169,235 square miles, while the Arabic-speaking areas of Anatolia cover only a small area. The native Arabic-speaking population in these two areas is about 11,500,000 in Iraq and 400,000 in Turkey (*Ethnologue* 2003). By the western Sudanic area, I understand the western extension of the Arabic-speaking belt beginning in Kordofan and stretching into Nigeria (Owens 1993*a*). I restrict the sample to Chad, Cameroon, and Nigeria. The total area of Chad is 499,755 square miles; Arabic is spoken as a native language only in, approximately, the southern third of the country. Pommerol (1997: 9) estimates that only 12 per cent of the population are native Arabic speakers, which would give a population of about 700,000 native speakers. It is further represented as a native language in the small finger of Cameroon separating Chad and Nigeria, and in Nigeria in about half of Bornu (69,436 square miles). Estimates for the number of native Arabic speakers in these areas vary wildly, though it is probably not more than 500,000 speakers. Arab nomads have now moved south into Adamawa State, though their extension there is not documented. In all, very approximately, the area where Arabic is spoken as a native language in WSA is perhaps 250,000 square miles and the total number of speakers just over 1,000,000.

Fourth, a minimal constraint on the choice of dialects was the availability of material covering all of the linguistic variables. Beyond this, the comparison was limited to the same number of dialect samples in each area. To have overweighted one area or the other would vitiate some of the arguments advanced in sect. 5.3. Practically these two considerations mean that relative to the number of descriptions available, the Mesopotamian area is underrepresented while the WSA is overrepresented.

I have used nine sample points for Mesopotamia (see sect. 5.2.2.1) and nine for WSA (see sect. 5.2.2.2). This allows for a direct statistical comparability. Alternatively one could attempt to construct proportionally representative samples based on any number of parameters, such as geographical size of the two regions or total population. These would constitute alternative statistical approaches, which I will not attempt to develop here.

I have strategically added two further dialects, Uzbekistan Arabic and Shukriyya Arabic (eastern Sudan on the Atbara River). These two function as a control both in terms of defining dialect areas, and in terms of a historical interpretation of the data. For historical linguistics Uzbekistan Arabic, as will emerge, is of particular importance, as it became cut off from the rest of the Arabic-speaking world at a very early date.

5.2.2.1. *Mesopotamian area*   The Mesopotamian area was defined as a dialect area by Haim Blanc (1964). He distinguished two large dialect groupings, dubbing them the qəltu group (here *qultu*) and the gələt (here *gilit*). *Qultu/gilit* means 'I said', and represents a form in which the characteristic differences between the two, /q/ vs. /g/ and -tu vs. -t for the 1SG perfect verb suffix, are found in a short, common word.

The Mesopotamian area, thanks in large part to the work of Otto Jastrow and his associates, is one of the better-described Arabic dialect areas, at least as far as the *qultu* dialects go. A recent work (Talay 1999: 15) divides the *qultu* dialects into four groups, the Anatolian, the Kurdistan, the Tigris, and the Euphrates groups. These are essentially geographically based, but serve for present purposes as an orientation. The current sample has three members of the Anatolian group, Daragözü (= Kozluk group, Jastrow 1973), Siirt (Jastrow 1978), and Mardin (Sasse 1971). The Anatolian group is itself quite differentiated dialectically (Jastrow 1978: ch. 1), and the three dialects used here are all members of different, parallel groups. The sample has two members of the Euphrates group (Hiit and Khaweetna, Khan 1997, and Talay 1999, respectively) and two of the Tigris group (Christian and Jewish Baghdadi, Blanc 1964; Abu Haidar 1991). The *gilit* dialects are under-represented, both in this sample and in the literature in general. I have used the Muslim dialect of Baghdad (Blanc 1964, Malaika 1959), and the southern Mesopotamian dialect as described especially by Ingham (1976, 1982) and Q. Mahdi (1985).

Blanc's summary of the introduction of these two dialects into Iraq is still relevant today (1964: 169). The ancestors of *qultu* speakers constituted the first major wave of Arab expansion into Mesopotamia, beginning in the seventh century. Beginning in the tenth century, in the face of a breakdown of centralized government control, Iraq began increasingly to be settled by nomadic groups, who, apparently are associated with the *gilit* dialect. This historical sequence of migration explains the current distribution of dialects in contemporary Iraq: a later spread of *gilit*-speakers (1) populated previously uninhabited rural areas, (2) probably assimilated many *qultu* dialects, and (3) fragmented the *qultu*-speaking areas. *Qultu*-speaking islands in northern Iraq and Anatolia, usually urban-based, would have been left unaffected by this later migration, though it is clear that a *gilit*-variety has become established as an Iraqi lingua franca which in Iraq at least continues to spread into *qultu* dialects (see 5.8.4). I should note that while in Iraq the *qultu* dialects may be regarded as the older of the two, this does not imply that *qultu* dialects are, in terms of the global history of Arabic, older than the *gilit*. They are simply older in this area.

5.2.2.2. *Western Sudanic Arabic*   The western Sudanic area is much more sparsely described, and some of the literature available is problematic in its interpretation. Two works of high quality are Roth (1979, also 1972) for Abbeche Arabic and Zeltner and Tourneux (1986) for a dialect spoken either in far western Chad or in Cameroon. The authors are not explicit on the point, though they note that the phonology of the dialect they describe (identified by tribe, *wulaad Ɂeeli*, not place) is identical to that of Zeltner and Fournier (1971). This was a description of a Cameroonian Arabic dialect.[2] Beyond these two, I have relied on my own data. This consists of a wide range of samples from Nigerian Arabic, as well as specifically elicited information from speakers from Chad. For Nigeria, I exclusively use samples from villages. The largest conglomeration of Arabic speakers is found in Maiduguri, a city of 500,000 inhabitants, with perhaps 50,000 native Arabic speakers. They come from different dialectal backgrounds, however, so it is not possible to speak of a characteristic Arabic dialect of Maiduguri (see Owens 1999 for sociolinguistic basis of this situation). From Nigeria, I use the village of Kirenawa, located on the southwest side of Lake Chad. Lake Chad expands and contracts, and whereas as late as the 1970s Kirenawa was on the lake, today it is well inland. A second Nigerian village is Mada. While this is less than 100 kilometers away, it lies in what I term the northern Bagirmi dialect area, quite distinct linguistically in certain ways from Kirenawa. The final village is Aajiri, near the town of Banki which lies on the border between Nigeria and Cameroon. It is taken as a representative of the southern Bagirmi area. To these five samples I added four from Chad via elicitation. Two of these were gathered at the border town of Banki, which has a large cattle market every Wednesday and Thursday. Most of the cattle sold there are driven across Chad, through Cameroon to Banki over a period of one to three months, and sold to cattle dealers who transport the cattle via truck to southern Nigeria. Speakers of various Chadian dialects can therefore be found there on any

---

[2] The epicenter of the Uleed Eeli tribe is located on either side of the Chari River, which separates Cameroon from Chad. One work which I explicitly do not use is Abu-Absi (1995). Though published recently, it is an antiquated work based on the author's work with Chadians in the USA some thirty years ago. The bibliography cites no works after 1984. The grammar itself deviates in many points from better descriptions, and it is not clear exactly what variety it describes.

market day, speakers whose home is Chad. The speakers presented here are one from Atia (Atia I), and one a nomad born south of Umm Hajar who lives nomadically between Umm Hajar and Am Timan. Two other interviews were conducted in Maiduguri, again from speakers who had recently arrived from Chad. One of these is from Am Timan, the other a nomad from outside Atia (Atia II, see Map 3).

It may be noted that Arabic was introduced into the western Sudanic region in the late fourteenth century by nomads who, at the behest of the Mameluke rulers, spread out of Upper Egypt. It is, however, noteworthy, that although there are clear and specific isoglosses linking WSA Arabic and that of Upper Egypt, it is impossible to establish a dialectal link in any detail with any single dialect or dialect region of Egypt.

5.2.2.3. *Uzbekistan and Shukriyya*   Finally, two further dialects have been included in the comparison. One is Shukriyya Arabic spoken in the eastern Sudan along the Atbara River (Reichmuth 1983) and the other Uzbekistan 'Arabic', as described in the village of Jogari, near Bukhara to the northeast (see Fischer 1961; Versteegh 1984*b*; Dereli 1999; Zimmermann 2002). There exist, unfortunately, no detailed dialect surveys of Uzbekistan Arabic. What information exists points to considerable dialect variability. It is therefore important to bear in mind that what is used here is the Uzbekistan Arabic of one village, Jogari (also 'Jugari' and 'Djogari').

Arabs began settling in Uzbekistan in the early eighth century in the wake of their conquest of Transoxiana, the area north of the Oxus river in contemporary Turkmenistan and Uzbekistan. When Arab speakers in this region became cut off from the main Arabic-speaking regions is an important, though so far as I know, unanswered question.[3] Barthold (1962) writes that in Bukhara, Arabic had ceased to be the official language as early as the beginning of the tenth century and that by this time the houses in the original Arab quarter of the city were in ruins. Uzbekistan Arabic itself has undergone such drastic influence in some grammatical domains, such as syntax, that a case can be made for viewing it typologically as a mixed language (Owens 2001*b*). There are thus various prima facie pieces of evidence arguing for a very early isolation from the Arabic-speaking world. As Jastrow (1998) notes,

---

[3] A question whose answer is not helped by fictionalized history, such as the story popular in Uzbekistan that the Arabs of Uzbekistan are the progeny of Arabs exiled from Damascus by Tamerlane in the fourteenth century. Jastrow (1998: 179 n. 11) is appropriately sceptical of Spuler's (1952: 244) suggestion that the present-day Arabic-speaking population of Uzbekistan does not trace its ultimate historical roots to the seventh and eighth centuries. The linguistic evidence, as presented in this chapter, argues strongly for the thesis.

this very isolation makes Uzbekistan an interesting source for divining the form of early Arabic. The status of Uzbekistan Arabic plays a major role in the discussion and argumentation in Ch. 5.

For Shukriyya Arabic, there are no reliable historical accounts for when the ancestors of the Shukriyya Arabs left Upper Egypt for the Sudan or when they settled in their current location. Reichmuth (1983: 2) suggests that they have been there at least since 1800. At the same time, he concludes (29) that no direct relation with an extant Egyptian Arabic dialect is discernible, though many similarities are found with various varieties in Egypt.[4] This is similar to the situation with the relation between the WSA area and Egypt (Owens 1993a, 2003), and it may be that my conclusions for the WSA area are extendable to the Shukriyya area as well: the WSA and Shukriyya dialects, and indeed the Arabic dialects of the Sudanic region in general, filtered into the region via Egypt. Their Arabic, therefore reflects earlier forms found in Upper Egypt, some of which have since disappeared in this homeland region, as well as innovations and mixtures which arose via contact in the Sudanic region itself.

5.2.3. *Procedure*

Each linguistic variable was given as many values as it has realizations in the data. The variable 1SG perfect verb suffix, for instance, has two values, either-*tu*, as in *qəl-tu* 'I said' (e.g. Christian Baghdad) or-*t*, *gil-it* (Muslim Baghdad). These two values were arbitrarily (see sect. 5.7.1 below) given the values '1' and '2'. The variable 1SG perfect suffix implies only the contrast–*tu* vs.–*t*. Other aspects of variation relating to this suffix, for instance whether an epenthetic vowel is inserted before the- *t* (as in the *gilit* dialect), or whether the 1SG suffix has the alternative morpho-phonological realization of Ø, as in Kirenawa (*gul* 'I said'), are coded in other variables, since they are accounted for by different rules (see discussion in sects. 5.8.2, 5.8.6). The number of variants range between 2 (as here) and 5 (for the realization of *ð*).

Simple sets of statistics were produced (using SPSS) by aggregating the individual values according to variable and according to dialect groupings of different kinds.

---

[4] De Jong (2002: 358) considers the 'Ababda, a group which lives to the north of the Shukriyya and extend into southern Egypt, to be a northern extension of the Shukriyya, influenced, however, by Upper Egyptian Arabic. He does not discuss the question whether the similarities to Upper Egyptian Arabic are due to later contact, or whether the group is a missing link of sorts between Egyptian and Sudanese Arabic.

5.2.4. Inheritance and independent change

There are many methodological and interpretive issues relating to individual variables, so many in fact that I have summarized the major issues in sects. 5.7 and 5.8, after the presentation of the main findings and arguments. There is one interpretive issue which I think should be discussed before the statistical findings are presented, however. A core issue in addressing a question in historical linguistics is whether similar or identical forms in related varieties (be they languages or dialects) are similar because of inheritance or because of chance change. This is a question with no all-encompassing answer, though for some linguistic variables the answer is easier than for others. For instance, throughout the WSA area is found a rule (simplifying matters somewhat) deleting the suffix -*t* of the 1 or 2MSG perfect verb, after C- and not before a -V (see (1) in sect. 1.4. This produces paradigmatic contrasts such as the following:

(1) *gul* 'you said'   vs. *maʃee-t* 'you went'
    ka'tab 'I, you wrote'   vs. *ka'tab-t-a* 'you wrote it.M'
    ka'tab maktuub 'I/you wrote a letter' vs. *ka'tab-t al-maktuub* 'I/you wrote the letter'[5]

This rule is found in all nine WSA dialects sampled. It is so unique among Arabic dialects (and indeed, when looked at in detail, rather odd in general linguistic terms) that it is safe to say that it originated only once before the ancestral speakers of WSA spread out over their current distribution. In cases such as these, I would surmise that the innovation took place in Upper Egypt, before the spread of Arabs into the WSA area. The alternative, that it originated independently in the different dialects of this region, and only in these, may be discarded. Innovations such as these I term historically contingent ones, as they occurred at one point in history, and did not repeat themselves.

At the other extreme is a feature such as loss of emphatic consonants. This is found in Uzbekistan, and in some Chadian dialects (e.g. Abbeche). There are two indications that these developments are independent events. First, the loss is not a general one in the WSA area. Nigeria has emphasis, for instance, so the Abbeche development is, probably, a specific one even in the WSA area. Second, in both areas there has been a great deal of contact between the original Arab-speaking populations and non-Arab speakers, speakers of languages without emphatic consonants.[6] Emphasis is a feature

---

[5] The *al-* of the direct object licenses the -*t* in the second example; its absence in the DO requires the t-less form in the first.

[6] In Uzbekistan, for instance, Tajik and Uzbek; in Abbeche Maba.

which could well have been lost in the course of second language learning. This latter point, of course, has to be read as one establishing a plausible, though not a necessary cause. Uzbekistan Arabic has *not* lost its pharyngeal consonants, which are structurally comparable to the emphatics in their typological rarity, and there are many dialects in the WSA area which have maintained emphatics, even though, it may be assumed, in these there has been a good deal of assimilation of originally non-Arabic speakers.[7]

Even ostensibly clear cases can become problematic in a broader comparative perspective. I would assume that the loss of pharyngeals in a number of WSA sample points, for instance, is a region-specific development. However, the WSA shares with the Tihama (Yemen, Saudi Arabia coastal area) the change ʕ → ʔ (Tihama maintains ħ, however), so it cannot be ruled out with complete certainty that the change in the WSA is partly ancestral.

Even more problematic are those cases in which changes may be due to one factor in one context, to another in another. For instance, WSA, in agreement in this case with the entire Sudanic region, for most lexemes has the change *ð → ḍ, ðahab → ḍahab 'gold'. As this is attested only in the Sudanic region, and as it is historically contingent, it may be assumed that it is the result of an innovation in the pre-WSA diasporic population in Upper Egypt. Elsewhere in the present data ð may remain ð (Mesopotamian *gilit*), may become fricative z (Daragözü, Uzbekistan), v (Siirt), or may become d (Jewish Baghdadi = JB, Christian Baghdadi = CB, Uzbekistan). The changes to d and z are also attested elsewhere (e.g. often d in North Africa). The widespread d value of this variable could thus have arisen by independent ð → d changes. In this perspective, reflexes of original *ð could be explained in terms of a single change in the case of the reflex in the WSA area, but as independent developments in the case of North Africa and the *qultu* dialects.

In other cases, changes which could plausibly be regarded as due to independent innovation, when looked at in a broader perspective, probably are not. A case in point is the deletion of the initial -h from the object pronouns after a consonant -ha 'hers', -hum 'their.M', and -hin 'their.F (see feature Ap 2.2.66 and sect. 8.6.4 for detailed discussion). Often in Arabic dialects word final -h is lost (cf. the word for 'face' Cairene wiʃ, Mardin wəcc, Nigerian wic, etc. <wujh), so one could argue that the current change is a specific instance of a more general one. Nonetheless, it is striking that among Arabic dialects this particular variant in the object pronouns is concentrated

---

[7] The realization of ṭ as ɗ in a number of WSA dialects, for instance, may best be explained as a combination of Fulfulde implosive ɗ with the emphasis of ṭ. The Fulani and Arabs have been in close contact for hundreds of years in the region.

in two areas, namely among the *qultu* dialects of Mesopotamia and parts of Syria and in the Sudanic area. Moreover, wherever it occurs, underlying stress rules are not affected. Thus in Nigerian Arabic, *'faham-a* 'he understood it.M' is distinguished by stress from *fa'ham-a* 'he understood it.F' < *fa'ham-ha* with normal stress assignment to the first heavy syllable from the end of the word. The phenomenon is little attested, at least in the prevailing literature, in the Arabian peninsula[8] and North Africa, for instance. In this case if one argues that it is natural development, one has to answer why it is so little attested in the majority of dialects. I take this to be an argument for the historical contingency of the development.

The rest of this section will be devoted to a discussion of the origin of the similarities and differences used in sect. 5.3. In my judgment most of the forty-nine variables which I treat represent historically contingent events. That is, if they are attested in two different dialects it is evidence of a common origin in respect of this one feature. The few features which I think more likely due to independent development are, with areas from the present sample where they are attested:

(2) Variables whose common values may be due to independent innovation
Loss of emphasis (Abbeche, Uzbekistan)
Loss of pharyngeals ħ/ʕ (WSA)
Loss of feminine plural (Abbeche, most *qultu* dialects).

Two which may be due in some cases to independent development, in others to a single historical event are:

(3)
*ð̣ → ḍ (Sudanic area)
Some cases of ð → d/z (Uzbekistan, some *qultu* dialects)
θ → t (non-Bagirmi WSA, some *qultu* dialects).

It is probably of significance that four of the five features in (2) and (3) are phonological. A reader for Oxford University Press points out that similar developments occur in other Semitic languages. Akkadian, Modern Hebrew, and Ethio-Semitic for instance, all attest the loss of pharyngeals, strengthening the case for independent development. Invoking Hetzron again (1976b, see ch. 3), one may view morphological cognation as having greater weight for purposes of comparative reconstruction, since such cognation implies both phonological and arbitrary semantic relationship. As will be seen, morphological cognation is well attested in the current sample.

---

[8] Occasionally in southern Gulf Arabic and in a few areas in Yemen; Behnstedt 1985: 87.

One might want to exclude these features from any consideration of historical relationship (see sect. 5.4.4 below). Doing so, however, does not materially affect the present conclusions.

5.2.5. Describing the variables in plain language

It is the logic of the comparative method that a reconstructed proto-Arabic is needed to 'explain' developments observed in contemporary Arabic dialects. Such a proto-Arabic entity does not yet exist, however, at least not in adequate detail. Nonetheless, statements have to be made about related forms in different dialects, for instance the form *CaCiiC*, as in Chadian Arabic *kabiir* 'big', Hiit *kbiir*, and Muslim Baghdadi *cibiir*. Lacking a reconstructed proto-form, and not wanting to conjure up such on the spur of the moment,[9] a methodologically neutral convention is needed to say that one is talking about reflexes of the same assumed proto-form in all three cases, even if the proto-form itself is not necessarily available. Conventionally, therefore, it is assumed that in cognate sets, as here, a proto-form is reconstructible. While cognate sets are the basic unit of comparison, transposing the description into plain English sometimes entails formulations which can be understood as assuming a particular proto-form. The form *kabiir*, for instance, might be said to 'maintain' the vowel /a/, *kbiir* to delete it. This manner of description appears to imply that *kabiir* is retentive, *kbiir* innovative. Lacking explicit reconstruction, however, there is nothing to say that the /a/ of *kabiir* hasn't been inserted in original **kbiir*.

As will be seen, little in the argumentation depends on assumptions about which forms, if any, are identical to a possible proto-form, and where the issue of proto-forms is crucial, as in sect. 5.4, their relevance will be explicitly spelled out. In the meantime, the formulation used to describe the variants of individual variables will be descriptively clear, without necessarily being descriptively pure from a historical linguistic perspective.

5.3. Statistical Results and their Meaning

The basic results are first presented in tables. Table 5.1 gives the range of standard deviations (SDs) and the means for the forty-nine variables. The means and SDs are calculated as follows. First, the mean is calculated for each of the forty-nine variables individually. The individual means and SDs are then aggregated and divided by the total forty-nine so that an overall mean/

---

[9] Certainly the form *kbiir* is to be seen as innovative relative to proto-Arabic.

TABLE 5.1. Means and standard deviations for 49 variables

	Mean	Mean of aggregated SDs of individual variables
WSA	1.68	.15
Mesopotamia	1.58	.39
Uzbekistan	1.46	
Shukriyya	1.38	

SD is obtained. Since Uzbekistan and Shukriyya have a single value, they have no standard deviation.

The important statistic in Table 5.1 is the means of the aggregated standard deviations. It is clear here that WSA with a lower mean of SD is a far more compact, less variable dialect than Mesopotamia. According to the measures here, it is more of a coherent dialect than is Mesopotamia. The standard deviation is a more telling statistic here than the mean, since it would not change, even if the values of individual variables were changed around. For instance, *k is given a value of '1', *c of '2'. Reversing these values so that *k = '2' and *c = '1' would not alter the fact that WSA has no deviation at all in this variable. In the current coding system it is uniformally '1', therefore an SD = 0; if the values were reversed it would be categorically '2', with an SD of 0.[10]

In Table 5.2, all forty-nine variables are combined into one super variable by summing the standard deviations. In these terms it may be said that the variation in WSA is less than half that of Mesopotamian Arabic, for the features treated.

Table 5.3 repeats Table 5.1 except that the features are divided into phonological (N = 25) and morphological (N = 24) classes.

These statistics show that phonology and morphology contribute approximately equally to the differences between WSA and Mesopotomia. In particular, the considerably larger SD of Mesopotamian Arabic found when all

TABLE 5.2. Sum of standard deviations

WSA	7.9
Mesopotamia	19.7

[10] For information, thirty-three of the forty-nine variables are bivalued. Of the remaining sixteen, one has 5 values, four have 4, and eleven have 3. Of the sixteen multi-valued variables, as far as WSA goes, ten have the same value (hence an SD of 0).

TABLE 5.3. Means and standard deviations for 49 variables, phonology and morphology

	Phonology		Morphology	
	Mean	Standard deviation	Mean	Standard deviation
WSA	1.72	.21	1.70	.10
Mesopotamia	1.62	.45	1.54	.33
Uzbekistan	1.58		1.34	
Shukriyya	1.40		1.35	

features are classed together reappears in the phonological and morphological subcomponents.

The next two tables are relevant to the discussion in sect. 5.4. In these the WSA and Mesopotamia dialect areas are compared to two specific dialects, the Shukriyya in the eastern Sudan and Uzbekistan. As these are represented by a single variant they themselves have no standard deviation. For these statistics, in Table 5.4 I have compared the value of a given feature of the Shukriyya or Uzbekistan dialect to the mean of the WSA and Mesopotamian ones, and noted to which mean it is nearer. For instance, for variable 45 (Ap 2.2.45), insertion of a long -aa- before a verbal pronominal object suffix (*katab-aa-ha* 'he wrote it', '1' = no insertion of *aa*, '2' = insertion), WSA has a value of 1.62, all other areas a value of '1' (i.e. uniformly no insertion). In terms of this feature, Shukriyya and Uzbekistan are considered closer to Mesopotamia than they are to WSA. According to Table 5.4, individual features of WSA/Mesopotamia in the sample are about evenly split as regards to their relative proximity to Uzbekistan and Shukriyya.

Without presenting the statistics here, it can also be noted that dividing the features between phonology and morphology yields a similar division as in Table 5.4, analogous to the difference between Tables 5.1 and 5.3.

Table 5.5 looks at the same data from a similar perspective as Table 5.4. A count is made comparing how many times the WSA and Mesopotamian

TABLE 5.4. Number of variables for which the means of WSA or Mesopotamia are closer to Uzbekistan/Shukriyya

	Closer to WSA	Closer to Mesopotamia	
Uzbekistan	24	22	3 ties
Shukriyya	26	20	3 ties

TABLE 5.5. Identical means, WSA and Mesopotamia compared to Uzbekistan, Shukriyya

	WSA	Mesopotamia
Uzbekistan	19	13
Shukriyya	22	14

dialect areas have exactly the same score (same mean value implying same linguistic value) as Uzbekistan and Shukriyya. The mean score used in Table 5.4 is subject to technical interpretive problems discussed in sect. 5.8, problems which Table 5.5 circumvents simply by counting only values which are identical. For instance, variable 12, absence/presence of word-internal *imala* (WSA = 1.00, Mesopotamia = 1.63, Uzbekistan = 1.00, Shukriyya = 1.00) is counted as being identical for WSA, Uzbekistan, and Shukriyya.

These two tables show that looking beyond the WSA and Mesopotamian borders for longer-range relatives, geographical proximity by no means guarantees structural similarity. Uzbekistan in particular is quite close to WSA, in terms of the identical means measure (Table 5.5). In terms of the similar means criterion, Shukriyya and Mesopotamia are as close to each other as are Uzbekistan and Mesopotamia.

The final table of statistics dismantles the Mesopotamian dialects into component parts. The justification for this is that, as seen above, the area is quite diverse. It stands to reason that this diversity would reduce in its constituent groups. The subgroups used here follow traditional ones in Mesopotamian dialectology: Anatolian *qultu* dialects (N = 3), non-Baghdad *qultu* dialects (N = 2), Baghdad *qultu* dialects (N = 2), and *gilit* dialects (N = 2). The present classification is based on reigning dialectological classification. The dialects or dialect groupings are arranged in order of increasing means. Groups with only one member have no standard deviation.

Table 5.6 has surprises of a number of types. From a purely statistical perspective, WSA remains a strikingly coherent dialect area (has a low SD), even though it has more than three times as many members as any other group on this list and covers a much wider geographical area. It has, for instance, a lower SD than the three Anatolian *qultu* dialects.

A more important point for present purposes is the coherency of the dialect areas as represented by the ranking of means. The *qultu* dialects of Mesopotamia are split in two, as it were, not by the *gilit* dialects of Mesopotamia but by Shukriyya and Uzbekistan Arabic. The Anatolian *qultu* dialects are closer

TABLE 5.6. Mesopotamian subdialects

Dialect or subdialect area	Mean	Mean of SDs (where applicable)
Non-Baghdad *qultu* (N = 2)	1.31	.12
Baghdad *qultu* (N = 2)	1.38	.06
Shukriyya	1.38	
Uzbekistan	1.46	
Gilit (N = 2)	1.51	.11
Anatolia *qultu* (N = 3)	1.61	.21
WSA (N = 9)	1.68	.15

to WSA than they are to the other Mesopotamian subdialects. Uzbekistan Arabic falls close to the middle of the entire range of mean values.

The main 'problem' which emerges from this statistical summary presented in Tables 5.1–5.6 resides in the Mesopotamian dialects. They are extremely splintered, and are, under the premises set out in this study, often as or more similar to dialects geographically far removed as they are to each other. Why should this be so? As a linguistic problem the answer will reside in a complex of causes: change through language contact, lack of change due to linguistic isolation and other causes, independent innovation, and, as a post-Islamic era diasporic variety, characteristics of the founding dialects. It is this last, historical component which I will concentrate on in greatest detail. I touch on other questions in summary fashion in sect. 5.6 below.

At this point it is relevant to suggest an initial historical hypothesis centered on the two dialects which are geographically most removed from each other, Uzbekistan and the western Sudanic area. Because of the immense distance, both spatial and diachronic, separating the two areas, focusing the issue on these two dialects brings to the foreground the importance of historical explanations in accounting for similarities, should they be significant.

> The statistical similarities between Uzbekistan Arabic and WSA Arabic are due to a common pre-diasporic ancestor, located probably on the Arabian pensinsula.

This hypothesis can be met with scepticism, as it has been stated without detailed discussion of the linguistic variables themselves. There are two initial answers to this. First, the logic of the method does indeed depend on numbers for developing hypotheses and the numbers are only as reliable as the coding system and statistical test used. As far as the coding system goes, the last third of this chapter is devoted to explication of the system I used. The statistics in fact are quite basic; I eschew the use of more advanced techniques until the basic approach is tested and the data base is expanded, however. Given these caveats, the hypothesis is commensurate with what little is known about the social and linguistic identity of the expanding Arabic groups. It is historically plausible in that populations of Arabs are known to have moved into both Uzbekistan and Egypt, in some cases both via the Syrian desert. In the early eighth century, for instance 'Qaysites' are reported to have been settled in Upper Egypt by the Umayyad rulers (Lewis 1970: 176). Qays is also a tribe reported among the soldiers of Qutayba ibn Muslim, the conqueror of Transoxiana (Agha 1999: 217). Of course, the Egyptian migration is, for the WSA area, a preliminary stopping point.[11]

It is not provable from the written sources at our disposal whether it was the same populations which split, one moving in one direction, one moving in the other. However, it is precisely a strength of comparative linguistics that language can be used to elucidate earlier migrations. Unless the high degree of similarity is due to chance independent development, it has to be assumed that the similar contemporary populations must at some time have shared a common ancestor.

As a second answer, I would argue that the use of statistics provides a necessary antidote to the prevailing tendency over the last sixty years for Arabic historical linguistics have worked with very general categories such as 'Neo-Arabic' or 'Mesopotamian Arabic'. The advantage of using statistics is that indices consist ultimately of individual cases and variables. While what comes out in the end is a single number, the number itself is dependent on individual, well-defined component parts. When the statistics quantitatively suggest a relation between two units, it is a relation defined across a range of variables.

At the same time, while the statistics may be suggestive of significant groupings, the ultimate linguistic test for measuring historical relationship is the comparative method and reconstruction of proto-forms. The nature of the comparative historical method, however, demands a relatively painstaking

---

[11] It is extremely difficult tracing the exact tribal migrations out of the Arabian peninsula, down the Nile, and into the Sudan. It is, however, clear that elements who are usually reckoned to be part of Qays, at least in Egyptian genealogies, were part of these migrations. MacMichael (1967: 183–4) for instance, states that the Mameluke army which made a major incursion into Dongola in northern Sudan in 1286 contained, inter alia, Banu Hilal, Banu Kanz and Rabiʕa. Garcin (1976: 75) has identified these three groups as being important Qaysites who had settled in Upper Egypt. There are other tribes mentioned by name spreading in different directions. Juhayna, for instance, is eponymous for a large grouping of tribes found throughout the Sudanic region. The same tribe is mentioned spreading eastward into Iraq (Kufa) at the beginning of the Islamic conquests (Donner 1981: 228). Kufa (and Basra) served as staging areas for the subsequent conquest of Iran and Uzbekistan.

reconstruction of individual forms. One does not reconstruct a dialect or an entity such as 'Neo-Arabic' but rather individual linguistic features, which are subsequently interpreted as forming larger units, such as dialects.

It is in this spirit that in the next section I consider two linguistic variables in detail which bear on the relations between the varieties discussed in this section, in particular on the relation between Uzbekistan Arabic and that of the other regions.

5.4. Interpretations

The statistics become more interesting when the comparatively detailed coverage of the WSA and Mesopotamian areas are used as a basis of comparison for other dialects.

5.4.1. *Uzbekistan Arabic*

In recent years a certain amount of attention has been directed towards Uzbekistan Arabic, both in terms of its dialectological and historical status. Whereas this status has usually been discussed in terms of its relations to Mesopotamian Arabic, Behnstedt (2000: 145) going so far as to claim it has its origins there, I have emphasized geographically long-range associations, in particular with Nigerian Arabic (Owens 1998*a*: 72).

The statistics in Tables 5.4 and 5.5 would support both associations. However, Behnstedt's peremptory dismissal of the Nigerian connection in favor of a Mesopotamian one cannot be upheld in the face of them: Uzbekistan Arabic has more variables close to values of WSA than to Mesopotamia, and its mean values, though globally considerably closer to Mesopotamia than to WSA (Tables 5.1 and 5.3), do not align with a single Mesopotamian subgroup (Table 5.6).

An initial conclusion is that the present statistical comparison does not contradict my suggestion of a special relationship between WSA and Uzbekistan. However, the statistical summary read as pure numbers is neutral as to historical interpretation. Similarities and differences may be due to common inheritance or to shared or divergent innovations. Given that the current set does comprise fundamental phonological and morphological features, they do give a broad basis of comparison. The WSA area is testimony to this. Its relative uniformity can plausibly be related in part at least to its historical roots (see above). By the same token, the fact that the WSA area does exhibit a good number of similarities to Uzbekistan encourages a closer look at the two varieties.

Turning to this question, Behnstedt says that Uzbekistan Arabic has its *origins* in Mesopotamian Arabic. To this point I have not treated historical linguistic questions systematically, so in a sense, what I have presented and what Behnstedt asserts have no direct connection with each other. However, Behnstedt himself does not show how Uzbekistan Arabic arose from Mesopotamian, so his assumption of direct genetic affiliation is unsupported.

In making his claim, Behnstedt refers to Jastrow's work (without a specific reference, however). In fact, Jastrow (1998) does treat the relation between Uzbekistan Arabic and Mesopotamian Arabic in historical linguistic terms, and in a more differentiated and detailed way than does Behnstedt. Jastrow begins by noting that in looking for relationships between Mesopotamian Arabic and dialects outside the area, one should not consider Mesopotamian Arabic globally. Rather, he divides it into the familiar *qultu* and *gilit* dialects, and proceeds, initially at least, in the same way that data has been organized in this chapter. He draws historical inferences on the basis of contemporary distributions of variables, though with considerably fewer than in the current data set. In Table 5.7, Jastrow's data (1998: 177) is reproduced in the first three columns, representing Uzbekistan Arabic, *qultu* dialects (Q), and *gilit* dialects (G). In addition, I have added my own data from Nigerian Arabic.[12] The variables used in the comparison are copied from Jastrow. The ones identical

TABLE 5.7. Uzbekistan Arabic compared to other dialects: 7 variables

	Uz	Q	G	Nig
Imperfect endings-*iin, uun* (Ap 2.2.52):	yes	yes	yes	no
M vs. F plural (Ap 2.2.30)	yes	no	no	yes
Linker-*in**	yes	no	no	yes
2FSG-*ki* (Ap 2.2.62)	yes	yes	no	yes
internal passive*	no	no	yes	no
1SG perfect-*tu* (Ap 2.2.44)	no	yes	no	no
qaaf (Ap 2.1.1)	yes	yes	no	no
Shared traits:				
Uz – Q: 4/7				
Uz – G: 2/7				
Uz – Nig: 5/7				

* See sect. 3.4.1 for discussion of linker-*in*. The internal passive (e.g. *iktib* 'it was written' vs. *kitab* 'he wrote') in the Mesopotamian *gilit* dialects in fact is quite variable. Many dialects e.g. Muslim Baghdad and some southern Iraqi, do not have it.

[12] Except for the feminine plural which is not universal in the WSA area, I could equally have used WSA instead of Nigerian Arabic.

to those used in my statistics are identified by the variable number in my data (see sect. 5.7). I have added one variable to Jastrow's list, namely the realization of 'qaaf', as this is, traditionally, one of the constitutive variables distinguishing the *qultu* and *gilit* dialects.

Below the table I have counted how many features of similarity there are between Uzbekistan Arabic and the other varieties.

Even more strikingly than in my own data, this abbreviated list confirms that a prima facie case can be made for linking Nigerian Arabic with Uzbekistan. It furthermore confirms the heterogeneous nature of the Mesopotamian area; the *gilit* dialects in this reckoning have only two features in common with Uzbekistan Arabic.

At this point it is time to move beyond tabular listings. Methodological clarification is needed, however. For Jastrow, Table 5.7 is not so much a taxonomic listing as a statement about historical relation. He says that his list is based on 'old characteristics' ('altertumliche Merkmale'). The idea appears to be that the variables listed in the comparison represent features going back to Old Arabic or proto-Arabic (see below), or at least, to a stage of Arabic before certain innovations occurred in the Mesopotamian dialect area.

As it stands, however, Table 5.7 is no more a statement of historical relations than are the forty-nine variables in my data. Lacking an explicit demonstration of which features on the list are old or proto-forms there runs the danger of claiming or assuming one feature to be older than another in a comparative linguistic sense, while in fact there is no linguistic basis for the assumption. A case in point pertains to a further element in Jastrow's presentation.

5.4.2. *What is not attested in writing is not necessarily non-existent*

As I noted, the statistics in sect. 5.3 are useful as general direction markers. Shared features which are relatively rare are a valuable diagnostic for establishing historical relationship. Thus, the fact that (1) above is shared among all WSA dialects is significant not only for its limitation to the WSA area, but also in its status as a morphologically unusual linguistic feature. Such unusual events are unlikely to be produced more than once.

Interesting in the present context is a feature shared between Uzbekistan Arabic and some WSA dialects (the Bagirmi dialects) whose chance of independent origin is quite small.[13]

Roughly speaking, in Arabic dialects there are three forms of an active participle with pronominal object suffixes. The three different forms are

---

[13] The feature was not included in the sample as for a number of the dialects data is missing in the sources used.

contrastive in the FSG. In all varieties the non-suffixal feminine takes the regular FSG adjectival suffix -*a* or -*e*, the vowel quality depending on harmony rules, if any, prevailing in the local dialect.

Turning to the object suffix forms, in one widespread alternative (e.g. Cairene, non-Bagirmi WSA dialects) the object suffix is suffixed to the F. participle form marked by -*ee*, or -*aa*, which otherwise is the FSG adjectival marker (see (4a)). In a second, when a pronominal object suffix is added to a feminine form the feminine participle takes the morpho-phonological alternative -*it*, otherwise used in a genitive construction (see (4b)). This is found for instance in eastern Libyan Arabic and in many Arabian peninsula dialects. The third alternative is to add an intrusive suffix -*in*- or -*inn*- on either the MSG or FSG form whenever a pronominal object suffix is added, as in (4c), using Bagirmi Arabic forms as examples in column (4c).

(4)   a   b   c
MSG   *kaatib-ha*   *kaatib-ha*   *kaatb-in-he* 'he has written it.F'
FSG   *kaatb-ee- ha* *kaatb-it-ta* *kaatb-in-he* 'she has written it.F'

The third alternative (4c) is by far the least common. It is found only in relatively small, isolated areas, so far reported only in Oman and western Hadramaut, Bahrain (among Shia Baharna), the Emirates (Holes 1990: 48, 58, 219), Uzbekistan, Khorasan (Seeger 2002: 635), and Bagirmi Arabic in the WSA area. There are differences between its form and use in these areas. In Uzbekistan Arabic the first person pronominal object suffix added to an active participle marks the subject of the sentence, as in (5) (see sect. 8.7.5).

(5a) *zorb-in-naa-kum*
     hit-IN-we-you.MPL
     'we have hit you'.

In all other areas only one pronominal object is allowed, and it marks the object. In Oman the intrusive -*in* is suffixed to the gender/number markers of the participle,

(5b) *ḏaarb-it-n-iʃ*
     hit-F-IN-you.FSG
     'she has hit you.F'
     ḏaarb-aat-inn-iʃ
     hit-FPL-IN-you.FSG
     'they.F have hit you.F' (etc., Reinhardt 1972 (1894): 139).

In Bagirmi the intrusive -*in* is suffixed directly to the participle stem, thereby neutralizing gender and number contrasts, (*hi*) *ḏaarb-in-he* '(she) has hit her', identical to masculine, *hu ḍaarb-in-he* '(he) has hit her'. Apparently with first and second person subjects, number and gender differences of the participle stem are neutralized in Uzbekistan Arabic as well (cf. (5a) above, where the plural suffix *-iin* would be expected), and in Dathina northeast of Aden, de Landberg (1909: 723) reports that a feminine subject is usually used with the masculine participle, not with the feminine form when an *–in* + object is added. In Bahrain Shia *-in* is added only to a singular participle (either to the M or F form). It may also be noted that in many Sudanic dialects outside of the Bagirmi area, an intrusive *-in* is added to the active participle feminine plural form, as in Shukriyya *ḍaarb-aat-ann-u* 'they.F have hit him' or Kirenawa *ḍaarb-aat-inn-a* (same meaning). I assume a common (as yet, unexplained) origin for this latter feature.

What is important for present purposes is the observation that it is unlikely that so unusual and specific a feature as the intrusive *-in* could have originated independently in four or five geographically separated areas. Formally it is similar or identical in these areas, and in some of them gender/number differences are neutralized through its insertion. It is plausible to think in terms of common place of origin, with the present-day geographical distributions being accounted for by migration out of this place of origin. Following Retsö (1988: 88, see Barth 1910/1972: 1–18 for original discussion), a common origin, however, could only be somewhere on the Arabian peninsula, so far as the present-day evidence allows us to deduce, on the eastern and northeastern littoral, and it would have had to have been pre-diasporic. Pre-diasporic Arabic, however, is contemporary with what I have termed Old Arabic. To my knowledge, the intrusive *-in* is mentioned nowhere in Old Arabic, either by a grammarian or in a Koranic reading tradition. It does not exist as a written, attested form. Nor can it be derived via grammatical rule from an Old Arabic form or forms, as Retsö (1988) against various suggestions demonstrates. Yet simple principles of reconstruction, as briefly described here, require its presence as a proto-form in the seventh or eighth century. It is a contemporary of all varieties mentioned in early written sources. Clearly then, Old Arabic as described in old sources does not exhaustively describe the forms of Arabic which were spoken during this era. The comparative method based inter alia on a consideration of modern dialects, forces us to reconstruct further forms into the era.[14] This is illustrated on Map 4, where the modern attestations of the intrusive *-in* on the participle, force the reconstruction in pre-diasporic Arabic, probably on the Arabian peninsula.

---

[14] Note that the same argument was applied in sect. 3.4.1 in the interpretation that the linker *-n* of modern dialects does not derive from the Old Arabic indefinite *tanwiyn*.

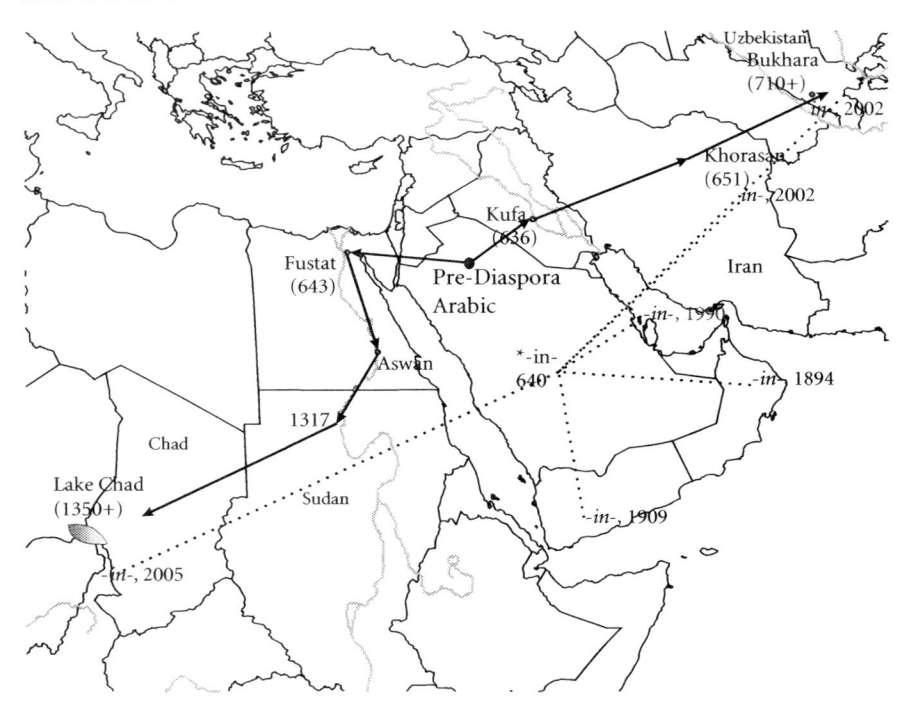

MAP 4. Reconstruction based on modern dialects of pre-diasporic *-in in participal forms

On the map, the year of most recent attestation for each dialect is noted, as well as the dates of settlement and and/or first intrusion of Arabic speakers to the areas where the -in forms are attested.

5.4.3. New is not new until proven new

Jastrow seeks to demonstrate that the Mesopotamian *qultu* dialects have collectively undergone certain innovations. This explains why Mesopotamian *qultu* dialects differ in certain respects from Uzbekistan Arabic: whereas Uzbekistan Arabic has retained archaic features, the *qultu* dialects in their post-diasporic phase innovated.

A case in point is the phenomenon of *imala* (Ap 2.1.12). *Imala* will be treated in much greater detail in Ch. 7, so here I will be very brief. *Imala* is a type of vowel harmony or assimilation, where a long *aa* changes to *ie* or *ee* in the presence of an *i* in a neighboring syllable. Though rare by the standards of contemporary Arabic dialectology, it was apparently at an earlier era a highly salient phenomenon.

Imala is one of the features Jastrow cites as representing a post-diasporic innovation characteristic of the Mesopotamian *qultu* dialects. He uses this observation to argue that 'Uzbekistan Arabic did not participate in either of the waves of innovation of the two [dialects, i.e. *qultu/gilit*]; it displays the innovations of neither the *qultu* nor the *gilit* dialects'.

Imala, however, is not a post-diasporic innovation and therefore the *qultu* dialects cannot be said to have innovated the feature. This can be seen on two counts. First, *imala* is described in great detail in the oldest detailed source which exists for Classical Arabic, Sibawaih's *Kitaab* (II: 279–94). Imala in the Old Arabic classical tradition is, moreover, at least a generation older than Sibawaih. In the *Qiraaʔaat* literature of Ibn Mujahid (146–52) we find in particular that Kisaʔi (Sibawaih's contemporary) and Abu ʕAmr Ibn ʕAlaaʔ (d. 154/770, see Ch. 4) were two readers who used *imala* regularly.[15] Ibn Mujahid summarizes the *Qurʔaan* recitation practices of seven readers, the earliest of whom Ibn ʕAamir (d. 118/736) lived in the first half of the eighth century. It may be assumed that *imala* was not innovative with them, but rather that they used a phonological trait whose origin is older, as yet undated in a comparative linguistic sense. Arabs began settling in Uzbekistan (Transoxiana) after 710. In terms of chronological time, therefore, *imala* is attested at a date contemporary with the Arabic settlement of Uzbekistan. For whatever reasons Uzbekistan Arabic does not have *imala*, one can be excluded, namely that *imala* did not exist at the time of the original Arab settlement of the country. It is not the case that it is only after Arabs were comfortably ensconced in Transoxiana that elsewhere in the Arabic-speaking world that *imala* emerged.

This is the first reason *imala* cannot be regarded as innovative in the *qultu* dialects. The second argument relates to the contemporary distribution of *imala* in Arabic dialects. As will be seen in Ch. 7, *imala* is found in the Mesopotamian *qultu* dialects, eastern Libyan Arabic, and Maltese, and was well attested in Andalusian Arabic. The distribution of the same phenomenon in such widely separated areas points to a single common point of origin. The simplest explanation is that *imala* of the present-day dialects originated in pre-diasporic Arabia, and spread from there in different directions. This indicates a pre-diasporic origin, i.e. one which can be reconstructed no later than the seventh century.

The comparative dating of *imala* impinges on the present discussion in the following way. Jastrow has argued that Uzbekistan Arabic is in some sense

---

[15] Ibn Kathiyr, Naafiʕ, Hamza, Ibn ʕAamir, and ʕAaṣim on the other hand frequently are mentioned as those who do not generally use *imala*, though all may use it on occasion, e.g. p. 151 of the Kufan reader Hamza is said to use *imala* in *ʔamaata* (*ʔamieta*) 'who granted death' (53: 44), stronger even than that of Naafiʕ and Abu ʕAmr (*ʔaʃadd min ʔimaalat ʔabiy ʕAmr wa Naafiʕ*).

older than the *qultu* and *gilit* dialects of Iraq in that it has innovations not found in Uzbekistan. Looking closely at how this one 'innovation' is characterized, however, shows that *imala* is a variable which in fact cannot be used to establish the relative age of Uzbekistan vs. Mesopotamian *qultu* Arabic, since *imala* can be reconstructed into pre-diasporic Arabic. The crucial point is a methodological one. Whereas Jastrow interprets the list in Table 5.7 in terms of historical change, without an unequivocal standard by which to measure the change, no historical linguistic interpretation is possible.

To conclude this section, the fact that in the present sample the *gilit* dialects, Uzbekistan and WSA, have no *imala* would constitute one small indication of very old affiliation between these varieties, despite the great geographical distance separating them. Note that in this respect Uzbekistan Arabic stands no closer to the *gilit* dialects than it does to WSA.

5.4.4. Innovations and retentions: western Sudanic Arabic?

The detailed case studies from the previous two sections serve as models for a broader interpretation of Arabic linguistic history. Both of them point to forms prevalent in peninsular Arabic in pre-diasporic times, and both point to a relatively profound dialect differentiation present at that early era. *Imala* and non-*imala* forms were clearly coexistent, as were various ways of marking participles, marking linkage between noun and modifier (see sect. 3.4.1), and so on. The broader implication is that diversity found today among the Arabic dialects can mirror diversity already present in pre-diasporic times.

It is clear, of course, that there have been innovations, sometimes striking ones, since the Arab diaspora of the seventh and eighth centuries. Pinpointing them, however, is problematic. It is beyond the scope of the present chapter to look at each of the forty-nine features treated here on a case-by-case basis, though eventually such a detailed treatment is necessary. Being brief, I believe that only the following elements are self-evidently post-diasporic innovations in western Sudanic Arabic. I will not treat Mesopotamian Arabic here, for as seen it has a more differentiated history than does WSA.

(6) Apparent innovations in WSA
   Phonology (features Ap 2.1.3/4/7/8/9/10; see 5.7 for discussion of interpretive problems)
   *ħ > h, ʕ > ʔ, ð > ḍ/d, θ > t/s, ð̣ > ḍ, ṭ (?)[16] > ɗ,

---

[16] The question mark pertains to the voice element of the proto-form. In Sibawaih, ṭ is classed as *majhuwr*, which is arguably descriptive of a voiced sound. In any case, the implosiveness of the WSA area is certainly innovative and may be due to contact with Fulfulde.

Morphology (features Ap 2.2.44/53/54/72)
Loss of -t 1/2M perfect verb suffix in certain contexts (as in (1) above),
n- 'I', n- ... -u 'we' in imperfect verb, 3FSG form of weak imperfect verb

As suggested in sect. 5.2.4, a number of phonological features are harder to interpret as to the shared vs. independent innovation parameter, than are most of the morphological. Except for the $\underset{\circ}{t} > \underset{\circ}{d}$ shift, all the phonological changes involve an element of simplification via loss of a marked characteristic (loss of emphasis, pharyngealization, interdental fricatives less common than dental or alveolar stops). Universal tendencies certainly play a role here.

That said, however, all other features included in this data set, I would argue, are candidates for pre-diasporic Arabic.[17] Note that I include in this latter set forms which at some point would disappear into deeper proto-Arabic forms. Feature Ap 2.1.6 for instance is the reflex of Standard Arabic ɣ. In WSA this has various reflexes, though the most common is q attested in six of nine sample points. In the present sample the reflex q is also attested in Shukriyya (especially in final position) and in southern Mesopotamia. Outside these areas it is found in the former North Yemen (five sample points in Behnstedt 1985: 44), in Syria in a long, continuous area on the Euphrates River, stretching to the Turkish border, and westward to Aleppo (Behnstedt 1997: 16), among the Arab of Bahrain (Holes 1987: 36), and in Mauritanian Arabic. Assuming this reflex did not innovate spontaneously over and over again, the broad distribution of the variant speaks for a single, pre-diasporic origin. At an older pre-diasporic level the innovation ɣ > q occurred among some groups of speakers. Populations with both variants then moved outside the peninsula.

The important point, however, is that the broad distribution of $q<*ɣ$ outside Arabia speaks for a reconstruction of the form in the pre-diasporic population as well. All features not included in (6) above, thirty-nine in all, I believe are candidates for a pre-diasporic variety, though of course ultimate justification depends on case-by-case argumentation.

I would note that with possibly one exception,[18] none of the innovations in (6) is shared between WSA and Uzbekistan Arabic, which means that any identical features shared between the two (see Tables 5.4–5.6 above) would be retentions.

---

[17] A reader points out that there are other features which may be due to 'drift' in Semitic languages, citing the development of the so-called analytic genitive (not documented here, see Table 3.2 in sect. 3.4.3). As argued in 3.4.3, however, this feature is not self-evidently a new tendency in Arabic, both Old Arabic and contemporary dialects having analytic and a synthetic (= ʔiḍaafa) genitives.

[18] θ > s is widespread both in Bagirmi Arabic in the WSA area and in Uzbekistan Arabic. Of course, this could also be due to common inheritance.

5.5. The interpretation of Arabic linguistic history

The discussion in the previous two subsections may be seen as complementing the use of the statistics in the following way. The statistics provide, as it were, a blunt instrument for suggesting where significant relationships lie. As raw data, they do not automatically reveal why dialect areas are similar or different, whether because of chance convergence, change due to contact and borrowing, innovation due to simplification or analogical formation, or to common inheritance. They can, however, help identify where it might be interesting to look for further evidence which helps disentangle what elements are at play. Thus, by one statistical measure of similarity and difference (Tables 5.4, 5.5), Uzbekistan Arabic turns out to be as similar to WSA as it is to Mesopotamian Arabic. These similarities, moreover, are most likely not due to independent innovation (see sect. 5.4.3). Looking further to features shared by these two varieties, it turns out that both have a highly contingent participial construction, whose origin goes back to pre-diasporic Arabic. The sharedness of this feature can only be explained in terms of an original pre-diasporic population with this feature in their language moving out of the Arabian peninsula, then splitting, one eventually settling in the eastern extremity of the Arabic-speaking world, the other at an extreme western end. In this case, statistics and reconstruction of the participial forms complement each other in a rather vivid way.

The statistics, furthermore, provide the basis for other, interesting, if not linguistically powerful hypotheses. I have, for instance, included Shukriyya Arabic only as a control group to provide a counterfoil for the emphasis on Uzbekistan Arabic. The statistics in Table 5.4, however, suggest that Shukriyya has no noteworthy affinity with WSA Arabic as compared to Mesopotamian Arabic. I do not think this is statistical trivia. Rather, it suggests that the form of present-day Arabic dialects (as, of course, measured in the current forty-nine variables) is as or even more dependent on inheritance than it is on geographical proximity. In dialectological terms, there is, in fact, no strong evidence here for a 'Sudanic Arabic' (as I term it) contrasting as a whole with Mesopotamian.[19] The historical linguist is challenged here on two fronts: where, historically, did the differences come from and to what extent does coterritorial contact hinder or abet dialect differentiation (see sect. 5.6)?

Lurking behind the discussion of the individual variables used in the statistics and reconstruction of specific linguistic forms is the more

---

[19] Even less so Behnstedt's (2000: 145) facile categorization of Sudanic Arabic as Hijazi (Saudi Arabia).

fundamental issue of how, generally, Arabic linguistic history is to be conceptualized.

Essentially there are two interpretive approaches, which were contrasted at length in Ch. 2. To recapitulate, one, developed mainly in Germany in the nineteenth century, is to regard Classical Arabic, conventionally termed Old Arabic (*Altarabisch*) as the ur-ancestor of the contemporary dialects, also known as Neo-Arabic (*Neuarabisch*, e.g. Brockelmann 1908; Blau 1988, 2002: 16; Fischer 1995). Jastrow's model follows this tradition. He assumes (rather than demonstrates) a division between old and new or innovative structures, and on this basis works out a historical linguistics. Thus, *imala* is assumed to be innovative or newer than non-*imala* varieties, and so Uzbekistan Arabic, which lacks *imala*, can be considered an older variety, relative to Old Arabic, than are the *qultu* dialects of Iraq, which have the innovative *imala*.

The problem with this approach is not in its basic logic. In some respects Jastrow's interpretations are certainly correct. The change of $r \rightarrow y$, characteristic of a few Iraqi *qultu* dialects (see Ap 2.1.13) is undoubtedly innovative for those dialects which have it. The problem lies in the assumption of what the ancestral variety is.

A second approach is to assume no predefined ancestral version, and to develop one according to customary principles of comparative linguistics. I have suggested that the second position is little developed among Arabicists,[20] and so what I have presented here represents only basic spadework. It leads to a reconstruction of pre-diasporic Arabic which is considerably more complex than traditionally assumed. The complexity in part, as seen in the discussion in the previous three chapters is already attested in some detail in the oldest texts, and in part it follows from a simple reconstruction of forms based on the distribution of post-diasporic elements, such as the intrusive -*in* treated in sect. 5.4.2. It can also lead to the postulation of forms which may even contradict aspects of Classical Arabic as described by the Arabic grammarians, for instance the postulation of caseless variety as the proto-ancestor of a case-based variety (Chs. 3, 4).

As will be evident from the preceding discussion, the position argued for here by no means leads to the reconstruction of a unitary proto-Arabic

---

[20] The two general, opposing positions which I define here are, in the contemporary state of Arabic linguistics, relatively poorly profiled. In fact, only the first has much currency. This is unfortunate, as I believe it may be associated with a highly scholarly, but at the same time highly orthodox and restrictive interpretation of Arabic linguistic history. Among its best-known representatives are Brockelmann, Nöldeke, and Fück. What today is little appreciated is that contemporaries of Brockelman and Nöldeke such as Vollers, de Landberg, and later Kahle argued for a broader reading of what the 'Arabiyya was. Even if I would not agree in all detailed interpretations with this latter group, I would see my position as reviving their perspectives.

located somewhere in the Arabian peninsula or in a neighboring area. By the same token, it does not preclude it either. It does argue for a stepwise reconstruction process, working first back to the pre-diasporic varieties of Arabic. Moving backwards beyond these varieties is a task left unaddressed here, though obviously is a desideratum for further research.

The problem treated in this chapter is not new. Indeed, it was summarized over a thousand years ago by Ibn al-Nadim (d. 990) writing about the origin of Arabic orthography in his *Fihrist: 7.* 'and each [pre-Islamic] tribe had its linguistic variety which distinguished it and by which it was recognized, all of which are a part of the original (*ʔaṣl*) variety'.

In a recent compendious survey of the term 'ʕarab' and its congeners in classical sources, Retsö suggests that the Classical language itself, as embodied in pre-Islamic poetry, had died out before Islam, and that it existed not in one form but rather as 'several 'languages of the Arabs' in pre-Islamic Arabia' (2003: 595).

The thrust of this chapter is sympathetic to these two perspectives. It is to suggest that old diversity is often directly reflected in contemporary diversity, and that contemporary diversity can be used both to reconstruct old diversity, and to explain contemporary diversity through the ultimately simplifying procedure of the comparative linguistic method. This can take place even in the absence of confirmation in old, classical sources. From this vantage point, modern scholarship has a further tool to discern what the *ʔaṣl* of Arabic is.

With this section ends the general discussion of the relation between a statistical summary of contemporary Arabic dialects, reconstruction, and the interpretation of the history of Arabic. In the next three sections I discuss individual problems in the interpretation of the linguistic features, of which there are many, and outline further uses to which a comparative data can be put. Those interested in the main thread of argument in this book, the conceptualization of proto-Arabic, may want to come back to these sections later.

5.6. Statistics, Reconstruction, Hypothesis Testing

Whereas I have thus far concentrated on the relation between the statistics and specific issues of historical reconstruction, the statistics can be invoked for many issues which impinge on the history of the language. One of their functions is that of broadly orientating contemporary dialectology. They provide, for example, an overview of what is out there, shorn of preconceived notions of what should or should not fit together. In this respect, and this remains a primary function of the statistics, it provides a general classificatory framework for understanding the diversity and unity of Arabic dialects in their contemporary form.

The further interpretation of the statistics belongs to a different conceptual order. One of the most important is to relate them to a historical interpretation of the development of Arabic. The statistics provide prima facie evidence for a significant relationship between, inter alia, Uzbekistan Arabic and WSA. This provides one lead in looking for other connections between the two areas. In fact, as seen in sect. 5.4.2, other, non-trivial links can be found. Still, without a precise, feature-by-feature reconstruction of the different linguistic variables, the citation of quantitatively based groupings alone does not prove anything as far as historical relationship goes.

Even if the statistics do not provide proof of relationship, coupled with reconstruction they are helpful in formulating hypotheses about how Arabic spread. A global interpretation, based on the foregoing discussion, is that the pre-diasporic Arabic was quite heterogeneous, and that as Arabic-speaking groups migrated outside the Arabian peninsula beginning in the seventh century, different varieties became dominant in different regions. The Arabs who settled Uzbekistan and those who made their way down the Nile and ultimately migrated into the western Sudanic area may well have derived from the same pre-diasporic group.

Beyond this general perspective, the statistics give insight into many aspects of developments in Arabic linguistic history. I mention seven of these cursorily in the form of open-ended hypotheses. These points are common issues in discussion of language spread, contact, and change, though they are only rarely stated explicitly in the Arabic dialectological tradition. These seven hypotheses are neither exhaustive, nor are they mutually exclusive. Unless otherwise stated the brief exemplifications relate to the observations in Tables 5.1–5.6 that the WSA area is, statistically a more homogeneous area than is the Mesopotamian.

> H1 The homogeneity of a dialect area is a direct reflection of its age of settlement. Newly settled areas are more homogeneous than older ones.

WSA is more homogeneous than the Mesopotamian because it was settled considerably later.

> H2 Low percentage forms are innovations more likely than relics. If they only are found in neighboring dialects, they are probably innovations.

Jastrow's example of $^*r \rightarrow r$ fits here. It is found in only two dialects in the sample, contiguous ones, Jewish and Christian Baghdadi. This feature is certainly an innovation.

> H3 The homogeneity of a dialect area is a function of the life style of its inhabitants.

Because Arabic culture in the WSA area has historically been strongly influenced by a nomadic and semi-nomadic lifestyle, intercommunication is facilitated (relative to the Mesopotamian area), and this militates against the development of marked dialect differences.

> H4 The homogeneity of a dialect area is a function of its geography. It should be recalled here that it is only in the course of the twentieth century that modern communication, roads, bridges, etc. have tended to level natural geographical boundaries.

Most of the WSA area is flat. Geographical boundaries have generally not been a hindrance to population movement. A significant exception is found in the Bagirmi dialect area, where during the rainy season, for four or five months a year, villages are effectively cut off from the outer world. The Bagirmi area in fact is a very distinct dialect area within WSA. In northern Mesopotamia at least, mountains hinder communication, and it is in this region where the greatest diversity is found.

> H5 The homogeneity of a dialect area is a function of the social status of the dialect speakers. This hypothesis is a complicated one, which can be extended in various ways. I will do this in only one way for the current data. I would suggest that minority speakers will tend to maintain differences, whereas speakers living where there is a related lingua franca variety will tend towards koinization and loss of inherited features when these differ from the koine, unless, it should be added, there are social factors sanctioning a dialectal diglossia (Owens 2001a: 442 n. 28).[21]

This hypothesis would appear to be substantiated by the *qultu* dialects, where minority traits such as *q* and *imala* are maintained. Moreover, comparing Anatolian *qultu* vs. northern Iraqi *qultu* dialects would appear to

---

[21] This hypothesis, as well as the previous one substantiate in a certain manner way Nettle (1998: 46, 52). He suggests, albeit on the basis of modeled rates of linguistic change, not actual data, that two key factors favoring language diversification are lack of population exchange between originally unitary groups, and social stratification in the population. As described in H5 and H6, geography and social stratification in the compared population do appear broadly to correlate with diversity.

further substantiate it: Iraqi *qultu* dialects are influenced by *gilit* traits (e.g. *k > c, q > g) to a far greater degree than are the Anatolian (see 5.8.4 below). This hypothesis was a major object of my investigation of spoken Arabic in Maiduguri (1998a, also quantitatively based), in which it was suggested that the lack of a city-wide koine (and inversely, maintenance of ancestral traits) is a direct reflection of the minority status of Arabic in the city.

> H6 The homogeneity of a dialect area is dependent upon its peripherality or centrality. Peripheral areas will maintain inherited categories longer than central areas.

So far as the current data base goes, WSA and Uzbekistan show significant similarities.

This hypothesis, however, is closely related to the previous H5. One might prefer to say that it is not peripherality as such which is the effective feature, but rather the minority status of the speakers which favors maintenance. Moreover, the hypothesis is contradicted in one respect: Uzbekistan Arabic shows greater similarity to the more central Shukriyya dialect than to WSA. Furthermore, non-circular definitions of central and peripheral are difficult to develop. Is Yemen more central than Nigeria? If yes, what does it mean when Yemen maintains the 2FSG suffix *-iʃ*, already attested in Sibawaih, whereas Nigerian Arabic has *-ki*, identical to Standard Arabic *-kī*? What non-circular arguments are there that *-iʃ* is innovative? Peripherality and centrality are, I believe, designations taken over from the social sciences (e.g. Political Science) which can be applied in linguistics only with considerable circumspection.

> H7 Phonology is more variable than morphology or, phrased as a historical proposition, phonology is more liable to variation and change than is morphology.

I think one of the more intriguing statistics is found in Table 5.3, where the means and standard deviations of the phonology and morphology are compared. For both WSA and Mesopotamia, the SD of the phonological variables is considerably higher than that of the morphological.

Note that this observation would tend to support Hetzron's point that morphology is a better index of ancient sharedness than is phonology. It also justifies the remarks of a reader for Oxford University Press that some of the common features could be independent innovations, even if it directs this tendency towards phonology.

5.7. Three Caveats

Three structural problems can be noted in the interpretation of the statistics.

5.7.1. Innovations

The statistics are a representation of contemporary Arabic. Ideally one would want to have similar statistics from varieties of Arabic in 1800, 1500, 1200, and so on. Obviously, lack of sources for spoken Arabic precludes such detailed accounting. In general it may be assumed that Arabic dialects are becoming more dissimilar with time and that the present statistics include many innovations. An obvious case in point are variables 3 and 4. These describe the reflex of *ħ and *ʕ, which in WSA is mostly h and ʔ (see Ap 2.1.3, 4). That these are innovations in WSA is shown by the contrast in Bagirmi Arabic of ʃaʰhar 'month' vs. leʰhem 'meat'. In these forms *ħ and *h have fallen together in WSA h. However, the indication of a former pharyngeal ħ is left behind in the different vowel quality. Low a remained low after *h, but was raised to e after *ħ. Ancestral Bagirmi Arabic must have had *ħ at some point.

The statistics, however, by their very logic, will in this respect show WSA to contrast with most other varieties of contemporary Arabic, which of course have retained *ħ.

This point underscores the necessity of using the statistics as a tool of historical interpretation only in the context of a plausible attempt at reconstruction. If, as suggested, WSA and Uzbekistan Arabic have a special historical affinity, the data cited here would allow one to remove one statistic separating the two contemporary reflexes, namely presence (Uzbekistan) vs. absence (WSA) of pharyngeals. Moreover, looked at in these terms the statistics help indicate not only what innovations have occurred in a given contemporary dialect area, but also the degree to which innovations have spread. The WSA area has a mean (1.86) for this variable which indicates that the change is close to complete in the region (2 = uniform h/ʔ).

5.7.2. Minority forms

A temptation should be avoided of valorizing the statistics to the detriment of other, relevant material and variant forms. The statistics will always be incomplete. I illustrated this in two separate places, so I will be brief here. In sect. 5.4.2 it was seen that the form of the active participle + suffix pronoun provides an interesting historical link between Uzbekistan Arabic and one variety of WSA. This has not been included as a variable, however, since in many dialect descriptions no information is given on the form. It would be a major mistake to ignore it, however.

In sect. 5.8.5 below are mentioned forms which are attested sporadically in my WSA data, always in texts, but which, so far as my experience in explicit elicitation of data goes, does not occur regularly. Unfortunately, even the best-researched dialect areas have gaps. Precisely in regard to the question of the spread of a given form, and its status as to retention or innovation, such minority forms may have an important interpretive role to play. The sporadic presence of a final *imala* form in verb, *maʃe* 'he went', suggests a link to Tripolitanian *mʃe*, the Daaxila oasis in Egypt (Behnstedt and Woidich 1985: 281) and to various Persian Gulf dialects (T. Prochazka 1981: 37).

5.7.3. *What features are criterial?*

A final caveat is not to lose sight of the fact that the statistics as I have developed them here are non-weighted. Each feature is of equal status as far as numerical calculations go. It is above all this aspect of statistics which perhaps will make philologically orientated Arabicists wary. One could add a feature, for instance, for the realization of *s. This is one of the most stable of all phonemes in Arabic (discounting assimilation for voicing, emphasis, and other regular allophonic effects). Were it added, it would have the same numerical weight as the realization of the 1SG perfect verb suffix as -*tu* or -*t*, a variable of greater significance than is *s. Why, however, is the 1SG suffix more significant? Dialectologists would simply intuitively regard it as such. Even statistically one could work out a justification for according it greater significance.

Each value of a variable could be given a variation index, for instance, ranging between 0 and 100. The index is formed by dividing the number of cases by the number of different realizations of a variable and multiplying by the percentage of each variety in the sample. So far as the present data goes, were *s entered as a variable it would have a value of 100, indicating that *s is realized as /s/ in all varieties. The 1SG perfect suffix, on the other hand, has a value of -tu = 33 per cent, -t = 67 per cent (8.2.40). For purposes of dialect comparison it is the more heterogeneous variables which are the more interesting.

5.8. Problems in Coding

In this section I would like to discuss a number of problems which, in a sense, have no solution, but which, at the same time, in all probability do not materially affect the main results of the present analysis. I add the proviso 'in all probability' because, since they are problems, their significance cannot be accurately gauged until they have been solved, or at least, worked on to a greater extent than what I have done. Furthermore, there are problems whose solution is fairly obvious, but which, for lack of more detailed data, are impossible to implement at the present time.

5.8.1. Coding values

The statistical summary relies on a numerical coding practice whose basis is, to a broad degree, arbitrary. It is hoped that this very arbitrariness, however, guards against skewing the results in one direction or another.

Statistics distinguishes between ordinal, interval, and nominal coding scales. Interval are those which measure the extent to which a case has a certain fixed property; ordinal define the relative order a set of cases have of a certain property, and nominal are those in which cases are defined to have a certain property in an arbitrary, though explicit way. The present statistics, like much found in language phenomena, are of a nominal order: they measure no fixed property, and the assignment of a number to one exponent or another is arbitrary. I have, however, followed certain guidelines in assigning values to the different cases: '1' is a form close to or identical with Standard Arabic; thus, between the two 2FSG object pronoun forms *-ki* and *-ik*, I have coded *-ki* with '1', *-ik* with '2'. I should emphasize that in according Standard Arabic the value '1' I am not making a statement of historical origin. This is simply an arbitrary starting point, which provides an orientation for any dialect. Note furthermore that I use Standard Arabic and not a presumed Classical Arabic as the hinge. Classical Arabic as seen in sect. 1.1 above is an interpretive problem. Thus I codify the form CaCVV, as in *kabiir* with '1', as this is the same as Standard Arabic. It is also broadly identical to Classical Arabic. However, if taking Sibawaih as a source for the language, Classical Arabic also has the adjective form *fiʕiyl* e.g. *siʕiyd* 'happy' (*Kitaab* II: 274), so that, barring an extensive justification of what one understands by Classical Arabic, many variables in this data base would be ambiguous in this respect. Standard Arabic as an artificial, conventionalized model is in this context a convenient starting point.

A second informal principle is that what I perceive as more widespread forms are codified with a lower number. My horizon extends here beyond the present data set. Thus, for the 2MSG object pronoun *-ak* is tagged as '1', *-ik* as '2'. Of course in this case the Standard Arabic form *-ka* is of no help.

In a few cases I have coded variables to allow for split categories, which are coded as a fraction of a number (see below). In CC-C sequence in nouns there are three outcomes in the current data, as illustrated in (7). In (7a and b) an epenthetic vowel is inserted between either the first and second or second and third consonants.

(7a) CəC-C, *akl-na* → *akəl-na* 'our food'
(7b) CCə-C, *aklə-na*
(7c) CC-C *aklna*

Some dialects (e.g. JB) have only (7a), some (WSA) have mainly (7b), and one (Uzbekistan) appears to have (7c). In addition some dialects have (7a) in some contexts, (7c) in others. Mardin, for instance, has (7a) when C2 is a sonorant, as in the example, otherwise (7c), as in *kalb-ki* 'your.F dog'. I code these 'both/and' dialects with a half point. In order for this to work, however, (7a) and (7c) need to be numerically contiguous, so in this instance (7a) has the value '1', (7c) the value '2', and (7b) the value '3'. In this reckoning Mardin gets a score of '1.5' (see Ap 2.1.23).

I would note that as more dialects are added to the data bank, and 'both/and' dialects fill in gaps, this system would probably break down (e.g. if there emerged a dialect with both (7a) and (7b), the value between would be '2', which is already occupied by (7c)). For present purposes, however, no contradictions arise.

Beyond these three points I use my own intuitions to one extent or another. While different codings would result in different individual values, in most cases they would not alter my final analysis. For instance, take the variable *ṭ*, emphatic *ṭ*. '1' is the Standard pronunciation *ṭ* (note arguably different from Sibawaih's description of *ṭ* as *majhuura*), '2' the variant *ḍ* (implosive emphatic), found in various WSA dialects, while '3' is *t*, a non-emphatic reflex found again in the WSA area, and in Uzbekistan. Why I have coded *ḍ* as closer to Standard Arabic than *t* is: (1) *ḍ* is still emphatic and (2) it maintains a systematic contrast to *t* in its dialects, whereas the de-emphasized form results in a phoneme merger. Still, it is relevant to see what would happen if the coding for '2' and '3' here were reversed. The difference is only relevant for the status of Uzbekistan Arabic. All the Mesopotamian dialects in the sample have *ṭ*, and most of the WSA have *ḍ*, though some have *ṭ* or *t*. Table 5.8 compares the results of two coding values.

The end effect is the same, when Uzbekistan is compared to Mesopotamia and the WSA area. In both cases it is closer to WSA. The effect is greater for the first manner of coding than for the second, though other than to assign Uzbekistan Arabic to Mesopotamian or to WSA Arabic, I do not consider 'degree of difference' as a relevant variable.

TABLE 5.8. *t coded two ways

1. $t = $ '1', $d = $ '2', $t = $ '3' (as in present data)	2. $t = $ '1', $d = $ '3', $t = $ '2'
Mesopotamia 9 × 1 = 9/9 = 1	Mesopotamia 9 × 1 = 9/9 = 1
WSA 8 × 2 + 1 × 3 = 19/9 = 2.1	WSA 1 × 2 + 8 × 3 = 25/9 = 2.7
Uzbekistan = 3	Uzbekistan = 2

5.8.2. Hierarchicalized variables

Linguistic variables, particularly phonological and morphological ones, may often be hierarchicalized. 'Emphasis' is a more general category than its instantiations in individual consonants, t, $ð$, and so on. There is an implicational relationship such that if a dialect lacks emphasis, it lacks t, $ð$ and all other emphatic consonants. The reverse does not hold. A dialect may lack a given emphatic consonant, say emphatic $ð$, but still may have other emphatic ones (e.g. s or d).

It is preferable to oppose dialects according to their most general parameter of contrast. Abbeche Arabic, for instance, should be opposed to Nigerian Arabic (all dialects), on the basis of non-emphatic vs. emphatic. This produces one feature of contrast. Another basis of comparison would be to oppose each consonant which realizes such as opposition. On this basis, Nigerian Arabic, with phonemic d, d, s, r, l, and m would differ in six ways from Abbeche Arabic (d, t, s, r, l, m).

I have followed neither accounting practice completely. The clear parameter of difference described in the previous paragraph is muddied through the following circumstance. Consonants in the emphatic series may differ not only in terms of emphasis, but also in terms of other phonetic contrasts. To continue the example from the beginning of this section, the alveolar plosive not only contrasts in terms of emphasis, but also in terms of buccal pressure, d (implosive) vs. t. I judge this latter to be an important parameter characterizing many WSA dialects. However, once the d vs. t contrast is included, so too must t (non-emphatic variant), since a number of dialects have this reflex for SA t.

The practice which I have followed here is that a difference in emphasis alone is not included as a parameter of contrast. The difference between s (*baṣal* 'onion', Nigeria) and s (*basal*, Abbeche), for example, is not included, since, so far as the present data goes, there are no further phonetic parameters of difference implied by the s - s contrast. As soon as another difference is implied in the contrast, however, individual emphatic phonemes are included. The Abbeche Arabic reflex *t* for SA *ṭ* is therefore included, since SA *ṭ* also differs in terms of the explosive/implosive contrast described above.

Note that the same principle applies to morphological differences. In many dialects the 2 and 3PL object pronoun forms have *-n* rather than *-m*, *-kun, -hun* 'your.PL, their.PL' (e.g. many Mesopotamian *qǝltu* dialects), vs. *-kum, -hum* (see sect. 8.7.3). To the extent that *-hun* always implies *-kun*, or the other way around, there would be no grounds for recognizing two separate variables here. Indeed, there are no dialects in this sample with *-m* in one of the forms and *-n* in the other. However, there are dialects with *-ku* in the 2PL, so a three-set *-kum, -kun, -ku* series has to be coded. This is, in the present analysis, different from the two-way *-hum, -hun* contrast, so the 2/3PL forms are entered as separate variables.

It would, perhaps, be possible to organize the analysis in a more subtle way, based on the following observation. Among the forty-nine dialects, a 2PL form *-kun* always implies *-hun*, whereas either *-kum* or *-ku* always imply *-hum* (there are no *-ku/hun* dialects). In this respect my classification errs on the side of caution in making a coding distinction. As it turns out, there are dialects in Syria, not included in the data bank, with *ku* (or *-ko*) and *hun* or *hin* (Behnstedt 1991: 243), so caution indeed has been rewarded in this case. As more and more details about Arabic dialects become known, experience has shown that what can occur, will occur, someplace.

Of course, other considerations are implied here, which I do not explicitly address. For instance, I would tend to recognize distinctions more in the realm of inflectional morphology than in phonology. To return to the *ṣ/s* difference noted above, I think it unlikely that a dialect should turn up where only this distinction occurs, but not in other emphatic sounds.

There are, however, issues within this broad thematic area which I leave unresolved. One, for instance, pertains to the class of second and third person plural forms. Some dialects have morphologically distinct masculine and feminine forms, while others do not. Among those that do, the exponence of the FPL may be variable. In Bagirmi Arabic, for instance, the 3FPL object suffix is *-han*, whereas in Kirenawa, as in most areas of Chad and Nigeria, it is *-hin*. I have not incorporated this vocalic difference into the comparison, since the variation cannot be applied in a broad way to the Mesopotamian area: few Mesopotamian dialects have a morphological FPL (only those in the extreme south). This case is analogous to the emphatic/non-emphatic contrast discussed above. In this instance, however, I recognize only the parameter, morphological FPL, yes or no. This means that any differences within the exponence of FPL forms are not considered. In this one instance the effect is slightly to increase the homogeneity of the WSA area vs. the Mesopotamian area. However, one would have to compare variation within a category in area A with a non-existent category in area B.[22] The issue is noted as a problem.

5.8.3. *One rule or two, one case or two*

A similar problem relates to the status of certain phenomena as linked or independent, in linguistic terms, one rule or two. A case in point is the status of a short vowel in pre-stress position in (reconstructed) open syllables, exemplified in (2) in sect. 2.4. In many dialects one needs but a single rule to account for all occurrences, or more accurately non-occurrences: short vowels do not occur in the context *CV'CVV. The quality of the vowels is irrelevant:

(8) JB, Hiit etc.: *kbiiγ/kbiir, kleeb* < **kabiir, kilaab* 'big, dogs'

In fewer dialects the vowel may be maintained in both contexts.

(9) Kirenawa: *kabiir, kilaab*

So far as these two sets of data go, and indeed the rules generalize to cover a variety such as JB in its entirety, a single rule accounts for the occurrence or non-occurrence of all short vowels in open, pre-stress syllables. On the basis of these cases the present statistics need only a single variable with two values: short vowel maintained or short vowel deleted (or not allowed).

Further data, however, indicates that the two cases do not always go hand in hand. In particular, there are a good number of dialects allowing a short low vowel, or reflex thereof, in an open pre-stressed syllable, but not a short high vowel.

(10) MB: *cibiir, cleeb* 'dogs'
     Khaweetna: *cabiir, cleeb*

In MB the short low vowel is raised to *i* in an open syllable (a very widespread phenomenon), but not deleted, while in Khaweetna it is maintained as *a*. Short high vowels, however, are categorically deleted in pre-stress position in both.

On the basis of this further data, two variables need to be recognized for vowels in pre-stressed open syllables, one for short high, and one for short low vowels (see discussion around Table 2.1 in sect. 2.4). Moreover, even this

---

[22] Lest it be thought that I am minimizing the variation within WSA by ignoring this feature, a comparable category would be the suffixal copular pronouns (Jastrow 1978: 131 ff.), which are unique to various *qultu* dialects (this could be captured by a 'yes/no' feature), and which within this group are internally variable. I have not included this variable.

differentiation is not adequate. In the Anatolian *qultu* dialects a short low vowel will often be maintained, either as *a* or as *ə* in nominal forms, but in derived verb forms the *a* is lost. In Siirt (Jastrow 1978: 62) one has, for instance, *ka'leem-i* 'my word', with *a* maintained in the pre-stress open syllable but in the same dialect *t'qaatal* 'quarrel' (<*taqaatal*) with the vowel of the derivational prefix *ta-* lost. Variable (17) is therefore phrased to cover only a short *a* in the pattern *CaCii(C)*. Separate variables apparently are needed to cover the reflexes of short *a* in different morphological forms.

In general in cases of doubt I over-differentiate or over-specify variables. There is, for instance, an important variable pertaining to medial CCHC-V sequences. This occurs, inter alia, in the basic imperfect verb when a vowel suffix is added. Prototypical variants are *yiktub-u* (no vowel rearrangement) vs. *yikitbu*.[23] Potentially comparable nominal forms are found with the feminine singulative suffix *-it* (*zib'dit-u* vs. *zibitt-u* 'his butter'), but the interpretation of the variants here is complicated by two factors. On the one hand in Mesopotamian Arabic in particular the maintenance or deletion of the short high vowel interacts with stress (which may protect the short high vowel). On the other hand, the situation in other dialects (Nigerian Arabic in general, see Ch. 6) is influenced by the nature of the consonants involved, which makes a simple rule formulation difficult. At this stage in a broad investigation, I limit the alternation to verbs only, where the situation is fairly clear.[24]

5.8.4. *Variation: morphophonological and sociolinguistic*

There are basically two types of variation in language, linguistically conditioned and sociolinguistically explicable. Both types are present in the current data.

The linguistic variation is, traditionally, the better known and theoretically better accounted for. In basic linguistic parlance, it is known as allo-variation (allomorph/allophone). Examples from the present data include the following:
The preformative vowel of verb: Abbeche = /a/ before -CC, /i/ or /u/ before CV, *ya-mrug* 'he leaves', *yu-murgu* 'they leave'; Shukriyya = /a/ before verb stems with /a/ as stem vowel, /i/ before verbs with high stem vowel (*yaʃrab* 'he drinks' vs. *yuktub* 'he writes').

---

[23] See sect. 6.1 for detailed discussion of the imperfect verb.

[24] In any instances of doubt, I present data as morphophonological rather than phonological. Jastrow (1978: 88–92) for instance reports that in nouns CC# sequences will frequently be broken up by an epenthetic vowel in Anatolian *qultu* dialects, e.g. Siirt *mahəd* 'cradle', but in verbs the *-t* of 2MSG is not accompanied by epenthesis, *nəmt* 'you slept'. In respect of epenthesis in these cases a distinction has to be drawn, inter alia, between nouns and verbs.

The 2FSG object suffix. In a number of dialects, -*ki* after a long vowel, -*ik* otherwise (similarly 3MSG objects suffix, either -*u*/-*hu* or -*u*/-*nu* in same contexts).[25]

A slightly different variation concerns the 3MSG object suffix. Generally it has a basic allomorphic variation between -V (usually either -u or -a) and -CV (either -*nu* or -*hu*), the latter after a long vowel (as in the immediately preceding -*ki/ik*). What is distinctive here are the allomorphic variants -*hu/nu*. Within the dialects with the -*u* suffix I distinguish further as to whether they take -*nu* or -*hu* after VV-. These instances differ from the preceding in that there are no dialects where only -*nu/hu* occur.

I have categorized these variants as having mid values. For instance, -*ki* has a value of '1', -*ik* a value of '2'. If a dialect has a conditioned -*ki/ik* variation it has the score of '1.5'.

A more difficult problem to handle is the issue of sociolinguistic variation, in part because it only rarely is systematically investigated. Dialects, however, increasingly are coming into contact, often under the influence of regional koines, and undergoing change as a result of this contact. Pure dialects in the sense that only a minimal amount of non-linguistically conditioned variation occurs are becoming rarer. Such variation is often remarked upon obliquely but unsystematically in standard dialect descriptions. Talay (1999: 30) for instance, notes that Khaweetna (Iraq *qultu*) has many occurrences of /g/ in loanwords from other Arabic varieties. While he suggests that /g/ enters the dialect via loanwords, rather than via substitution of native dialect words, he has both *baaq* 'steal' (native /q/) and *bawwaag* 'thief' (with 'bedouin' /g/), indicating that /g/ is insinuating itself into 'native' vocabulary as well. Remarking on the same alternation, Khan (1997: 56) notes that in his recordings, the *gilit* /g/ is largely limited to a story about a bedouin. The alternation g~q is thus conditioned in complex ways: lexical conditioning plays an important role[26] and situational and discourse factors are relevant. Ideally one would want a dialectology which systematically takes into account quantitative variation. In Owens (1998a: ch. 5) I use dialect maps, for instance, which divide binary variables into percentiles, so that, for instance, the sampling points for rural Nigerian Arabic for the preformative vowel /a ~ i/(see Ap 2.2.51) are

---

[25] Other variables here include *CC#* nouns (viewed in synchronic, syllable-structure terms). In Kirenawa, for instance, a consonant cluster is allowed where C1 is sonorant (*kalb* 'dog'), otherwise *CVC#*, *laham* 'meat'. In CB only CəC is allowed, *kalib*, whereas in JB CC# is categorically allowed, *laḥm*. A second is the stem vowel of *CCVC-V* imperfect verbs, for which see Ch. 6.

[26] In Arabic sociolinguistics lexical conditioning has been relatively well studied for the influence of Standard Arabic on spoken Arabic (e.g Abdul Jawad 1981; Holes 1987); it is equally relevant to the study of dialect contact, however.

given as categorically *a*, categorically *i* or as falling somewhere in between. The contrasts, moreover, are based on statistically distinctive differences. Lacking such quantitative data, however, one is left to make judgment calls about how to represent the linguistic variation. Based on the discussion in Khan and Talay, for instance, I consider both dialects to have both /q/ and /g/, marked with a score of '1.5'. On the other hand for a parallel variable which is spread from the dominant *gilit* dialect, it appears that whereas Khaweetna has both /k/ and /c/(< *k), Hiit has only /k/.[27]

Ideally features should be coded with differentiated sociolinguistic and lexically marked features.

5.8.5. *How many variants should be recognized?*

I think there really is no obvious place to stop a survey of this kind. The temptation is to continue adding as much detail as possible. A broader survey will certainly account for a greater degree of variation than that represented here. Two aspects of this problem can be briefly cited. First, greater attention could be given to morpho-phonological and allophonic variation. For instance, the verbal 3FSG suffix is given as *-at* for WSA, yet there is a widespread alternative with weak middle verbs before V-initial suffixes, namely -t, *jaab-at* 'she brought' vs. *jaab-t-a* 'she brought it.M'. Such alternation specific to weak middle verbs is fairly rare among Arabic dialects, hence its broad distribution in the WSA is significant and worthy of classificatory note. At the same time, it is morpho-phonologically restricted, and for this reason I do not include it in this survey.[28] A detailed look at the grammars I have used as the basis of this survey will reveal a number of comparable forms which I have not included. Such second-order variables, as they can be termed, will await a more detailed treatment.

A second type of feature worthy of note here is that which in a given dialect is rare, yet potentially of significance in understanding the spread of certain forms on a pan-Arabic basis. To mention two examples here, very occasionally there are found in Nigerian Arabic weak-final 3MSG forms of the type *maʃe*

---

[27] Though again another variable is at play here. Khaweetna is a dialect still in situ, constantly exposed to influences from surrounding Iraqi dialects, whereas Hiit was recorded among Jewish Arab emigrants residing in Beersheva, Israel.

[28] In fact, the values of the 3FSG perfect suffix before a vocalic suffix is a small chapter in itself. In eastern Libyan Arabic and Alawitan Hatay and Cilicia, for instance, it lengthens, ELA *iktib-aat-a* (or *iktib-iet-ih*) 'she wrote it', Hatay *qatl-iit-u* 'she hit him', in southern Mesopotamia the *-t* doubles, *kitb-att-a* 'she wrote it' (urban), in Cairene it attracts irregular stress, *ḍara'b-it-ak* 'she hit you', etc. Ignoring purely phonologically determined variants, Nigerian Arabic has three segmental values for it: *-t* after hollow verbs before a V-initial suffix, as in *ʃaaf-t-ak* 'she saw you', *-it* after weak final high-V verbs before a V-initial suffix, *lig-it-a* 'she got it.M', otherwise *-at*, *lig-at-hum* 'she got them.M'.

'he went'. I have never elicited them, though they do occasionally crop up in texts from the Bagirmi dialect area. They are also found in Tripolitanian Arabic, Daaxila, and some Gulf dialects. A similar case is the imperfect of stem II verbs, where occasionally ablaut stems such as *bi-diffin* 'cover with earth' are found. Such ablaut forms are the normal ones in Uzbekistan Arabic and are found in Upper Egypt as well (Behnstedt and Woidich 1985: 226). These might be interpreted as remnant forms brought originally from Upper Egypt: these forms spread from Upper Egypt and became established in Tripoli, but not, ultimately, in the WSA area.[29]

My point in citing this second class of occurrences which are not treated in these statistics is to remind one that it may be the unusual, rare form, but one which appears to link up with similar or identical forms located far afield, that helps to determine the historical status of a feature. Ablaut imperfect verb stems are rare, historically contingent developments. Rather than interpret their presence in three widely separated areas as due to independent innovation, it is more likely they go back to common point of origin.

5.8.6. *Structural, not lexical features in the index*

The data used here is largely structural (phonological and morphological structure), not lexical. Thus, when it is noted that Khaweetna (Talay 1999: 111) has CəCy stems (*ʕəm-yit* 'she became blind'), the point of identity with, say Abbeche Arabic is in the existence of a common morphological structure. The fact that the lexical distribution of these patterns is not identical (Khaweetna *laq-it* vs. Abbeche *ligiy-at* 'she got') must be explained and described elsewhere.[30]

Similarly, in regards to CVCC# nouns, both WSA and various *qultu* dialects have both CVCC# and CVCəC# nouns, the presence or absence of the epenthetic vowel determined in each case by the value of the consonants. In my coding CVCC# has the value '1', CVCəC# the value '2' and dialects which have both classes of nouns get the middle '1.5'. Note, however, that the precise rules that sanction the CVCəC# forms are different in the two areas. In the WSA area, one has CVCəC, unless C_2 is a sonorant, in which case the CVCC# form occurs (*darb* 'road' vs. *digin* 'beard'). In the Daragözü *qultu* dialect (Jastrow 1973: 78–9, also in Mardin, Sasse 1971: 78) CVCəC# is required if C_3 is a sonorant *ħajər* 'stone', vs. *daħʃ* 'young donkey'. Again, more detail is needed

---

[29] Though cf. the verbal noun of second stem verbs, *ti-diffin* 'covering with earth', which is common in the WSA area.

[30] It appears that Khaweetna has largely regularized the low vs. high stems according to the transitive/intranstive parameter.

to distinguish the two, though the current classification does not contradict basic facts of the two cases.

5.8.7. *Other points*

Opposing forms within a variable are minimally contrastive. This is perhaps a type of hierarchical relation (sect. 5.8.2), though phonology and morphology are not logically hierarchizable relative to each other. The minimal point of contrast in the 2FSG object suffix is whether the vowel occurs before or after the consonant (*-ik* vs. *-ki*). In these terms no contrast is made between MB *-ic* and CB *-ik* (post-C form), since the $c \sim k$ contrast is a phonological one accounted for elsewhere (see Ap 2.1.2). Should there be a dialect which has *-ic* 2FSG object, but no other forms with *c* (I am not aware of such), the 2FSG object suffix in this case would be given a separate value, as the *c* in this case would not be accountable for under other rules.

The variants of variables are opposed in their surface realizations. It might be argued that Kirenawa *buktubu* (with maintenance of stem *u*) and Shukriyya *bukutbu* (with deletion and epenthesis, Ch. 6) have the same underlying form and therefore are not to be differentiated. However, at some point a differentiation can be made, either at an inspection of surface forms (as done here) or in terms of application of rules (Shukriyya applied rules which Kirenawa does not).

6

Nigerian Arabic and Reconstruction of the Imperfect Verb

It was argued in the previous chapter that there is dialectal data, non-existent in Old Arabic sources, which forces reconstructions into the pre-diasporic era. This data is found equally in so-called core areas as well as in geographically peripheral regions. In this chapter, I provide a further illustration of this state of affairs. The starting point is again a 'peripheral' dialect, Nigerian Arabic. I begin by outlining the synchronic facts. These, it will be seen, are pivotal to understanding the wider history of the imperfect verb in Arabic.

6.1. The Basic Imperfect Verb

The scope of this analysis is restricted to the basic imperfect stem. In earlier analyses (e.g. Owens 1993b) alternations such as the following:

(1) *burgud* 'he lies down'
    burugd-an 'they.F lie down'

were analyzed as follows:

(2) *burgud* basic stem, with the stem vowel /u/ lexically determined

(3) *burgud-an*
    burgd-an deletion of /u/ in an open syllable
    burugd-an epenthetic insertion of [a] to break up a prohibited CCC sequence.

This analysis follows a phonological tradition going back at least to Mitchell's (1960) classic analysis of epenthesis in eastern Libyan Arabic.

(4) ELA epenthesis in imperfect verb
    yiktib-u base form
    yiktb-u deletion of short high vowel in open syllable, producing unacceptable CCC
    yikitbu epenthetic insertion to break up resulting CCC sequence

With minor adjustments, this analysis works for a great many dialects (see list in Kiparsky 2003), including many North African dialects, many Syrian and Iraqi dialects, Shukriyya in the eastern Sudan and many Egyptian varieties, for instance in Upper Egypt and the northern Sinaitic litoral.

Against my earlier analysis, closer inspection of the Nigerian Arabic data shows that it does not work particularly well for this variety. It will be seen that a different modeling of the imperfect verb in NA provides a key to understanding the diachronic development of the verb in other varieties of Arabic as well.

In Owens (1993b: 32) Nigerian Arabic was described as having four different types of rules of epenthesis (introduced in Ch. 3, (17)–(19)).

(5) CCC → CəCC *burgd-an* → *burugdan* (as in (3))
(6) sonorant epenthesis, CC_{son} → $CəC_{son}$, *bitni* → *bit̪ini* 'he folds' where sonorant = /r, l, m, n, w/
(7) guttural epenthesis, $C_{gut}C$ → $C_{gut}əC$, *biʔrif* → *biʔarif* 'he knows', guttural = /x, q, h, ʻ/ and ə = [a]
(8) CC-C → CCə-C, *ʃif-t-ha* → *ʃifta-ha* 'I saw her', where '-' = morpheme boundary

As will be shown now, these rules can be simplified and essentially reduced to two,

(9) CC-C → CCə-C (= (8))
(10) CC_{son} → $CəC_{son}$, Sonority epenthesis (= (5)–(7)).

The first rule, (9), inserts an epenthetic vowel when sequences of three consonants arise across morpheme boundaries. This occurs in particular when object suffixes beginning with a consonant are attached. This configuration occurs only in the perfect verb and in nominal forms, so does not concern the immediate problem. The rule will be met with again in sect. 6.3 below, however.

The justification for collapsing (5)–(7) into one rule, (10), resides essentially in a better data coverage than presented in previous work. The following data is illustrative. The decisive paradigms are indicated by comparing forms with and without vowel-initial suffixes. For the V-initial suffixes I use the 3FPL suffix -an, though any vowel-initial suffix (whether subject or object marker) would suffice. In (11a) are unsuffixed verbs, in (11b) the verbs with the V-initial suffix. It may also be noted that equivalent to the suffixless forms in (11a) are forms with C-initial suffixes. For instance, *biʔarif* + ha yields *biʔarif-ha* 'he knows her', with no change in the stem voweling.

186 *The Imperfect Verb*

(11a) (11b)
   i. 'bu*d*ufun 'he buries'   bu'*d*ufun-an
      'buzugul 'he throws'   bu'zugul-an
      'bus̩ufun 'he is quiet'   bu's̩ufun-an
      'bu*d*uxul 'he enters'   bu'*d*uxul-an
  ii. 'biharij 'he quarrels'   bi'harj-an
      'butubuz 'he cuts off (plant)'   bu'tubz-an
      'busubug 'he finishes first'   bu'subg-an
      'budubuz 'he slaps on back'   bu'dubz-an
      'bukubus 'he attacks'   bu'kubs-an
      'buduguʃ 'he crashes into'   bu'dugʃ-an
      'bijibid 'he pulls'   bi'jibd-an
      'bu*d*urud 'he chases'   bu'*d*urd-an
 iii. 'bungul 'he moves'   'bungul-an
      'buns̩ul 'it falls out of a socket'   'buns̩ul-an
      'bulbuk 'he pounds'   'bulbuk-an
      'bufs̩ul 'it separates'   'bufs̩ul-an
      'bufzur 'he stretches s.t.'   'bufzur-an
      'bibdan 'it spoils'   'bibdan-an
      'bustur 'he covers'   'bustur-an
      'buktub 'he writes'   'buktub-an
      'bug*d*uf 'he trims'   'bug*d*uf-an

There are two aspects to understanding the alternations observed in (11). It is easiest to begin with the suffixless forms, those in column (11a). First, in the suffixless forms each verb has a vowel before the final -C. This of course is the stem vowel. The contrast of high vs. low vowel is lexically determined. A high vowel can be either [i] or [u], front or back. This is partly lexically, partly phonologically determined, according to the conditions described in sect. 2.4.1.1.

Second, some verbs have an epenthetic vowel before the second consonant, while others do not. Set (11 iii) does not have an epenthetic vowel whereas sets (11 i) and (11 ii) do. The conditions for the insertion can be stated in terms of constraints which I will term, 'extended sonority constraints'. I call them 'extended', because the hierarchy requires a greater differentiation of consonants than treatments of sonority customarily allow.[1] In the sequence C_1C_2, an

---

[1] In Clements (1990: 286) six sonority categories are recognized, in sequence of increasing sonority: oral stops, fricatives, nasals, liquids, glides, and vowels. In the NA hierarchy, nasals, liquids, and glides form a single class, while stops and fricatives have internal differentiation.

epenthetic vowel is inserted if C_1 is less sonorant than C_2. The sonority hierarchy is:

(12) Extended sonority hierarchy, Nigerian Arabic
   1. r, l, m, n, w: liquids and nasals
   2. b, f: bilabials
   3. s, ṣ, ʃ: voiceless, aveolar (alveopalatal), fricatives
   4. k, g, j: velars, alveopalatal
   5. t,[2] d, ɖ, z, ḏ: alveolars, dentals (coronals)[3]
   6. ʔ, h, q, x: velar, uvular, glottal   decreasing sonority

The entire system can be summarized as follows.

(13) Extended sonority hierarchy and epenthesis
   for C_1C_2, then $C_1əC_2$ if C_1 is lower on hierachy than C_2
   (less sonorant) $6 > 5 > 4 > 3 > 2 > 1$ (more sonorant)

In the sequence C_1C_2, an epenthetic vowel is inserted if C_1 is less sonorant than C_2. The epenthetic vowel is /a/ after a guttural, otherwise a high vowel (front or back, [i/u] depending on harmonic factors discussed in sect. 2.4.1.1). I would note that this rule replicates what Clements (1990: 287, following Murray and Vennemann) terms the syllable contact law, which states that in a CC cluster, the first consonant tends to be more sonorant than the second.

To elucidate how the system works, 'minimal pairs' can be summarized from the list, where the presence or absence of an epenthetic vowel follows from the sonority relationship of the consonants. The first column sanctions epenthesis while the second does not.

---

[2] -t is in the second lowest sonority group, which means that an epenthetic vowel will relatively rarely be inserted before it. This observation may be part of the explanation for the deletion of the 1 and 2MSG subject suffixes in Nigerian and western Sudanic Arabic, when they are not themselves suffixed, *ʃif-t → ʃif 'I saw' (see (2) in sect. 1.4). The lack of epenthesis leaves the suffix unsyllabified and renders it non-salient, making it a more prominent target for deletion.
I would note that there are not enough examples of /j/in my sample to be sure at this time where exactly it belongs. It is no higher than level 4, however.
[3] Adapting observations from Jun (2004: 65), one line of explanation for the propensity of the alveolars and dentals (coronals) to support epenthesis might be in terms of speed of lingual gesture. Coronals have a fast gesture, velars, by comparison, are slow. The CC difference between bigɖa 'he cuts' vs. buduguʃ 'he crashes into' is thus one between a slow-fast and a fast-slow gesture. Furthermore, the 'slow' consonant (/g/in this case) extends its influence on the formant transitions on the preceding vowel, even when it is in the C_2 position. In a hypothetical *budguʃ, the /g/has an effect on the transitional formants of the /u/, thereby interfering with the typical formant transitions which help identify the following /d/. With an epenthetic vowel between /d/and /g/, this interference is avoided.

(14) buṣufun vs. bufṣul: ṣ-f epenthicizes, but not f-ṣ
    buduguʃ vs. bugduf d-g but not g-d
    budubuz vs. bubdan d-b but not b-d
    budubuz vs. bubzur d-b but not b-z
    bukubsan vs. bubgus k-b but not b-g

The examples from column (11b) can be understood in the same rule complex, except that here a further variable is added, namely that the stem vowel (the vowel before the final -C) occurs in an open syllable. Using a very descriptive format, a further rule can be stated: delete the stem vowel in an open syllable, unless this leads to a violation of the sonority hierarchy.

For instance, in

(15) 'buṣufun, bu'ṣufun-an

the singular form inserts because /s/ is lower than /f/. When a V-initial suffix is added placing the final stem in an open syllable, the stem /u/ is not deleted, since /f/ is less sonorant than /n/ on the hierarchy. By contrast, in

(16) 'bukubus, bu'kubsan

the stem vowel /u/ does delete in the plural, since /b/ is less sonorant than /s/. The epenthetic vowel between /k/ and /b/ remains, since /k/ is lower than /b/. In

(17) buktub, buktub-an

there is no insertion anywhere, since /k/ is more sonorant than /t/. In the plural the /u/ is not deleted in an open syllable, since /t/ is less sonorant than /b/, and hence requires a vowel separator. In (11b), sets i. and iii. have no deletion, since C_3 is less sonorant than C_2. Set ii. does have deletion, since C_2 is more sonorant than C_3.

Sonority makes itself felt in further phonological alternations. In the following perfect–imperfect pairs, where the perfect verb has k-s as the first two consonants, converting this to the imperfect would theoretically involve placing /k/ next to /s/. /k/ is below /s/ on the sonority hierarchy, so an epenthetic vowel would be inserted. Instead, sequences of k-s (and others of the /s/class) metathesize in the imperfect, resulting in:

(18) kasar 'he broke'   biskar, biskar-an (instead of *bikasar)
     kaʃa or kaʃah 'he opened'   biʃki, biʃk-an.

A similar explanation lies behind

(19) waagif 'standing', waafg-e 'standing.F'.

Here the open syllable deletion rule applies, but on the metathesized f-g sequence.

It can be seen how the interplay of epenthesis as defined by the sonority hierarchy along with the deletion of a short vowel in an open syllable, as in (16), produces the effect which was described in (1)–(3) above.

6.2. Historical Significance

To introduce this section, it can be noted that there is a degree of variation attested in certain forms. A detailed quantitative treatment of the alternation, *burgud* 'he lies down', *burgud-an* ~ *burugd-an* is found in Owens (1998*a*: 29). While *burugdan* is not expected from the sonority hierarchy, in fact its tokens in an extensive text count outnumber the unepentheticized *burgudan*. Also, I have noted that while *buskutan* 'they.F are quiet' is the normal form, conforming to the sonority hierarchy, in one village *busuktan* (etc.) was regularly observed. In both these cases the exception moves in the same direction, namely that the epentheticized form becomes categorical, regardless of sonority context. Epenthesis occurs where a sequence of three consonants, CCC, arises.

I will ignore these two 'exceptions' for present purposes, because so far as the Nigerian Arabic data goes they represent isolated cases. Nonetheless, they serve as an introduction to the main theme of this section, namely the historical development of epentheticized forms. The basic argument is that already in some pre-diasporic varieties sonorant-determined epenthesis gave way to what I term linearly determined epenthesis. As in the examples cited in the previous paragraph, sonority gives way to consonantal sequence, as the determinant of epenthesis.

The starting point of this discussion is an article by Kiparsky (2003) in which he offers a tripartite division of Arabic dialects into -*VC*, *C*-, and -*CV*-dialects.[4] His treatment covers many types of syllabification phenomena, not only those exhibited in the imperfect verb, to which this chapter is limited. I will summarize it only to the extent that it impinges on the current historical problem. Neither *C*-nor -*VC* dialects allow a short high vowel in an open syllable, hence *CV is prohibited. As far as the verb goes, in synchronic terms this constraint produces alternations such as the following (as in (4) above):

(20) *yiktib*
    (a) *yiktib-u*
    (b) *yiktb-u*
    (c) *yikitb-u*.

---

[4] See Watson 2007 (ms.) for criticisms of many of the linkages suggested in Kiparsky's article.

As with Nigerian Arabic, the input is a verb with a VC# stem. When a vowel-initial suffix is added, a disallowed CV syllable (*ti-*) is produced (20a). The vowel deletes (20b). This leads to another unacceptable situation, namely a CCC, *ktb*, syllable. To alleviate this problem an epenthetic vowel is introduced between the first two consonants (20c). As already noted, in many Arabic dialects this rule is categorical when the stem vowel is high.

C-dialects, as Kiparsky notes, are similar to -VC dialects, in that they have (20). After high vowel deletion, however, the resulting CCC sequence is allowed. Kiparsky includes here both most North African dialects, and certain Arabian peninsular dialects, particularly southern Hijazi (see (21) below). As will be seen below, this synchronic class of C-dialects collapses historically different developments.

CV-dialects, finally, essentially maintain a stem vowel in all positions. Examples are many Yemeni dialects and Bahariyya in Egypt, as described in Ch. 2, Table 2.1.

What I would like to suggest here is that the contemporary Nigerian Arabic situation is the key to understanding a development which may be described as in Table 6.1.

There are four tiers in Table 6.1. It will be easiest to begin with the bottom one (level d), as it describes the relative chronology of actual varieties. Beginning on the left, three different varieties are identified. All of them are reconstructed into pre-diasporic times. The first position is represented by Classical Arabic, and by the ancestor of various modern varieties. These have no rules at all which affect the imperfect stem, neither rules of deletion nor of epenthesis.

The ancestor of various southern Hijazi dialects represents a second situation. Here a short high vowel is deleted in an open syllable. There is, however, no epenthesis, as CCC sequences are tolerated. This produces imperfect verb paradigmatic contrasts such as in (21), where low vowels are maintained in open syllables, high vowels deleted.

TABLE 6.1. Basic imperfect stem: relative chronology of stem change

a. Non-linearly determined	Linearly determined
b. Stem constraint	No stem constraint
c. No epenthesis or epenthesis by sonority	Regular epenthesis
d. *Proto-NA> NA> *Proto-Southern Hijazi *CA Etc.	ELA etc. > (?) > North African

The Varieties listed in row d in the left half of the table have the properties specified above them, and those on the right have the properties specified above them.

(21) tuktub   tuktb-iin 'you.F write' (T. Prochazka 1988: 32, 35)
     taʃrab   taʃrab-iin 'you.F drink'

A third situation is sonorant epenthesis, with Nigerian Arabic an approximate living reflex. It will be argued below that sonorant epenthesis began with the most sonorant consonants, essentially as in (6) above, and became generalized from there to the situation which is currently attested in Nigerian Arabic. The sonorant hierarchy of Nigerian Arabic thus derives directly from an earlier proto-variety, but is not an exact relic of the original situation itself.

Up to Nigerian Arabic all the varieties share one basic feature: either they undergo no phonological perturbation to their basic form or if they do, as with Nigerian Arabic, it is not stems but rather consonant sequences which are the domain of epenthesis.

With ELA, on the other hand, there emerges a phonological rule which is generalized to all high-vowel stems: CCVC-V changes to CVCC-V. Unlike Nigerian Arabic, consonant quality plays no role in the process. I therefore call it linearly determined epenthesis, since it depends solely on linear sequences of consonants. Tiers a and c in Table 6.1 divide the dialects and proto-varieties according to whether or not the imperfect verb has linearly based epenthesis.

I would propose that the ELA-type epenthesis grew directly out of a Nigerian-type. It is clear from the list in (11) that the sonorant hierarchy introduces a large number of epenthetic vowels, and at the same time sanctions a large number of vowel deletions when a -V initial suffix is added. Speakers generalized the insertion/deletion alternations from ones being governed by specific consonantal constraints, to ones governed by the global sequence of consonants and vowels. From the diverse inputs, for the forms without a vowel-initial suffix, a pattern of the type in (11 a iii) became the norm, and in those with a vowel-initial suffix, the pattern in (11 b ii) did.

That a process of generalization in favor of linearly determined epenthesis could have become dominant is supported by the evidence cited in the first paragraph of this section, that on a variational basis in Nigerian Arabic such a 'shift' is observable.[5]

Since the sonority hierarchy in (12) is attested in this form only in Nigerian and other western Sudanic dialects, it is to be seen as the endpoint of a continuous development which began in pre-diasporic times. It may be further suggested that the input for expanding the hierarchy began at the

---

[5] This is not to suggest that the shift will ever go to completion to reach a system such as in eastern Libyan Arabic. As seen in the discussion of short high vowel quality in Nigerian Arabic in sect. 2.4.1.1, there appear to be strong social factors supporting a non-directed variation.

extremes of the hierarchy, step 1 and step 6. Note that these two contexts have already been introduced as general phenomena in Arabic dialects (sect. 3.4.2, e.g. (17), (18)). Step 1, insertion of an epenthetic vowel before a liquid or nasal, as will be reiterated in sect. 6.4 below, is a process already described by Sibawaih. Step 6, so far as I know, is not attested in the Old Arabic literature. In the modern dialectological literature, it represents a phenomenon so widespread that it has a fixed designation, namely the 'gahawa' syndrome. This refers to the /h/in the word for 'coffee', a letter which is eponymous for any guttural consonant (as in (12)). After a guttural consonant, in many dialects an [a] is inserted (e.g. Najdi, southern Jordanian and the Sinaitic littoral, most dialects of the entire Sudanic region, eastern Libya, see sect. 1.6.6). From this wide distribution it may be surmised that it is a pre-diasporic event. There is thus very strong evidence that steps 1 and 6 in (12) were found in a fairly large number of pre-diasporic varieties. I would suggest that these two contexts represented initial models for sonorant epenthesis which generalized in some varieties to other contexts, resulting in the contemporary situation in Nigerian Arabic (and western Sudanic in general).

I should note that from a comparative historical basis I am not saying that eastern Libyan Arabic, or the rule of epenthesis in ELA, developed from Nigerian Arabic. Rather, the generalized linearly determined epenthesis developed out of a sonority-based epenthesis. It could be that the ancestral variety of linearly based epenthesis developed from a more impoverished version of a sonority hierarchy than in (12), though at this point such thinking is speculative. What is argued is that the Nigerian Arabic situation today is closer to the ancestral variety of the ELA than is ELA itself, and it is in this sense that Nigerian Arabic is the key to interpreting the development of a linearly based epenthesis.

From the relative dating of the rules follows the pre-diasporic provenance of the forms in (12). Epenthesis based on sonority preceded linearly determined epenthesis. Linearly determined epenthesis is found today, inter alia, in eastern Libyan Arabic and in the dialects of southern Jordan, the Negev and the northern Sinai littoral (see de Jong 2000: 190, 229, 516). De Jong notes that the Sinaitic dialects can be dated to pre-Islamic times. Assuming the ancient and present-day populations to be related linguistically, it would follow that the linearly determined epenthesis was already in place in pre-diasporic times. Since in the argumentation developed in this chapter this logically assumes the sonority-determined epenthesis, this form of epenthesis as well must be pre-diasporic.

The exact status of North African dialects in this historical typology is not crucial. My guess (hence the question mark) is that they derive from an

ELA-type epenthesis. However, since the high–low vowel contrast was lost in most North African varieties, it affects all stems. Note that in this respect it contrasts with southern Hijazi, where the low-vowel stems are stable (see (21)). Otherwise, both southern Hijazi and North African allow CCC-V stems.[6] Whether there is a residual southern Hijazi element in the North African data is an issue requiring separate study. Given the current reconstructions, the southern Hijazi type is pre-diasporic, and therefore could have served as a pool for the North African forms.

6.3. Epenthesis

In all varieties of Arabic situations may arise where a rule of linear epenthesis is needed. This does not pertain to the imperfect stem. It does, however, apply to the perfect verb, in the configuration:

(22) Stem-t-OBJ, t = 1, 2 MSG subject suffix where object is -C initial.

Given:

(23) ʃif-t 'I saw'

if a C-initial suffix is added, a CCC sequence will result.

(24) ʃif-t-ha 'I saw her'

In southern Hijazi, which as seen allows CCC sequences, no further action need be taken (e.g. ḍarabthum 'I hit them.M', T. Prochazka 1988: 185). In both Najdi and Nigerian Arabic, on the other hand, the sequence needs to be broken up, *CCC being disallowed. A vowel is inserted between the second and third consonants, giving,

(25) ʃift-aha 'I saw her' (see (15) in Ch. 3).
    CVC-CV-CV

In principle the vowel could have been inserted between the first two consonants. This is not the insertion of choice. Militating against this position of insertion are the following. This insertion is typically found with the suffix -t. In the Nigerian sonority system, /t/ is low on the list, hence insertion before it would be disfavored but insertion after it favored. Furthermore, the resulting CV-syllable (ta) produces only minimal disruption to the syllabification of the basic stem. The CVC stem (ʃif) is not affected by the epenthesis. This is

---

[6] Though it is often reported in the literature that a very short epenthetic vowel will appear in a $C^ə CC$-V sequence.

represented in tier b in Table 6.1. Up to Nigerian Arabic there is effectively a constraint which does not allow generalized epenthesis in a verb stem. In CA, ancestral varieties of Yemeni etc, and in southern Hijazi no epenthesis at all occurs or is allowed in the stem. In Nigerian Arabic, epenthesis occurs, but it refers to consonantal quality, not an abstract notion of stem. There is thus a rough isomorphy between the morphological stem and the stem syllable structure, and the morphological suffix and the suffix syllable structure: a stem is represented in a syllable and the suffixes by their syllables.

A syllabification of the type ʃifitha, on the other hand, breaks up the stem ʃif into two syllables, ʃi-fit, CV-CVC. Here, and in the ELA-type syllabification of the imperfect verb (see (20) and (26), (27) below), the rules are purely phonological, so no constraints based on the construct 'stem' are relevant.

That the ELA system confirms the purely phonological nature of epenthesis can be seen in its solution to the current predicament:

(26) ʃif-i̱t-ha.

Here the epenthesis between the first two consonants parallels the epenthesis in

(27) yiki̱tb-u
   'they write'

which as seen above, is based purely on consonantal sequence. Of course, in this system epenthesis as in Nigerian Arabic or northern Najdi Arabic is ruled out, since the insertion would create an open syllable.

(28) *ʃifti̱-ha

6.4. The Old Arabic Evidence

I have proposed three reconstructed forms of the imperfect verb which all date into the pre-diasporic era. Each of them finds identical or analogous reflexes in the Old Arabic literature, though to differing degrees. As noted in Table 6.1, no deletion, no epenthesis is characteristic of Classical Arabic. Deletion of a high vowel leading to a CCC sequence is not attested as such in the Old Arabic literature. However, as seen in Ch. 2, deletion of a short high vowel in an open syllable, similar to (21), is well attested. It may be suggested that the southern Hijazi forms are directly related to Old Arabic varieties where deletion of a high vowel in an open syllable was widespread.

Sonorant epenthesis also is attested in Old Arabic, particulary in Sibawaih. This was summarized in sect. 3.3.2.1, where it was seen that Sibawaih describes

The Imperfect Verb 195

as an alternative to *bakr*-'Bakr-NOM', *bakur*, with the case vowel inserted before the final stem consonant. It can be inferred from the few examples which Sibawaih supplies, that the epenthesis occurs in the context CC$_{liquid/nasal}$. Liquids and nasals in the Nigerian Arabic rule (12) are also the most sonorant consonants of the set, and as pointed out in sect. 3.3.2.1, the epenthesis before a liquid or nasal, the so-called *bukura* syndrome (*bukura*, the word for 'tomorrow'), is fairly widespread in Arabic dialects generally.

It can thus be said with a high degree of certainty that the three reconstructed forms are also adumbrated in the Old Arabic literature, or, if they are not, comparative evidence argues strongly for postulating them. Of course, high vowel deletion and even more, sonorant epenthesis have a much more circumscribed role in the Old Arabic accounts than they do in the current reconstructions. This is ancillary to the current argument, however. As often emphasized in this work, reconstruction can be practiced by definition on whatever data source allows it, and the results therefrom have an internal validity independent of other linguistic sources. In my judgment what is striking is that reconstruction and attestation in Sibawaih complement each other at all in issues of rather small detail.

6.5. The Reconstructions and the Classical Arabic Verbal Mode Endings

As a final issue in this chapter, it is relevant to consider the historical status of the mode endings on the imperfect verb. The Classical Arabic verb parallels the noun in having a set of inflectional endings marked by short vowels.

(29) *yaktub-u* 'he writes-IND'
  yaktub-a 'he writes-SUBJUNCTIVE'
  yaktub 'he writes-JUSSIVE'

The indicative verb is marked by-u, the subjunctive by -a, and the jussive by Ø.

As with the case system, the system of short vowel markings on the verb plays no role in understanding the genesis of the forms in the contemporary dialects (see (11) in Ch. 8 for parallel situation in nominal paradigm). This follows from the following considerations. The addition of a vowel in both the southern Hijazi and the Nigerian Arabic-type systems triggers, or in the case of Nigerian Arabic, potentially triggers the deletion of a short high vowel. There are no Old Arabic sources which mention the mode endings as triggering such a process. So far as the old sources go at least, the reconstructed

The Imperfect Verb

southern Hijazi and Nigerian Arabic types have to be seen as parallel to and independent of a variety with verbal mode endings.

As for the 'no deletion, no epenthesis' type, the presence of mode endings in Classical Arabic cannot be related linguistically to the absence of mode endings in the modern typological equivalent (equivalent in the sense that a short high vowel is maintained in the stem under all conditions). There is no relation because there is no logical causal connection: the mode endings *could* once have existed on the ancestral variety, but there is no historical linguistic trace allowing such an inference to be made.[7]

---

[7] The present chapter skirts around further epenthetic phenomena, such as the CA rule, *radd-tu* → *radadtu* 'I returned', and requires a complete treatment of stress.

7

Imala

In the final two chapters, I draw on data from both modern dialects and Old Arabic sources. In each chapter, I begin with the Old Arabic sources.

Arguably, the most complicated treatment of a subject in Sibawaih in relation to variational properties is that of the *ʔimaala* (*imala*, as I term it). The term is Sibawaih's and like much terminology from the Arabic tradition has been taken over in the modern Arabistic literature. *ʔimaala* means 'inclining, bending to'. Essentially *imala* involves the change of a long *aa* to an *ee*-like value in the context of an /i/ in a preceding or following syllable. As will be seen, the examples Sibawaih gives are often identical forms found in the modern dialects which have *imala*, e.g.:

(1) *kilieb* 'dogs' (II: 279.21)
    masiejid 'mosques' (II: 279.11).

Imala involves a long /aa/, medial or final, and it can, in Sibawaih's terminology, be applied to short /a/ as well, though this is much more restricted. *Imala* of final /aa/ and /a/ treated in comparative perspective involves a prohibitively large data set. In this chapter, the comparative goals of the work are served by a concentration on the medial *imala* of long /aa/, with one exception in sect. 7.1.3 where I treat short /a/ *imala*. In describing Sibawaih's summary of *imala*, I do, however, occasionally describe *imala* of final long -aa, as it allows elucidation of Sibawaih's systematic linguistic thinking.

7.1. *Imala* in Old Arabic

7.1.1. *Phonetics and phonology*

Before summarizing the various, sometimes contradictory rules pertaining to where *imala* occurs, I will first attempt to ascertain its phonetic form. Sibawaih describes *imala* as a type of assimilation (*ʔidɣaam*), comparing it to assimilation of one consonant to another in terms of emphasis or voicing. The long *aa* is assimilated by a following or preceding *i*. He describes *imala* as an inclination of the tongue in which the phonetic configuration of /aa/ is made to resemble and approach that of /i/ (II: 279.16). Most Western scholars (e.g. Jastrow 1978; Levin 1998) who have worked on *imala*-dialects have not interpreted Sibawaih's description of the sound phonetically. They merely refer to it as *imala*. As phonetics is an important aspect of any linguistic reconstruction, however, some attention needs to be given to this issue. Schaade (1911: 23) represents it with the German umlaut [ä], which would imply a front [a]. He does not explain his orthography, however. Similarly, al-Nassir (1993: 92) suggesting only that the value of *imala* lies somewhere between [ee] and [ɛɛ], conventionally uses the symbol [ee]. He does not recognize a diphthongal value for it. Fleisch's interpretation is treated briefly in sect. 7.3.4 below.

Grünert (1875), although an early treatment among Western Arabicists, is a good one. Unlike some contemporary Arabicists (see sect. 7.3.4), he recognizes the close connection between classical *imala* and all the then-known modern dialectal varieties (Andalusia, Lebanon, Syria, Malta, even noting evidence in old Sicilian sources, 1875: 453).[1] Again in contrast to most contemporary sources (see above), Grünert attempts a very specific phonetic interpretation for classical *imala*. Unfortunately he bases his interpretation on post-Sibawahian texts only, and in the tradition of his compatriots (see Ch. 2), does not apply the comparative method to the contemporary dialectal sources.[2] The description of *imala* in later texts is quite unitary. Zamaxshari serves as an example. Zamaxshari says (*Mufaṣṣal* 335) that 'you incline an [aa] towards a [y]' (tumiyl al-ʔalif naḥw al-yaaʔ). Crucially, Grünert recognizes in this formulation a diphthongal value. However, there is nothing in it which specifies an

---

[1] Grünert (1875: 453) specifically relates the *imala* of the Arabic grammarians to North African dialects, citing the forms *biib* and *lisiin* (= *lsiin* if at all correct). This would imply the *imala*-induced change of [aa] > [ii]. In fact, outside the special cases of Maltese and eastern Libyan Arabic treated in detail in sect. 7.2, North African Arabic does not, according to contemporary descriptions, have this reflex for *[aa]. Marçais (1977) is an extensive review of North African dialects and in all examples where *imala* is expected (i.e. on the basis of comparison with other *imala*-dialects), his examples have [aa], e.g. *kaan* ('he was' p. 71, *lsaan* 'tongue' p. 119, *θmaanya* 'eight' p. 174). Similarly, Caubet in her edition of Marçais's studies on the Arabic of Fezzan (Southwest Libya) gives a low vowel, non-diphthongal reflex for these words (Marçais 2001: 162, 221–2, 255).

North Africa does have the change *[ay] > [ii], as in *biit* 'house' < *bayt*, but as will be discussed in greater detail in sect. 7.2.5, relating this change to Sibawaih's classical description of *imala* is quite problematic. Marçais does state that *imala* is found in Central Tunisian dialects, though gives no examples so it cannot be judged what are to be understood as lexical and phonetic reflexes of *imala* in this case (I thank Catherine Taine Cheikh, p.c., January 2005, for discussion of this point).

[2] In fact, Grünert (1875: 453) would appear to explain the various manifestations of modern *imala* as a result of spread of Arabic and foreign language contact, rather than as a reflex of pre-diasporic developments, as argued for in this chapter. He justifies his view through a prioristic assumptions rather than by case-by-case argumentation ('what occurs to every language under similar conditions, which undergo vowel modification', 'wie das bei jeder Sprache unter denselben Vorbedingungen der Fall ist, der Vocalismus immer mehr modificiert').

on-glide [ia] or an off-glide [ai]. Grünert, without discussion, opts for the latter (1875: 465). To be fair, reading Zamaxshari and other later descriptions linearly, this is probably the most neutral reading. Zamaxshari begins with the [aa] which you incline towards a [y]. Logically, however, the reverse could also be intended, with the [y] value in the beginning. Note that if the on-glide interpretation developed in detail below is correct, this would already indicate that Zamaxshari's reading is based purely on a philological reading of the *imala* value (or based on those who developed such), not on actual aural phonetic interpretation. Zamaxshari's *imala* description is treated in more detail in Appendix 3.

By comparison, Sibawaih, probably not by chance, used a passive formulation, 'the [aa] is inclined (imalized) if there is a consonant after it with [i]' (fa-al-ʔalif tumaal ʔiðaa kaan baʕdahaa ħarf maksuwr...). This betrays no bias for on-glide or off-glide value. To decide between the two further textual material may be adduced, along with an application of the comparative method.

In this section, I first suggest a phonetic interpretation of the *imala* of long /aa/, then summarize basic distributional properties.

The phonetic realization of *imala* can be interpreted as a high falling diphthong: the tongue begins in the position of [i] and moves towards [a] under the influence of an [i] in a neighboring syllable. This same *imala* is attested even earlier than Sibawaih in the Koranic reading tradition (see Ch. 4). In fact, it is associated above all with the Kufan readers Abu ʕAmr ibn ʕAlaaʔ, the main protagonist of Ch. 4 whom Sibawaih sometimes took as an authority on Arabic (Talmon 2003: 43–7) and al-Kisaaʔi, who has also been met above (see sect. 2.4.1.2, Didactic manuals). In Ibn Mujaahid *imala* is represented as the orthographic mark of a kasra placed before an alif, as in 'one who envies' حاسد, this token attributed to Abu Amr (Ibn Mujahid, 703).[3] In Sibawaih *imala* is signaled by a straight line (a type of kasra) written beneath the line, similarly placed before the alif, kiḷaab. A direct phonetic reading of these phonetic signs gives the diphthongs *ħiaasid*, *kiliaab*. Further in the reading tradition, Dani (49) describes Abu Amr and Kisaaʔi's reading of the *imala* of the -aa in *kaafiriyn* (= kiefiriyn) as 'imalizing... the [a] of the [k-]' (wa ʔamaala Abu ʕAmr wa al-Kisaaʔiy ʔaydan fiy riwaayat al-Duwriy fatħat al-kaaf min 'al-kaafiriyn' '). On a componential reading of this statement, the -aa = alif is stable, whereas the short vowel /a/(fatħa) which comes before the alif is said to imalize. Taking 'imalize' as an i-like pronunciation (see below),

---

[3] Similarly in the hand-written manuscripts described by Grünert (1875: 488), a kasra is usually placed before the alif.

thus gives the form *kiafiriyn*. This falling diphthong is basically the phonetic shape assumed here for Sibawaih's *imala* value.[4]

Furthermore, as will be seen, emphatic and guttural consonants such as /q/ are *imala* inhibitors. They favor the maintenance of /aa/ as /aa/.

(2) *qaaʕid* 'standing'

In the Arabic terminology *imala* is often referred to as a kasra = /i/ quality, whereas the lack of *imala* is referred to as a naṣb = /a/ quality.[5] As is well known, gutturals also have a lowering effect on imperfect verbs, so that as a rule verbs with a guttural (x, ɣ, q, ʕ, ħ, ʔ) at C_2 or C_3 will tend to have /a/, rather than /i/ or /u/ as stem vowel (Sibawaih II: 270, Ch. 470). In both instances the gutturals tend to favor a low, [a]-quality in the following vowel.[6] The important point for phonetic interpretation is that for *imala* the guttural consonant can be seen as inhibiting the high-falling diphthong at the beginning of the vowel, i.e. because *imala* is a high falling diphthong, the tongue raising is prevented in the guttural context.

An alternative interpretation would have *imala* as a low rising diphthong, [ai]. The main problem with this interpretation is that this gives a value identical with the already existent diphthong [ay], as in *bayt* 'house', and Sibawaih nowhere draws attention to any similarity between the two sounds. To the contrary, he appears to emphasize the unique phonetic character of *imala*. Furthermore, in a chapter after the discussion of *imala*, Sibawaih discusses the case of certain Arabs (he names some Qays and Lafazaara) who change a final long /aa/ to /ay/ in pausal position.

(3) *ħublaa* → *ħublay*
    'pregnant' (II: 314. 8)

This is a clear change of a long /aa/ to a rising diphthong, but Sibawaih does not include it in the category of *imala*. Were the *imala* similar to /ay/, one

---

[4] The *imala* alone recalls a chain-shifted variant, as described by Labov. Labov (1994: 116) notes that in a chain shift long vowels tend to rise. Given the diphthongal value, *imala* falls within this category of change (*aa* → *ie*). In fact, the North Frisian phonetic change [æː] → [ia] (ibid. 126, 135) is, alone, very close to what is proposed here as the original *imala* variant of /aa/. In the Arabic case, however, in general no chain is involved in *imala*; it is a conditioned variant. There are other vowel shifts attested, for instance *ay* → *ee*, summarized in various sections in 7.3 below, though this appears largely to operate independently of *imala*. A detailed discussion would take one outside the immediate subject of this chapter.

[5] This terminology recalls the early use of *naṣb* purely as a phonetic designation for [a] (see e.g. Versteegh 1993b: 125 ff. on the early exegetical tradition).

[6] Though the status of [ħ] and [ʕ] is problematic. In Sibawaihi they are not among the *imala* inhibitors. There are dialects, however, e.g. Maltese, where *[ʕ] is an *imala* inhibitor.

might have expected here mention of similarity. In fact, in this case there is a minimal contrast with the alternative

(4) ħublaa → ħublie (287. 18).

Example (4) is an alternative *imala* realization of the final *-aa* of ħublaa, and is discussed among the various issues in the chapters on *imala*. There are, therefore, two realizations for the final *-aa*, practiced, it appears, by different groups. The crucial point is that the *imala* realization has to be distinguished from a different realization, a difference which can be interpreted as [ie] (*imala*) vs. [ay] (Qaysi realization).

In this regard, as will be seen below in sect. 7.2, dialects with *imala* tend to preserve the diphthong *ay*. This supports the contention that the direction of tongue movement in the two cases is quite different, different articulatory movements being involved.

Where modern dialects do not have a monophthongal reflex of *imala*, the realization is always a high falling diphthong. In eastern Libyan Arabic (ELA), for instance the phonetic value of *imala* is [ie] and in Maltese variously [ie], [eɛ], etc., always higher to lower. I take the ELA value to be close to the interpretation of Sibawaih's description, a point which will be expanded upon in sect. 7.2.2 below, and therefore use [ie] as the canonical *imala* value.

As a final phonetic remark, in the Koranic reading tradition (though not in Sibawaih) certain readers or certain readings of *imala* are sometimes referred to as 'in between' (*bayna bayna*).[7] This is said to be a value between [a] and [i] (Ibn Mujahid, 145), though unfortunately it is not specified more closely. I return to this terminology in sect. 7.3.3 below.

Turning now to distributional matters, while I concentrate in the rest of this section on issues of phonological distribution, it is ultimately impossible to separate the linguistic treatment from dialectological and sociolectal variation, as will be seen.

In Sibawaih *imala* is basically an allomorph of *aa*. *Imala* does not affect a long *aa* when /a/ or /u/ rather than /i/ occurs in the context, hence not in *taabal* 'coriander' or in *ʔaajur* 'baked brick'. It is also usually prevented from occurring in the context of the so-called 'raised' consonants (ħuruwf musta ʕliya), which include the emphatics and gutturals, *q, x, ɣ, ð̣, ḍ, ṭ,* or *ṣ*. (II: Ch. 480). In addition, /r/ may act as a *imala*-inhibitor as well (II: Ch. 481), a context which I return to in sect. 7.1.3 below. Another way of looking at the phenomenon is to say that /aa/ imalizes unless prevented from doing so by one of the inhibiting consonants (Cantineau 1960: 96–7, Corriente 1977: 22).

---

[7] The reading tradition also has degrees of *imala* where some *imala* is stronger than others (see Ch. 5 n. 16).

Levin (1998: 77–80) summarizes the context of Sibawaih's *imala* in three main categories (C = category).

C1. In the context of an [i], as in (1). This may be termed allophonic *imala*.

C2. Lexically conditioned: when a weak medial verb has an [i] in the paradigm. In these verbs *imala* can occur even in the context of an inhibiting consonant, as in *xief* 'he feared' (cf. *xif-tu* 'I feared', for the [i] in the paradigm). Other verbs cited here include *ṭaab* 'be good' and *haab* 'fear' (II: 281. 13).

C3. Weak medial nouns, so long as no inhibiting consonant occurs, as in *bieb* 'door', *nies* 'people'.

(C3), it should be noted, is Levin's observation, correct I should add. Sibawaih (II: 285) views these as exceptional (ʃaaðð), a point taken up in sect. 7.3.3 below. It should also be born in mind that (C1) and (C3) serve as reference to types of *imala* that are also found in modern dialects, discussed in sect. 7.2.

In fact, the situation is more complicated than represented in (C1)–(C3), both linguistically and dialectally/idiolectally.

First, individual sounds have idiosyncratic effects, in particular /r/. Sibawaih devotes an entire chapter (481, 3 1/2 pages in all) to describing the effect of /r/ on *imala*. As always, there is a great deal of detail, which will be pared down to the essentials, as relevant to a later comparison with eastern Libyan Arabic (sect. 7.2.2). Sibawaih's basic observation is that an /r/ before /aa/ is an *imala* inhibitor, whereas an /r/ after /aa/ tends to favor it.[8] As usual, there must be an /i/ in the environment to induce *imala*.

(5) *ḥimier-i-k* 'donkey-GEN-your.M' (II: 290. 5)

vs.

(6) *firaaʃ-i* 'bedding.GEN'
    raaʃid 'directing' (II: 289. 20)

In regard to *ḥimier-i-ka* it is interesting that Sibawaih considers this to be equivalent to *faʕaalil* plural noun, i.e. with the suffixes -i-k conceived of as part of the stem. I return to this point in sect. 7.2.2 below.

Though less common than (6), the *imala*-abetting effect of pre-r /aa/ can even induce *imala* after a guttural sound.

(7) *qierib* 'nearing'
    ṭierid 'chasing' (II: 290. 6)

---

[8] Post-aa /r/ as *imala* abettor is also treated in the *QiraaʔAat* tradition (Ibn Mujahid, 147, 149–50).

The /aa/ need not immediately precede the /r/, as in

(8) *kiefir* 'unbeliever'.

With an initial guttural sound, however, the /r/ generally must come immediately after the /aa/, though even here *imala* is attested among some speakers.

(9) *qaadir* 'able' more often than *qiedir* (II: 291. 12)

In terms of frequency of imalization, and leaving off further details, Sibawaih gives the following hierarchy of *imala* in the context of /r/.

(10) Given an *imala*-inducing environment:
 raa, ier > G*ier* > GaaCir
 G = guttural consonant

Imala does not occur after /r/, does occur before it, can occur even after a guttural consonant, and generally does not occur after a guttural if the /r/ is not adjacent to /aa/.

Besides (C2) above, describing word-final *imala*, Sibawaih notes that there is a tendency for a final /aa/ to imalize, even if the stem has no /i/ or /y/ in it, as in *daʕie* 'he called' < *daʕawa* and *ʕaʃie* 'show dim-sightedness' < *ʕaʃaw*. He notes that such /w/ final nouns and verbs undergo *imala* because the vast majority of weak final verbs have /y/ rather than /w/ (II: 280. 10) and because there are forms, the passive of verbs, where even /w/ -final verbs have a /y/ in the paradigm (*duʕiya* 'he was called'). Further complications are discussed below.

Furthermore, the three categories identified by Levin are not necessarily mutually exclusive. This can be exemplifed in Sibawaih's discussion of the *imala* of weak-medial nouns (II: 282). It should be emphasized that the following discussion is representative of a number of different cases, all of which display a great deal of internal variation.

Sibawaih notes that some speakers imalize /aa/in /i/ contexts, as in (11). Anticipating sect. 7.1.2, in the following it is relevant to introduce briefly the groups whom Sibawaih associated with some of the *imala* variants. The designation 'group' identifies the people who Sibawaih says use the variant in question.

(11) *bi-l-miel-i*
 with-the-wealth-GEN
 group: *qaaluw* 'they (unspecified people) said' (II: 282. 11)

This practice would seem to correspond to (1) above, as he gives the non-pausal variant (12):

(12) *bi-l-maal*
 'with the wealth'
 group: minhum man yadʕuw ðaalika fi l-waqf ʕalaa ħaalihi [i.e. in *imala* form because of genitive context] wa minhum man yanṣibu fiy l-waqf (II: 282. 11), 'among them are those who leave the form in pausal position as it is in context, and those who leave it as /aa/ in all circumstances' (see (13) below)

where lacking the conditioning force of /i/, the /aa/ of *maal* remains in its non-*imala* state.

However, Sibawaih goes on to note that there are also those (minhum man, see above) who imalize even when the conditioning genitive suffix does not occur, in the context of pause.

(13) *bi-l-miel*
 group: as in (12)

Sibawaih, who always searched for parallels to help understand a given observation (see Owens 2005) suggests that the deleted -i suffix still has imalizing force. He cites as a precedent the active participle variant of weak-final participles, such as

(14) *mieʃiy* ~ *mieʃ* ~ *maaʃ*
 'walking'.

The active participle has in addition to its 'usual' variant *mieʃiy* or *maaʃiy* a variant without the final *-iy* (see Carter 1990) and here an *imala* variant is attested, even though the conditioning *-iy* is deleted.

In this set of examples it appears that Sibawaih is basically talking about the same group of speakers, though this is not explicitly spelled out. If this is so, then there are among these speakers those who conform to (C1), i.e. speakers who have the usage (C2) and (C3), and those, who, in Sibawaih's description, conform to (C1), and to yet another category, namely:

(C4) *imala* in a non-*imala* context, on the basis of a lexicalized genitive, as in (13).

However, even this summary does not cover all cases. In a later chapter (II: ch. 479, 285) he notes the further variant:

(15) haaðaa mielun
 'This is wealth' (II: 285. 11)
 group: wa qaala naas yuwθaq bi-ʕarabiyyatihim 'people whose Arabic is reliable'

This is an unconditioned *imala*, as indeed Sibawaih notes, since *maal* comes from the stem *mwl*, with /w/ rather than /y/ as medial consonant, and the context does not have an-i suffix. Sibawaih explains this case as he does *daʕie* discussed above: /y/ tends to predominate over /w/ as a stem consonant, and forms associated with /y/ stems spread analogically to other classes.

In Levin's classification this is a case of (C3). The interpretive problem, however, is whether (11), (13), and (14) are in fact separate cases. While (15) is treated in a separate chapter from (13), the groups using the variants are identified so vaguely that one cannot say with certainty how many sociolinguistic groups one is dealing with. This problem is discussed in greater detail below. Linguistically, one can represent the three cases on a cline of values, moving from most *imala* to least *imala*:

(16) a. haaðaa mielun (*imala* in all cases)
 b. bi-l-miel-i, bi-l-miel, maal-un (*imala* in non-pausal and pausal genitive context, not with nominative suffix)
 c. bi-l-miel-i vs. bi-l-maal (*imala* before surface -i, otherwise /aa/).
 d. bi-l-maal-i (never *imala*)

(16) looks very like a change-in-progress type hierarchy, with *imala* generalizing from a conditioned (16c) to a non-conditioned (16a) variant of an original /aa/. Unfortunately, one can do no more than speculate that this was the situation Sibawaih was observing, as precise data is lacking. While one can extrapolate a very neat hierarchy out of Sibawaih's various descriptions, one should not lose sight of the fact that Sibawaih's goal was to make order out of chaos, and one can construct a case for Sibawaih idealizing his grammatical rules at the expense of ignoring alternative explanations.

I would like to follow up this point with two further examples. First, Sibawaih notes that some Arabs imalize *miet* < *maata* 'he died'. Ordinarily, according to (C2) above this lexeme should not imalize, since *maata* has a lexical /w/ as its medial consonant (cf. *mawt*, 'death'). Sibawaih rationalizes this by noting that those Arabs who do imalize *miet* also say *mit-tu* 'I died' in the perfect, i.e. do have an /i/ in the overall paradigm (wa hum allaðiyna yaquwluwna 'mittu'). While there are modern dialects with /i/ as the perfect vowel (Nigerian Arabic *mit*), most have /u/ (*muttu*) and this is the usual form in Classical Arabic.⁹ Of course, Sibawaih's linkage (see below), i.e. all who imalize actually have /i/ as the perfect vowel, may be correct. On the other hand, given the variation described below, it is equally plausible that Sibawaih is idealizing his grammatical rule to the case of a verb which in fact should not have *imala*, i.e. some Arabs do indeed say *miet*, but these could be those who say *mut-tu*. Given the information at our disposal, it could equally be that the imalization of *miet* is of the same category of the unconditioned *imala* of *bieb*, discussed below. Sibawaih interprets the matter in another way, however, since he, like any good linguist, is above all concerned to explain as many variants as possible according to a general rule.

A similar point pertains to Sibawaih's observation that *maal* is sensitive to the influence of an /i/ in a preceding word. He notes that those who use *maal* in pausal context (= (13) above)

(17) *bi-l-maal*

can imalize when an /i/ occurs in a preceding word,

(18) *li-zayd-in miel*
    to-Zayd-GEN wealth
    'Zayd has money'.

Again, this may be the actual situation. But it is equally possible that Sibawaih has observed a speaker who always uses *imala* in this word (as in (15)). Sibawaih, however, ascribes to him the conditioned *imala*, since this is explicable by phonological rule.

The cautionary note I am introducing here is that while Sibawaih's observations were certainly cogent as far as they pertained to the usage of certain individuals, in a few cases groups of individuals, Sibawaih, unlike present-day linguists, did not have at his disposal models for describing language variation as a general or group-based phenomenon, nor did he develop them.¹⁰ There is no way of controlling in his descriptions who uses which variants to what extent, though it is clear that the use of *imala* cuts across all segments of the speech community (see sect. 7.1.2 below). For this reason (16) is an interesting summary of what forms did occur, but cannot be used to draw detailed inferences about how the language was developing in the late eighth century. What one can say is that *imala* was a very widespread phenomenon with a plethora of conditioning factors.

---

⁹ In the *Lisaan al-ʕArab* (2: 91) the variant *mittu* is given, based on Sibawaih.
¹⁰ In contrast, in a certain manner, to the *QiraaʔAat*, the Koranic reading tradition which at least made an exhaustive listing of variants ordered against various readers and chains of transmission.

7.1.2. Imala: *a variationist's dream*
How confusing the situation was is attested directly by Sibawaih.

Know that not everyone who imalizes the /aa/ agrees with others of the Arabs who do so. Rather, each one of the two groups might differ from the other, in that one might use /aa/ [in a word?] where his neighbor imalizes, while he will imalize where his neighbor uses /aa/. Similarly, someone who [basically?] has /aa/ will differ from another who [basically?] has /aa/, in a way similar to those who [basically?] use *imala*. So if you should encounter an Arab with such forms, don't assume that he is simply mixing up forms. Rather, that is how the matter stands. (II: 284. 1)[11]

Sibawaih's style is obscure in certain respects here (as often elsewhere) and I have edited in words (marked with a question mark) to facilitate an understanding of the text. In any case, his observation is fully consistent with the data as it is presented. To give some quick examples here, regarding (C1), he says that many Tamim and others do not use it at all (281. 4). Previously he had said that none of the Hijaz use it, so it may be surmised that (C1) is a non-Hijazi application, though variable. (C2) on the other hand, is used by 'some of the Hijaz' (281. 12). *biyyieʕ* 'seller' may be imalized, but many Hijazi, as well as many Arabs do not apply the *imala* to it (281. 21). In general Sibawaih notes that *nies* 'people' and *miel* 'wealth' (see (13) above) may imalize, but that this is to be regarded as exceptional and most Arabs do not imalize these words (ch. 479).

What characterizes this topic, more than perhaps any other in the *Kitaab*, however, is the extent to which Sibawaih points to linkages between different groups. This was met in the discussion of *miet* ∼ *mit* above. A typical formulation is to observe that those speakers who say form x, also use y; in the above example, those who use /i/ in the perfect also use *imala* in the third person form of the weak medial verb.

All in all, the discussion of *imala* is marked by Sibawaih's frequent reference to various groups of speakers, or to individual experts. These can be termed 'social identities'. What one traditionally terms 'dialects', as illustrated in a previous paragraph, in fact represent only a small minority of all such group-based references. Individual grammarians figure hardly at all, and the Koranic readers are not well represented.[12] By far the largest groups are the bedouins

---

[11] In the light of this passage, which Fleisch himself cites, Fleisch's statement is incomprehensible: 'In the writer's opinion, in addition to a conditioned *imala*, there exists an unconditioned *imala* which is widely used, which Arab grammarians have not recognized as such and have forced into the framework of the first, without, however, leaving us the means to discriminate precisely between the two' (Fleisch 1961: 1162). Besides the passage quoted, Sibawaih's category of 'ʃaaðð', (exceptional) to describe the *imala* of *nies* 'people' takes cognizance precisely of the situation Fleisch summarizes.

[12] Examples of (C2) are also found in the reading tradition. Sibawaih does note that the Koranic readers (unnamed ʕaamma) use *imala* in verbs where the medial consonant is /y/, as in *xaaf* (II: 281,

(ʕArab), and the grammar-internal groups marked by linkages. In all I have counted fifty references to groups of speakers who are referred to with an independent noun or pronoun. The figures are presented in Table 7.1. Plural verb forms alone, such as *qaal-uw* 'they said', often referring to bedouins, are not counted. With the table I include an index, formed of the total social identities divided by the pages per topic.

By way of comparison, I also counted references to social identities in the chapters on noun modifiers which themselves govern a complement (*marartu bi rajulin muxaaliṭin ʕalayhi daaʔun* 'I passed a man afflicted with an illness', see Carter 1972). This is a topic which covers twelve pages and hence is roughly comparable in length to the fifteen pages in which *imala* is discussed.

There are two striking differences between the social identities found in the two topics, one quantitative, the other qualitative. For present purposes the first is the more important, though I will first comment briefly on the second. The section on noun modifiers deals with syntactic matters, which in Sibawaih are often subject to analogical reasoning. In these particular chapters he

TABLE 7.1. Social identities in the chapters on *imala*, Sibawaih II: 279–94

Entities	Observations
ʔAhl al-ḥijaz	3
Tamim	2
ʔAsad	1
Qays	1
Al-ʕaamma = (consensus) of Koranic readers	2
Xalil	1
Abu ʔIsḥaaq*	1
Bedouins, (al-ʕArab)	10
Those of reliable Arabic	3
'those who say x ...' (man qaala x/allaðiyna qaaluw x)	14
Many people (naas kaθiyr)	1
People (qawm)	4
Some of them (baʕduhum)	4
These (haʔulaaʔ)	2
The two groups	1
Total: 15	50
Index	3.3

* A Basran Koranic reader, d. 129/746 (or 117/735). He is reported to have heard xiefa 'fear' as ṣiera 'become' (Kitaab II: 281).

see n. 9). Dani (48) reports that the reader Hamza (one of the seven) used *imala* in ten verbs, more than the number Sibawaih attributes to the readers. All these follow Sibawaih's rule whereby the medial consonant must be /y/.

TABLE 7.2. Social identities, noun modifiers (Sibawaih I: 195–207)

Entities	Observations
Bedouins	11
Xalil	7
Yunus	3
Grammarians (naḥwiyyuwn)	2
ʕIysaa	1
Common language (*kalaam al-naas*)	1
Those who say x (linkages)	3
Total: 7	28
Index	4

takes issue with a number of other opinions on various constructions, and therefore almost half the social identities cited are grammarians (see Talmon 2003: 48, 57). There appears to be a lower need to cite native speakers, since here matters of correctness are decided by grammatical rules. Clearly, it is a question of general import beyond the scope of this chapter, what the relation is between social identities and individual grammatical topics.

In the discussion of *imala*, on the other hand, Sibawaih is confronted with various usages by native speakers, which he appears to record faithfully, even if, as suggested above, he probably idealizes the homogeneity of the forms in regards to individual speakers or groups of speakers. As far as the realization of phonological forms goes, he cannot reject them on the basis of false grammatical reasoning. At best, and this is to his enduring empirical credit, he can note them as exceptional (*ʃaaðð*).

As far as the actual count goes, there are both a larger number of social identities and observations for *imala*, overproportional to the number of pages in the two topics (fifteen for *imala*, twelve for modifiers). The lower index for *imala* indicates that Sibawaih was noting linguistic variation on a finer scale for *imala* than for the nominal modifiers in that he invoked a larger number of entities to account for a larger number of observations. The high number of linkages indicates a complex web of phonological dependency, at least in Sibawaih's way of thinking, and it is probably this phonological complexity which underlines Sibawaih's invocation of many grouping categories.

7.1.3. Imala *of short* /a/

Before leaving Sibawaih and turning to the situation in the modern dialects, it is necessary to consider the last chapter of the section on *imala*, which deals, inter alia, with *imala* of short /a/ (II: 293, ch. 482). The general theme of the chapter concerns the *imala* of an /aa/ or /a/ before an /r/. An /r/ has an imalizing effect on a preceding /aa/ or /a/. Rather than *min maṭar-in*, for instance, one has *maṭier-in*. The diphthong, however, is not indicated as long.[13]

Among the forms cited are *xieyr* < *xayr* 'better' and *ʕieyr* < *ʕayr* 'insult'. As will be seen in sect. 3.2 below, the phonetic interpretation of this form is important, so it is relevant to look at Sibawaih's description in greater detail. He adds in relation to these two examples:

(Q 2) 'and you don't sniff them, because otherwise it would disappear in the /y/[of *xayr*], just as an /i/ does' (fa-lam tuʃmim liʔannahaa taxfaa maʕa l-yaaʔ kamaa ʔanna al-kasra fiy l-yaaʔ ʔaxfaa).

This phonetic description is somewhat difficult for the use of two technical terms. *Paʃamma* 'give the phonetic coloring to, lit. smell, sniff', is generally used in form IV, with the verbal noun *Piʃmaam*. *Paxfaa* is 'hide'. Discussion of each is necessary.

Wehr (1974: 485) gives as a translation of *Piʃmaam* the pronunciation of a sound with a trace of [i]. This is only a partial translation. In Sibawaih, two distinct usages of *Piʃmaam* are discernible. In the first, Sibawaih discusses *Piʃmaam* along with other pausal phenomena in chapter 494 (II: 307). In all there are four different ways to effect a pausal form. One of these is termed *Piʃmaam*. As noted in sect. 1.6.3, it appears that *Piʃmaam* is realized as a voicelessness of a final nominative /u/. This can be seen in two places. First, Sibawaih notes that *Piʃmaam* occurs only in the nominative, not genitive or accusative (II: 309. 1). This rules out an interpretation of *Piʃmaam* in this context as lip rounding. /u/ is already a round vowel, and the case ending which would make an otherwise unrounded vowel into a rounded vowel is the genitive. This, however, cannot have *Piʃmaam*. Second, Sibawaih very carefully explains that when one uses *Piʃmaam*, it is only a visible feature, not an audible one; if you were to do *Piʃmaam* before a blind person he would not recognize it.

In other contexts *Piʃmaam* is used to describe lip rounding. This occurs in the discussion of passivization, for instance in the example:

(19) *Puxzüya* < *Puxziya*
    'it was attacked', 447. 6 (also II: 280. 10, II: 398. 4)

---

[13] One hundred and thirty years after Sibawaih, Sarraj (III: 169) summarizes this type of *imala* simply as *imala* of short /a/ (*fatħat al-ʔimaala naħw al-kasra*, as title), without specifying the /r/ conditioning context. In general later grammarians systematized and summarized Sibawaih's treatment of *imala* in a concise fashion, but added nothing new as far as its workings go. In App. 3, I show this on the basis of a comparison between Sibawaih's treatment of *imala* and that of Zamaxshari.

where Sibawaih suggests that the lip rounding of the vowel before /y/, which in the passive model should be [i], is due to the fact that the stem *ɣazaa/ yaɣzuw* is originally a /w/ final verb. This has to be seen as a different usage from the first, as the vowel is in non-pausal position.

In passing it can be noted that *ʔiʃmaam* is also used elsewhere in the larger Arabic grammatical tradition. In Ibn Mujahid (105), for instance, the quality of the the /ṣ/ in ṣiraaṭ 'way' (Q 1.5) is discussed in which four variants are noted, [ṣ, s, z, *ʔiʃmaam*]. The first three are values represented in the normal Arabic script. The last is said to be a value between ṣ and z.

The term *ʔiʃmaam* is used to designate a medial value, this usage derivable from its original etymology. A sound has the scent of something else, without being that.

Turning to the second term, Sibawaih uses the stem *ʔaxfaa* 'be hidden' in various forms, adjectival *xafiyy* 'hidden', *xafaaʔ* 'hiddenness', *ʔaxfaa* 'more hidden', etc. (see Troupeau 1976: 84). It has a complex of meanings, in a phonological sense related to the idea that some sounds are inherently less perceptible or less salient than others. These are in particular /aa/, /iy/, /uw/, /h/, and /n/. Additionally, *ʔaxfaa* describes a process whereby a sound may (1) not appear, as when an underlying /i/ does not appear between two ys, as in *ʔahiyya* < *ʔahyiya* 'she camel's private parts' (pl. of *hayyaaʔ*, II: 431. 9, *Lisaan* 14: 219), (2) have a moric value, but not necessarily a vocalic realization,[14] as in *tətanaajaw* 'you speak together secretly' (II: 457. 10), an alternative to *ttanaajaw*, and (3) assimilate to another, as when an /n/ is said to assimilate to oral consonants (II: 464. 24). In the last case, it appears that *xafaaʔ* is an al ternative to *ʔidɣaam* 'assimilation' when the assimilated consonant has the property of *xafaaʔ*.

Having briefly considered Sibawaih's technical terminology, I return to the interpretation of *bi-xieyr* in (Q 2) above. The term *ʔiʃmaam* remains problematic. It could be that Sibawaih is saying that the imalized short /a/, here given the phonetic interpretation [ie], does not have a rounded vowel (lam yuʃmam), i.e. not *bi-xüeyr*. What would remain unexplained, however, is why *ʔiʃmaam* in the sense of lip rounding would be mentioned in this context at all, since *ʔiʃmaam* in this sense usually occurs only when an [u] or a /w/ is somewhere in the paradigm, to induce the rounding, as in (19). In any case, should an *ʔiʃmaam* quality be contemplated here, it cannot occur because the

---

[14] In this context, the property of *taxfiyya* is qualified with 'with the weight of a short vowel' (*bi- zinat l-mutaharrik*), i.e. a vowel is 'hidden', but it still has metrical weight.

[i] value which arises from the *imala* is so close to the /y/ that no *ʔiʃmaam* is possible.

I would note in passing that if this interpretation is plausible, it would be another argument for the [ie] quality of *imala* as opposed to [ai] or [ei]. The latter would give a geminate y, *xaiyr* = *xayyr*, which is a value Sibawaih nowhere hints at.

7.2. *Imala* in the Modern Dialects

In this section, I summarize the reflexes of *imala* in the modern dialects. Today there are three separate areas with reflexes of word-internal *imala*, eastern Libya, Malta, and the *qultu* dialects of Mesopotamian Arabic. In addition, *imala* was well attested in the Arabic of Spain (Andalusia), and this will also be included in this summary. One further related reflex from southern Iraq will also be summarized in this section.

While the reflexes of *imala* in all four locations are broadly similar, they always differ on points of detail. *Imala* is summarized according to conditions of occurrence and for phonetic reflex.

Before beginning, some general distinctions can be noted which have been applied in the description of modern-day *imala*.

Imala can be lexical or allophonic. While lexical *imala* often has a phonological origin when examined in a historical perspective, it is irregular in that a comparable context in a paradigmatically related word will not display *imala*. Allophonic *imala*, on the other hand shows a regular alternation between *imala* and *imala*-less forms. (C1) is a classic example of this, and indeed will be met with below. Allophonic *imala* has often been termed productive *imala* (e.g. Blanc 1964: 47). However, there are various degrees of productivity. As will be seen, Mesopotamian *imala*, for instance, is largely restricted to the allophonic conditioning element of the plural suffix -*iin*. ELA *imala*, on the other hand, is unrestrictedly allophonic, any suffix -i inducing *imala*.

The word-internal *imala* of /aa/ which I restrict myself to here is also sometimes termed i-*imala*, as it is induced by an underlying or overt [i]. I prefer not to use this terminology, as it implies that the *imala* of, say, *klieb* 'dogs' (ELA) is somehow conditioned differently from that of *nies* 'people'. This may or may not have been the case historically ((C1) vs. (C3) above, see sect. 7.3.2). However, the two can be subsumed under a common rule (imalize unless an inhibiting factor occurs) and hence can be conceptualized as a single phenomenon, something the 'i-*imala*' formulation prohibits.

7.2.1. Andalusia

For Spain, Corriente (1977: 22) simply formulates *imala* in the converse way from Sibawaih (type (C1)). Sibawaih takes the non-*imala* form as the input, and specifies conditions where it occurs. Corriente says that in Andalusia the unmarked case is for *imala* to occur, 'whenever this tendency (*imala*) was not checked by inhibiting factors'. As seen above, Sibawaih was describing a speech community where *imala* and non-*imala* varieties existed side by side. In Corriente's Andalusian data, apparently, the *imala* variant had become so widespread that it was easier to note exceptions than to give rules for *imala*. For the inhibiting factors Corriente refers the reader to Cantineau's summary of *imala*, which are basically those of (C1) above. It thus appears that Andalusian Arabic and the classical description are similar.

In Spanish Arabic the value of *imala* is generally /ee/, though /ii/ also occurs. Both varieties are attested throughout the existence of Arabic in Spain, though it appears that the /ii/ variant became more common in later sources.

(20) *yibede* 'worship' (< *ʕibaada*)
moneeda [almoneda] 'auction'
niis 'people' (Ferrando, p.c., citing Pedro de Alcala, early fifteenth century, < *naas*)
kiin 'he was' (Corriente 1977: 24 n. 6, < *kaan*)

Corriente (1977: 23 n. 3) also notes examples of *imala* occasionally occurring in inhibiting contexts.

(21) *ribeete* 'strip' < *ribaaṭa*
maqeem 'holy place' < *maqaam*

As far as the diphthong *ay* goes, it is generally maintained as *ay* in Spanish Arabic (Corriente 1977: 29).

(22) *al-qaṣr-ayn*
'the two castles'

7.2.2. Eastern Libyan Arabic

In eastern Libyan Arabic conditions for *imala* are very like those in (C1) above. Emphatic consonants and an /a/ environment prevent *imala*. Otherwise a long /aa/ is realized as [ie].[15]

---

[15] In Owens (1984) *imala* in Benghazi Arabic is described as a palatalization of the preceding consonant, followed by a low front vowel, *iħð ʸaa* 'near him'.

(23) *iCaa* or *aaCi* → *ie*

Mitchell (1975: 52–7) offers a detailed discussion of sometimes singular conditions for *imala*, but by and large it can be said that inhibiting contexts are emphatics, /x/ and /ɤ/ and following /a/.

(24) No change   ʔimaala
    a. *ṭaaliʕ* 'leaving'   *mieʃi* 'going'
    b.   *misieʒid* 'mosques'
    c. *aṭfaal-hin* their.F. children
    d. *baal-kam* 'look out.MPL.'   *biel-ik* 'look out.FSG' (Mitchell 1975: 56)
    e. *saamaħ* 'he forgave'   *siemiħ* 'forgive!'
    f. *mooz-aat* 'banana-PL'   *mooz-iet-ik* 'your.F bananas'
                                          (Owens 1980: 42)

This *imala* is allophonic in that the occurrence of *imala* is conditioned by the suffixation of an *imala*-inducing front vowel, as in (24d) and (24f). Mitchell (1975: 52) notes that the allophony is sensitive to the status both of a potentially inhibiting consonant, and to the morphological status of the following front vowel. Emphatics and gutturals always inhibit (24c).

The behavior of /r/ in ELA is interesting, because it allows a direct comparison with Sibawaih's detailed description of /r/ in *imala* (see (10)). Distilling over a long discussion, the four main conditions in Mitchell regarding /r/ and *imala* in ELA may be summarized thus: /r/ does not inhibit if a following /i/ is in the same stem as the /aa/, but if it is in a suffix it does.[16]

Before /aa/ a /r/ is an *imala* inhibitor.

(25) *ṛaami* 'having thrown'

An /aa/ before /r/ allows *imala* (in Sibawaih's terms, is an *imala* abettor), provided the /i/ is within the word stem.

(26) *dieri* 'take care of!' (< *daari*)

A word-final post-aa /r/ is an *imala* inhibitor.

(27) *uħmaaṛ* 'donkey'
     daaṛ 'house'

---

[16] Mitchell gives the further example *siemiħ-ih* 'he forgave him' < *saamaħ* + *-ih*, where the /a/ of the final syllable in the verb is raised to /i/ in an open syllable, by regular phonological rule in the dialect. This raised /i/ then induces *imala* in the long /aa/. The effects of a phonological rule in turn inducing *imala* may be compared to a form such as *ʕimied-ie* 'support.ACC' < *ʕimaad-aa*, cited as a variant of some people, where the initial /i/ induces *imala* of the following /aa/, and this in turn of the accusative suffix (282. 14).

Imala does not work across morpheme boundaries, so that given (26), if a suffix such as *-i* 'my' is added, no *imala* is induced, in contrast to (24d, f).

(28) *daa̱r-i* 'my house'

Summarizing these contexts:

(29) *raa, aar#, ieri*

What is noteworthy is that broadly speaking two of the three contexts are comparable to Sibawaih's observations on /r/ *imala* summarized in (10) above. An /aa/ in post /r/ position does not imalize while an /aa/ before /r/ does. The main difference is that an /aa/ before /r/ does not imalize in ELA across morpheme boundaries, which it does in Sibawaih's description. However, even here it was noted that Sibawaih conceived of *ħimierik* as a single stem (see (5) above). This is a somewhat mysterious classification. Perhaps Sibawaih expected *imala* not to occur across a morpheme boundary here, as in ELA, and therefore assumed that a type of post-morphemic phonological realignment was needed to explain the *imala* of *aar*. In these terms, the difference between ELA and Sibawaih's description in this third respect would be that in Sibawaih's variety *aar-i* realigns to *aari* allowing→*ieri*, whereas in ELA no realignment occurs, so *aar-i* remains *aar-i*.

In ELA *imala* occurs only in stressed syllables, so alternations such as the following are found.

(30) *ki'tab-na* 'we wrote'   *kitab-'nie-hin* 'we wrote them.F'
    saa'miħ-li 'forgive me'   *'siemiħ* 'forgive'

Lacking inhibiting consonants, *imala* will occur in monosyllabic nouns ((C3) above).

(31) *nies* 'people'
    bieb 'door'

The diphthong *ay* is either maintained, particularly after a guttural consonant, or, and this is more common in Benghazi, monophthongized to *ee*.

(32) *ʕayn* 'eye'
    beet 'house'

7.2.3. Malta

In general Maltese *imala* is similar to that of ELA, except that, having lost emphatic consonants, *imala*-induced *aa has a wider distribution than in ELA. Maltese is dialectally diverse, so I begin with standard Maltese (Aquilina 1973: 53–6) and then briefly consider dialect differences.

216   Imala

Imala is realized as [iə], represented as 'ie' in Maltese orthography.

(33) *baab > bieb 'door'
      θalaaθa > tlieta 'three'
      banaat > (?binaat) > bniet 'girls'
      xaddaam > haddiem 'workman'
      kaan > kien 'he was'

As in ELA, the diphthongal realization occurs only in stressed syllables. When unstressed the vowel shortens to [i] or [e],

(34) bniedem 'man', but bnedm-iin 'men'
      bi'rik-t 'I blessed', 'biərk-u 'they blessed, n-'biərek 'I bless'
      (Vanhove 1993: 28).

When final /a/ is unstressed it does not imalize. If a suffix is added, lengthening the /aa/, it does.

(35) ktib-na, 'we wrote', ktib-nie-hum 'we wrote them'
      sewa 'he did', swie-l-a 'it cost her' < sewaa-l-ha (Aquilina 1973: 56)

Maltese has lost the classic inhibiting contexts of imala. Nonetheless, one trace of a former emphatic context, ɣ or x is the lack of imala in the vowel. This pertains to r,[17] etymological emphatic consonants, ɣ, and x and also ʕ. Imala inhibition appears particularly strong when the former inhibiting context preceded *aa.[18] Unless otherwise stated, the following examples were culled from Borg and Azzopardi-Alexander 1997.

(36) dyaar 'houses' < diyaar (Aquilina 1973: 22, 43)
      ʔaali 'expensive' < ɣaali (ibid. 22, 43)
      rhaam 'marble' < rxaam (Ambros 1998: 26, 34)
      sfaar-u 'they got yellow' < ṣfarr (Vanhove 1993: 29)
      am 'he swam' < ʕaam (għam)
      il-ħames 'the fifth' < il-xaamis
      sittaʃ '16' < siṭṭaaʃ
      ndafa 'cleanliness' < nḍaafa
      saʔ 'he drove' < saaq or ṣaaq
         In addition the suffix -an < *aan does not undergo imala.
      daħk-an 'laughing'

---

[17] Presumably *r̥, see Schabert 1976: 51.
[18] Schabert (1976: 46) explicitly observes that etymological /aa/before ʕ imalizes, ʔi·ɛɛ·t 'sitting' < ʔaaʕid, even in the context of etymological emphatics, *ṭaaʕam > tiam 'taste,

Nonetheless, *imala* may still occur in etymologically inhibiting contexts,

(37) *tielaʔ* 'going up' < *ṭaaliʕ*
      rieʔed 'sleeping' < *raaqid*
      sieʔ 'leg' < *saaq* (cf. above)
      ʔiet 'staying' < *qaaʕid*

In recent textbooks describing Standard Maltese (Borg and Azzopardi-Alexander 1997: 305; Ambros 1998: 24) the dominant realization of *imala* is stated as [iː]. Ambros notes that [iə] is heard in slow, careful speech, while Borg and Azzopardi-Alexander give this realization in open, phrase-final contexts. However, Vanhove (1993) notes the usual realization as [iə].

Turning to Maltese dialectology, the Standard Maltese situation appears to reflect closely the dialect of the eastern end of the main island, Malta, as described in Schabert (1976). Aquilina and Isserlin (1981) describe the dialectology of the second island, Gozo. The contexts of occurrence of *imala* are identical as for Standard Maltese. In their description of individual lexical reflexes, *imala* is realized either as a diphthong along the lines of [iə], or as a pure vowel, as they describe it, in the region of cardinal vowel 1 [i], 2 [e] or 3 [ɛ]. In the following are given words with various phonetic realizations in different Gozo dialects.

(38) *wiət* 'valley', *weet*, *wɛɛt* (81) < *waadi*
      lsiin 'tongue', *lseen* (87) < *lisaan*
      tlietɐ 'three', *tliitɐ*, *tleetɐ*, *tlɛɛtɐ* (93) < *θalaaθa*

Commenting on the diphthong *ie*, Aquilina and Isserlin state (104): 'Maltese spelling frequently features *ie*, but a corresponding realisation in the range of [ie] is rarely found in Gozitan pronunciation (though it is found in Standard Maltese).' They go on to note that the common realizations are variously [ii], [ee], [eɛ], or [iɪ].

The diphthong *ay* is generally maintained in Maltese.

7.2.4. Northern Mesopotamia, Cyprus

Imala is found in a wide band of dialects stretching from northern Iraq across the isolated Anatolian Arabic dialects, northern Syria as far as Damascus and Lebanon, central southern Turkey including Hatay province, and ending in the isolated dialect of Cyprus. It is usually associated with the so-called *qultu* dialects of the area, though there are some dialects with [q] as reflex of classical 'qaaf' in the region which do not have *imala* (e.g. Hiit, Khan 1997).

As Levin (1998: 84) points out, the *imala* contexts in this area in general are like those described in Sibawaih, though the original conditioning environment may have been subsequently lost. In *kleeb* 'dogs', for instance, the short high vowel has been elided, but presumably after it had induced *imala* in the following vowel, *kilaab* > *kileeb* > *kleeb*. The realization of the imalized /aa/ is either /ee/ or /ii/. A representative set of examples is as follows, taking examples from Jewish and Christian Baghdad (= JB, CB respectively), Mardin in Anatolia (Sasse 1971), Cilicia (S. Prochazka 2002), and the Cypriot dialect of Kormikiti (Borg 1985) as examples.

(39)		JB	CB	Mardin	Cilicia	Cyprus
kilaab 'dogs'		*kliib*	*kleeb*	*kleeb*	*kleeb*	*klep*
miizaan 'scale'		*miziin*	*mizeen*			*mi'zan*
naas 'people'		*niis*	*nees*	*nees*	*nees*	*nes*
θamaaniya 'eight'		*θmiini*	*tmeeni*	*θmeenye*	*tmeeni*	*xmenye*
θalaaθa 'three'		*tlaaθi*	*tlaati*	*θaθe*	*tlaati*	*tlaxe*

In general, *imala* inhibitors are the usual emphatic consonants, as well as /x/, /ɣ/, /q/, and /r/. However, there are many individual variations according to dialect, worthy of an individual study. It will suffice here to note some patterns of variation in the realization or not of *imala*, as well as to note individual lexical variation.

On the whole, Cypriot Arabic displays a robust system of historical lexical and allophonic *imala* (Borg 1985: 54–63). However, there are regular exceptions. Class 3 verbs, for instance, do not have *imala* in the imperfect, *pi-saʕed* 'he helps' (96). There are also irregular exceptions. The participial pattern CaaCiC has members both with and without *imala*. In some instances the non-*imala* variants go back to old inhibiting consonants, e.g. emphatics, which have been lost in the dialect, e.g. *ʃater* 'smart' < *ʃaaṭir*. In other cases, however, historical inhibiting factors may play no role, *qetʕe* 'passing' < *qaaṭiʕ* (58). Similarly in Mardin and other Anatolian *qultu* dialects usually *imala*-inhibitor contexts may allow *imala*, *qeeʕid* 'standing' (Sasse 1971: 218; Jastrow 1978: 66). In Cilician Arabic, S. Prochazka (2002: 47, 88) notes that in class 3 verbs weak final verbs never undergo *imala*, *ydaawi* 'he heals', and that in other class 3 verbs some have *imala* in the imperfect only, some in the perfect and imperfect, and others in none, *yqeerib/qeerib* 'he is related/was related' vs. *yṣaaliħ/ṣaalaħ* 'he reconciles/reconciled'.[19] Similar irregular application of *imala* is found in nominal patterns, e.g. *minxeel* 'sieve' with *imala* despite the /x/ vs. *minʃaar̞* 'saw' without. In JB and CB, Blanc (44) notes that

---

[19] This situation, in fact replicates the overall situation for form III verbs described in Behnstedt's Syrian language atlas (1997: 123): some dialects have no *imala*, *saafar/ysaafir* 'he traveled/travels', others have *imala* only in the imperfect, *ṣaalaħ/yṣeeliħ* 'he reconciled', others only *imala*, *ṣeelaħ/yṣeeliħ*.

neither variety has *imala* in class 3 verbs, *asaameħ* 'I forgive'. All in all a broad tendency is for *imala* to occur in what are historically *imala* (non-inhibiting) contexts, and for *imala* to intrude into inhibiting contexts on an irregular basis (see Jastrow 1978: 63–70 for more examples). The example of the word '3' in (39) underscores the lexical irregularity of the *imala* process in this region. In Maltese '3' undergoes *imala* as expected, *tlieta* 'three' (Borg and Azzopardi-Alexander 1997: 356). At the same time, it is a consistent exception in the Mesopotamian region.[20]

Another source of irregularity is the realization of *imala* as /ee/ or /ii/. In most Mesopotamian dialects it is /ee/. In a few, for instance JB, its usual reflex is /ii/, but in the active participle of form I verbs has *ee, weeqef* 'standing'.

Looking at the region as a whole, allophonic *imala* as found in Maltese and ELA does not occur, where *imala* and non-*imala* forms co-vary on a fully automatic basis. The exemplification of class 3 verbs above illustrates this point. In CB and JB no *imala* occurs in form 3 imperfect verbs, though this is a classical conditioning context, in other dialects *imala* may extend to the perfect, though this is not an *imala* context, and in others *imala* may occur, according to the standard rule as it were, in the imperfect only. Apparently in the dialects in this region the only inflectional suffix which regularly induces *imala* is the plural suffix -*iin* (e.g. *nəjjaar, nəjjeer-in* 'carpenters', Sasse 1971: 99, cf. sect. 7.2.2 for ELA, with object suffixes inducing *imala*).[21]

The diphthong *ay* is usually maintained in the more northerly *qultu* dialects.

(40) *bayt* 'house' (Jastrow 1978: 78, for Aazex)
 rm-ayt 'I threw' (Mardin, Sasse 1971: 165, Cypriot, Borg 1985: 89)

In the more southerly ones it may be realized as *ee* (Blanc 1964: 50; Jastrow 1978: 79).

(41) CB *beet, rmeet*

7.2.5. Southern Mesopotamia and other areas

In southern Mesopotamia an *imala*-like form is found as the reflex of the diphthong *ay.

(42) *biet* < **bayt*, 'house', *miʃiet* 'I went' < *maʃayt*

---

[20] In Behnstedt's Syrian atlas (1997: 585) there are only about twenty individual sample points out of 567 with *imala* in the word '3', e.g. *tleeta, θaleeθi* etc., and one large area, Qariiteen, northeast of Damascus.

[21] Sasse (1971: 55) reports that in Mardin the FSG imperfect verb suffix does induce *imala, tnam* 'you.M sleep' vs. *tnem-in* 'you.F sleep'. Jastrow, however, observes only *tnaam-iin* (1978: 69).

220 Imala

So far as I know, these forms, little discussed apart from Ingham (1982: 80), are not considered *imala* reflexes. They have, however, the same phonetic reflex as ELA *imala* and they play a role in the analytical discussion in sect. 7.3 below.

Outside of these five regions, there are no reflexes of word-internal *imala*. As far as the diphthong *ay* goes, its most common reflex is probably *ee*, *beet* 'house' (the entire Sudanic region, most of Egypt), though *ay* (*bayt*) is still maintained (most *qultu* dialects, Najdi, most northern Yemen). In a number of dialects it falls together with *ii* (e.g. most Tunisian, Algerian, and Moroccan dialects).

7.3. Reconstruction

In these summarizing sections, I will consider a reconstruction of *imala* in Arabic from two perspectives. First, I will work out lines of development for each of the four dialects where *imala* occurs. Thereafter, I will bring the results of this endeavor into line with the earlier description of Sibawaih and present an overall synthesis. In the following I begin with the simpler cases and move to the more complex.

7.3.1. Individual dialect reflexes

Before beginning it will be useful to refer to the contexts where *imala* does or does not occur by a single binary term. In general there are two broad categories of *imala* inhibitors, a low vowel and an emphatic or guttural context. This conditioning difference is evident in ELA today (see sect. 7.2.2). A high, front context on the other hand favors *imala*, the vowel [i] and consonants not marked by the feature of emphasis or backness. I will use the contrast palatal–non-palatal to represent this broad class of differences. Palatal contexts (high vowel, non-back, non-emphatic consonants) favor *imala*, non-palatal ones (low vowel, back, and emphatic consonants) do not.

I begin with ELA, as it is the simplest to describe. [ie] is an allophone of /aa/, which occurs in non-guttural contexts, non -*a* contexts. A negative formulation, 'not in palatal contexts' seems to be the most appropriate, as what Sibawaih termed exceptional *imala* in forms such as *nies* 'people' are covered in the statement. Gutturals are /x, ɣ, emphatics (sometimes including r)/, while an -a context is one where a long /aa/ is followed by /a/, or a back vowel. This is probably close to the original situation, as the dialect was brought to the ELA area. There is no need to reconstruct intermediate phonetic values of *imala*.

```
        aa
        |\
        | \ non-palatal
        |  \
        ie  aa
```

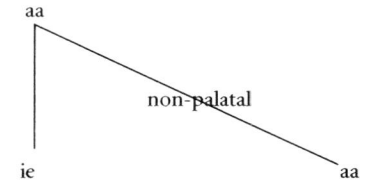

FIGURE 7.1. Eastern Libyan Arabic *imala*

In Andalusian Arabic, the context is similar to ELA, though apparently there is less detail in the written texts at our disposal, so that it can be said with certainty only that the guttural context inhibits *imala*. Phonetically the situation is more complicated as there are two realizations, [ee] and [ii], and neither of these are identical to the original reconstructed value [ie]. A development such as the following needs to be proposed, with [ie] developing into [ee] or [ii]. This looks like an unconditioned split in Andalusian Arabic. A progressive development might be imagined on the basis of the changes attested in Maltese (Fig. 7.3 below). Since [ie] is not attested in Andalusian Arabic texts (Ferrando, May 2004, p.c.), it needs to be postulated as a reconstructed form.

In Maltese the situation gets more complicated for two reasons. First, all phonetic values of *imala* are attested in one dialect or another. Secondly, when emphasis was lost, *imala* was still a living phonetic process, so former inhibiting emphatic contexts became non-inhibiting. Original guttural contexts, however, remained inhibitors. Furthermore, it appears that historic [ʕ] was an inhibitor. The situation can be sketched as in Fig. 7.3.

Finally, the situation in Mesopotamian Arabic is essentially similar to Andalusian, except for one important complication, namely the reflex [ie]

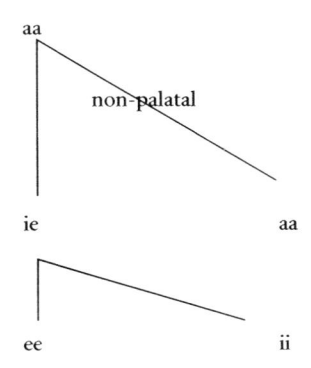

```
        aa
        |\
        | \ non-palatal
        |  \
        ie  aa
        |\
        | \
        ee  ii
```

FIGURE 7.2. Andalusian *imala*

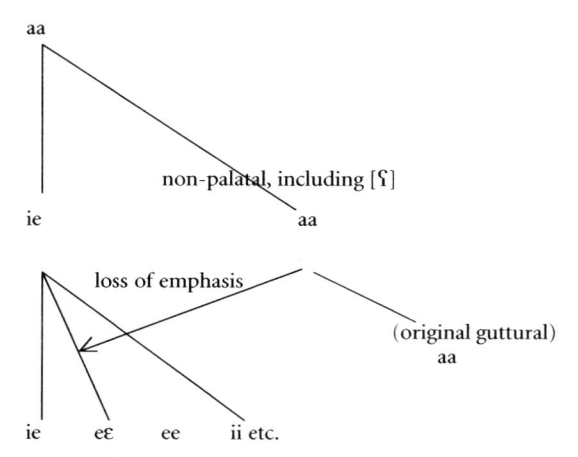

FIGURE 7.3. Maltese *imala*

for *ay* discussed in sect. 7.2.5. I assume that it is no coincidence that precisely the same phonetic reflex as *imala* should appear in precisely the area Sibawaih described 1,200 years ago. What is anomalous, of course, is its very different lexical distribution. In Fig. 7.4, *ay* is represented as converging with the [ie] reflex of the *imala*.

7.3.2. *A synthesis*

Given the overlap between both the realization and the contexts of *imala*, as well as the broad similarities with Sibawaih's description of *imala* (see below) it is clear from a linguistic perspective that *imala* is not to be reconstructed as

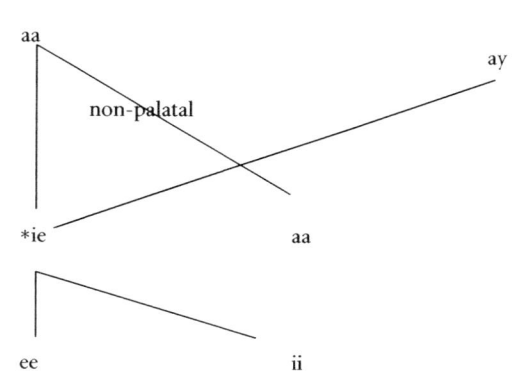

FIGURE 7.4. Mesopotamian *imala*

arising in four separate events. Except for the ay > *ie change, the Andalusian tree (Fig. 7.2), for instance, is a clone of the Mesopotamian one. Rather, one is dealing with a pre-diasporic phenomenon which happened once, and was spread from a central point to Andalusia, ELA, Maltese, and the Mesopotamian *qultu* dialects. I outline this development in Fig. 7.5.

I assume that at some stage proto-Arabic had no *imala*, though I have presented no evidence in favor of this, and at this point in our research at least, nothing depends on this assumption. While I have argued that Sibawaih's description of the *imala* variant is [ie], I have also included the other variants among them as well. These are to be understood as unattested in the early grammatical literature, but nonetheless reconstructible *imala* variants. They are reconstructible to Sibawaih's time, which is what I term pre-diasporic Arabic, since the variants [ee] and [ii] are found in Andalusia and Malta, and in the *qultu* Mesopotamian dialects. Parallel, independent development may be ruled out. Furthermore, the *qultu* dialects themselves are spread throughout a number of discontinuous areas, and have apparently been out of contact with each other for some time, yet the *imala* reflex is fairly uniform throughout the region. Further and rather speculatively, one might relate the monophthongal realization [ee] to the 'intermediate *imala*' (*bayna bayna*) noted in sect. 7.1.1. This is found in the Koranic reading tradition, and indicates that there was more than one rendition of *imala*, at least by the time Ibn Mujahid had compiled his work. Unfortunately, the phonetic description of the *bayna bayna* form is not specific enough for firm conclusions to be drawn. ELA, as well as the [ie] variant of Standard Maltese, are the same as Sibawaih's phonetic variant.

It is assumed that the original *imala* variant was [ie]. This either remained [ie], or monophthongized to [ee] or [ii]. In the latter instance *imala* falls together with /ii/, as in JB *kliib* 'dogs' < *klaab* and *ktiir* < *ktiir*. In the former it usually forms a new phoneme, as the diphthong *ay* is usually maintained

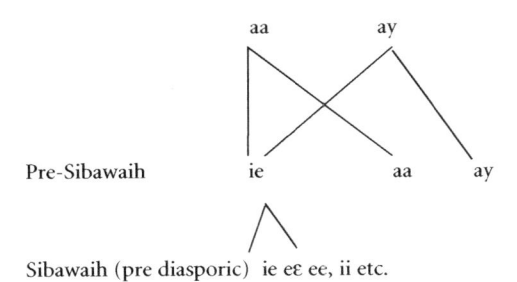

```
                        aa            ay

Pre-Sibawaih            ie            aa      ay

                        /\
Sibawaih (pre diasporic) ie eɛ ee, ii etc.
```

FIGURE 7.5. *Imala*, a synthesis

where *ee imala* occurs (Andalusia, the more northerly Mesopotamian *qultu* dialects). In some dialects *ee* < *imala* merges with *ee* < *ay*, as in CB *kleeb* < *klaab* and *beet* < *bayt*. Given that this merger is mostly attested in Iraq and Syria where *imala* dialects are in close contact with dominant *imala*-less dialects with the *ay* > *ee* change, it is probably best to regard the latter as a later borrowing or substrate-induced shift into a dialect originally with *ay*. More work needs to be done to confirm this.

(43) **bayt* > *bayt* >   *beet* (Muslim Baghdad, borrowing influence)
     klieb >   *kleeb*

Note that in ELA, while *ay* > *ee* is spreading in the dialect, it remains distinct from *imala*, which has the reflex [ie].

As far as the monophthongization process to [ii] or [ee] goes, the detailed phonetic observations of Aquilina et al. for Maltese are instructive. All their diphthongal variants have a high to low tongue movement, but in some variants the movement is slight, e.g. mid-high to mid-open [eɛ]. This perhaps indicates that monophthongization proceeded in stages, reducing gradually from a saliently-differentiated diphthong [ie] as in ELA, to [eɛ] and then finally to [ee].

It may be necessary to put in another step in historical derivation between *[ie] and the various Sibawaih-era reflexes, namely (1) a conditioned *imala*, followed by (2) an unconditioned one. Conditioned or allophonic *imala* would be the original reflex, followed by a spread to unconditioned contexts (as in (C3) above). By Sibawaih's time, conditioned and unconditioned clearly lived side by side.

The most problematic aspect of the reconstruction is the [ie] reflex of *ay in southern Mesopotamia (e.g. *biet* 'house'). Very tentatively, this can be seen as a reflex of Sibawaih's short /a/*imala* discussed in sect. 7.1.3 above. As mentioned above, I assume it is not a coincidence that this is the reconstructed and attested *imala* value. The problem is how to account for its historical relation to *imala*.

The southern Mesopotamian dialect (otherwise) does not have *imala* reflexes. Its relation to *imala* can be assessed in two ways. First, *ay* would have merged with *imala* [ie] in [ie], as in *xieyr*, discussed in sect. 7.1.3 above. *Imala* in Sibawaih is an allophonic process (C1), so speakers would always have had the non-*imala* [aa] in their repertoire. That group of speakers who had merged *ay* with *imala* in [ie] could subsequently have come into close contact with those who did not have *imala*. They would have converted their *imala* allophones into non-allophonic [aa], while maintaining the *imala* variant of

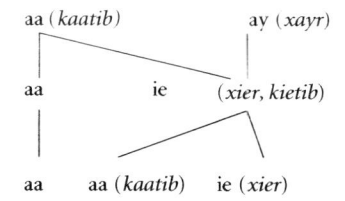

```
        aa (kaatib)              ay (xayr)
        ┌──────┐                    │
        aa     ie              (xier, kietib)
        │         ╲─────┐
        aa    aa (kaatib)    ie (xier)
```

FIGURE 7.6.

ay. These are the speakers of the southern Mesopotamian dialect described by Ingham. This can be sketched as in Figure 7.6:

While this accounts for the present-day facts, as it were, there is no independent evidence for it, and it involves the merger of *ay* and *imala*, followed by their demerger. Such an explanation would probably be ruled out on a priori grounds, lexical demerger being an unlikely process (Labov 1994: 33–5), but for the fact that *imala* is allophonic, not lexical. While there are no variational studies on the matter, it has been observed that *imala* and non-*imala* usages can reside in the same speaker (sect. 7.1.2). I observed (1980) that Mitchell (1975) described an *imala* operative in more contexts than I described for Benghazi Arabic. Thus, de-imalization alone is not only plausible, but in fragmented ways, actually attested. Since the *imala* of *xieyr* would not have been allophonic, there being no *imala*—non-*imala* alternation associated with these forms, they could have survived an allophonically based general de-imalization of the dialect.[22]

Looking to analogies elsewhere in the history of Arabic dialects, contemporary variational studies attest to a part of the demerger process, at least in local contexts. As is well known, many Arabic dialects throughout eastern Arabia, Jordan, Syria, and Israel have undergone the change $k > c$ in front contexts, *kammal* > *cammal* in Jordanian (see sect. 8.7.1). Abdel-Jawad (1981) observes in urban areas a tendency for *c* to re-merge with *k*, essentially under the influence of what Abdel-Jawad sees as a dominant prestige variant ʔ/k. This can be compared to the suggested remerger of *ie* > *aa*. It would become a complete parallel if the remerger would go to completion, except for a residue in a certain morphological pattern, or a certain morpheme, e.g. the 2.F.SG. suffix -*ic*. This of course is not yet attested, though is at least in principle conceivable.

---

[22] Labov treats apparent mergers with subsequent demergers as actual near mergers, with subsequent differentiation (1994: 371–90). There is not adequate phonetic detail either in the historical record or in the contemporary dialects (e.g. southern Mesopotamia, eastern Libya) to follow up this possibility at this time.

Note that this account feeds into the further development of the diphthong to *ii* (see above). It could be that [ie] was a stage in the development of North African *biit* etc., the de-diphthongization of *biit* running parallel to the de-diphthongization of *imala*.[23] Such an analysis would imply that *imala* was an ancestor of more dialects than where it is found in present-day Arabic.

7.3.3. The reconstruction and Sibawaih

By and large the reconstruction of *imala* based on application of the comparative method to attested post-Old Arabic variants reproduces the same phenomenon as that described in Sibawaih. The main points of identity are as follows.

I. /aa/ is realized as [ie] or a related value
II. *Imala* is conditioned by an /i/ in a neighboring syllable.
III. This value is inhibited in the context of emphatic consonants and gutturals /x/, /ɣ/, /q/ and sometimes /r/.
IV. The phenomenon is not completely regular: many lexical and morphological pattern exceptions occur.

In addition, there are points of difference which distinguish Sibawaih's *imala* from one or more of the four dialects where *imala* is attested today.

V. The class of inhibitors may differ.
VI. The realization may be [ee], [ii], or various other values (as in Maltese).
VII. According to Sibawaih's description, there are types of *imala* for which there is no direct correspondence in the dialects, (C2) for instance.

In this section I expand upon points V–VII.

Regarding V, in Maltese *ʕ inhibits *imala* (see sect. 7.2.3). Given that *ʕ as an inhibiting consonant is attested only in Maltese it should probably be seen as a local innovation relative to tree 5 (Fig. 7.5). Whether this local innovation took place in Malta or among an ancestral pre-immigrant group is an open question.[24] For VI, I have noted above that the reconstruction of the pure vowel variants follows from the widespread distribution of *imala* in today's dialects.

---

[23] As pointed out in n. 1 above, this was already suggested by Grünert (1875: 453), though on the basis of false lexical correspondences.

[24] Given that it is only in Maltese that [ʕ] is an *imala* inhibitor, it should probably be seen as an innovation. However, given the recognized class of guttural consonants (mustaʕliya) to which [ʕ] traditionally belongs, it is a natural extension for *imala* inhibition to spread from some members of the class [x, ɣ, q] to others.

As for VII, one has to distinguish between Sibawaih as a theoretical linguist and Sibawaih as a field linguist, who was trying to accommodate many observations in his grammatical description. A basic precept of Sibawaih's methodology is that no observation should go unexplained. I believe it is in the context of this approach that one needs to understand (C2) and (C3) above. Sibawaih very acutely observed that the basic conditioning factor of *imala* was an [i] in a syllable preceding or following an [aa] (C1). He also noted the inhibiting effect of various consonants.

Observationally, however, *imala* in the Basra of his day was a form expanding out of its basic realization. Phonetically the change [ie] → [ee]/[ii] can already be postulated. Distributionally Sibawaih notes that it occurs even when no conditioning [i] context is present in a word. This is a problem for Sibawaih, as indeed it would be for any linguist true to his or her principles of accounting for data in a principled fashion. Observing that *imala* occurred even in back contexts, as in *xiefa* 'he feared' and *ṭieba* 'be good', Sibawaih solved the contradiction by observing that such verbs have an [i] elsewhere in the paradigm (e.g. *xiftu* 'I feared'). With Fleisch (1961) I would agree that what is involved here is something beyond regular, phonologically specifiable variation, and that Sibawaih's explanation is unconvincing. After all, every verb minimally has an [i] in the passive form (*fuʕila*). Indeed, this is perhaps why Sibawaih could accommodate irregular verbal *imala* with less problem than irregular nominal *imala*, since nouns do not always have cognate forms with an [i] somewhere in the paradigm. It is clear, however, that Sibawaih is rather overwhelmed by what he observes. This is clear in the quote at the beginning of sect. 7.1.2, and it is further in evidence in his ultimate observation that *imala* in nominal forms such as *bieb* (< *bwb*) and *maal* (< *mwl*), both from roots with a medial /w/, not /y/, are simply exceptional (*ʃaaðð*). For Sibawaih, who valued theoretical accountability above all else, this is indeed a radical categorization. Interestingly, these forms are considered exceptional, but are not judged pejoratively (*qabiyħ* 'ugly', *radiyʔ* 'bad', or the like). In the context of these observations categories (C2) and (C3) above can be understood as Sibawaih's solution to the problem of accounting for a great deal of variation, within a relatively simple rule-based grammar which does not allow for such contemporary constructs as variable rules or statistically representable realizations. Sibawaih's solution should be regarded as an extremely clever way of integrating variational observations without seriously compromising basic linguistic precepts.

The variation observed in Sibawaih obviously bears on an interpretation of the variation in the modern dialects. An initial perspective would be that variation in the modern dialects continues a situation already initiated during

Sibawaih's era. At the same time, local developments reflected in regularizations of paradigms, development of lexical irregularities, or the expansion of *imala*-inhibiting contexts as noted for Maltese above, certainly must have occurred. A clarification of these issues, however, requires a much closer historical treatment of development in individual dialects.

7.3.4. *European Arabicists' accounts of* imala

The historical interpretation of *imala* among Arabicists can be roughly divided into two categories.

In the first category are treatments which basically recognize the identity between the Old Arabic *imala* and that found in the modern dialects. These identities are always noted for the individual dialect the researcher is working on, and not generalized to the overall history of Arabic, understandably, given the specific dialectal nature of these works. Corriente (1977) for Spanish Arabic, Aquilina and Isserlin (1981) for Maltese, Levin (1998, 2002), Borg (1985) and other researchers for Mesopotamian Arabic can be mentioned in this regard.

The second are those where the writers for one reason or another simply do not mention that the given phenomenon is related to Old Arabic *imala* (Borg and Azzopardi-Alexander 1997 and Ambros 1998, both for Maltese). Particularly critical in this regard is the summary of Fischer and Jastrow (1980: 55). Without argumentation, they assume that *imala* in Malta and Spain was an unconditioned development, not related to the *imala* of Mesopotamia or of Sibawaih.[25] In more than one place (1978: 66, 1980), Jastrow misses Sibawaih's ch. 479 which explicitly mentioned the unconditioned *imala* of *nies* and other forms. Furthermore, Fischer and Jastrow observe that *imala* in Mesopotamia was of a different status from *imala* in Maltese (for instance), in that in Mesopotamian *qultu* dialects it leads to a phonemicization of /ee/, whereas in Malta *imala* does not lead to the creation of a new phoneme. This statement is, however, (1) incorrect and (2), for historical purposes, irrelevant.

[25] I conclude this by triangular logic. Fischer and Jastrow relate Sibawaih's *imala* to that found in the Mesopotamian *qultu* dialects. The other dialects have a completely different type of *imala*, i.e. one unrelated to Sibawaih's. Fischer and Jastrow relate this second type of *imala* to a general fronting of /a/ in non-emphatic contexts. Such fronting is found in many dialects. They then observe that this general fronting can lead to [ie] or [ii]. That is to say, dialects with [ie], they give the example of Maltese, arise historically by a different process of imalization from the Mesopotamian dialect.

However, given the identity of form between Mesopotamian *imala* and, for instance Andalusian (both have [ii] and [ee] variants), and the near identity of basic conditioning contexts, and the basic historical fact that the Arab diaspora evolved out of the same demographic milieu, the onus of proof is surely on those who would see two completely independent developments to show under what conditions basically the same phenomenon arose independently. Fischer and Jastrow merely claim them to be different.

It is incorrect because the variant [ie] in Maltese is a 'new' phoneme (cf. the contrast *sieʔ* 'leg' vs. *saaʔ* 'drive' in (36), (37) above). It is irrelevant because for historical purposes it is not the synchronic status of *imala* which is crucial, but rather the systematic similarity and/or difference between purported stages in linguistic history. As argued here, in both the C1 category of Sibawaih's Old Arabic and in ELA (sect. 7.2.2) *imala* is allophonic, conditioned by broadly the same conditions, as well as sharing the same form. ELA simply continues the Old Arabic *imala* as described by Sibawaih. Indeed, a systematic allophonic similarity can provide cogent evidence of close relationship, since conditioning contexts need to be maintained over long periods of time.

Finally, I would note that few scholars have dealt with the question of the phonetic value of *imala* in Sibawaih. Most simply term it *imala*, as if it were an abstract entity. Sibawaih, however, was an acute phonetician, and he attempts a specific phonetic characterization of *imala*, as described above, even if ultimately his description is not completely unambiguous. Old Arabic *imala* did have a specific form, and using the comparative method and drawing correlations with Sibawaih's description, a specific ur-form can be reconstructed. I have suggested *[ie], which is also the same as the realization of *imala* in ELA and some Maltese varieties (as well as, paradoxically, the reflex of *ay* in southern Mesopotamian dialects). This reconstruction is commensurate with Sibawaih's phonetic description, orthographic practice, e.g. in the *Qiraʔaat* tradition, with the observation that *imala* and the other 'a' diphthong [ay] are different phenomena, with realizations in modern dialects, and the phonetic logic of deriving the widely attested [ii] and [ee] variants historically from *[ie]. Fleisch (1961: 1162) does suggest a phonetic realization for Sibawaih's *imala*, giving [e] or [ä]. These two are distinguished as strong vs. weak *imala*, a distinction probably referring to the *bayna bayna* realization in the *Qiraʔaat* tradition. The problem with Fleisch's suggestion recapitulates that often found in the Western Arabicist tradition. It is based simply on a reading of Sibawaih's text, without working through the implications of the interpretation for the history of the grammar as a whole. A simple problem is, given *[e], how does one get ELA *imala* [ie] on the one hand and [ii] on the other? To my knowledge, no Western Arabicist has addressed the issue.

8

Suffix Pronouns and Reconstruction

8.1. Pausal and Context Forms and Case Endings

As discussed in sects. 1.6.3 and 3.3.2.3, every Classical Arabic word has two sets of phonological forms, one pausal (waqf), the other non-pausal (waṣl). Traditionally, non-pausal forms are fully inflected, while pausal forms lack short final vowels. These include, but are not limited to, the grammatical case endings on nominals and mode endings on verbs. In (1), the translations are for the non-pausal forms. In the pausal variants the differences indicated by the suffix morpheme are lost.

(1) Non-pausal   pausal
    bayt-un   *bayt* 'house-NOM'
    al-bayt-u   *al-bayt* 'the house-NOM'
    bayt-in   *bayt* 'house-GEN'
    al-bayt-i   *al-bayt* 'the house-GEN'
    al-bayt-a   *al-bayt* 'the house-ACC'
    yaktub-u   *yaktub* 'he writes-IND'
    ʔayna   *ʔayn* 'where?'
    etc.

An exception is the indefinite accusative case, which in pausal form has a long-aa, *bayt-aa* 'a house'.

Were the linguistic situation as simple as this, there would perhaps be no obstacle in reconstructing the non-pausal forms as the 'original' ones. The assumption follows from this that modern dialects continue pausal forms (Nöldeke 1897: 10).

Problems in this assumption were raised in sect. 3.3.2.3, where it was pointed out that actual evidence in any post-'Old Arabic' variety showing the transition from a stage where both non-pausal and pausal forms existed to pausal forms alone is exiguous and always ambiguous at best. In this section, I continue the discussion begun in Ch. 3. A logical and key question is whether pausal or context forms are basic. Note that on an a priori basis there is no way to decide which is basic. Viewed as alternative synchronic realizations, they are simply conditioned alternates. Arguments need to be advanced motivating one or the other as basic, on a comparative basis.

Harris Birkeland (1940) made the most detailed study of pausal forms in Arabic. For Birkeland, the non-pausal forms are historically antecedent and as seen in sect. 1.6.3 he worked out a set of steps by which pausal forms came into being. He points out that in Old Arabic poetry one alternative of pausal position, defined as (half-) line-final position, was to recite a final vowel long. This is termed *tarannum* 'reciting, chanting'. In (2), the well-known opening half-line (ʃaṭr) of the Muʕallaqa of Imr al-Qays, the genitive suffix -*i* on *manzil-i* is lengthened to *manzil-iy*.

(2) *qifaa nabki min ðikraa ḥabiybin wa manzil-iy*
     'Let us stop to bewail the memory of my lover and her abode'
     (Sibawaih II: 325)

This, he says, is only possible if the relevant short vowels were at some stage in the proto-history 'there' to be lengthened in what came to be pausal position.

Sibawaih, who is the oldest explicit source in the matter, in fact notes three ways of pronouncing the final syllable in poetry. One is vowel length, as illustrated in (2), a second is to drop the final short vowel.

(3) ... *manzil#*

A third, attributed to the Tamim, is to close the line with an invariable -*n*, as in

(4) ... *yaa abataa ʕalla-ka ʔaw ʕasaa-ka-n#*

'O father your wish or your fear' (Sibawaih II: 326, trans. follows *Lisaan* 11: 473).

This is a purely phonological reflex of pausal position, since in (4) the -*n* is added to the 2MSG possessive pronoun -*ka*, which of course cannot bear an indefinite tanwin.

There is, as already noted in sect. 1.6.3, no indication in the Old Arabic literature that the full vowel pausal version as in (2) is historically the oldest. As I explained in that chapter, Sibawaih's description of pausal phenomena in poetic recitation is not amenable to an internal reconstruction that leads to postulation of the non-pausal forms as basic. Logically, the possibility needs to be considered, as outlined in Ch. 3 above, that the non-pausal forms are basic. The evidence for this is found precisely in the extensive pausal system documented by Sibawaih and others, summarized briefly in sect. 1.6.3, and in the phenomenon of *ixtilaas*, discussed in sect. 2.4.1.2, old Arabic sources, and *tamṭiyt/ʔiʃbaaʕ* (see below).

I would therefore like to adduce the following point in further support of my position, based on data from Old Arabic, and devote the greater part of this chapter, beginning with sect. 8.2, to the search for traces of short vowel case suffixes among contemporary Arabic dialects.

Concerning the lengthened pre-pausal vowel in (2), vowel lengthening of /i/ and /u/is also noted in non-pausal position. Sibawaih (II: 324) terms the phenomenon *tamṭiyt* 'pulling, lengthening' or *ʔiʃbaaʕ* 'satiating'. It applies to a /i/ or /u/. Instead of *manzil-i-ka* 'your abode' the genitive -*i* can be lengthened. Importantly, in (5a) the genitive -*i* is not in pausal position, as it is protected by the final -*ka*.

(5a) *manzil-iy-ka*

tamṭiyt would appear to produce a final vowel parallel to the long vowel version of poetic pause, as in ((2) = (5b)).

(5b) ... *manzil-iy*

For metrical purposes, however, there is no motivation lengthening a final vowel pre-suffix, as in (5a).

Just as lengthening of a case suffix occurs in pausal and non-pausal position, so too does shortening. In pausal position in poetry, two of the three recitational styles involve creating a final -C, either by closing the syllable with an -*n*, as in (4), or by deleting the final vowel as in (3). In non-pausal position Sibawaih notes that parallel to and opposed to *tamṭiyt* (lengthening), a final -*i* or -*u* can be reduced to a murmur vowel. This is termed *ixtilaas*.[1]

(6a) *manzil-ə-ka*

Further, in poetry Sibawaih cites instances where the case vowel is deleted altogether.

---

[1] In the QiraʔAat tradition, *ixtilaas* is opposed to *waṣl*, designating a short-vowel realization of a final vowel, whether in pausal or context position. The short vowel may be either of lexical or grammatical status. Its opposite realization is *waṣl*, a long vowel realization (see sect. 8.9 below for some examples). This 'weakening' phenomenon is also attested in the *taxfiyf* or lightening tendencies attributed to Abu ʕAmr, discussed in greater detail in Ch. 4 above. All in all, terms in the grammatical and reading traditions for lengthening of a short vowel include *ʔiʃbaaʕ*, *tamṭiyt*, *itmaam*, and *waṣl* (these last two used only for word-final position), while those for shortening or reduction of quality are *ixtilaas* and *taxfiyf*. Other terminology such as *ʔiʃmaam* and *rawm* further specify the vowel quality of a reduced vowel.

(6b) ... wa qad badaa han-ki min miʔrazi
'and your private parts showed from your skirt'

(instead of *han-u-ki* with nominative *-u*) (Sibawaih II: 325, see *Lisaan* 15: 367).

It thus emerges that the contrast between a voweled and unvoweled or neutralized [i] – [u] contrast noun runs throughout Sibawaih's description, both in what is traditionally termed pausal position, but also in non-pausal ones. My conspiratorial interpretation can be summarized as follows. The *tamṭiyt* of a long vowel is unusual. If the case vowels -i and -u were universally present, there would be no need to lengthen them. *Tamṭiyt* can thus be seen as a device to highlight what normally is non-distinctive. In other words, in non-pausal position there normally was no contrast between the short high case vowels. The *tamṭiyt* rendition is a normative counterweight to this state of affairs. I thus consider *ixtilaas* to be a normal pronunciation. By extension to the verse-final position, the pausal rendition is equally normal.[2]

I can note two objections to this interpretation. It could be, *pace* Birkeland, that *ixtilaas* may simply reflect a later stage of the language where case endings have become indistinct, as Birkeland suggests. My main point which argues against this position is that the lack of nominative/genitive contrast as reflected in the neutralization of the -u/i contrast in the *ixtilaas* variant reflects the general non-contrastive status of the high vowels in the Classical language, as documented extensively in Ch. 2. The weak functional load of the case endings, documented as seen in Ch. 3 by Corriente (1971, 1973), is merely a reflection of the lack of functional contrast in short vowels in general. Historically, the short high vowels in Arabic never developed into a fully contrastive system, either in lexical or in grammatical terms.

In a historical linguistic perspective, the *ixtilaas* variant does not need to be interpreted as the reflex of a case system breaking down. Further arguments in this respect are adduced in sects. 8.2–8.8. It is more likely that a functional contrast between what was originally a single high short vowel developed, probably influenced by phonological context, and that this developed into a contrast between nominative and genitive case in that variety which was the basis of Classical Arabic.

---

[2] While having much sympathy for Zwettler's (1972: 145) broadly argued conclusion that no spoken variety at the time of Mohammed or even in the era of pre-Islamic poetry still employed case endings, I believe an interpretation based on early grammatical sources does not permit so simple a dichotomy: Zwettler argues that case inflection was present only in a poetic register, not in spoken language. The problem goes in two directions. As pointed out in this work, even in poetic and Koranic rendition (see Ch. 4) can be found evidence for the lack of a functioning case system. On the other hand, it is hard to deny that Sibawaih and the early grammarians were drawing on a living case system in their detailed grammatical observations.

The second objection is that this interpretation flies in the face of received interpretations of pausal phenomena. Here, however, a careful reading of the original texts allows a detailed enough description of both a case and caseless rendition of forms to throw the question of which is original into the interpretive arena of comparative linguistics.

In the rest of this chapter I introduce further considerations into this debate, which continues the search begun in sect. 3.4 for traces of case endings in dialectal forms.

8.2. Suffix Pronouns and Case Endings

The relevance of the preceding discussion to the main theme of this chapter resides in a simple observation. Were a case variety the basis of the modern Arabic dialects, one would expect some residue of the former case endings in some part of paradigms somewhere. There is one obvious place to look, namely in the position before the object suffix pronouns. Object suffix pronouns are suffixed to the case ending of a noun or to a verb, to create a possessive construction in the case of nouns, a direct object with verbs. Examples are given in (7) (see e.g. (5) in sect. 1.6.4 for more complete paradigm).

(7) *bayt-u-ka* 'house-NOM-your.M' 'your house'
    bayt-u-ki 'house-NOM-your.F', 'your house'
    yusaaʕid-u-ka 'help-IND-you.M', 'he helps you.M'

The positions before the object suffixes, here the nominative -u and the verbal indicative ending -u, by definition are non-pausal, and hence in theory would be protected from the pausal reduction. An analogy with another morphological alternation in Arabic will help elucidate this inference. As described in sects. 1.4 (1) and 5.2.4 (1), in western Sudanic Arabic the first person perfect suffix is 'protected' from deletion when a suffix pronoun is added, as (8b).

(8a) *ka'tab-Ø* 'I wrote' vs.

(8b) *ka'tab-t-a* 'I wrote it'

It is reasonable to ask whether in an analogous non-pausal, non-word final protected position the case suffixes did not at least leave traces of their alleged former presence behind. The central question I will discuss in this chapter is whether there are not traces of case endings to be found in such protected positions.

8.3. Pronominal Suffixes, Case Endings and Epenthetic Vowels in Dialects

This idea in fact has been put forward by prominent Arabicists, including Birkeland himself.[3] In discussing the presence of the vowels highlighted in boldface in the following paradigm from Cairene Arabic, Birkeland (1952: 12, 19) suggests that they derive from the three case endings, -u, -a, -i.

(9) rigl-**u**-hum 'their leg'
    rigl-**a**-ha 'her leg'
    rigl-**i**-na 'our leg'

As will be seen in sect. 8.7 below, there is an obvious and regular phonological explanation for these vowels as epenthetic insertions. Here it may simply be noted that Birkeland offers no independent motivation for his explanation, other than, implicitly, the phonetic identity with CA case suffixes. There is no obvious explanation, for instance, as to why the genitive -i should have been preserved before -na, -u before -hum, nor does Birkeland explain how the case endings were converted to non-morphological epenthetic status.

Another excellent Arabicist who suggested that epenthetic vowels were remnants of case endings was Cantineau (1937: 180). His suggestion comes in a discussion of dialects in northeast Saudi Arabia, Jordan, and Syria (tribes of the ʕAnazi confederation) pronominal suffixes, in this instance his explanation for the alternation -ak ~ -k of the 2MSG object suffix:

(10a) raas-**a**k 'your head'

(10b) bgaṛ-at-k 'your cow'.

Cantineau assumes that the -**a** of (10a) is the remnant of a case vowel (*voyelle de flexion*), which in (10b) gets reduced after a short syllable, at-ak > at-k.

There are a number of problems with Cantineau's explanation for the -ak ~ -k variation in terms of a case remnant, and it will be instructive to dwell on these.

First, similar to the problem with Birkeland's account of the epenthetic vowels in Cairene Arabic, it is not explained why the accusative -a should be maintained to the exclusion of the other flexional vowels with this suffix. Second, given an underlying form such as bgaṛat-ak or perhaps *baǧaṛat-ak, Cantineau offers no general rule explaining why the ultimate -a is deleted, not the penultimate (yielding *bgart-ak). As will be seen below, on the other

---

[3] And much earlier than him, Wallin (1858: 673), discussed briefly in Ch. 2 n. 16.

hand, assuming the historical epentheticity of -a renders the distribution of the vowels susceptible to explanation by general rule.

Thirdly and finally, the ʕAnazi dialect described by Cantineau has a general constraint preventing sequences of two open syllables. Thus, *bagar* 'cattle' may occur, but **bagar-ih* is impossible. In this case, the vowel of the first syllable is elided, giving *bgar-ih* > *bgir-ih* 'his cattle'. The vowel-initial pronominal suffix *-ih* induces the initial vowel reduction. If *-a* were a remnant accusative case suffix, one would expect that the effect of adding *-a* to the stem would have induced the elision of the stem *bagar*, as in (11).

(11) *bagar-a*
      *bgar-a

After loss of the case suffixes in pausal form, this should give stems like

(12) *bgar*.

These are not attested in this dialect, however.

Of course, one could say that the sequence of events was as follows:

S1. Case suffixes: *bagar-a*
S2. Loss of case suffixes: *bagar*
S3. Inception of 2 open syllable constraint: *bagar*, *bagar-ih* → *bgar-ih*.

This explains why the ostensibly identical forms in (S1) and (S3) yield different results. (S1) existed when (S3) did not. However, if this is the case, it is unclear how the vowel in (10a) could historically be a reduced case vowel. According to (S1)–(S3) all case vowels need to have been deleted from the system, in order to explain (S3).

In both Birkeland and Cantineau, therefore, the assumption that non-stem suffixal vocalic material is a residue of a short case vowel becomes problematic, as soon as the implications of the assumption are thought through systematically. Nonetheless, the hypothesis may be held open that case traces are to be found somewhere in stem or suffixal material. In the remainder of this chapter I will offer a reconstruction of the object suffix pronouns, in order to ascertain definitively whether some aspects of the reconstructed forms do not in fact go back to case vowels.[4]

---

[4] Brockelmann (1908: 309) as well interprets the vowels of the 2SG suffixes *-ak*, *-ik* as original case vowels. His observation that these original nominal suffixes were also carried over to verbal object endings begs far more questions than it answers (see also Behnstedt and Woidich 2005: 25). Abdo (1969: 102) opts for an explanation which calls for metathesis of the final vowel of the pronoun suffix, e.g. *-ka* → *ak* via metathesis. However, no independent arguments justifying this solution are offered.

8.4. Syllable Structure

In order to understand a reconstruction of pronominal forms based on their form and distribution in the modern Arabic dialects, basic syllable structure rules found in the dialects need to be referred to. Various dialects, of course, are characterized by different rules. Three rules need to be cited. The first relating to epenthetic vowel insertion was already summarized in sect. 3.4.2 (examples (14), (15)) and so need be repeated here in skeletal form only.

(13) Linear epenthesis

(13a) CCC → CəCC (ə = epenthetic vowel), *galb-na* → *galib-na* 'our heart'

(13b) CCC → CCəC, *galbna* → *galbi-na*

A second widespread rule raises a low vowel in an open syllable.

(14) Low vowel raising
kabiir → *kibiir* 'big'
katab → *kitab* 'he wrote'

A third rule is a constraint allowing only one open syllable. Given two open syllables in sequence, either the first will be deleted, or, depending on morpheme and dialect, the second syllable will be altered in some way. This rule was met in S3 above.

(15) Open syllable structure constraint
katab-at → *ktib-at* 'she wrote'
bagara → *bgura* 'a cow'

Note here that the second syllable is raised before the open syllable, according to the previous (14).

8.5. A Data Survey

For the following analysis the object pronouns from forty-nine dialects were collected and analyzed according to parameters described in the following sections. The data points are indicated on Maps 1–3 (139–41) and the data itself listed in Appendix 4. In some instances dialects have been included for their perceived comparative value, even though not enough information is available about them for a comparison along every parameter (e.g. Khorasan Arabic). Mostly, however, I strove to have two–four data points per country, depending on its size and intuitively perceived dialectal diversity. Yemen, for instance, though geographically small, is extremely diverse dialectally, so four data points are included for it. In some cases I generalized to dialect areas, so that for instance Nigeria, Cameroon, and Chad, three countries, have in total only four sample points, as the Arabic spoken in this region belongs to one dialect area (see Ch. 5). These forty-nine dialects serve as the raw data from which a set of reconstructed forms will be derived. In the process of reconstruction, I will in places allude to secondary developments in certain dialects. However, the main focus of the reconstruction is to derive for each pronoun a form or in some cases, forms, which plausibly needs to be postulated into pre-diasporic Arabic. These reconstructed forms will then be examined for traces of case suffixes.

The methodology, end product, and immediate goal of this reconstruction should be clarified here. In sects. 8.5–7, I reconstruct object pronouns based on contemporary dialects only. There is no dependence on Classical Arabic, Old Arabic, or assumed proto-Arabic forms. In fact, it will be seen in sects. 8.8 and 8.9 that forms which are often assumed to be proto-Arabic, e.g. the 3FPL suffix **-*hunna* (e.g. Behnstedt 1991: 235) themselves are problematic.

Unless otherwise stated, the reconstruction itself is understood to be that of pre-diasporic Arabic (see sect. 1.1). The '*' thus means 'pre-diasporic form'. This was seen in Ch. 5 to be a variety or varieties found in the Arabian peninsula and adjoining areas at the time of the Arabic-Islamic expansion. Admittedly, the sample of forty-nine dialects, though relatively large, is not adequate for a detailed reconstruction, and I would fully expect that a larger sample would lead to a more complicated set of reconstructions.

However, the major goal of this exercise is not reconstruction per se. Rather, minimally, I intend to show that whatever detailed reconstructions are ultimately developed, none of them will require positing traces of case vowels. The broad sample of dialects which I use I believe ensures the plausibility of this claim.

It is, however, interesting to correlate the results of the reconstruction with the relatively rich descriptions of suffix pronouns in the Arabic grammatical tradition in order to determine the extent to which reconstruction based on modern dialects is compatible with eyewitness observations from the eighth century. This is done in sect. 8.9.

I should note that in some cases it is interesting to go beyond a reconstruction of pre-diasporic forms to proto-Arabic ones. This is done in particular when the instrument of comparative reconstruction[5] leads to a fairly

---

[5] As opposed to cases where the reconstruction of a proto-form also involves ancillary problems such as substrate effects, which entails a digression into the historical circumstances of the groups in contact, as outlined for instance in sect. 8.6.6 in the discussion of the 3MPL object suffix.

unambiguous reconstruction. In these cases the proto-form will be identified as 'proto-Arabic' and marked with a double asterisk.

Before beginning, for orientation I give a sample paradigm from Standard Arabic of the SG and PL suffix pronouns.

(16)   SG   PL
1   -iy, -niy   -naa
2M   -ka   -kum
2F   -ki   -kunna
3M   -hu   -hum
3F   -haa   -hunna

In the 1SG, *-iy* is suffixed to nouns and prepositions while *-niy* is suffixed to verbs.

8.6. Unproblematic Cases, Some Easy Generalizations

A number of analytic parameters are unproblematic. The following pronominal forms, for instance, show little or no variation. In the following, to the left of the equals sign I place the Standard Arabic rendition of the suffix for ease of reference, not as a claim of historical origin. Note that general phenomena such as generalizations on the FPL (sect. 8.6.3) are factored out and treated in individual sections.

8.6.1. *1SG*

1SG, -iy, niy = *-i, *'-i, *-ni

All forty-nine sample points have the same segmental form for the 1SG object pronoun. The only variation is the different stress. In most dialects the suffix is not stressed. In five it is. Four of these are the sample points in the western Sudanic Arabic region. In Chadian Arabic both nominal and verbal object suffix are stressed, in Nigerian only the nominal. Were the stressed version restricted only to the WSA region, they would be seen as an innovation, the unstressed variant being reconstructed as the proto-form. However, the Bdul dialect in southern Jordan (Petra) also has the same stress, and in fact stressed 1SG forms are found throughout the Sinai and into northeast Egypt (de Jong 2000, Behnstedt and Woidich 1985). The WSA forms probably are related to these, i.e. ancestral speakers of stressed 1SG forms broke away, some eventually migrating into the WSA area. Since the Sinai dialects are quite old— de Jong (2000: 13) states that their speakers settled in the region in pre-Islamic times—the two variants, stressed and unstressed, can be reconstructed into pre-diasporic Arabic.[6]

8.6.2. 1Pl

1PL naa = -*na

All but two sample points have the 1PL form as -na. Khorasan and Oman have -ne. The raising of /a/ is quite common in Arabic. Extensive discussion of one aspect of this process is found in Ch. 7 on *imala*. In the present data, raising of the 3FSG suffix -*ha* to -*he* is also attested, in Hofuf, Bagirmi Arabic, and Khorasan (see next point). Oman has -*ha*. It is therefore possible that the -*ne* variant is old. However, there is otherwise little support for reconstructing a unitary proto-split, say joining the ancestors of Khorasan and Oman Arabic (*na → na/ne), at least not in this data. It is equally possible that -*ne* arose independently in each area, by analogy to other $a \to e$ changes. The systematic -*ne*, -*he* forms in Khorasan are certainly significant, though at this point can be regarded as a local analogical leveling. Note that since there is almost no variation on this point, the starred *-*na* can be taken as a proto-Arabic form as well.

8.6.3. *Feminine plural*

The remaining persons may or may not have a distinct feminine plural. FPL as a morphological category is found throughout the Arabic-speaking world. If a variant has it, it has it throughout the grammatical system (e.g. subject marking on verb, object marking in pronouns, FPL demonstratives, etc.). Loss of morphological FPL is to be regarded as innovative. Those dialects which retain it are as follows, also indicated on Maps 1–3. In all nineteen sample points have morphological FPL, 40 per cent of the sample: Khartoum, Shukriyya, eastern Libya, northern Israel, Ajarma, Bdul, Najdi, Abu Dhabi, Rwala, Oman, Basra, San'a, Al-Nadhir, Suwwadiyye, al-Mudawwar, Uzbekistan, Khorasan, Bagirmi, Nigeria.

---

[6] An anonymous reader for OUP points out that Hebrew as well stresses the final -*iy* of the 1SG suffix, which would make a case for parallel development. In general, however, Semitic linguistics needs to consider the effect of language contact and shift when parallel features are found. A feature, for instance, could have entered some varieties of Arabic via contact or contact abetted by shift, and spread from that variety onwards. A stressed -*iy*, for instance, could have entered a variety of Arabic in southern Jordan or the Sinai via shift from a Hebrew-speaking population contact in this case being historically plausible, this feature then continuing on into the WSA area. For purposes of the time frame covered in this book, however, such a development would indeed link WSA with the southern Jordanian/Sinaitic varieties, since the original point of entry would have been southern Jordan or the Sinai.

8.6.4. *Dropping the h, -*h, *Ø*

Three suffixes begin with *h, 3FSG -*haa*, 3MPL -*hum*, and 3FPL -*hunna* (using Standard Arabic here as a citation form). The 3MSG form is treated separately (see sect. 8.7.6). In a number of dialects the initial -*h* may be dropped. Two general patterns which pertain to all h-initial suffixes may be summarized here.

In many Mesopotamian dialects the presence of -*h* is phonologically conditioned, at least as represented in the grammars. Christian Baghdadi may be taken as typical.

(17) -ha, -hum after V-, katab-uu-ha 'they wrote it.F'
      -a, -um after C-, katab-a 'he wrote it.F'

Dialects represented with this pattern in the sample are Cypriot, Aazex, Mardin, CB, JB, Tripoli (Lebanon), Khorasan, Uzbekistan, Teerib (Syria). In Daragözü (Jastrow 1973) -*h* deletion has gone so far that it occurs in all contexts, even after a vowel (e.g. *katab-uu-a*), so the *h*-less forms are completely generalized. Roth-Laly (1979: 161), writing about Abbeche Arabic in Chad, also represents -*h* deletion as a conditioned variant, as in (17). In addition, two dialects, al-Mudawwar in Yemen and Andalusia have h-less forms in the 3FSG only.

In the current sample, twenty dialects have -h deletion as a categorical or variable phenomenon. As is often the case with variable phenomena, precise conditions governing the variation are more complex than a simple distribution such as (17) describes. Example (17) does capture the basic situation in WSA as well. However, more precise variable data may be introduced here. Analyzing a 400,000 word corpus of Nigerian Arabic (personal data), 4,995 tokens of -*h* deletion are found. The most basic contexts are as (17), after a V- and after a C-. Examples of forms and their percentages in the corpus are given in (18). In the examples, the 3FSG -*ha* suffixed to a form of the verb *katab* 'write' is used for basic illustration, though the phenomenon applies equally to -*hum* and -*hin/han*. Note that in addition to simple presence or absence of an /h/, the /h/ can also be completely assimilated to a preceding obstruent, devoicing a voiceless consonant. I note the statistic for this category without further comment (Table 8.1).

It is interesting to note that -h deletion occurs even in the presence of epenthetic vowel insertion, as in (18c, < *katab-t-a-ha* where -a-is epenthetic).

As a broad percentage of all cases, the h-deletion rules in WSA follow the categorical rule in (17), though there is a good deal of leakage. In (18b) /h/ is more frequently maintained than deleted after V-. The same tendency is discernible in (18a), though even here -*h* is maintained more than it is

TABLE 8.1. Deletion and assimilation of pronominal-*h* in Nigerian Arabic

	-h	No h-	Assimilated –h
(a) C-	katab-ha: 3,020	katab-a: 1,842	katap-pa: 421
(b) V-	katab-oo-ha: 5,225	katab-oo-a: 2,725	
(c) CC-	katabt-a-ha: 428	katabt-a-a*: 85	

* The sequence of two a's is pronounced with a HL tone contour, áà or áâ, which clearly gives each vowel a separate identity.

deleted. However, the distribution shows a significant association, with -*h* maintained significantly more often after a V-than after a C- (p < .000, chi sq = 17.1, df = 1).

It would not be surprising to find that in a corpus analysis of Mesopotamian Arabic variation of the kind in (18) is not also found, though for our historical purposes this point is not essential.[7] As far as the historical interpretation goes, pre-diasporic Arabic may be reconstructed as having both dialects where -*h* is always maintained, and those where -*h* was deleted. This follows from the basic correspondence between *qultu* Mesopotamian Arabic on the one hand and WSA on the other. Such identical phenomenon do not arise independently.

It may also be noted that Sibawaih's description of /h/ as a 'transparent' or 'hidden' consonant (*xafiyy*, see 7.1.3) may describe a state of affairs in which /h/ was deleted. Citing Xalil, Sibawaih says that the form *rudd-a-haa* is as if the speakers say *rudd-aa*, without an /h/ present (II: 163. 15). This would reinforce a pre-diasporic reconstruction of both h-and h-less suffixes.

In the Mesopotamian dialects -h deletion is related to another development, namely the shift of stress to the syllable before the object suffix. Historically stress shift is conditioned by a -CC sequence, so that in Nigerian Arabic for instance there is a contrast between:

(18a) 'katab-a 'he wrote it.M'

(18b) ka 'tab-ha 'he wrote it.F'

With deletion of -h, the only difference between the 3MSG and 3FSG object suffix after a consonant is the stress placement.

(19) ka 'tab-a 'he wrote it.F'

These rules of stress placement are identical in WSA and in the Mesopotamian Arabic. Mesopotamian Arabic has taken the stress shift a step further,

---

[7] In a quantitative study of the identical *h*-deletion rule in Damascene Arabic, Ismail (2004) also documents a variable realization of -*h* after a consonant.

shifting stress to all pre-object suffix stem syllables, even when the object suffix begins with a vowel. For instance, the 1SG object suffix (nominal) is unstressed -i. In Mardin, normally addition of a V-initial syllable to a 'CVCVC form has no effect on stress, 'CVCVC-V, as in 'baqar 'cattle', 'baqar-a 'one cow'. When an object suffix is added, however, stress uniformally shifts to the pre-pronominal suffix, no matter what its phonological shape.

(20) ba'qar-i 'my cattle'
ba'qar-u 'his cattle'
ba'qar-a 'her cattle' (< ba'qar-ha, note, minimally contrastive with 'baqara 'one cow') etc.

What apparently happened is that once the V-initial suffixes deriving from initial *-h became stressed, the stress shift was generalized to all V-initial pronominal suffixes.

Excepting Uzbekistan Arabic, this pre-pronominal stress shift is found throughout the Mesopotamian area, but it does not occur in WSA. It therefore should be regarded as innovative in the Mesopotamian area.

In the following three subsections the three third person object pronouns with initial h-are discussed, the factor of presence or absence of h-being largely factored out of the discussion, it having been treated here.

8.6.5. *3F.SG*

3FSG -haa = *ha/*he

There are three variants of the 3FSG in the data, -ha (43 tokens), -he (4), and -a(h) (3).[8] The forms without -a are due to h-deletion discussed in the previous section, though interestingly one of the dialects without h- is al-Mudawwar in Yemen. The forms with -he are found in Khorasan, mentioned in sect. 8.6.2 above, Bahariyya, Hofuf, and al-Mudawwar. In addition, -he occurs as a conditioned variant after a front [i] or [e] in the Bagirmi dialect of WSA, as in

(21)
bagar-ha
beet-he.[9]

Given the wide, if relatively rare distribution of the -he variant, I recontruct both variants into pre-diasporic Arabic. Independent development in Bahariyya in Egypt, Khorasan in eastern Iran, al-Mudawwar in Yemen, Hofuf in

---

[8] The form -ee from al-Mudawwar (Yemen) is counted twice here, once for -ee and once for lacking h-.

[9] In this dialect the distribution -he of the 3FSG suffix parallels the variant -e of the 3MSG suffix, beet-e 'his house' and the variant -e of the FSG adjective suffix, kabiir-e 'big.F'.

Saudi Arabia, and Bagirmi in Chad/Cameroon/Nigeria is unlikely. It is perhaps tied to the *imala* phenomenon, discussed in Ch. 7. Sibawaih explicitly cites *imala* forms of the 3FSG suffix, as in *ʔan yanziʕa-hie* 'that he take it.F out' (II: 282. 21). A complete treatment of *imala* including final -aa would shed more light on the issue. Furthermore, as seen in sect. 7.1.3, /h/ was observed by Sibawaih to be a 'transparent' consonant (xafiyy) which allows harmonic influence from a preceding front vowel. This is the same conditioning factor as behind the Bagirmi forms.

8.6.6. 3.MPL

-hum = *hum/*hun

The 3MPL essentially has two forms, -hVm (thirty-eight cases) and -hVn (eleven). The vowel is usually /u/, though it may also be /i/ or /o/, in one case in the sample (Soukhne) /a/. It is tempting to see the -*n* variant as a local development characterizing many of the dialects in the Syrian and northern Mesopotamian area. All but two of the -*n* sites in the current sample are from this area. Indeed, it has been proposed that the -*hVn* variant arose via contact and shift with Aramaic, which has the PL suffix -*hon* (Brockelmann 1908: 310). Responding to this suggestion, Diem (1973) proposes an Arabic-internal development in which the masculine pronoun shifts its original -*m* to -*n*, via analogy to the feminine form, -*hunna*.

Behnstedt (1991), on the other hand, observes differences between the realization of -*n*-final pronouns in Yemen and in the Mesopotamian/Syrian area. He suggests that the masculine -*n* forms in the Mesopotamian/Syrian area could have been influenced by an Aramaic substrate. He adduces in this respect the Aleppo *hinnen* 'they', which he compares to MaʕIula Aramaic (Syria) *hinnun/hinnen* 'they M/F'. The final -*n*, in particular points to Aramaic influence. For Yemen, Behnstedt would appear to accept the analogical analysis of Diem, though does note Yemeni specificities.

Neither Diem nor Behnstedt take account of the -n variant in Shukriyya Arabic in the Sudan. Given the morphological specificity of this feature—there is no general rule which converts an /m/ to an /n/ in Shukriyya Arabic—a unitary source is most likely. This in turn implies that the innovation, whatever its source, occurred once and spread. There are two possibilities: it innovated in the Syrio-Mesopotamian area and spread into the Arabian peninsula and into the Sudan, or in the Arabian peninsula and from there into the other two regions. The general trend of migration argues for the latter, though here, as elsewhere, corroborating evidence needs to be worked out. In the first case the -*hVn* development could be a post-diasporic development.

In the second *-hVn* would be a pre-diasporic development, originating in Yemen (Tihama in particular) and spreading from there.

8.6.7. *3.F.PL*

3FPL, hunna = *hin/*han

As noted above, only nineteen of the dialect samples have a feminine plural. Seventeen of these have *-hin*, two have *-han*. Despite the rarity of **han*, its distribution in Bagirmi (WSA) and al-Suwwadiyya in Yemen suggest it may have a common origin, which would be pre-diasporic. The status of a geminate *-nn*, as in Standard Arabic, is discussed in sect. 8.9 below.

8.7. More Difficult Cases

The following reconstructions are more complicated.

8.7.1. *k ~ c variation in second person forms*

The second person pronouns have an initial k- or k-like element. In general this consonant displays the k ~ c alternation which characterizes Arabic dialects as a whole. Many dialects, including all of those in Africa in this sample, have invariable k-. Eastern Arabian, southern Mesopotamian, Jordanian, Israeli, Palestinian, and Syrian Arabic have a palatalization rule, whereby, historically k → c [tʃ] or ts before a front vowel (see Johnstone 1963, 1967; Holes, 1991) as in *ceef* < *keef* 'how', *diic* (*diits*) 'rooster' < *diik*. The palatalization often generalizes to the other velar consonant as well, g → dʒ, dz or even y (*giddaam, dʒiddaam, dziddaam, yiddaam* 'in front'). The palatal variants of *-k are part of this broader palatalization phenomenon and therefore will not be treated as a separate variable in this chapter.

In some cases, *k → c* generalizes outside of its basic palatal context, as in Soukhne (Syria) 2PL *-cu*. What probably happened here is that the 2FSG palatal form, *-ci* generalized lexically throughout the second person pronoun paradigm, cf. 2MSG *-ac*, as happened in certain other dialects in the region (northern rural Palestinian, see Abdel-Jawad 1981).

In the following four sections, I factor out the more general *k ~ c* alternation, using a simple realization with 'k'.

8.7.2. *2F.PL*

2FPL kunna = *-kin/*kan

For the second person forms I depart from the previous order (SG > PL, M > F) in the interest of summarizing the easiest cases first. This begins with the 2FPL, which is either *-kin* or *-kan*. Variation between /i/ and /a/ was already met in the 3FPL. Contrary to what might be expected, a far larger number of sample points have /a/ in this form than in the 3FPL, seven of the nineteen. Both of the *-han* 3FPL dialects have *-kan* as well, so an implication goes from *-han* > *-kan*. In this instance, given the rarity of *-han*, one could entertain the hypothesis that *-han* arose independently in different areas, by analogy to the 2FPL *-kan*.

8.7.3. 2M.PL

kum = *kum/*kun/*ku

The variant *-kun* is fully isomorphic with the 3MPL variant -hun (sect. 8.6.6.3): dialects in this sample with *-hun* as 3MPL have *-kun* as 2MPL, and vice versa (though against this see sect. 5.8.2). The discussion around -hun therefore covers this variant. Most sample points (thirty-three) have -kum. Four of the six with -ku are in the WSA area. However, the Bdul dialect in Jordan as well as Soukhne in Syria have *-ku* (*-cu* in the case of Soukhne), so independent innovation can be ruled out. The *-ku* variant is a second significant isogloss linking the WSA area with the Bdul, the first being the stressed 1SG object suffix (see 8.6.1), which strengthens the case of WSA speakers having specific ancestral links with those of Bdul.

8.7.4. 2F.SG

ki = *-ik/*ki (pre-diasporic), proto-Arabic **-ki

The remaining three forms, 2FSG, 2MSG, and 3MSG are the most complicated, each requiring detailed individual attention. I begin with the 2FSG.

The reconstruction of the 2FSG object suffix entails two main problems, one the final vowel -i and one the form of the consonant. I will deal with these in turn.

As far as the syllable structure goes there are three forms, -Ci (thirteen attestations), -iC (thirty) and -C (two). Four dialects have no distinctive 2FSG pronominal forms at all (Malta: Borg and Azzopardi-Alexander 1997: 195; Susa: Talmoudi 1980: 73, 148; Djidjelli: Marçais 1956: 155, 436; and Tunis: Singer 1980: 250, 325; see sect. 1.5), and in one the data is apparently lacking (Andalusia). As indicated in the section heading, *-ki* is also the same as the reconstructed proto-form. This form also happens to be the same as the Standard Arabic form. The basic argument for **-Ci as the proto-form is that this form is not otherwise derivable via general rule. The form -iC on the other hand can be accounted thus:

The *-ki* form in many dialects when suffixed to CC-requires insertion of an epenthetic vowel. As seen in sect. 3.4.2 ((14), (15)) this vowel will harmonically be [i] before *-ki*.

(22) *galb-i-ki* 'your.F heart'

Given the proto-form *galb-i-ki, the final -i was lost in the majority of dialects (or only once in the proto-ancestor of these dialects) yielding *galb-i-k*. Subsequent to this, what was originally an epenthetic vowel was reinterpreted as the vowel of the suffix, *-ik*. The vowel of the *-ik* variant is thus an original epenthetic vowel, not an original case vowel as Birkeland and others would have it.

The following argues for this interpretation. First there are dialects, two in the present sample, where the 2FSG is simply -C, as in Rwala.

(23) *galb-its* 'your.F heart' (with *ki → *ts* palatalization as in sect. 8.7.1)

Rwala along with other northeastern Arabian peninsular dialects, has the following distribution of epenthetic vowels (Ingham 1994a: 17):

(24) Epenthesis rule, northeast Arabian peninsular dialects

CCC → CC-ə-C   *ʃift-c* → *ʃift-ic* 'I saw you.F'
VVCC → VVC-ə-C   *rijaal-c* → *rijaal-ic* 'your.F men'.

In these dialects a three-consonant sequence is equivalent to a long vowel plus two consonants, an equivalence also found sporadically elsewhere, as in the Bagirmi dialect of WSA. After VC sequences no epenthesis occurs.

(25) *min-c* 'from you.F'

According to the present analysis, these dialects represent an intermediate stage between those dialects which exclusively have *-ki*, an epenthetic vowel being inserted before it under appropriate circumstances, and those dialects where the epenthetic vowel has been reinterpreted as a part of the 2FSG suffix. The final [i] has been lost in these dialects (see below), but a short [i] before the suffix is still epenthetic.

A second argument pertains to allomorphic variation in the 2FSG suffix. A number of dialects have the alternative forms *-k* ~ *-ki*. The form *-ki* occurs after a long vowel and before a further suffix, as in Cairene.

(26) *ʃaaf-ik* 'he saw you.F'
     ʃaaf-uu-ki 'they saw you.F'
     ʃaaf-kii-ʃ 'he did not see you.F'

Dialects with one or both of these distributions of the 2FSG include Baskinta, Cypriot, Alawite Turkey, Damascus, and Shukriyya. Given original -*ki*, the maintenance of the final [i] in these dialects can be accounted for by appeal to complementary conditioning: The final -/i/ is lost only after a C-, so long as no further suffix is added.

Third, in general after a vowel no dialect has a 2FSG with -*ik*. This fact is accounted for if the [i] was originally epenthetic. It is not inserted after a long vowel, since this is not a context for epenthetic vowel insertion (see (24)).

The general line of development can be represented in four steps as follows.

$$(27) \quad \overset{1}{-^{*}ki} \quad \overset{2}{\rightarrow (i)\text{-}ki^{10}} \quad \overset{3}{\rightarrow (i)\text{-}k} \quad \overset{4}{\rightarrow \text{-}ik}$$

Some dialects (WSA, Mesopotamian *qultu*, Uzbekistan) maintain the original -*ki* in all contexts, others only the consonant (Najdi, step 3), while in most the original epenthetic vowel [i] has been reinterpreted as a part of the morpheme (step 4).

Why the final [i] was lost in some dialects but not in others cannot be answered definitively. A number of dialects with -*ki* are fairly tolerant of open syllables, whether filled by short high or short low vowels. All four WSA dialects in the sample, for instance, have -*ki* and are liberal in allowing high vowels in open syllables (see sect. 2.4.1.1). The Bahariyya dialect, Uzbekistan Arabic, and the Bdul dialect in Jordan are the same in this regard. The tolerance for -*ki* may thus be a general reflection for tolerance of a CV syllable.

However, many of the *qultu* dialects have -*ki* invariably, and others have it according to the variation in (26), and these do not readily tolerate short high vowels in open syllables. By the same token, dialects in Yemen are very tolerant of open syllables, yet only three sample points have -*ki* after a consonant, according to Behnstedt's atlas (1985: 83). In general those of the Arabian peninsula are fairly tolerant of open syllables, and yet only one in the sample (Qauz) has -*ki*. However, in the case of many peninsular dialects the form of the 2FSG suffix is complicated by affrication, summarized in sect. 8.7.1 and discussed below. Still, it is noticeable that invariable -*ik* is found throughout North Africa, whose varieties tend to avoid open syllables with short vowels, while in many *qultu* dialects, as noted above, -*ki* occurs only word-finally after a long vowel, VV-ki. This is a context, in these dialects, which readily allows VVCi (e.g. *raami* 'having thrown'). Otherwise here, and in the

---

[10] To the extent that epenthetic vowels themselves should not be part of proto-Arabic; see discussion in sect. 3.4.2. It is probably more accurate to represent the first two stages as contemporary, allomorphic variants: *-ki ∼ *-iki → -(i)k → ik.

North African varieties, there is a strong tendency to end the word with a closed syllable, which the *-ik* form provides. The maintenance of the reconstructed proto-form may thus be broadly correlated with syllable structure rules, though working out details is beyond the scope of this book.[11]

Turning to the affrication of the suffix, this may be reconstructed as follows:

(28) *-ki* → (*i*)*ci* → (*i*)*c* → *ic*
 ? → ʃi → (*i*)ʃi → *iʃ*

As noted above, affrication of the 2FSG suffix is part of a general affrication tendency found in northern Arabian dialects and those adjacent to this area. A full reconstruction cannot therefore be carried out here, though the reader can be referred to Holes (1991) for a detailed proposal.[12] The affricated forms in any case would indicate an earlier *-ki*.

---

[11] I count the Qauz form *-ky* as -CV (T. Prochazka 1988: 126, 140). A crosstabs correlation shows the clear tendency for -ki dialects to allow short open syllables. For this, I correlated two variables from the data set. One is the form of the 2FSG object pronoun, in which there are two classes, forms with final -*i*, and those without (i.e. -*ik* etc.). Affrication and other variables were ignored. The second variable is the form of a *CaCaC* verb when a suffix is added which begins with a vowel. The 3FSG suffix -*Vt* was chosen as the representative V-initial suffix. This potentially creates a sequences of two open syllables. In Nigerian Arabic the sequence stands, *katab* + *at* = *katabat* 'she wrote'. In Najdi Arabic the sequence is not allowed and the first vowel is deleted, = *iktib-at* 'she wrote' (see (15) above). Here as well other factors such as the raising of a low vowel in an open syllable and affrication are ignored. Generalizing across a number of further variables (see below), the correlation is as follows. The first column represents dialects where a sequence of *CaCa* is allowed to stand, while the second represents those in which reduction is called for.

	katab-at	katb-at/iktib-at/kitb-it etc.
-ki	10	3
-ik	13	18

df 1, chi sq = 4.5, p < .034

The correlation gives the following results. On the one hand the 2FSG *-ki* form also favors the maintenance of short low vowels in open syllables, as exemplified in the 3FSG perfect verb form. *-ik* forms are distributed between the syllable-structure types. In a chi square test, the two factors reach significance, indicating that the two variables, form of 2FSG suffix and maintenance of open syllables (as exemplified in 3FSG perfect verb from) are not independent factors. I would note that in the dialects which do not allow two open syllables in sequence in these verb forms, a number of subcategories exist. In some (e.g. Damascus) the second syllable is reduced (*katabat* → *kat-bit*), while in others (e.g. Najdi) the first is (*katabat* → *ktibat*). I also included North African dialects, where the perfect verb does not usually display a high–low stem vowel contrast. A more precise consideration of relevant factors, from a statistical perspective, is outside the scope of this work, however. I did not include the four dialects where there is no distinction at all between a M/F form in the second person (Malta, Djidjelli, Susa, Tunis). The 2FSG in Andalusia is unclear.

[12] The fact that affricated variants are rarely found outside the Arabian peninsula and its immediate vicinity to the north—only Khorasan has -*ic* outside this region in the present sample—may be one support for Holes's (1991: 671), reconstruction of the phenomenon only to the eleventh century, which would make it post-diasporic. The diasporic populations would have already established affrication-less varieties.

The affricated forms, therefore, usually indicate an earlier *i, which in any case is reconstructed as a part of the proto-form.

It may be noted in passing that however old the change in (28) is, the affrication and the loss of final [i] apparently occurred at about the same time, as there are dialects with -*ki* and -*c* (reconstructing **ci*) as well those with -*ik* and -*ic*. There is also a dialect in the sample with -*ci*, namely Soukhne in Syria. As this dialect occurs along the *qultu–gilit* dialect boundary, it may be that the -*ci* in this case arose in part via contact between original *gilit* -*ic* speakers and *qultu* -*ki* speakers (see Behnstedt 1994: 114).

A final set of forms found in four peninsular dialects (Hofuf, Oman, San'a, Al-Suwwadiyya) have -*iʃ* as the 2FSG suffix. These forms are cognate with the form -*ʃi* discussed at some length by Sibawaih.[13] In (28) this line of development is represented as parallel to that of the affricate variant. The -*ʃi* variant is attested only in Sibawaih.

In this pronoun I have indicated two reconstructions. The wide distribution of both -*ki* and -*ik* indicates a pre-diasporic provenance of both. At the older proto-stage I assume–*ki*, for reasons given above.

8.7.5. 2M.SG

-ka, 2MSG, *-k/*-ka = proto-Arabic **k or **ka

There are two consonantal variants in the data, one [k], and in one case the affricated variant [c], [ts], etc. (see sect. 8.7.1). The affricated variant -*ic* occurs only in Soukhne, and would be explained as a general, local leveling of the second person suffixes in favor of [c], (see sect. 8.7.4 above). This is a local post-diasporic development.[14]

As far as the vowel goes, the majority of the dialects, thirty-four in total, have /a/, -*ak* (-*ac* in one case as noted). Four sample points have -*k*, all in the Arabian peninsula, mainly the eastern part, Hofuf, Rwala, Najdi. The remaining eleven have -*ik*.

In this case I suggest two alternative pre-diasporic forms, both *-*k* and *-*ka*, and as a proto-form either **-*k* or **-*ka*, but not both. Both solutions involve steps more arbitrary than have hitherto been encountered in the current pronominal reconstructions.

The easier solution is to assume *ka as the proto-form. Given this, the development of the most widespread form, -*ak*, follows the same line of development as the FSG -*ik*, given in (27) above.

---

[13] The Old Arabic variant -*kiʃ* and its possible congeners in Yemeni Arabic are discussed in Watson (1992). She suggests that -*ʃ* derives at an earlier stage from -*ki*. There are a number of views on this, however.

[14] Also attested in other Levantine varieties, such as some rural Palestinian dialects.

(29) *ka → *a-ka → -ak

The [a] before the prefix was originally an epenthetic vowel inserted in the same contexts as (27). In this instance the value [a] for the epenthetic vowel is itself a reconstructed form, as there are no contemporary varieties with this value of epenthetic vowel in this context. However, the contemporary paradigm in sect. 3.4.2 ((15), (16)) indicates that the epenthetic vowel is basically harmonic with the vowel of the pronominal morpheme, which in this case would have been -[a]. The final [a] was then lost, parallel to the loss of [i] of the feminine -ki in many dialects. The epenthetic vowel was reinterpreted as part of the 2MSG suffix.

This derivation is possibly supported by one dialectal observation. In Uzbekistan Arabic there exists what was etymologically a participial construction in which the original object suffixes came to represent an agent. The basic form of this construction was the subject of sect. 5.4.2. The 2MSG -ak suffix can therefore represent a subject. This same construction allows expression of both subject and object via pronouns, in the first and second persons the same object pronoun series being used for both. In (30) the suffix -ak is the subject.

(30) *zoorb-in-ak baqara* 'you.M hit the cow'

In (31), the object is represented pronominally via -*ni*. In this case, the 2MSG suffix, otherwise -*ak*, takes the form -*akaa*-

(31) *hint zoorb-in-ak-aa-ni*
      'You.M hit me' (Zimmerman 2002: 93).

It could be that the -aa which appears before a pronominal object represents the reconstructed [a] of *ka.

There are two interpretive problems with this. First, when a Subject–Object sequence is represented in this construction by two pronouns, the subject always ends in a long vowel. Thus, whereas unsuffixed the 2MPL is -*kum*, when a further suffix is added the form -*kuu* appears.

(32) *hintu*   *zorb-in-kum*
      you.MPL   hit-in-you.MPL
      'You.MPL have hit'

(33) *hintu zorb-in-kuu-nii*
      'You have hit me' (Zimmerman 2002: 96)

In this verbal construction in Uzbekistan Arabic third person plural subject forms use the etymological sound plural suffixes, -*iin*, -*i*. Here again, when a further object suffix is added, an -*aa* may appear before the suffix. In this case -*aa* appears to be optional.

(34a) *haloo*   *zorb-iin-aa-ha*
       they   hit-PL-aa-her
       'They have hit her'.

(34b) *halaan zorb-aat-aa-hum*
      'They.F have hit them' (Zimmerman 2002: 97–8)

Whereas in the masculine form (34a) the *-aa* is conceivably etymological *-a* of **-iina*, in (34b) it has no correspondence in Old Arabic. Looking at ((30)–(34)), there is thus clearly a morpho-phonological constraint operative, militating against a C–C sequence at the subject–object suffix boundary. *-aa* insertion alleviates this sequence. Given this synchronic situation, the *-aa* which is inserted could derive from etymological *-ka*, *-iina*, but it could equally stem from a later morpho-phonological rule specific to Uzbekistan Arabic which alleviates C–C sequences, as stated.

While *ka works perfectly for those contemporary dialects with *-ak* as the 2MSG suffix, it is problematic in other cases.

In four dialects, all in the northeast Arabian peninsula, the 2MSG is *-k* alone. Parallel to the 2FSG suffix in these dialects (all affricated *-c*), an epenthetic vowel is inserted after VVC- or CC-. Example (35) replicates (24) exactly.

(35) Epenthesis rule, northeast Arabian dialects, 2MSG
     CCC   CC-ə-C   *ʃift-k*   → *ʃift-ik* 'I saw you.MSG'
     VVCC   VVC-ə-C   *siyuuf-k* → *siyuuf-ik* 'your.MSG. swords'
     vs. *min-k* 'from you.MSG'

It is of course possible that the [a] was lost, and the suffix *-k* was left, to pick up an epenthetic vowel as needed. There is no evidence for or against this as far as I can tell. It can equally be proposed, however, on the basis of contemporary forms as in (35), that the original suffix was **-k* alone. This obviates the need for arbitrarily 'deleting' the final *-a*, and it replicates the contemporary situation in the above four dialects. Furthermore, most *qultu* dialects have the 2MSG form *-ik*, all in fact in the present sample (Cypriot, Aazex, Mardin, Daragözü). In addition, Bahariyya has *-ik*. This form is explicable as the 2MSG reflex in exactly the same way the phonetically identically, though morphologically distinctive reflex *-ik* of the 2FSG is derived (see (27)). The epenthetic vowel [i] in (35) became reinterpreted as a part of the 2MSG suffix, now *-ik*.[15]

---

[15] From the region can be found examples such as, *law ḍərab-kə fi məkaan* 'if it (a small bullet) hits you.M anywhere'. The morphemic form is *ḍərab-k* 'it hit you', with the ə added as an epenthetic vowel in close juncture to prevent a CCC sequence. The *kə* gives a vocalic model for a -CV suffix, which could be morphologized by analogy to the reconstructed FSG **-ki.

It should also be noted that the pausal form -k 2MSG is noted in Sibawaih, *bi-ḥukm-i-k* 'by your judgment' (II: 304. 18). Interestingly, his example in the genitive formally replicates the allomorphemic form -ik which would appear after two consonants in northeast Arabian dialects, as stated in (35). In passing, it hardly needs repeating that there is no comparative linguistic justification for seeing the modern variant -ik as arising from the genitive -i + pausal form -k. Note also that there are a number of instances cited in this book where modern dialectal attestations are formally identical to citations in Sibawaih, even if the underlying rules accounting for them are different (see e.g. in Ch. 3 (19) and n. 31). This mutual shadowing requires resolution at the deeper level of proto-reconstruction.

In many North African varieties (Fez, Tripoli, Mzab, Tunis), the form -ik, common second person masculine/feminine singular form probably derives from the 2MSG -ak > ik, not from original -ik. In most North African varieties a short low vowel in an unstressed closed syllable is raised.

(36) *kammil* 'he finished' < *kammal*

The normally unstressed -ak would regularly raise to -ik under the same rule.

The problem for the 2MSG reconstruction *k is accounting for the [a] in other dialects. As in (29), its origin would be seen as epenthetic. However, motivation for the value [a] as opposed to [i] needs to be found. Here one could to appeal to analogy with the final vowel of independent pronouns, e.g. 2M *inta* 2F *inti*, as well as appeal to an avoidance factor: all dialects with 2FSG -ik have 2MSG -ak.[16] The [a] value would be a default value to disambiguate the 2SG object suffix. However, whereas here one avoids the problem of the arbitrary deletion of final [a], the resultant vowel [a] of -ak is partly arbitrary as well.

8.7.6. *3M.SG.*

hu = *-hu, possibly also *Vhu

The final suffix is basically reconstructed using procedures already found in 8.7.4, with the feminine singular suffix -ki. No contemporary dialects have invariable -hu. There are, however, a few *qultu* dialects like Mardin and Aazax with the variant -hu after a long vowel and dialects with -hu before another suffix (Cairene). This parallels the alternation of the 2FSG suffix, -ik ~ -ki noted in (26).

(37) ʃaaf-uu-hu 'they saw him'
      ʃaaf-uu-huu-ʃ 'they didn't see him'

---

[16] Except of course those North African dialects where -ik and -ak have fallen together in -ik.

In a few dialects, -h alone appears after a long vowel, as in Najdi and Hofuf.

(38) ʃaaf-uu-h

That there was an [h] in the suffix is confirmed by the Cypriot Arabic variant -x after a long vowel.

(39) ʃaaf-uu-x

In Cypriot Arabic, *h regularly is realized as /x/.

Most dialects have -u alone. These would be explained by the same chain as the second person singular chains in (27) and (35).

(40) *hu → (u)hu → uh → u[17]

Under this interpretation, the -u of these suffixes is an epenthetic vowel etymologically.[18] Note that in this interpretation the -hu variant might also be taken as the proto-form as well.

Five dialects, Rwala, San'a, Bahariyya, Najdi, and Suwwadiyye have the variant -ih. In addition, eastern Libyan Arabic, according to Mitchell has both -ih and -ah. One explanation for this variant will be given below.

Eleven dialects in the sample have a low vowel, -a, as in WSA ʃaaf-a 'he saw him'. These include WSA, ELA, and Mesopotamian gilit, and Abu Dhabi and Khorasan, so the extension of the feature argues for pre-diasporic status. These might be explained as a special consonantal harmony rule. In many dialects there exists a so-called gahawa syndrome in which a guttural consonant induces a low vowel epenthetic vowel after it (see sect. 3.4.2 (18)).

(41) gahwa → gahawa 'coffee'

---

[17] This chain resembles Nishio (1986), who similarly reconstructs object pronouns on the basis of dialectal evidence to the exclusion of Classical Arabic. He deals only with the two third person singular forms. Nishio (1986: 11) suggests the immediate ancestor of 3MSG forms in various northern Arabian dialects (e.g. Shammar) is *uh/hu. This would almost be comparable to my second stage, -uhu (with epenthesis) vs. -hu (without). In fact, the chain in (40) runs into a problem in the context -VC, as in ɣanam-? 'his sheep'. No epenthesis is predicted in this context, so the form *hu is expected, ɣa'nam-hu (I assume the stress without argumentation here). However, such a reflex is unattested. Instead, in this context all dialects go back to a -V suffix, e.g. WSA ɣanam-a 'his sheep', ELA uɣ'nim-ih or uɣnim-a, Shammar ɣnem-o, etc. In the present schema, the vowel-initial suffix is provided by a vowel epenthesis rule. I leave this context open as a problem. Various solutions might be proposed, but one can be ruled out which is crucial to this chapter, namely that the vowel goes back to a case suffix.

[18] It does not appear possible to assimilate this form to the h-deletion third person pronouns (sect. 7.6.4). Given the pre-diasporic *-hu, -u could be reached simply by deleting the -h. A major problem is that many dialects which do not have the h-deletion rule, all those in Morocco, Mauritania, Algeria, and Tunisia as well as Maltese in this sample, for instance, have the 3MSG suffix -u. It would be necessary to postulate the -h deletion only in the 3MSG for them.

In (41), the /h/ induces insertion of /a/ after it (similarly *aḥamar* < *aḥmar* 'red', *biSarif* < *biSrif* 'he knows' etc.). It could be that in this case the following -h induces insertion of the epenthetic vowel [a] rather than [u], as in (42).

(42) *hu → a-hu → ah → a

One problem with this suggestion is that in attested contemporary dialects, the epenthetic vowel is either harmonic with the vowel of the suffix, or has the default value [i]. As an alternative, one could reconstruct two variants of the 3MSG, one a high vowel, one a low. One small piece of evidence in favor of this perspective comes from eastern Libyan Arabic. This has two variants, *-ih* after a high vowel/non-guttural consonant and *-ah* or *-a* after a low vowel/guttural consonant. ELA is one of a number of dialects where [i] and [a] alternate morpho-phonemically elsewhere as well, for instance harmonically with the vowel of the stem. In the following, for instance, the preformative vowel has the values [a] or [i] according to the stem vowel.

(43a) *t-a-ʃrab* 'she drinks'

(43b) *t-i-ktib* 'she writes'

If this alternation goes back to pre-diasporic Arabic, which I believe to be the case (see sect. 2.4.2 (25) for related evidence), it could be that the epenthetic vowel was determined harmonically, some varieties (Rwala, Bahariyya, etc.) then generalizing *-ih*, others, as above, *-a*, and ELA maintaining both.

(44) (a)C_{gut}-h → (a)C_{gut}-a-h
     (i/u)C-h → (i/u)C-i-h

Under this interpretation there are two 3MSG pre-diasporic forms, distinguished primarily by epenthetic vowel rule. One form, *-hu*, induces the epenthetic vowel [u], as in (40). The other, either *-hu* or *-h*, is tied to the rule (44). Final vowel length is not dealt with in this book (see Ch. 3 nn. 25, 27).

8.8. Case Traces?

In the following table for a general orientation the results of the reconstruction of pronominal suffix forms into pre-diasporic times, based on dialectal evidence is compared to the forms in Classical Arabic. I put in bold variants which are identical in Classical Arabic and the current independent reconstruction based on modern dialects.

(45) Classical Arabic   Reconstruction on basis of comparative dialectal
                         evidence

1
SG
-iy, -niy   **-i, ni,** 'i
PL. -naa   **na**
2
MSG. -ka   **ka** or k
F -ki   **ki**
PL
M -kum   **kum**/ku
F -kunna   kin/kan
3
SG
M -hu   **hu**
F -haa   **ha**/he
PL
M -hum   **hum**/hun
F -hunna   hin/han

Note 1. In -CVC pronouns, a reconstruction of V, rather than specifying a particular vowel quality, or of CHC, where H = a high vowel, is perhaps appropriate. As described in Ch. 2, the short high vowels /i/ and /u/ are often non-contrastive and often in free variation both in classical sources and in modern dialects. Final vowel length is not dealt with systematically in this book (see Ch. 3 nn. 25, 27).

Note 2. The two paradigms range from outright identity to minor difference.

Note 3. The biggest difference is in the feminine plural forms, where CA has a final *-na* (*-kunna/hunna*), lacking in the dialects. This difference will be relativized considerably in sect. 8.9 below, however.

In this section it is relevant to discuss in detail the historical status of the vowels which I term 'epenthetic', which either occur in various contexts before the object pronouns, as in the third person plural forms, or have been reinterpreted as a part of the suffix, as in the second person singular forms (sect. 8.7.2/3).

In the Arabicist tradition, as already noted above in the discussion of Cantineau and Birkeland in sect. 8.2, one assumption has been that the vowels of say 2F *-ik* and 2M *-ak* are former inflectional vowels. This idea goes back at least to Brockelmann (1908: 309). As noted already in a number of places, the existence of case vowels in Old Arabic and their 'loss' in Neo-Arabic has been used as a prime structural marker of the difference between the two varieties. However, there are few convincing instances of traces of these vowels in the dialects. Such would be expected if a case-variety was at all an ancestor of the modern dialects. The suffix pronouns therefore are an important test case. The question here is in what sense the relevant vowels are in fact a missing link between Old Arabic and Neo-Arabic.

Problems relating to this interpretation have already been alluded to in sect. 8.2. In this section I will outline five reasons why the reconstruction of pronominal suffixes argues for an epenthetic vowel status, either in a synchronic or in a synchronic and diachronic sense. They have no etymological relationship to an original case vowel. Furthermore, there is, in general, no evidence from the protected stem + object suffix position which shows a trace of a case vowel. All discussion here relates to data discussed above already, so I will be perfunctory. The main argumentation refers to reconstructed forms, those which can be taken back to pre-diasporic Arabic.

1. *-h* deletion and assimilation. In the third person forms in many dialects the initial *-h* (*-hu, ha, hum, hin*) is lost in various contexts. Most frequently, they are lost after a consonant, maintained after a vowel. Obviously, the post-consonant deletion is explicable only in a system where there is no intervening vowel, which the case marker is (see paradigm in (7) above). Since the h-deletion varieties are reconstructed back to pre-diasporic Arabic, it follows that this variety lacked the case inflectional vowel. A similar argument applies to those cases where an *-h* is assimilated to a preceding voiceless consonant (not discussed extensively in this chapter).

2. Stem form change. This argument has been explained above, in the discussion of Cantineau's observations. Cantineau assumes that the /a/of the 2MSG *-ak* is a remnant of the accusative case. However, in the ʕAnaza dialect in the form *bgaṛ-at-k* 'your cow' from **bagarat-a-ka*, there is no explanation as to why the syllabification has the outcome which it does, with the first vowel and the case vowel but not the other vowels deleted.

3. Epenthesis. The epenthesis rules needed to account for the appearance of vowels before object suffixes are in many dialects identical to those in other contexts. In the eastern Libyan dialect, for instance, there is a general rule which inserts a vowel in a CCC context, as CCC → CəCC. This is illustrated in sect. 8.4 above, as well as in Chs. 3 and 6.

(46) *galb-na* → *galib-na* 'our heart'
 yi-ktb-u → *yikitbu* 'they.M write'

This rule has a wide distribution among dialects, suggesting that it is a pre-diasporic relic which acted on caseless forms.

Similarly, a number of Arabian peninsular dialects have an epenthetic rule which is sensitive only to the quantity of the final stem syllable. For all suffixes beginning with a consonant (-k, -c, -ha, -na, -kum, -cin, hum, -hin) the rule is:

(47) insert an epenthetic vowel after VVC- or CC- stems, otherwise do not insert.

This yields, for instance, the contrast,

(48) *rijaal-ic* 'your.F men'
bugar-c 'your.F cattle'.

The phonological basis of the rule is clear, and I think it would be linguistically perverse to suggest that the [i] of -*ic* is somehow a remnant of a genitive case suffix.

4. Vowel harmony. The form of the epenthetic vowels are adequately accounted for by simple rules of vowel harmony or assimilation. The value [i] vs. [a] in the following is straightforwardly a function of the vowel of the pronominal suffix.

(49) *darb-i-ki* 'your.F road' (Nigerian Arabic)
darb-a-ha 'her road'

There is no need to see in these the remnants of a genitive (-*i*) or an accusative (-*a*) suffix. Positing such would lead to the question, why a genitive survives before a 2FSG form and an accusative before a 3FSG. As pointed out in n. 31 in Ch. 3, already in Sibawaih an identical rule of epenthetic vowel insertion with vowel harmony determined by the pronominal suffix can be found (II: 163, Ch. 409).

5. Conversion of epenthetic vowel status. In the 2FSG, 2MSG (under one interpretation), and 3MSG object reconstructions it was posulated that an original epenthetic vowel became morphologized as part of the object pronoun suffix. In fact, according to the reconstruction chain in (40), the 3MSG suffix -*u* of many contemporary dialects arises solely as an epenthetic vowel. The conversion is clearly that of an original epenthetic vowel, whose presence is required by general phonological rules (see point 3 above), not of an original case vowel.

There are three crucial points in these five phenomena. (1) Some of the phenomena require suffixation to a vowelless stem for their realization, (2) a vowel before a suffix can be exhaustively explained as an epenthetic vowel, and (3) there is no need to see in these epenthetic vowels the remnants of a case suffix origin, nor is there any evidence from reconstruction that the epenthetic vowels derive from old case markers. In short, there is nothing in a comparative study of the origin of the dialectal object pronoun suffixes which hints at case traces.

8.9. Harris Birkeland and Old Arabic Object Pronoun Reconstruction

It is appropriate to end this chapter by returning to Birkeland's ideas. Birkeland reconstructs only the object pronouns to the extent that they are problematic within the Old Arabic literature. Four forms he deals with are relevant to the current discussion. In these Birkeland follows August Fischer (1926) and others (e.g. Reckendorf 1895/1967): 390; Brockelmann 1908: 309–10) assuming the following proto-forms. It should be noted, however, that A. Fischer, whom Birkeland most heavily relied on, can hardly be said to have reconstructed anything. While his 1926 article has a wealth of observations from a panoply of Old Arabic sources, his conclusion (1926: 402) has more the character of a census than a reconstruction. He writes, for instance that '*hu* generally was realized as *huu*' ('*hu* lautete im allgemeinen *huu*'). That more sources cite *huu* than *-hu* or another variant is hardly criterial in the comparative method, however. In any case, Birkeland assumes the following proto-forms, which are also often assumed today (e.g. Fischer 1972: 126).

(50) *-huw 3MSG[19]
       *-hiy 3FSG
       *-humuw 3MPL
       *-kumuw 3FPL

Birkeland derives variant forms as later developments. There is a problem in this approach, however, when the issue is limited to the Old Arabic sources. The basic problem is that the set of forms in (50) is not the only variants attested in the classical literature, which means that (50) is a reconstruction which itself needs to be justified.

---

[19] Nishio (1986: 13) on the basis of reconstruction from Arabian peninsula dialects reconstructs an allomorphic 3MSG object suffix *hu/huu, the former after CV, the latter after CVC or CVV. The reconstruction of this form, however, appears motivated by a parallel reconstruction of the 3FSG form -ha/haa. I will not go into details here, other than to note that whereas for the 3FSG a length allomorphy may be needed to account for developments in some dialects (e.g. Shammar *jmal-ah* 'her camel' < -ha vs. *ḍreboo-ha* 'they struck her' < -haa, Nishio 1986: 7), no such parallel paradigms are found for the 3MSG suffix.

I begin the discussion here with the 3SG forms. There are three forms noted for the 3MSG. A basic distribution for these, found for instance in FarraʔI (I: 223) and in the Qiraaʔaat literature (Ibn Mujahid, 130), are described as being in complementary distribution, -hu and -huw: -hu occurs after a long vowel, -huw after a short vowel or consonant.

(51) ḍaraba-huw 'he hit him'.
    ʕalay-hiy 'on him'

vs.

(52) ʔabaa-hu 'his father'
    xuðuw-hu 'take.MPL-him' (Sibawaih II: 318, ch. 502)

This distribution is often represented as Classical Arabic par excellence. Sibawaih, however, notes variants here. Besides (52), he notes (II: 318. 13) that the short form after a long vowel as in ʔaṣaabat-hu 'she hit him' is 'Arabic' as well, even if the full form (ʔitmaam) is better here. The complementarity in fact appears to be a variable phenomenon. In pausal position only the short forms are reported by Sibawaih, though it is not always clear whether they are -hu or -h or both (II: 313. 9, 319. 3).

Farraʔ notes a further 3MSG alternative in the Koranic readings of ʕAaṣim and al-ʔAʕmash, where the form ends in -h (I: 223, also I: 388).

(53) ʔaxaa-h 'his brother'

There are also bedouins who realize the pronoun with -h after a vowel.

(54) ḍarab-tu-h
    'I hit him'.

Farraʔ further notes that there are bedouins who, it may be inferred, invariably use the form -hu, never -huw.

In the Qiraaʔaat literature Ibn Mujahid's basic, which is to say initial summary is essentially like Sibawaih's ((51), (52)), with the short vowel realization as in (51) referred to as having an ixtilaas (130) realization (see sect. 8.1). However, Ibn Mujahid also notes that there are reports of readers such as Kisaʔi who in certain contexts where one might expect -huw instead have the realization -hu, yara-hu 'should see him' and others who have -h, like ʕAṣim and Ibn Amr, yara-h (237). Ibn Kathir on the other hand is reported always to have recited with a long -huw, e.g. ʔansaaniy-huw 'he made me forget it'. In the Qiraaʔaat literature, therefore, all variants are attested.

For the two plural forms in (50), Sibawaih notes that in context position there is free variation (kunta bi-l-xiyaar ʔin ʃiʔta haðafta wa ʔin ʃiʔta Paθbatta, II: 319. 8).

(55) ʕalay-kumuw ~ ʔalay-kum maal 'You.MPL have wealth'
laday-himiy ~ laday-him maal

Sibawaih explains here that the -uw or -iy may avoid a short variant, -kumu, -humu, since one motivation for using the -m final form is to avoid sequences of open syllables, and retaining a short vowel at the end would be counterproductive to this purpose (see Ch. 2 (21)). However, should the need for a short vowel occur, a -u or, harmonically, an -i will be appended. From Sibawaih's examples the need arises when in context a sequence of three consonants would otherwise occur. In the following, the final -u is considered a shortened form of -humuw, not an epenthetic vowel.

(56) ʕalay-himu l-maal 'they owe money'

In the QiraaʔPaat as well both V-final and m-final forms vary (Ibn Mujahid, 108–12).

Before coming to a general conclusion, it is relevant to discuss remaining object pronominal forms, even if these were not explicitly dealt with by Birkeland. These are the feminine plural forms and the second person singular:

(57) -kunna 2FPL
-hunna 3FPL
-ka 2MSG
-ki 2FSG.

As noted above in sect. 8.8, in regards to the feminine plural forms, the reconstruction in the dialect forms (see sect. 8.6.7), appears to differ slightly from Sibawaih's forms, represented in (57). However, this difference needs to be relativized. In most dialects with a feminine plural, there are no or few contexts where a further morpheme can be added to an object pronoun. Dialects with the FPL, for instance, happen not to be those which suffix a negative -ʃ at the end of a word. One can look at the comparable FPL subject suffix on verbs, however, either -in or -an, depending on dialect. In WSA it is -an. When a further vowel-initial suffix is added, the [n] doubles, as in Nigerian Arabic,

(58) katab-an 'they.F wrote'
katab-an-n-a 'they.F wrote it.M'

The [n] also geminates before a direct object beginning with the definite article:

(59) ʔirf-ann aj-jaar
know-FPL DEF-neighbor
'They know the neighbor'.
fihim-ann   al-kalaam
understood-FPL DEF-matter
'They.F understood the matter'.

Such forms are comparable to the CA FPL object suffix forms - *kunna, -hunna* in having a geminate *-nn*.

In Old Arabic the pausal status of the FPL forms are somewhat puzzling. According to standard interpretation, in pausal position the final short /a/ should be lost (see (1) above).

(60a) *bayt-u-kunna#* → *bayt-u-kunn#* 'your.FPL house'

(60b) *bayt-u-hunna#* → *bayt-u-hunn#*

This, however, produces an unacceptable double consonant sequence in pausal position, *-nn#*

Sibawaih does note via example that the verbal subject 2FPL - *tunna* may in pause appear before an intrusive - *h*.

(61) *ðahab-tunna-h#* 'you.FPL. went' (II: 303. 7)

This certainly generalizes to the object suffix *-kunna* as well, not explicitly mentioned in Sibawaih. Nonetheless, Sibawaih also notes that many Arabs do not add an *-h* in pausal position. In this case (57a, b) are particularly problematic. It could be that the pausal forms here maintain the final *-a*, though this seems unlikely given Sibawaih's specific mention of the *-h* alternative, which effectively takes a pausal position and makes it non-pausal. If the final *-a* is elided, as noted, a CC# sequence arises. However, *nn#* is not allowed, so the expected pausal forms probably would give *-kun, hun*. These are essentially identical to the suffixes reconstructed here (sects. 8.6.7, 8.7.2).[20]

For the two second person singular forms Sibawaih notes the following variants:

(62) 2MSG: -ka, -kaa-, -k
     2FSG: -ki, -kii-, ʃi, kiʃ.

---

[20] Alternatively, a CC# sequence induces epenthesis, as in the imperative of doubled verbs, rudd# → urdud# (Sibawaih II: 162).

-*ka* and -*ki* are non-pausal forms and correspond to Standard Arabic. -*kaa* and -*kii* occur among some Arabs before a pronominal suffix:

(63) *ʔu-ʕṭiy-kaa-haa*
'I-give-you.M-it.F'
'I give you it.F'
ʔuʕṭiy-kii-hi
'I give you.F-it.M' (II: 323. 17).

Sibawaih cites pre-pronominal variants with the short variant as well:

(64) *ʔaʕṭaa-ka-niy*
'He gave you.M me' (I: 355. 19).

The two feminine variants -*ʃi* and -*kiʃ* are noted as variants among the Tamim and Banu Assad (II: 322, ch. 504; see sect. 8.7.4 above). In discussing the cause for these forms, Sibawaih notes that -*ʃi* and -*kiʃ* are motivated by the desire to distinguish between the M and F forms in pause, since the masculine form is realized as -*k*. This point is elliptic. It seems to imply that elswhere, against the general rules for pause, -*ka* and -*ki* do not fall together in pause, but that in this dialect they would, but for the realization of the 2F as -*ʃ*.

The main point of the discussion in this section is that looked at as a group, object pronouns are exceptional to Birkeland's purported development, whereby in pausal position long vowels are shortened, short vowels are deleted. Regarding the short vowels in -*ki*, -*ka*, -*kunna*, and -*hunna*, it may be interpreted that in fact there were variants described by the Arabic grammarians in which these vowels are not deleted at all, the -*a* being left in tact against the rules of pause. If normal pausal behavior is assumed, then forms like those in sect. 8.6.7 are implied.

The situation with the long vowels in Birkeland's reconstruction in (50) is problematic in its own way. Birkeland himself in his characteristic meticulousness recognized the problem and devoted an entire chapter (1940: 89–91) to the realization of the 3MSG *-*huw*. Context -*huw* should give rise to pausal -*hu*. As seen above, however, besides -*hu*, -*h* is attested as well. Moreover, even in context, -*huw* alternates with -*hu* according to rules discussed in relation to ((51), (52)). Birkeland's (1940: 90) comparative historical explanation envisages three stages, thus:

(65) 1. **huw*
    2a. *huw* after V
    2b. *hu* after VV
       3. dialect split, some dialects take 2b as basis of all pausal forms, giving -*h*.

This is a logical possibility, of course, but there is no independent motivation for it. On the basis of stage 2, there should be pausal forms in -*hu*. Birkeland, however, takes the form in 3, -*h* to be the normal pausal form. Taking 2b as the source, this gives the expected pausal form. Since, however, 2a, 2b, and 3 are all contemporary, Birkeland has to appeal to the *deus ex machina* of multiple, coexisting dialects; otherwise one would expect a pausal symmetry, -*hu/h* paralleling the context symmetry -*huw/hu*. Such a pausal symmetry is nowhere described in the grammars or Koranic commentaries, however. The Arabic grammarians, according to Birkeland, therefore took a dialect as their norm which uniformly generalized 2b as the basis of pausal forms.

As by now should be familiar, other explanations for the development of forms attested in the classical literature should be entertained. The easiest one, which I would adopt, in fact is as follows:

(66) 1. **hu*
    2a. *huw* after short vowel
    2b. *hu* after long vowel
    2c. *h* in pause.

Given a proto-form **hu*, the variants -*huw*, -*hu* and -*h* follow by rule. Note that it is even possible to begin with the pausal form:

(67) 1. **h*
    2a. *huw* after short vowel
    2b. *hu* after long vowel
    2c. *h* in pause.

The only preference for (66) over (67) resides in the need to specify the vowel /u/ in (67).

The independent evidence which I offer in favor of (66) over (65) and (67) is that (66) is the same reconstruction which a consideration of modern dialects yields (see sect. 8.7.6). Very probably a much closer look at Old Arabic sources, especially a closer study of the variants of the Koranic readers, would indicate how widespread the long and short vowel variants in fact are, and this in turn would shed further light on the issue of whether **hu* or **huw* is a more likely proto-form. In the current study, in any case, **hu* is preferred.

Furthermore, in a recent study Hasselbach (2004), basing her sources entirely on comparative Semitic excluding Arabic dialects, concludes that proto-Semitic object pronouns were short, except for the 1SG, 1PL, 3FSG. If this position is the correct one, it would again suggest that Arabic dialects are in certain respects more 'archaic' in a proto-Semitic context than is Classical

Arabic, and at the same time confirm that evidence from the dialects is directly relevant to proto-Semitic reconstruction.

Before closing this chapter, I should point out that the interpretation of Arabic history advocated here is at its core very close to that expressed by Carl Vollers (1892: 154) over a hundred years ago. Basing his argument on Arabic phonetics, he suggested, 'As regards the vulgar Arabic, it is very probable that it is an older layer than the classical language, and that therefore the classical Arabic is, from the phonetic point of view, the youngest prehistoric offshoot of the Semitic stock.' Vollers, to my knowledge, never developed his argument in a more detail than this, and like his contemporaries he did not work out his argument in the framework of a rigorous comparative methodology, in particular not indicating what the older vulgar Arabic phonetic stock was as compared to Classical Arabic. Moreover, the bulk of the argumentation in the present work only allows the conclusion that modern dialects often maintain features which either are identical with forms attested somewhere in Old Arabic but for whatever reason are not necessarily recognized as being part of Classical Arabic, or allow reconstruction into the pre-diasporic era. No claims are made about the ancientness of 'vulgar Arabic' vs. 'Classical Arabic', constructs which in any case are dangerously a prioristic from a comparativist perspective. Nonetheless, it appears to be the case that interpretations of Arabic language history in Western scholarship were once more variegated and nuanced than they are today.

9

Summary and Epilogue

The main linguistic points of this work can be represented in three categories. The basis of the three is the comparative historical relation between Arabic in what I have termed the pre-diasporic period and the present-day dialects. I list only the issues which have been dealt with in detail. There is no point in presenting a longer list of potential supporting evidence so long as the comparative arguments are outstanding.

9.1. Reconstruction and Continuity with Old Arabic

1. In the first category are phenomena which essentially are identical in at least some varieties of contemporary Arabic and Old Arabic. As will be recalled, Old Arabic in my terminology is the corpus of written attestations between around 650–850. There are four main topics which fall into this category.

- Variation in short high vowels: contrastive if at all only in restricted positions, often lexically determined (Ch. 2);
- *imala* (Ch. 7);
- suffix object pronouns (Ch. 8);
- reconstruction of imperfect verb (Ch. 6).

The conclusions for this category, it should be recalled, were reached by reconstructing pre-diasporic Arabic solely on the basis of the modern dialects, and correlating these results with the earliest grammatical descriptions. In each case, results of the reconstruction dovetailed nicely with early descriptions, though the correspondence is also based on generalized inferences in the case of the imperfect verb.

2. Reconstructible forms not identical to attested Old Arabic, but on a comparative basis, at least as old:

- intrusive *-in*, linker *-n* (Chs. 3, 5);
- many features discussed in Ch. 5.

The elements in this category are solely artefacts of reconstruction. However, given the very wide contemporary distribution of the features, at an extreme attested both in Nigerian Arabic and in the Arabic of Uzbekistan, independent parallel development can in most instances with certainty be ruled out. Pre-diasporic Arabic thereby becomes an object characterized by a good deal more variation than is found Old Arabic alone.

3. Discontinuity with some varieties of Old Arabic

- lack of case endings (Chs. 3, 4).

This class has elements of the first two. The universal lack of case endings in the contemporary dialects is as the second category; indications that the short vowel case endings were not a robust system in Old Arabic, however, allows an interpretation as with the first category. Moreover, the short vowel case endings are phonologically nothing more than the same short vowels with restricted contrastive status.

Certainly the conclusions of these three categories can be graded for their adherence both to a result commensurate with an application of the comparative method and to an interpretation of the given phenomenon in Old Arabic sources. In this sense for instance, the interpretation of *imala* given here I believe is a relatively clear issue. On the other hand, my reading of the case endings though compatible with comparative arguments, is less certain, in particular because an explanation for how case evolved remains to be worked out. However, the conclusions of the book do not stand or fall on the reading of one issue. The overall argument that a comparative linguistic interpretation of the Arabic language is possible only in the light of a serious integration of contemporary dialect sources transcends judgment on a single topic.

9.2. Epilogue

What I have presented is less a definitive account of the history of Arabic than a way of thinking about it. In my view, there are far too many open questions to expect a comprehensive account now or any time soon. Four broad domains of research I think need to be integrated into a historical interpretation.

First, any results from an internal reconstruction of Arabic, which is the basis of the current work, will need to be integrated into broader Semitic comparisons. If proto-Arabic was in fact caseless, what does that imply for comparative Semitic? Or is the evidence from proto-Semitic in fact so overwhelming (against the arguments in Ch. 3 and elsewhere) that case is a proto-category, and if this is so, how would this be reconciled with the argument advanced here (sect. 3.4, Chs. 4 and 8) that there is no internal evidence for a transition from a case to a caseless variety of Arabic? The point here is to recognize that different sources, different languages will claim their own individual histories, as it were, and that a broader comparative treatment needs to be open to the many nuances and imponderables internal to the individual languages whose linguistic history they explain.

Second, though I have attempted in my dialect surveys, for instance in Chs. 5 and 8, to be broad and representative, they are by no means detailed enough. Ultimately there can be no reasonable synthesis of Arabic language history until far more historical comparative studies are carried out on individual features in individual dialects and dialect areas.

Thirdly, it would be obtuse to claim that no significant changes are to be found among Arabic dialects. This is a perspective which I have purposely downplayed, for two reasons. First is the strategic one: it is a major argument of this book that Arabicists have avoided a linguistically realistic representation of Arabic language history because of the facile assumption that Arabic neatly dichotomizes into Old and Neo-Arabic. These, I have argued, are basically logical, not comparative linguistic categories. It is a provisional fear on my part, expressed in a number of places in this work, that as soon as historical changes within a dialect are identified, that such changes will be cited as proof of the validity of the Old/New difference as a whole. By not addressing the issue of individual dialect change (see Kusters 2003 for this approach), this problem is avoided and broader issues in Arabic historical linguistics can be confronted. Second, and this follows from the first point, changes have to be worked out individually for individual dialects. However, as pointed out above, studies in this direction are broadly absent. Eventually, however, given a clearer idea about what proto-Arabic is, and a better historical treatment of individual dialects, individual histories can be developed and integrated into the broader fabric of Arabic language history.

Finally, a last point I think is a special challenge to Arabicists, namely developing a historical sociolinguistics of the language. Crucial here are questions such as who wrote early Arabic grammar, why they wrote it, what sources they used, why they used these sources, what they made of them, what sources were not used (see sect. 9.1, category 2 above) and how the teaching and preservation of Arabic developed. These and other issues will prove to be extremely pertinent to the question of why there may be discrepancies between linguistic reconstruction such as developed here and Old Arabic sources.

Summary and Epilogue   269

The language continues to hold its secrets. The insights of linguists are as relevant today as they were over 1,000 years ago, when the ninth-century legal scholar and contemporary of Farraʔ, Shafiʕi (d. 204/820) stated, 'ʔashaab al-ʕarabiyya jinn al-ʔuns, yubsiruuna maa laa yubsiru ɣayruhum',[1] 'Scholars of Arabic are the spirits among men; they perceive what others don't.'

---

[1] Astutely noted in Versteegh (1989: 291). Versteegh (p.c.) himself has the quotation from Nabia Abbot, *Studies in Arabic Literary Papyri*, iii. 34, from *'Adab al-Shafi'i*. In the *Lisaan* (6: 13) *ʔins* is 'man, mankind'. The variant *ʔuns* is rare, but noted with the meaning, 'opposite of savagery, roughness'. An alternative translation would be 'the spirits of civilized society'. *Jinn* can also be 'devils'.

Appendix 1. Dialects Cited

In this appendix is found a listing of all the dialects cited, in particular those used in the two surveys in Chs. 5 and 8. A short commentary is also included which specifies the time of first Arab migration to the given region and when, if this should be different, Arabicization became dominant. The dialect labels are basic heuristics only. It was seen especially in Ch. 5 that geographical labels often hide longer-range historical relationships among dialects and an overlapping of varieties caused by migrations at different periods, post-migration contact, and so on.

The dialects listed here are entered on Maps 1–3. On the maps, those descriptions which are represented by a single location (village or city) are represented by a point, while those which represent an area (e.g. Najdi) are represented by name over the approximate area of the dialect.

Western Sudanic Arabic (Map 3)

I term the Arabic established in the Lake Chad area beginning in the late fourteenth century 'western Sudanic Arabic'. Dialectally, it includes the Arabic of northeast Nigeria, Cameroon, and Chad, as well as Darfur and Kordofan in the Sudan. This is not to be confused with the area of western Sudan, which in Islamic history practice refers to Mauritania and adjoining regions. In Nigeria it is still expanding, as nomadic Arabs continue their spread, so that there now exist permanent Arab villages in Adamawa state, south of Borno.

Included in samples are:

    Bagirmi Arabic
        Mada
        Aajiri

    Western Nigerian Arabic
        Kirenawa
    Abbeche
    Ndjamena
    Amm Timan (2)
    Umm Hajar (2, nomads)

Arabic of the Sudan (Map 3)

Arabic was brought to the Sudan permanently in the same invasion which brought the Arabs to the Lake Chad region. The date customarily cited is 1317, as that was when the northern Nubian kingdom of Mariis was defeated by a Mameluke force, setting the stage for the rapid expansion of Arabs directly south and west. The Shukriyya settled in their current home along the Atbara River by the eighteenth century. They apparently have affinities with Arabs in the eastern Egyptian desert (de Jong 2002). Included in samples are:

Shukriyya
Khartoum

Egypt (Map 1)

Pre-Islamic dialects were present in Sinai (see below). Arabic spread throughout Egypt with the Islamic conquest. Fusṭaṭ at the site of present-day Cairo was founded in 640/1 and Aswan was reached by 630. Until about 900 the large Coptic population maintained their own language, but thereafter a gradual language loss set in. Upper Egypt in particular was an important demographic staging area from which large-scale populations moved both into North Africa (e.g. the Banu Hilal) and into the Sudanic region to the south. Included in samples are:

Cairene Arabic
Bahariyya Arabic (western desert oasis)
Nile Valley (Ṣaʕiid)

Libya (Map 1)

Arabic was first introduced with the Islamic conquest, beginning about 640. Western Libya was strongly Arabicized with the Banu Hilal invasion from Upper Egypt, beginning about 1040.

Eastern Libyan Arabic
Tripoli (western)
Gharyan (western)

Tunisia, Algeria, Morocco, Mauritania (Map 2)

Along with Libya, Arabicization proceeded in these regions basically in two waves. The earlier one was the original Arab-Islamic conquest, completed by the end of the seventh century. At this point Arabic was largely confined to urban areas. A more complete Arabicization followed in the wake of the Banu Hilal invasion of the eleventh century. The Banu Hilal established themselves first in western Libya and Tunisia. In the twelfth century a large group of their descendants were settled in the central Moroccan coastal area, which greatly increased the number of Arabic speakers in Morocco. The Arabicization of Mauritania began in the fourteenth century with the arrival of the eponymous Banu Maʕqil and accelerated considerably in the fifteenth and sixteenth centuries (Catherine Taine-Cheikh, p.c. November 2004 (Taine-Cheikh, 2008)).

Fez (Morocco)
Mauritania
Mzab (Algeria)
Djidjelli (Algeria)
Susa (Tunisia)
Tunis

Andalusia (Map 2)

Andalusia was first invaded in 711, and Arabic was spoken as a native language until the sixteenth century (Ferrando p.c., November 2004). Documents attesting the Arabic dialect become available in the tenth century, though the most detailed reports are relatively late in the fifteenth.

Maltese (Map 1)

Established either late ninth century or eleventh century, it was cut off from the Arabic-speaking world by the end of the eleventh century.

Jordan, Syria, Israel, Palestine, Lebanon (Map 1)

Arabs had spread throughout this region, particularly into the desert regions of Jordan and Syria, in pre-Islamic times. It was largely in the wake of the Arab-Islamic conquests, however, that Arabic displaced Aramaic on a large-scale basis as the mother tongue of most speakers of the region. The northern region of Syria and Lebanon shades dialectically into a northern Mesopotamian type. The part of the region running from the Sinai, across the Negev desert and into southern Jordan and northwest Saudi Arabia is dialectally quite different. Arabs have lived in the Sinai continuously since the third century BC (de Jong 2000: 13).

Tripoli (Lebanon)
Baskinta (Lebanon)
Soukhne (Syria)
Teerib (Syria)
Damascus
Ajarma (Jordan)
Bduul of Petra (southern Jordan)
Galilee (northern Israel)

Cypriot Arabic (Map 1)

Arabic is spoken by a small Maronite community in Kormakiti in northern Cyprus, which was established between the ninth and twelfth centuries (Borg 1985: 5, 6). The most recent information comes from Borg (2004: 1) whose work is based on a community of 1,300 Cypriot Maronites. Before the invasion of 1974 they lived in the village of Kormakiti in northern Cyprus, but thereafter most migrated south of the armistice line.

Mesopotamian Arabic (Map 1)

This designates the varieties found in Iraq, parts of northern Syria, and Turkey. Cypriot Arabic as well can be reckoned as belonging to this dialect area. It is characterized by two broad dialect types (see Ch. 5). The first, the *qultu* dialects, are the first to have been brought to the region in the immediate aftermath of the Arab-Islamic conquests. The second, the *gilit* dialects, arrived later, beginning around AD 1,000 or 1,100, probably pushing in from either the Arabian peninsula or from Jordan (Blanc 1964: 1). The dialect of the pre-Islamic tribes who lived in southern Iraq, such as the Tanukh, has not been speculated upon to my knowledge. More sharply than in many regions of the Arabic world, the different dialects in this area are often associated with confessional differences. It should be noted, however, that some of the dialects are dying out. The Jewish dialect of Hiit, for instance, is attested only through a description carried out in Israel of the diasporic population from that city (Khan 1997).

In Iraq:
Jewish Baghdadi
Christian Baghdadi
Muslim Baghdadi
Basra and other areas in southern Iraq
Hiit
Khaweetna

In Anatolia:
Siirt
Daragözü
Mardin
Aazex

South Central Turkey (Map 1)

Arabic was first brought to this area of south central Turkey (in and around the cities of Mersin, Adana, and Tarsus) in the seventeenth century, from Hatay. It is thus essentially a continuation of the varieties of that area (S. Prochazka 2002).

Hatay (Alawite dialect)
Cilicia

Hatay essentially continues the dialect complex of northern Syria (Arnold 1998).

Uzbekistan and Khorasan (Map 1)

Settled in the early eighth century and cut off from the broader Arabic dialect world by the beginning of the ninth, Uzbekistan represents an important Sprachinsel. While often characterized as Mesopotamian, as discussed in Ch. 5, Uzbekistan in fact shares significant affinities with dialects in a number of regions. The Jogari dialect spoken near Bukhara is used here.

The Arabic of Khorasan is known through a single description (Seeger 2002). It has interesting affinities to Uzbekistan Arabic, as well as some remarkable traits of its own (e.g. a complete *s → θ shift in some dialects).

Arabian peninsula (Map 1)

The pre-Islamic Arabian peninsula knew a number of languages, the closely related North Arabian type which includes the ancestor of Arabic (Macdonald 2000), as well as various South Arabian languages, five of which are still spoken today. No significant work has been done to discern evidence of language contact and shift among the historical populations, and there is not even agreement upon where the ancestral homeland of Arabic is. Petrácek (1988), for instance, locates it in the region north of the peninsula in modern Jordan and Iraq, whereas Retsö (2003: 37, 48–51) would appear to suggest the Arabian peninsula itself, between Yemen and Mecca, or perhaps an area northwest of Medina (*al-qura al-ʕarabiyya*). Throughout the history of the peninsula there have been a large number of population movements both to the north and to the south. It appears that in the immediate pre-Islamic era the dominate movement was already out of Yemen towards the north, due to the effect of dryer conditions (Caskel 1960/1986: 528). With the Islamic expansion, emigration increased considerably. Within the Arabian peninsula there continued to occur significant population movements, for instance from the central Arabian peninsula towards Bahrain and the trucial coast, and thence into Oman (Wilkinson 1987: 76).

Oman
Abu Dhabi
Saudi Arabia
  Rwala (northern Najd)
  Najdi
  Hofuf
  Qauz
Yemen
  Ṣanʕaaʔ
  As-Suwwaadiyyeh
  an-Nadhiir
  Al-Mudawwar

Appendix 2. Summary of Variables, Mesopotamia, Western Sudanic Region, Uzbekistan, Shukriyya

1. These variables are referred to in the text under Ap 2.1 for phonology or Ap 2.2 for morphology plus the number in brackets, which is the number by which the variable is identified in the data bank. /k/ for instance is sect. 2.1.2. The numbering sometimes has gaps in the sequence, these being left for related features.

Unless otherwise specified, the suffixal elements in the data do not themselves have another suffix. The addition of further suffixes often induces allomorphy of different types, which is not accounted for here.

2.1. Phonology

(1) qaaf (reflex of SA /q/); 1. q, *baqar* 'cattle': Mardin 2. g, *bagar*: Kirenawa. (2) /k/.1. k: *kalib*: CB, 2. c [tʃ]: *calib*: MB

In those dialects with a *k* ~ *c* alternation, *c* basically occurs in the environment of front vowels, or high front vowels but not back ones. The precise conditions vary from area to area, however.

(3, 4) /ħ//ʕ/; 1. *laħam*, 'meat', *baaʕat*, 'she sold', 2. *laham*, *baaʔat*: Kirenawa. (5) *ħa/ʕa; 1. *laħam*, *gaʕad* 'he stayed', 2. *leħem* 'meat', *geʕed*: Bagirmi

In the Bagirmi area proto *ħa/ʕa raise to *ħe/ʕe. Subsequent to this raising of /a/ to /e/, (3, 4) above occur.

(6) /ɣ/; 1. ɣ: *ɣasal* 'wash': MB, 2. q: *qasal*: Kirenawa, 3. x: *xasal*: Abbeche, 4. G (=[ʛ]) (pre-glottalized voiced velar stop or injective) *Gasal*: Awlad Eli (Cameroon/Chad). (7) /ð/; 1. ð, *dabaħ* 'slaughter': Hiit, 2. z, *zahab* 'go': Daragözü, 3. d, *daba(h)* 'slaughter': Abbeche, 4. ḍ, *ḍaba(h)*: Kirenawa, 5. v, *vahab* 'go': Siirt. (8) /θ/; 1. θ, *θlaaθa* 'three': Hiit, 2. t, *ṭa̱laata*: Kirenawa, 3. s, *sa̱laasa*: Aajiri, 4. f, *faafe*: Siirt

This correspondence applies to basic vocabulary.

(9) /ð̣/; 1. ð̣, *ð̣all* 'remain': Hiit, 2. ḍ: *ḍahar* 'back': Kirenawa, 3. ẓ: *ẓahar*: Daragözü, 4. v̱: *v̱ahar*: Siirt. (10) ṭ; 1. ṭ: *ṭaaɣ* 'it flew': JB, 2. ɗ: *ɗaar*: Kirenawa, 3. t: *taar*: Abbeche. (11) Realization of 'jiim' 1 j, *jimal* 'camel': (MB), 2. y, *yimal*: (southern Mesopotamia). (12) Word-internal *imala* 1. No *imala*, *kaatib* 'has written': Kirenawa, 2. Imala, *keetib*: CB

The *imala* in the Mesopotamian area has two degrees, with some dialects (e.g. JB) having a further raising to *ii* in some forms (e.g. nominal but not participial, *kliib* 'dogs').

(13) r; 1. r, *baarid* 'cold': Kirenawa, 2. ɤ, *beɤid*: CB. (14) CCVC-V (verb); 1. CCVC-V, *bu-ktub-u* 'they write': Kirenawa, 2. CəCC-V *ykitb-uun*: Hiit, 3. CCC-V: *yiktb-o* Daragözü.

Jastrow (1973: 27) considers the stem /a/in the Daragözü form *təftaħe* 'you.F. open' to be an epenthetic vowel. This creates an interpretive problem. In terms of underlying form this would be classified in category '3', but in surface realization as '1'. I have classified it as '3'.

(15) CC-C (verb) 1. CəC-C, *jibət-hum* 'I brought them': MB, 2. CC-C, *jəbtna*: 'you brought us': Khaweetna, 3. CCə-C, *jibt-u-hum*: Kirenawa

(17) CaCii; 1. CaCii, *kabiir*: Kirenawa, 2. CCii, *kbːiir*: Hiit, 3. CiCii, *cibiir*: MB

Sasse (1971: 238) notes that both (1) and (2) occur in Mardin, *naḏiif* 'clean', *gbiir* 'big', on a lexically (i.e. irregular) governed basis.

(18) CaCa(C); 1. CaCa(C), *katab* 'he wrote', *bagar* 'cattle': Abbeche, 2. CiCa(C), *citab, bugar*: MB. (19) CaCaC-V (verb); 1. CaCaC-V, *katab-at* 'she wrote': Kirenawa, 2. CiCC-V, *kitb-at*: MB, 3. CaCC-V, *katb-it*: JB. (20) CaCaC-C(V) (verb); 1. CaCaC-C, *katab-tu* 'I wrote': Mardin, 2. CCaC-C, *ktab-it*: Hiit, 3. CiCaC-C, *kitab-t*: MB (or *ktab-t*). (21) CiCaaC; 1. CiCaaC, *kilaab* 'dogs': Kirenawa, 2. CCaaC, *klaab*: Hiit. (22) CVCC# (noun); 1. CVCC, *əxt* 'sister': JB, 2. CVCVC, *uxut*: MB. (23) CC-C (noun); 1. CəC-C, *calib-hum* 'their dog': MB, 2. *CC-C: kalb-ki*: 'your.F dog': Mardin, 3. CC-əC: *kalb-uhum*: 'their dog' Kirenawa

(24) C$_{gut}$Ca *gahwa* (guttural = x, ɤ, q < ɤ, ʕ, ħ, h, ʔ); 1. C$_{gut}$Ca, *gahwa*: Mardin, 2. C$_{gut}$aCa *gahawa*: Kirenawa. (26) CVCV(C) stress; 1. 'CVCVC, 'bagar 'cattle': Kirenawa, 2. CV'CVC, *ba'gar*: Aajiri. (27) Emphasis; 1. Emphatic consonants, *ṭaaɤ* 'it flew': CB, 2. No emphatic consonants, *taar*: Abbeche

2.2. *Morphology*

(30) feminine plural; 1. yes, *buktub-an* 'they F. write': Kirenawa, 2. no, *ykitb-u* (common plural): MB. (31) two verb conjugations, low vs. high vowel (perfect verb); 1. yes, *katab-tu /kbəɤ-tu* 'they F. I wrote/I grew': CB, 2. no,: *ktab-it* 'I wrote', *lbas-it* 'I wore': MB

The two conjugations are characterized by an opposition between a high stem vowel and a low stem vowel.

(40) First person singular perfect suffix; 1. -tu, *katab-tu* 'I wrote': CB, 2. -t, *ktab-it*: MB

I have not included the variant *-eet* which occurs in some southern Mesopotamian dialects (e.g. Shaṭṭ al-Arab), *kitb-eet* 'I wrote'.

(41) 3 F.SG. perfect suffix; 1. -at, *katab-at* 'she wrote': Kirenawa, 2. -it, *katab-it*: Mardin. (42) 2 plural perfect suffix; 1. -tum, *ktab-tum* 'you PL wrote': MB, 2. -tun, *katab-tun*: Mardin, 3. -tu, *katab-tu*: Kirenawa, 4. -to, Daragözü

The variant *-taw* found in southern Mesopotamia is included under value '4' here. In Daragözü *-to* is minimally contrastive with the 1SG perfect suffix *-tu*.

(43) 3 masculine plural; (non-suffixed form) 1. -u, *katab-u*: 'they wrote': Khaweetna, 2. -o, *katab-o*: Kirenawa, 3. -aw, *katb-aw*: Hiit

In some *qiltu* dialects, before a pronominal suffix the variant *-aw* may appear, *katab-o* ~ *katab-aw-ha*

(44) 1SG perfect suffix; -t or (t); 1. always -t (or -tu), *katab-tu*: Mardin, 2. -t morphologically conditioned, *ka'tab* 'I wrote': Kirenawa

The conditioning factor for (2) is complicated. (see Owens 1993b: 104).

(45) verb C-aa-object suffix; 1. no, *katab-ha* 'he wrote it.F': Kirenawa, 2. yes, *katab-aa-ha*, *ʃaaf-aa-ha* 'he saw her': Abbeche. (51) preformative vowel a, i or a/i; 1. a: *yaktub* 'he writes', 2. i, *yiktub*: Kirenawa

There are no dialects in this sample with only /a/(southern Borno Arabic does have such). If there are two values, *a, i*, the quality is usually determined by harmony with the stem vowel. Other distributions are possible, however. In Umm Hajar in Chad, for instance, *i* occurs in open syllables while *a* occurs in closed, *t-i-biiʕ* 'she sells', *t-a-ktub* 'she writes'. Dialects with both *i* and *a* have a value of '1.5'.

(52) imperfect suffixes (without object suffixes); 1. -uun, -iin, *yikitb-uun* 'they write': MB, 2. -u, -i, *yiktub-u*: Kirenawa

Siirt has a special stressed form, without *-n*, *yənkəsˈruu* 'they were broken'. I have coded this as 1.5, since it lacks *-n* (coding = '2'), but in its special stress is differentiated from all other dialects which do not have *-n*. Alternatively, one could give it a separate coding of '3'. Before suffixes, in some dialects (many Anatolian *qiltu*) the *n* is deleted, Mardin *yiktub-uu-ha* 'they write it.F'. As noted in sect. 8.6, I do not usually catalogue variants of suffixes with a further attached suffix.

(53) 1 singular imperfect; 1. a-, *a-ktub* 'I write': Kirenawa, 2. n-, *n-uktub*: Abbeche

The 1SG prefix is *a-*. In the indicative it will often be prefixed with *b-*, *ba-ktub*.

(54) 1 plural imperfect; 1. n-, *n-uktub* 'we write': Kirenawa, 2. n- ... -u, *n-uktub-u*: Abbeche (55) Harmony-determined imperfect suffixes in strong verb 1. Only one form, *-iin/uun*: *təkbaɤ-uun* 'you.PL grow', MB, 2. Two forms, high or

low vowel -*i*, -*e*/-*u*, *o*, determined by stem vowel (see 6.2 (21)): *tiktub-u* 'you.PL write', *tigɟaʔ-o*, 'you.PL cut', Kirenawa. (61) 1 singular object suffix on noun 1. -*i* (unstressed), *'beet-i* 'my house': CB, 2. *'-ii*, *beet-i:* Abbeche

Nigerian is distinguished from Chadian Arabic in that in Nigerian Arabic the verbal object suffix -*ni* is not stressed, whereas it is in Chadian. This difference is not catalogued.

(62) 2 F.SG object suffix; 1. -*ik*, *beet-ik* 'your house': CB (after C-), 2. -*ki*, *beet-ki:* Kirenawa

A number of dialects (e.g. CB) have both variants on a conditioned basis, e.g. -*ki* after a long vowel, otherwise -*ik*.

(63) 2 M.PL object suffix 1. -*kum*, *beet-kum* 'your PL. house': MB, 2. -*kun*, *beeti-kun:* Mardin, 3. -*ku*, *beet-ku:* Kirenawa. (64) 3 Pl. object suffix; 1. -*hum*, *beet-hum* 'their house': Hiit, 2. -*hun*, *beet-hun:* Mardin

I do not classify according to the vowel of this suffix, which can be distinctively front or back. In Hiit it is in fact [-him]; similarly, for the preceding 2M.PL suffix.

(65) 3 M.SG. object suffix; 1. -*u*, *beet-u* 'his house': Hiit, 1.2. -*u*, VV-*nu*, *katab-uu-nu* 'they wrote it', CB, 1.3. -*u*, VV-*hu*, *ijiib-uu-hu* 'they bring him': Mardin, 2. -*a*, *beet-a*: Kirenawa

Bagirmi Arabic has -*e* after a front vowel (*beet-e*), otherwise -*a*. This variable is an exception to my practice of not treating post-suffix allomorphy. However, the allomorph *u* ~ *nu* ~ *hu* is defined by any vowel, not only a suffix vowel, e.g. *ʕaʃaa-nu* 'his supper'. Variants with the -*nu* ~ *hu* post-vocalic allomorph are given a per cent classification which is closer to '1' than to '2', since the component vowel -*u* is closer to -*u* than to -*a*. After a vowel, dialects classified here as '1' or '2' both have the variant ':' (stress shift and length), e.g. *ʕaʃaa* 'his supper' (both Hiit and Kirenawa, allowing for pharyngeal change).

(66) H-deletion from object pronouns; 1. no h-deletion: *beet-hum* 'their house': Khaweetna, 2. h-deletion: *beet-um*: Kirenawa

There is a large amount of variability in the deletion of the /h/. For example in Daragözü in Turkey the /h/ has apparently completely disappeared, so that even after a vowel only the h-less form occurs, e.g. *kəl-tuu-a* 'I ate it.F'. This variant has not been given a different coding.

(67) Stress shift before V-initial object pronouns; 1. no shift, *'masak-a* 'he grabbed him': Kirenawa, 2. shift: *ma'sak-u*: Mardin. (68) Form of 2MSG object pronoun; 1. -*ak*, *beet-ak* 'your house' (MB), 2. -*ik*, *beet-ik* (Siirt). (71) Doubled verbs 3MSG; 1. *CaCCa*, *tamma* 'he finished': Kirenawa, 2. *CaCC*, *tamm:* CB. (72) weak final verb, vowel suffix; 1. -*Vt*, -*o*/*u*, *nis-at* 'she forgot: Kirenawa,

2. (i)y-Vt, *nisy-ət*: Mardin. (73) Initial vowel of imperfect of *aCaC* verbs; 1. prefix + *aa*, *yaaxud* 'he takes': Kirenawa, 2. prefix + *oo*, *yooxud* or *yooxuz*; Uzbekistan

Dialects used in survey (number represents the code):

Western Sudanic Arabic: 1. Kirenawa; 2. Mada; 3. Aajiri; 4. Wulaad Eeli; 5. Amm Timan; 6. Umm Hajar; 7. Abbeche; 8. Atia I; 9 Atia II.

Mesopotamia (dialect subgroup as in Table 5.4 given in brackets): 10. Christian Baghdadi (Baghdad *qultu*); 11. Jewish Baghdadi (Baghdad *qultu*); 12. Muslim Baghdadi (*gilit*); 13. Mardin (Anatolia); 14. Daragözü (Anatolia); 15. Siirt (Anatolia); 16. Khaweetna (non-Baghdadi *qultu*); 18. Hiit (non-Baghdadi *qultu*); 19. southern Mesopotamia (*gilit*).

30. Uzbekistan; 31. Shukriyya.

Appendix 3. Imala *in Zamaxshari*

It is a general and important issue to determine the degree to which post-Sibawaihian grammarians added significantly to the phonological, morphological, and syntactic data base of Classical Arabic. In this issue I agree with the observation of Carter (1999), that the data base was largely closed after Sibawaih, or shortly thereafter.

The extent to which later grammarians depended on the description of Sibawaih is, however, an empirical question which, as always, needs to be worked out on a case-by-case basis. While studies such as Alhawary (2003), which summarizes the methodology of how early grammarians worked on the basis of reports compiled by later grammarians are interesting, an essential metric is a comparison between the material found in Sibawaih (or Farraʔ or other early grammarians) and later ones. Alhawary (2003: 14), for example, in reporting on Ibn Jinni's (d. 392/1002) elicitation techniques would imply that Ibn Jinni was actually extracting new information. The example he gives, however, an elicitation frame built around *ḍarabtu ʔaxaa-ka* 'I hit your brother', clearly cannot add information about Arabic which by Ibn Jinni's day was not already well known. Ultimately, the only way to know the extent to which Ibn Jinni added new interpretations about Arabic based on new facts is to compare his examples and his analyses thereof, with those of his predecessors.

In this short appendix, I make such a short data comparison, based on the example of *imala*, discussed in Ch. 7. Phonological phenomena have a physical basis which, in the perspective of this work, can be given a concrete articulatory interpretation, even on the basis of phonetic descriptions from the classical period. It will therefore be apparent whether later grammarians merely mimicked the phenomenon as described by Sibawaih on the basis of his written description, or whether they refined them and added their own interpretations based on actual aural observations.

In these terms, a comparison between Sibawaih's description of *imala* and that of Zamaxshari (d. 538/1154) clearly indicates that the former is the case. Zamaxshari in this instance adds little to Sibawaih's observations, and in fact it may be suspected that he based his analyses on written philology rather than on first-hand aural observations, which was a hallmark of Sibawaih's methodology. A summary will make this clear.

Zamaxshari divides his description (pp. 335–8) into fourteen subcategories. That Zamaxshari basically takes over Sibawaih's description is first of all apparent in the description of *imala* conditioning factors, even allowing for the fact that in the two and a half pages Zamaxshari clearly cannot treat the phenomenon in anywhere near the detail of Sibawaih's fifteen pages. Zamaxshari, for instance, singles out in separate subsections *imala* in suffixes (such as 3FSG-*haa*), context-determined *imala* in *bi-baabihi* 'with his door', the harmonic nature of *imala* in *ʕimaadaa* ([ʕimiedie]) 'support', the *imala*-inhibiting effects of raised consonants, the effects of /r/ on *imala*, *imala* of short [a], and the *imala* in hollow verbs such as *xaaf* 'he feared'. There is only one class, the particles, singled out by Zamaxshari which Sibawaih did not render prominent as a class. All in all Zamaxshari's fourteen subcategories give an adequate overview of *imala*, though aspects of *imala* prominent in Sibawaih are filtered out of Zamaxshari's description. For instance, there is no mention of *imala* as an individual variational phenomenon. If Zamaxshari was interpreting written words rather than oral signals, this is not surprising.

Zamaxshari's dependence on Sibawaih is furthermore clear in his choice of lexemes illustrating *imala*. He cites about 110 individual lexemes, most with long [aa], four with short [a]. Of these, twenty-three are not found in Sibawaih, the rest already cited by Sibawaih. Eighty per cent of the actual words used to illustrate *imala* are therefore identical. I assume that Zamaxshari's *naaqif* is a printing mistake for Sibawaih's (II: 286) *naafiq* 'marketable'. Eight, or one-third of the non-cited total, are found in the longest set of lexemes, comprising forty-four examples in all, namely the context of raised consonants which inhibit imala, examples such as ʕ*aariḍ* 'obstruction' and *ṭullaab* 'students'. Another seven not found in Sibawaih are in the class of particles (e.g. ʕ*alaa* 'on', *Piðaa* 'if'), as noted above not singled out as a separate *imala* subcategory in Sibawaih. In identifying this *imala* subcategory Zamaxshari probably follows Mubarrad (d. 285/898; III: 52).

Zamaxshari is therefore clearly dependent upon Sibawaih for his general phonological and lexical description of *imala*. The one issue of interest is that noted at the beginning of Ch. 7, namely that Zamaxshari perhaps gives *imala* a different phonetic value from Sibawaih. If this is the case, it could be because Zamaxshari was dependent on Sibawaih's (or other earlier grammarians') written description, which Zamaxshari interpreted as [ai] (if this is correct; see discussion in sect. 7.1). Alternatively it could be that Zamaxshari in fact transmitted a twelfth-century *imala* norm which was [ai], or perhaps [ee]. Zamaxshari was from the eastern Arabic region (Iran), closest to today's *qultu* dialects with the *imala* value [ee]. It may be that what is interpreted in this book as the original *imala* value [ia] had died out in the eastern region, and that Zamaxshari was following local norms. As noted in sect. 7.3 (Fig. 7.5), already by Sibawaih's day different, competing phonetic reflexes of *imala* were already present. Whatever the explanation, Zamaxshari may be ignored for purposes of Old Arabic reconstruction on this issue.

Appendix 4. List of object pronouns used in reconstructions in Chapter 8

Table A1

	variety	SG1	SG2M	SG2F	SG3M	SG3F	PL1	PL2M	PL2F	PL3M	PL3F
1	western Nigeria	ii	ak	ki	low vowel	ha	na	ku	kan	hum	hin
2	Bagirmi	ii	ak	ki	low vowel	ha	na	ku	kan	hum	han
3	Ndjamena	ii	ak	ki	low vowel	ha	na	ku	—	hum	—
4	Abbeche	ii	ak	ki	low vowel	ha	na	ku	—	hum	—
5	Khartoum	i	ak	ik	u	ha	na	kum	kan	hum	hin
6	Shukriya	i	ak	ik	u	ha	na	kun	kan	hun	hin
7	Egypt, Cairo	i	ak	ik	u	ha	na	kum	—	hum	—
8	Sa'iidi	i	ak	ik	u	ha	na	kum	—	hum	—
9	Bahariyya	i	ik	ki	ih	he	na	kum	—	hum	—
10	Eastern Libya	i	ak	ik	low vowel	ha	na	kam	kan	hum	hin
11	Tripoli	i	ik	ik	low vowel	ha	na	kum	—	hum	—
12	Gharyan	i	ak	ik	low vowel	ha	na	kum	—	hum	—
13	Tunis	i	ik	—	u	ha	na	kum	—	hum	—
14	Susa	i	ik	—	u	ha	na	kum	—	hum	—
15	Djidjelli, Algeria	i	ik	—	u	ha	na	kum	—	hum	—
16	Mzab, Algeria	i	ik	ik	u	ha	na	kum	—	hum	—
17	Fez	i	ik	ik	u	ha	na	kum	—	hum	—
18	Mauritania	i	ak	ik	u	ha	na	kum	—	hum	—
19	Andalusia	i	ak	—	u	a(h)	na	kum	—	hum	—
20	Maltese	i	ik	—	u	ha	na	kom	—	hom	—
21	Cypriot	i	ak	ik	u	ha	na	kon	cin	hon	—
22	North Israel	i	ak	ic	u	ha	na	kam	cin	hum	hin
23	Baskinta	i	ak	ik	u	ha	na	kun	—	hun	—
24	Tripoli, Lebanon	i	ak	ik	u	ha	na	kon	—	hun	—
25	Damascus	i	ak	ik	o	ha	na	kon	—	hon	—
26	Soukhne	i	ac	ci	u	ha	na	cu	—	ham	—
27	Teerib	i	ak	ik	u	ha	na	kun	—	hun	—
28	Christian Baghdad	i	ak	ki	u	ha	na	kum	—	hum	—
29	Jewish Baghdad	i	ak	ik	u	ha	na	kum	—	hum	—
30	Muslim Baghdad	i	ak	ic	low vowel	ha	na	kum	—	hum	—
31	Basra	i	ak	ic	low vowel	ha	na	kum	can	hum	hin
32	Daragözü, Turk	i	ik	ki	u	a	na	kun	—	un	—
33	Mardin	i	ik	ki	u	ha	na	kum	—	hun	—
34	Aazex	i	ik	ki	u	ha	na	kun	—	hun	—
35	Alawite, Antakya	i	ak	ik	u	ha	na	kin	—	hin	—
36	Uzbekistan	i	ak	ki	u	ha	na	kum	kin	hum	hin
37	Khorasan	i	ak	ic	low vowel	he	ne	kum	cin	hum	hin
38	Abu Dhabi	i	ak	ic	low vowel	ha	na	kum	kin	hum	hin
39	Oman	i	ak	ish	o	ha	ne	kum	kin	hum	hin
40	Najdi	i	k	c	ih	ha	na	kum	cin	hum	hin
41	Rwala	i	k	ts	ih	ha	na	kum	kin	hum	hin

TABLE A1 (cont.)

	variety	SG1	SG2M	SG2F	SG3M	SG3F	PL1	PL2M	PL2F	PL3M	PL3F
42	Qauz	i	k	ky	uh or ih and ah	ha	na	kun	—	hun	—
43	Hofuf	i	k	ish	uh or ih and ah	he	na	kum	—	hum	—
44	San'a	i	ak	ish	ih	ha	na	kum	kin	hum	hin
45	an-Nadhiir	i	ak	icr	o	ha	na	kum	tsin	him	hin
46	As-Suwwaadiyyeh	i	ak	ish	ih	ha	na	kum	kan	hum	han
47	Al-Mudawwar	i	ak	ik	u	ee	na	kum	kin	hum	hin
48	Bdul, Jordan	ii	ak	ki	uh or ih and ah	ha	na	ku	kin	hum	hin
49	Ajarma, (Balqa)	i	ak	ic	o	ha	na	kum	cin	hum	hin
50	Classical	i	ka	ki	hu	haa	naa	kum	kunna	hum	hunna

References

Abbreviations:

AL	*Anthropological Linguistics*
BSOAS	*Bulletin of the School of Oriental and African Studies*
EI	*Encyclopedia of Islam,* new edition
JAOS	*Journal of the American Oriental Society*
ZAL	*Zeitschrift für arabische Linguistik*
ZDMG	*Zeitschrift der deutschen morgenländischen Gesellschaft*

Reprinted works are given in the format 'date of original publication/date of reprint'

ABBOT, N. (1972). *Studies in Arabic Literary Papyri,* iii. *Language and Literature.* Chicago: University of Chicago Press.

ABBOUD-HAGGAR, S. (2003). *Introducción a la Dialectología de la Lengua Arabe.* Granada: Fundación El Legado Andalusí.

ʿABD ALLAH, A. (1984). 'The Variant Readings of the Qurʔaan: a Critical Study of their Historical and Linguistic Origins'. Ph.D. thesis, Edinburgh University.

ABDO, DAUD (1969). 'Stress and Arabic Phonology'. Ph.D. thesis, University if Illinois.

ABDUL JAWAD, H. (1981). 'Lexical and Phonological Variation in Spoken Arabic in Amman'. Ph.D. thesis, University of Pennsylvania.

ABU-ABSI, S. (1995). *Chadian Arabic.* Munich: Lincom Europa.

ABU HAIDAR, F. (1979). *A Study of the Spoken Arabic of Baskinta.* Leiden: Brill.

—— (1991). *Christian Arabic of Baghdad.* Wiesbaden: Harrassowitz.

AGHA, S. (1999). 'The Arab Population in Xuraasaan during the Umayyad Period', *Arabica* 46: 211–29.

Al-ʕArabiyya (1987). Vol. 20.

ALHAWARY, M. (2003). 'Elicitation Techniques and Considerations in Data Collection in Early Arabic Grammatical Tradition', *Journal of Arabic Linguistics Tradition* 1: 1–24.

al-Koran. Trans. Yousuf Ali. Beirut: Dar al-Fikr.

ALLEN, R. (1998). *The Arabic Literary Heritage.* Cambridge: Cambridge University Press.

AL-NASSIR, A. (1993). *Sibawayhi the Phonologist.* London: Kegan Paul.

AMARA, M. (2005). 'Language, Migration and Urbanization: The Case of Bethlehem', *Linguistics* 43: 883–902.

AMBROS, A. (1998). *Bongornu, kif int.* Wiesbaden: Reichert.

ANTILLA, R. (1972). *An Introduction to Historical and Comparative Linguistics.* New York: MacMillan.

AQUILINA, J. (1973). *The Structure of Maltese.* Valletta: The Royal University of Malta.

AQUILINA, J. and ISSERLIN, B. S. J. (1981). *A Survey of Contemporary Dialectal Maltese*. Leeds.
ARNOLD, W. (1998). *Die arabischen Dialekte Antiochiens*. Wiesbaden: Harrassowitz.
—— and Bobzin, H. (eds.) (2002). *Sprich doch mit deinen Knechten aramäisch, wir verstehen es. Festschrift for Otto Jastrow*. Wiesbaden: Harrassowitz.
ASBAGHI, A. (1988). *Persische Lehnwörter im Arabischen*. Wiesbaden: Harrassowitz.
AUROUX, S., KOERNER, K., NIEDEREHE, H-J., and VERSTEEGH, K. (eds.) (2001). *History of the Language Sciences*. Berlin: Walter de Gruyter.
BAALBAKI, R. (1990). '*ʔIʕrâb* and *Binâʔ*, from Linguistic Reality to Grammatical Theory', in Versteegh and Carter (eds.), 17–33.
—— (2008). *The Legacy of the Kitaab*. Leiden: Brill.
BANI YASIN, R., and OWENS, J. (1984). 'The Bduul Dialect of Petra', *Anthropological Linguistics* 26: 202–32.
BARTH, J. (1898). 'Die Casusreste im Hebräischen', *ZDMG* 53: 593–9.
—— (1910/1972). *Sprachwissenschaftliche Untersuchungen zum Semitischen*. Amsterdam: Oriental Press.
BARTHOLD, V. (1928/1962). *Turkestan down through the Mongol Invasion*. London: Luzac.
BECK, E. (1945). 'Der ʿuthmanische Kodex in der Koranlesung des zweiten Jahrhunderts', *Orientalia* NS 14: 355–73.
BEHNSTEDT, P. (1985). *Die nordjemenitischen Dialekte*, i. *Atlas*. Wiesbaden: Reichert.
—— (1987). *Die Dialekte der Gegend von Ṣaʕda (Nord-Jemen)*. Wiesbaden: Harrassowitz.
—— (1991). 'Noch einmal zum Problem der Personalpronomina *hənne* (3.Pl.), *-kon* (2.Pl.) und *–hon* (3.Pl.) in den syrisch-libanesischen Dialekten'. *ZDMG* 141: 235–252.
—— (1994). *Der arabische Dialekt von Soukhne (Syrien). Part 2, Phonology, Morphology, Syntax*. Wiesbaden: Harrassowitz.
—— (1997). *Sprachatlas von Syrien*. Wiesbaden: Harrassowitz.
—— (1998). 'La Frontière orientale des parlers maghrébins en Egypte', in J. Aguade, P. Cressier, and A. Vicente (eds.). *Peuplement et Arabisation au Maghreb Occidental: Dialectologie et Histoire*. Zaragoza: Case de Velazquez, 85–96.
—— (2000). Review of Owens (1998a). *Afrika und Übersee* 83: 144–6.
BEHNSTEDT, P. and WOIDICH, M. (1985). *Die ägyptisch-arabischen Dialekte*, ii. Wiesbaden: Reichert.
—— (1988). *Die ägyptisch-arabischen Dialekte*, iii. *Nildialekte, Oasendialekte*. Wiesbaden: Dr Ludwig Reichert.
—— (2005) *Arabische Dialektgeographie: Eine Einführung*. Leiden: Brill.
BELL, R. (1958). *Introduction to the Qurʾan*. Edinburgh: Edinburgh University Press.
BELLAMY, J. (1985). 'A New Reading of the Namaarah Inscription', *JAOS* 105: 31–51.
BELNAP, R. K., and GEE, J. (1994). 'Classical Arabic in Contact: The Transition to New Categorical Agreement Patterns', in M. Eid, V. Cantarino, and K. Walters (eds.). *Perspectives on Arabic Linguistics* (Amsterdam: Benjamins), vi. 121–49.
BENDOR-SAMUEL, J. (1990). *The Niger-Congo Languages*. Lanham: University Press of America.

BERGSTRÄßER, G. (1933). 'Nichtkanonische Koranlesearten im Muḥtasab des Ibn Ginni', Sitzungsberichte der bayerischen Akademie der Wissenschaften, ii.
BIRKELAND, H. (1940). Altarabische Pausalformen. Oslo: Norske Videnskap-Akademie.
BIRKELAND, H. (1952). 'Growth and Structure of the Egyptian Arabic Dialect', Avhandlinger utgitt av det Norske Videnskaps-Akademi 1: 1–57.
BLACHÈRE, R. (1980). Histoire de la littérature Arabe, i. Paris: Librairie d'Amerique et d'Orient.
BLANC, H. (1964). Communal Dialects in Baghdad. Cambridge Mass.: Center for Middle Eastern Studies.
BLAU, J. (1966). A Grammar of Christian Arabic (3 vols.). Louvain: Secrétariat du Corpus.
—— (1969). 'Some Problems of the Formation of the Old Semitic Languages in the Light of Arabic Dialects', Proceedings of the International Conference on Semitic Studies. Jerusalem: Israel Academy of Sciences and Humanities, 38–44.
—— (1976). A Grammar of Biblical Hebrew. Wiesbaden: Harrassowitz.
—— (1981²). The Emergence and Linguistic Background of Judaeo-Arabic. Jerusalem: Ben Zvi Institute.
—— (1982). 'Das frühe Neuarabisch in Mittelarabischen Texten', in W. Fischer (1982a), 96–109.
—— (1988). Studies in Middle Arabic. Jerusalem: Magnes.
—— (2002). A Handbook of Early Middle Arabic. Jerusalem: Max Schloessinger Memorial Foundation.
BOHAS, G., and GUILLAUME, J-P. (1984). Études des théories des grammairiens arabes. Damascus: Institut Français de Damas.
BORG, ALBERT and AZZOPARDI-ALEXANDER, M. (1997). Maltese. London: Routledge.
BORG, ALEXANDER (1985). Cypriot Arabic. Wiesbaden: Steiner.
—— (2004). Comparative Glossary of Cypriot Maronite Arabic (Arabic–English). Leiden: Brill.
BOSWORTH, C. E. (1989). 'The Persian Impact on Arabic Literature', in A. Beeston, T. M. Johnstone, R. B. Serjeant, and G. R. Smith (eds.). Arabic Literature to the End of the Umayyad Period. Cambridge: Cambridge University Press, 483–96.
BROCKELMANN, C. (ed.). (1898). 'Al-Kisaʔi's Schrift über die Sprachfehler des Volkes', 1898. Zeitschrift für Assyrologie. 13: 29–46.
—— (1908, 1913/1982). Grundriss der vergleichenden Grammatik der semistichen Sprachen, i and ii. Hildesheim: Olms.
BRAUKÄMPER, U. (1993). 'Notes on the Origin of Baggara Arab Culture with Special Reference to the Shuwa', Sprache und Geschichte in Afrika 14: 13–46.
BUSTANI, B. (1977). Muḥiyṭ al-Muḥiyṭ. Beirut: Maktabat Libnan.
CALLENDER, J. (1975). 'Afroasiatic Cases and the Formation of Ancient Egyptian Constructions with Possessive Suffixes', Afroasiatic Linguistics 2: 95–112.
CANTINEAU, J. (1937). 'Études sur quelques parlers de nomades arabe d'Orient', Annales de l'Institut d'Études Orientales, Alger. 4: 119–237.

CANTINEAU, J. (1960). *Études de linguistique arabe*. Paris.
CARBOU, H. (1913). *Méthode pratique pour l'étude de l'arabe parlé au Ouaday et à l'est du Tchad*. Paris: Geuthner.
CARTER, M. (1972). 'Twenty Dirhams in the *Kitaab* of Sibawaih', *BSOAS* 35: 485–96.
—— (1973). 'An Arabic Grammarian of the Eighth Century A.D.: A Contribution to the History of Linguistics', *JAOS* 93: 146–57.
—— (1990). '*Qâḍî, Qâḍi, Qâḍ*: Which is the Odd Man Out?' in Versteegh and Carter (eds.), 73–90.
—— (1999). 'The Struggle for Authority: A Re-Examination of the Basran and Kuwfan Debate', in L. Edzard and M. Nekroumi (eds.). *Tradition and Innovation: Norm and Deviation in Arabic and Semitic Linguistics*. Wiesbaden: Harrassowitz, 55–70.
CASKELL, W. (1960/1986). 'The Expansion of the Arabs: General and the 'Fertile Crescent', *EI* i. 527–9.
CASTELLINO, G. (1978). 'The Case System of Cushitic in Relation to Semitic', in P. Fronzaroli (ed.). *Atti del Secondo Congresso Internazionale di Linguistica Camito-Semitica*. Florence: Instituto di Linguistica e di Lingue Orientali.
CAUBET, D. (1993). *L'Arabe Marocain*, i. Paris: Peeters.
CHAUDENSON, R. (1979). *Les Créoles francais*. Paris: Nathan.
CHEJNE, A. (1969). *The Arabic Language*. Minneapolis: University of Minnesota Press.
CHOUÉMI, M. (1966). *Le Verbe dans le Coran*. Paris: Klincksieck.
CLEMENTS, G. (1990). 'The Role of the Sonority Cycle in Core Syllabification', in J. Kingston and M. Beckman (eds.). *Papers in Laboratory Phonology*, i. Cambridge: Cambridge University Press, 288–333.
COHEN, D. (1963). *Le Dialecte arabe Hasaniya de Mauritanie*. Paris: Klincksieck.
—— (1972). 'Koiné, langues communes et dialectes arabes', *Études de Linguistique Sémitique et Arabe*. The Hague: Mouton, 105–25.
COLLINS, R. (1962). *The Southern Sudan, 1883–1898, a Struggle for Control*. New Haven: Yale University Press.
—— (1971). *Land Beyond the Rivers; the Southern Sudan, 1898–1918*. New Haven: Yale University Press.
—— (1983). *Britain in the Southern Sudan, 1918, 1956*. New Haven: Yale University Press.
CORRIENTE, F. (1971). 'On the Yield of Some Synthetic Devices in Arabic and Semitic Morphology', *Jewish Quarterly Review* 62: 20–50.
—— (1973). 'Again on the Functional Yield in Some Synthetic Devices in Arabic and Semitic Morphology', *Jewish Quarterly Review*. 63: 151–63
—— (1975). 'Marginalia on Arabic Diglossia and Evidence Thereof in the Kitab al-Aghani', *Journal of Semitic Studies* 20: 38–61.
—— (1976). 'From Old Arabic to Classical Arabic Through the Pre-Islamic Koine: Some Notes on the Native Grammarians' Sources, Attitudes and Goals', *Journal of Semitic Studies* 21: 62–98.
—— (1977). *A Grammatical Sketch of the Spanish Arabic Dialect Bundle*. Madrid: Instituto Hispano-Arabe de Cultura.

Cowan, W. (1960). 'A Reconstruction of Proto-Colloquial Arabic'. Ph.D. thesis, Cornell University.
Croft, W. (1990). *Typology and Universals*. Cambridge: Cambridge University Press.
Cuvalay, M. (1997). *The Verb in Literary and Colloquial Arabic*. Berlin: Mouton de Gruyter.
de Jong, R. (2000). *A Grammar of the Bedouin Dialects of the Northern Sinai Littoral. Bridging the Linguistic Gap between the Eastern and Western Arab World*. Leiden: Brill.
—— (2002). 'Notes on the Dialect of the 'Ababda', in Arnold and Bobzin (eds.), 337–59.
de Landberg, le Comte. (1909). *Études sur les Dialectes de l'Arabe Méridionale*. Leiden: Brill.
Dereli, B. (1997). 'Het Uzbekistaans Arabisch in Djogari'. MA thesis, Nijmegen University.
Diakonoff, I. (1988). *Afrasian Languages*. Moscow: Nauka.
Diem, W. (1971). 'Zum Problem der Personalpronomina *henne* (3pl), -*kon* (2pl) und -*hon* (3pl) in den Syrisch-Libanesischen Dialekten', *ZDMG* 123: 227–37.
—— (1973). 'Die nabatäischen Inschriften und die Frage der Kasusflexion im Altarabischen', *ZDMG* 123: 227–37.
—— (1978). 'Divergenz und Konvergenz im Arabischen', *Arabica* 25: 128–47.
—— (1984). 'Philologisches zu den arabischen Aphrodite-Papyri', *Der Islam* 61: 251–75.
—— (1991). 'Vom Altarabischen zum Neuarabischen. Ein neuer Ansatz', in Kaye (ed.), 297–308.
Ditters, E. (1990). 'Arabic Corpus Linguistics in Past and Present', in Versteegh and Carter (eds.), 129–41.
Donner, F. (1981). *The Early Islamic Conquests*. Princeton: Princeton University Press.
Doss, M. (1995). 'Some Remarks on the Oral Factor in Arabic Linguistics', in Harviainen et al. (eds.), 49–62.
Durie, M., and Ross, M. (eds.) (1996). *The Comparative Method Reviewed*. Oxford: Oxford University Press.
Ehret, C. (2000). 'Testing the Expectations of Glottochronology against the Correlations of Language and Arachaeology in Africa'. In Renfrew et alii eds, 373–400.
Einhauser, E. (2001). 'Die Entstehung und frühe Entwicklung des junggrammatischen Forschungsprogramms', in Auroux et al. (eds.), 1338–50.
Eksell, K. (1995). 'Complexity of Linguistic Change as Reflected in Arabic Dialects', in Harviainen et al. (eds.), 63–74.
Elgibali, A. (ed.) (2005). *Investigating Arabic: Current Parameters in Analysis and Learning*. Leiden: Brill.
Ferguson, C. (1956). 'The Emphatic *ḷ* in Arabic', *Language* 32: 446–52.
—— (1959*a*). 'Diglossia', *Word* 15: 325–40.
—— (1959*b*). 'The Arabic Koine', *Language* 35: 616–30.
Ferrando, I. (2000). 'Le Morphème de liason /an/en arabe andalou: notes de dialectologie comparée', *Oriente Moderno* 19: 25–46.

FERRANDO, I. (2001). *Introducción a la Historia de la Lengua Arabe*. Zaragoza: Navarro & Navarro.
FISCHER, A. (1926). 'Die Quantität des Vokals des arabischen Pronominalsuffixes *hu* (*hi*)', in C. Adler (ed.), *Oriental Studies Published in the Commemoration of Paul Haupt*, Baltimore, Johns Hopkins Press, 390–402.
FISCHER, W. (1961). 'Die Sprache der arabischen Sprachinsel in Uzbekistan', *Der Islam*, 36: 232–263.
—— (1972). *Grammatik des klassischen Arabisch*. Wiesbaden: Harrassowitz.
—— (ed.). (1982*a*). *Grundriss der Arabischen Philologie*, i. *Spachwissenschaft*. Wiesbaden: Reichert.
—— (1982*b*). 'Das altarabsiche in islamischer Überlieferung', in W. Fischer (1982*a*), 37–48.
—— (1982*c*). 'Das Neuarabische und seine Dialekte', in W. Fischer (1982*a*), 83–96.
—— (1995). 'Zum Verhältnis der neuarabischen Dialekte zum Klassisch-Arabischen', in Harviainen et al. (eds.), 75–86.
FISCHER, W. and JASTROW, O. (eds.) (1980). *Handbuch der arabischen Dialekte*. Wiesbaden: Harrassowitz.
FLEISCH, H. (1961/1986). 'Imala', *EI* iii. 1162–3.
—— (1974²). *Études d'Arabe Dialectal*. Beirut: Dar el-Machreq.
FLEISCHER, H. (1847). 'Griechisch-arabischen Codex rescriptus der Leipziger Univeritäts-Bibliothek', *ZDMG* 1: 148–60.
—— (1854/1968). *Kleinere Schriften*, iii. Osnabrück: Biblio Verlag.
FÜCK, J. (1950). *Arabiya*. Berlin: Akadamie Verlag.
GARBELL, I. (1958). 'Remarks on the Historical Phonology of an East Mediterranean Arabic Dialect', *Word* 14: 303–37.
GARCIN, J-C. (1976). *Un centre musulman de l'Haute Egypte médiévale: Quuṣ*. Cairo: Institut français d'archéologie orientale du Caire.
GILLIOT, C. (1990). *Exégèse, Langue et Théologie en Islam*. Paris: Vrin.
—— (1990/1999). 'The Beginnings of Qur'aanic Exegesis', in Rippin (1999), 1–28.
GLENDENING, P. J. (1961). *Teach Yourself Icelandic*. London: Teach Yourself Books.
GOLDZIHER, I. (1877/1994). *On the History of Grammar among the Arabs*, ed. Kinga Dévényi and Tamás Iványi. Amsterdam: Benjamins.
GORDON, C. (1965). *Ugaritic Textbook*. Rome: Pontificum Institutum Biblicum.
GRAND'HENRY, J. (1976). *Les Parlers arabes de la région du Mzaab*. Leiden: Brill.
GREENBERG, J. (1972). 'Linguistic Evidence Regarding Bantu Origins', *Journal of African History* 13: 189–216.
—— (1978²). 'Some Universals of Grammar with Particular Reference to the Order of Meaningful Elements', in J. Greenberg (ed.), *Universals of Language*. Cambridge, Mass.: MIT Press, 73–113.
GROTZFELD, H. (1965). *Syrisch-arabische Grammatik*. Wiesbaden: Harrassowitz.
GRÜNERT, M. (1876). "Die Imala, der Umlaut im Arabischen". *Sitzungsberichte der bayerischen Akademie der Wissenschaftler*. 81: 447–542.

GUTHRIE, M. (1962). 'Bantu Origins: a Tentative New Hypothesis', *Journal of African Languages* 1: 9–21.
HAJJE, H. (1954). *Le Parler arabe de Tripoli (Liban)*. Paris: Klincksieck.
HARRAMA, A. (1993). 'Libyan Arabic Morphology: Al-Jabal Dialect'. Ph.D. thesis, University of Arizona.
HARRISON, S. (2003). 'On the Limits of the Comparative Method', in B. Joseph and R. Janda (eds.). *The Handbook of Historical Linguistics*. Oxford: Blackwell, 213–43.
HARVIAINEN, T. et al. (eds.) (1995). *Dialectologia Arabica (= Festschrift for Heiki Palva)*. Helsinki: Finnish Oriental Society.
HASSELBACH, R. (2004). 'Final Vowels of Pronominal Suffixes and Independent Personal Pronouns in Semitic', *Journal of Semitic Studies* 49: 1–20.
HAYWOOD, J. (1965). *Arabic Lexicography*. Leiden: Brill.
HEATH, J. (2002). *Jewish and Muslim Dialects of Moroccan Arabic*. London: Kegan Paul.
HECKER, K. (1982). 'Das Arabische im Rahmen der semitischen Sprachen', in W. Fischer (1982a), 6–16.
HETZRON, R. (1976a). 'The Agaw Languages', *Afroasiatic Linguistics* 3: 31–75.
—— (1976b). 'Two Principles of Genetic Reconstruction', *Lingua* 38: 89–108.
HILLELSON, S. (1925). *Sudan- Arabic – English-Arabic Vocabulary*. London: The Sudan Government.
HIRSCHFELD, H. (1926). *Literary History of Hebrew Grammarians and Lexicographers*. London. OUP.
HOFFIZ, B. (1995). 'Morphology of U.A.E. Arabic, Dubai Dialect'. Ph.D. thesis, University of Arizona.
HOLES, C. (1987). *Language Variation and Change in a Modernising Arab State*. London: Kegan Paul International.
—— (1990). *Gulf Arabic*. London: Routledge.
—— (1991). 'Kashkasha with Fronting and Affrication of the Velar Stops Revisited: A Contribution to the Historical Phonology of the Peninsular Arabic Dialects', in Kaye (ed.), 652–78.
—— (1995). *Modern Arabic: Structures, Functions and Varieties*. London: Longman.
—— (2001). *Dialect, Culture, and Society in Eastern Arabia*, i. *Glossary*. Leiden: Brill.
HUDSON, G. (1976). 'Highland East Cushitic', in L. Bender (ed.), *The Non-Semitic Languages of Ethiopia*. East Lansing: Michigan State University, 232–77.
INGHAM, B. (1976). 'Urban and Rural Arabic in Khuzistan', *BSOAS* 36: 533–53.
—— (1982). *Northeast Arabian Dialects*. Kegan Paul International: London.
—— (1994a). *Najdi Arabic, Central Arabian*. Amsterdam: Benjamins.
—— (1994b). 'The Effect of Language Contact on the Arabic Dialect of Afghanistan', in J. Aguadé, F. Corriente, and M. Marugán (eds.). *Actas del Congreso Internacional sobre Interferencias Lingüísticas Arabo-Romances y Paralelos Extra-Iberos*. Zaragoza: Navarro & Navarro, 105–18
—— (1995). 'Texts in the Dialect of the Rwalah of Northern Arabia', in Harviainen et al. (eds.) 121–40.

ISMAIL, H. (2004). 'The Sociolinguistic Situation in Damascus: an Investigation into the Linguistic and Social Structures in Two Neighbourhoods in the City', Conference paper, Urban Arabic Vernaculars. Aix en Provence.

JANKOWSKY, K. (2001). 'The Crisis of Historical-Comparative Linguistics in the 1860's', in Auroux et al. (eds.), 1326–38.

JASTROW, O. (1973). *Daragözü.* Nuremberg: Hans Carl.

—— (1978). *Die mesoptamisch-arabischen Qiltu-Dialekte.* Wiesbaden: Steiner.

—— (1998). 'Zur Position des Uzbekistan-Arabischen', in H. Preissler and H. Stein (eds.). *Annäherung an das Fremde: XXVI Deutscher Orientalistentag.* Wiesbaden: Steiner, 173–84.

JOHNSTONE, T. M. (1963). 'The Affrication of "kaaf" and "qaaf" in the Arabian Dialects of the Arabian Peninsula', *Journal of Semitic Studies* 8: 210–26.

—— (1967). *Eastern Arabian Dialect Studies.* London: Oxford University Press.

JUN, J. (2004). 'Place Assimilation', in B. Hayes, R. Kirchner, and D. Steriade (eds.). *Phonetically-based Phonology.* Cambridge: Cambridge University Press, 58–86.

KAHLE, P. (1948). 'The Qur'an and the 'Arabiyya', in S. Löwinger and Samogyi, J. (eds.), *Ignace Goldziher Memorial Volume I.* Budapest, 163–182.

KAYE, A. (1976). *Chadian and Sudanese Arabic in the Light of Comparative Arabic Dialectology.* The Hague: Mouton.

—— (ed.) (1991). *Semitic Studies in Honor of Wolf Leslau.* Wiesbaden: Harrassowitz,

P. KERSWILL (2002). 'Koinization and Accommodation', in J. Chambers, P. Trudgill, and N. Schilling-Estes (eds.). *The Handbook of Language Variation and Change.* Oxford: Blackwell, 669–702.

KHALAFALLA, A. (1969). *A Descriptive Grammar of Saʕiidi Egyptian Colloquial Arabic.* The Hague: Mouton.

KHAN, G. (1988). *Studies in Semitic Syntax.* Oxford: Oxford University Press.

—— (1997). 'The Arabic Dialect of the Karaite Jews of Hiit', *ZAL* 34: 53–102.

KIPARSKY, P. (2003). 'Syllables and Moras in Arabic', in C. Féry and R. van de Vijver, (eds.). *The Syllable in Optimality Theory.* Cambridge: Cambridge University Press, 147–82.

KNOOP, U. (1982). 'Das Interesse an den Mundarten und die Grundlegung der Dialektologie', in W. Besch, U. Knoop, W. Putschke, and H. Wiegand (eds.). *Dialektologie.* Berlin: Walter de Gruyter, 1–23.

KOFLER, H. (1940–2). 'Reste altarabischer dialekte', *Wiener Zeitschrift für die Kunde des Morgenländs,* 47: 61–130; 48: 52–88; 49: 15–30.

KRUMM, B. (1940). *Wörter orientalischen Ursprungs in Suaheli.* Hamburg: Friederischsen, De Gruyter & Co.

KUSTERS, W. (2003). 'Linguistic Complexity'. Ph.D. thesis, Netherlands Graduate School of Linguistics (<www.lotschool.nl>, accessed August 2005).

LABOV, W. (1994). *Principles of Linguistic Change.* Oxford: Blackwell.

LARCHER, P. (2001). 'Moyen arabe et Arabe moyen', *Arabica* 48: 578–609.

—— (2003). 'Du jussif au conditionnel en arabe classique: une hypothèse dérivationnelle', *Romano-Arabica* 3: 185–97.

—— (2004). 'Théologie et philologie dans l'islam médiéval: Relecture d'un texte célèbre de Ibn Faris (Xe siècle), dans "Le discours sur la langue sous les régimes autoritaires"', *Cahiers de l'ILSL*, Université de Lausanne, 17: 101–14.

—— (2005a) 'Arabe préislamique, Arabe coranique, Arabe classique: un continuum?', in K.-H. Ohlig and G. Puin (eds.), *Die dunklen Anfänge: Neue forschung zur Entstehung und frühen Geschichte der Islam*. Birlach: Schiler.

—— (2005b). 'D'Ibn Faris à al-FarraɁ ou un retour aux sources sur la *luɣa al-fuṣḥaa*', Asiatische Studien/Études Asiatiques 59: 797–814.

—— (2006). 'Neuf traditions sur la langue coranique rapportées par al-FarrâɁ et alii", B. Michalak-Pikulska and A. Pikulska. (eds), *Authority, Privacy and Public Order in Islam, Proceedings of the 22nd Congress of L'Union Européenne des Arabisants et Islamisants, Cracow, Poland 2004, Orientalia Lovaniensia Analecta*, 148, pp. 469–484. Louvain: Peeters.

LATHAM, J. D. (1990). 'Ibn al-MuqaffaÇ and Early Abbasid Prose', in J. Ashtiany, A. Beeston, T. M. Johnstone, R. B. Serjeant, and G. R. Smith (eds.). *The Cambridge History of Arabic Literature. ʿAbbasid Belles Lettres*. Cambridge: Cambridge University Press, 48–77.

LETHEM, G. (1920). *Colloquial Arabic: Shuwa Dialect of Borno, Nigeria and of the Lake Chad Region*. London: Crown Agent for the Colonies.

LEVIN, A. (1985). 'The Syntactic Technical Term *Al-Mabniyy Ƹalayhi* ', *Jerusalem Studies in Arabic and Islam* 6: 299–352.

—— (1989). 'What is Meant by ɁAkalûnî l-Barâɣiθu', *Jerusalem Studies in Arabic and Islam* 12: 40–65.

—— (1998) (1992). 'The Authenticity of Sibawaiyhi's Description of the "Imaala"', in A. Levin, *Arabic Linguistic Thought and Dialectology*. Jerusalem: Institute of Asian and African Studies.

—— (2002). 'The Imaala in the Modern Arabic Dialect of Aleppo', in Arnold and Bobzin (eds.), 425–46.

LEWIS, B. (1970). 'Egypt and Syria', in P. Holt, M. A. Lambton, and B. Lewis (eds.). *The Cambridge History of Islam*, i. Cambridge: Cambridge University Press, 175–230.

MACDONALD, M. C. (2000). 'Reflections on the Linguistic Map of Pre-Islamic Arabia', *Arabian Archaeology and Epigraphy*. 11: 28–79.

MACMICHAEL, H. (1922/1967). *A History of the Arabs in the Sudan* (2 vols.). London: Cass.

MCWHORTER, J. (1998). 'Identifying the Creole Prototype: Vindicating a Typological Class', *Language* 74: 788–818.

—— (2001). 'The World's Simplest Grammars are Creole Grammars', *Linguistic Typology* 5: 125–66.

MAHDI, M. (ed.) (1984). *Kitaab ɁAlf Layla wa Layla*. Leiden: Brill.

MAHDI, Q. (1985). 'The Spoken Arabic of Baṣra, Iraq'. Ph.D. thesis, Exeter University.

MALAIKA, N. (1959). *Grundzüge der Grammatik des arabischen Dialektes von Bagdad*. Wiesbaden: Harrassowitz.

MARÇAIS, P. (1956). *Le Parler arabe de Djidjelli*. Algiers: Cellunaf.

—— (1977). *Esquisse grammaticale de l'Arabe magrébin.* Paris: Maisonneuve.
—— (2001). *Parlers arabes du Fezzaan,* collected and edited by D. Caubet, A. Martin, and L. Denooz Geneva: Droz.
MATISOFF J. 2000. 'On the Uselessness of Glottochronology for the Subgrouping of Tibeto Burman'. In Renfrew et al., 333–372.
MATRAS, Y. (2000). 'How Predictable is Contact-Induced Change in Grammar?' In Renfrew et al. (eds.), 563–85.
MERX, A. (1891). 'Reflections historiques sur l'origine de la grammaire arabe', *Bulletin de l'Institut Egyptien,* 13–26.
MILLER, C. (2005). 'Between Accommodation and Resistance: Upper Egyptian Migrants in Cairo', *Linguistics* 43: 903–56.
MITCHELL, T. (1960). 'Prominence and Syllabication in Arabic', *BSOAS* 23: 369–89.
—— (1975). *Principles of Firthian Linguistics.* London: Longmans.
—— (1986). 'What is Educated Spoken Arabic?' *International Journal of the Sociology of Language.* 61: 7–32.
MOL, M. (2003). *Variation in Modern Standard Arabic in Radio News Broadcasts.* Leuven: Peeters.
MOLAN, P. (1978). *Medieval Western Arabic.* Ann Arbor, Mich.: University Microfilms.
MOSCATI, S. (1958). 'On Semitic Case Endings', *Journal of Near Eastern Studies.* 17: 142–4.
—— SPITALER, A., ULLENDORF, E., and VON SODEN, W. (1980²). *An Introduction to the Comparative Grammar of the Semitic Languages.* Wiesbaden: Harrassowitz.
MÜLLER, W. (1982). 'Das Altarabische der Inschriften aus vorislamischer Zeit', in W. Fischer (1982a), 30–6.
NETTLE, D. (1999). *Linguistic Diversity.* Oxford: Oxford University Press.
NISHIO, T. (1986). 'On the Pronominal Suffixes in Proto-Colloquial-Arabic', *Linguistic Research* 5: 1–24.
NÖLDEKE, T. (1897/1963). *Zur Grammatik des classischen Arabisch.* Darmstadt: Wissenschaftliche Buchgesellschaft.
—— (1910). 'Zur Sprache des Korʔaans', *Neue Beiträge zur semitischen Sprachwissenschaft.* Strasburg: Trübner.
OWENS, J. (1980). 'The Syllable as Prosody: a Reanalysis of Syllabification in Eastern Libyan Arabic', *BSOAS* 48: 277–87.
—— (1985). *A Grammar of Harar Oromo.* Hamburg: Buske.
—— (1988). *The Foundations of Grammar: An Introduction to Medieval Arabic Grammatical Theory.* Amsterdam: Benjamins.
—— (1989). 'Zur Pidginisierung und Kreolisierung im Arabischen', *Afrika und Übersee.* 72: 91–107.
—— (1990). *Early Arabic Grammatical Theory: Heterogeneity and Standardization.* Amsterdam: Benjamins.
—— (1993a). 'Nigerian Arabic in Comparative Perspective', *Sprache und Geschichte in Afrika.* 14: 85–176.
—— (1993b). *A Reference Grammar of Nigerian Arabic.* Wiesbaden: Harrassowitz.

—— (1993c). 'Imâla in Eastern Libyan Arabic', in Otto Jastrow and Hartmut Bobzin (eds.). *A Festschrift for Wolfdietrich Fischer* (= *Zeitschrift für Arabische Linguistik* 25: 251–9).
—— (1995). 'Minority Languages and Urban Norms', *Linguistics* 33: 305–58.
—— (1996). 'Idiomatic Structure and the Theory of Genetic Relationship', *Diachronica* 13: 283–318.
—— (1997). 'Arabic-based Pidgins and Creoles', in S. Thomason (ed.), *Contact Languages: A Wider Perspective*. Amsterdam: Benjamins, 125–72.
—— (1998a). *Neighborhood and Ancestry: Variation in the Spoken Arabic of Maiduguri, Nigeria*. Amsterdam: Benjamins
—— (1998b). 'Case and Proto-Arabic', *Bulletin of the School of Oriental and African Studies* 61: 51–73 and 217–27.
—— (1999). 'Uniformity and Discontinuity: Toward a Characterization of Speech Communities', *Linguistics* 37: 663–98.
—— (2000). 'Medieval Arabic Morphological Theory', in G. Booij, C. Lehmann, and J. Mugdan, (eds.). *Morphology: A Handbook on Inflection and Word Formation*. Berlin: Walter de Gruyter, 67–75.
—— (2001a). 'Arabic Sociolinguistics', *Arabica* 48: 419–69.
—— (2001b). 'Arabic Creoles: the Orphan of all Orphans', *Anthropological Linguistics*: 43: 348–78.
—— (2002). '*Al-Idghaam al-Kabiyr* and the History of Arabic', in Arnold and Bobzin (eds.), 503–20.
—— (2003). 'Arabic Dialect History and Historical Linguistic Mythology', *Journal of the American Oriental Society*. 123: 715–40.
—— (2005). 'The Grammatical Tradition and Arabic Language Teaching: A View from Here', in A. Elgibali (ed.), 103–16.
PALVA, H. (1976). *Studies in the Arabic Dialect of the Semi-Nomadic əl-ʕAjaarma Tribe* (al-Balqaa District, Jordan). Göteberg: Acta Universitatis Götheburgensis.
PELLAT, CH. (1960/1986). 'Laḥn al-ʕAamma', *EI* v. Leiden: Brill, 605–10.
PETRÁCEK, K. (1988). *Altägyptisch, Hamitosemitisch*. Prague: Univerzita Karlova.
POMMEROL, J-C. (1990). *Da Hayyin*, iv. Ndjamena: CEFOD.
—— (1997). *L'Arabe tchadien: émergence d'une langue véhiculaire*. Paris: Karthala.
—— (1999). *Grammaire practique de l'arabe tchadien*. Paris: Karthala.
PRETZL, O. (1934). 'Die Wissenschaft der Koranlesung', *Islamica* 6: 290–331.
PROCHAZKA, S. (2002). *Die arabischen Dialekte der Cukurova (Südtürkei)*. Wiesbaden: Harrassowitz.
PROCHAZKA, T. (1981). 'The Shii'i Dialects of Bahrain and their Relationship to the Eastern Arabian Dialect of Muḥarraq and the Omani Dialect of al-Ristaaq', *ZAL* 6: 16–55.
—— (1988). *Saudi Arabian Dialects*. London: Kegan Paul.
PUIN, G. (1996). 'Observations on the Early Qur'an Manuscripts in Ṣanʕa' ', in S. Wild (ed.) *The Qur'an as Text*. Leiden: Brill, 107–12.
QAFISHEH, H. 1997. *Gulf Arabic–English Dictionary*. Chicago: NTC.
RABIN, C. (1951). *Ancient West Arabian*. London: Taylor's Foreign Press.

—— (1955). 'The Beginnings of Classical Arabic', *Studia Islamica* 4: 19–37.
—— (1960/1986). 'Arabiyya', *EI* i. 561–7.
—— (1969). 'The Structure of the Semitic System of Case Endings', *Proceedings of the International Conference on Semitic Studies*. Jerusalem: Israel Academy of Sciences and Humanities, 190–204.
RAWI, R. (1990). *Studien zum arabischen Dialekt von Abu Daby*. Heidelberg: Groos.
RECKENDORF, H. (1895/1967). *Die syntaktischen Verhältnisse des Arabischen*. Leiden: Brill.
REICHMUTH, S. (1983). *Der arabische Dialekt der Shukriyya im Ostsudan*. Hildesheim: Georg Olms.
REINHARDT, C. (1894/1972). *Ein arabischer Dialekt gesprochen in Oman und Zanzibar*. Amsterdam: Philo.
RENFREW, C., MCMAHON, A., and TRASK, R. (eds.) (2000). *Time Depth in Historical Linguistics*. Cambridge: McDonald Institute for Archaeological Research.
RETSÖ, J. (1988). 'Pronominal Suffixes with -n(n)- in Arabic dialects and other Semitic Languages', *ZAL* 18: 77–94.
—— (1994). 'ʔIʕrab in the Forebears of Modern Arabic Dialects', in D. Caubet and M. Vanhove (eds.), *Actes des premières journées internationales de dialectologie arabe de Paris*. Paris: INALCO, 333–42.
—— (1995). 'Pronominal State in Colloquial Arabic: A Diachronic Attempt', in Harviainen et al. (eds.), 183–92.
—— (2003). *The Arabs in Antiquity*. London: Kegan Paul.
RIPPIN, A. (1983/1999). 'Ibn ʿAbbas's Al-Lughaat fī 'l-*Qurʾaan*', in Rippin (ed.), 109–19.
—— (ed.) (1999). *The Qurʾan: Formative Interpretation*. Aldershot: Ashgate.
ROGERS, D. (1987). 'The Influence of Panini on Leonard Bloomfield', *Historiographia Linguistica* 14: 89–138.
ROSENHOUSE, J. (1984). *The Bedouin Arabic Dialects*. Wiesbaden: Harrassowitz.
RÖSSLER, O. (1950). 'Verbalbau und Verbalflexion in den semito-hamitischen Sprachen', *ZDMG* 100: 461–514.
ROTH, A. (1972). 'Esquisse de la phonologie du parler arabe d'Abbeché', *Études Chamito-Semitiques* 16: 32–79.
—— (1979). *Esquisse grammaticale du parler arabe d'Abbeché*. Paris: Geuthner.
SAEED, J. (1987). *Somali Reference Grammar*. Wheaton, ILL.: Dunwoody.
SASSE, H-J. (1971). 'Linguistische Analyse des arabischen Dialekts der Mhallamiye in der Provinz Mardin (Südosttürkei)'. Ph.D. thesis: Munich University.
—— (1984). 'Case in Cushitic, Semitic and Berber', in J. Bynon (ed.). *Current Progress in Afroasiatic Linguistics*. Amsterdam: Benjamins, 111–26.
SCHAADE, A. (1911). *Sibawaihi's Lautlehre*. Leiden: Brill.
SCHABERT, P. (1976). *Laut- und Formenlehre des Maltesischen anhand zweier Mundarten*. Erlangen: Palm & Enke.
SEEGER, U. (2002). 'Zwei Texte im Dialekt der Araber von Chorasan', in Arnold and Bobzin (eds.), 629–46.

SHAHIN, A. (2004). '*Kitaab Faʕaltu wa ʔAfʕaltu:* Edition und statistische Auswertung', MA thesis (Magisterarbeit), Bayreuth University.
SINGER, H. (1984). *Grammatik der arabischen Mundart der Medina von Tunis.* Berlin: de Gruyter.
SMART, J. (1990). 'Pidginization in Gulf Arabic: a First Report', *AL* 32: 83–119.
SPITALER, A. (1953). 'Rezension von Fück, Arabiyya', *Bibliotheca Orientalis* 10: 144–50.
SPULER, B. (1952). *Iran in den früh-islamischen Zeiten.* Wiesbaden: Steiner.
SULEIMAN, Y. (1999). *The Arabic Grammatical Tradition: a Study in Taʕliil.* Edinburgh: Edinburgh University Press.
TAINE-CHEIKH. C. (2008). "Mauritania". *Encyclopedia of Arabic Language and Linguistics, III.* K. Versteegh et al. (eds), Leiden : Brill, pp. 169–176.
TALAY, S. (1999). *Der arabische Dialekt der Khaweetna.* Wiesbaden: Harrassowitz.
TALMON, R. (1990). 'The Philosophizing Farraʔ: an Interpretation of an Obscure Saying Attributed to the Grammarian θaʕlab', in Versteegh and Carter (eds.), 265–80.
—— (2003). *Eighth-Century Iraqi Grammar.* Winona Lake: Eisenbrauns.
TALMOUDI, F. (1980). *The Arabic Dialect of Susa.* Göteborg: Acta Universitatis Götheburgensis. *The Ethnologue* (2003), internet version.
THOMASON, S., and EL GIBALI, A. (1986). 'Before the Lingua Franca: Pidginized Arabic in the eleventh century', *Lingua* 68: 317–49.
—— and KAUFMAN, S. (1988). *Language Contact, Creolization and Genetic Linguistics.* Berkeley: University of California Press.
TOSCO, M. (1993). 'On Case Marking in the Ethiopian Language Area', *Atti della 7ª Giornata di Studi Camito-Semitici e Indoeuropei.* Milan.
TRIMINGHAM, J. (1946). *Sudan Colloquial Arabic.* Oxford: Oxford University Press.
—— (1959). *Sudan Colloquial Arabic.* Oxford: Oxford University Press.
TROPPER, J. (1999). 'Kasusverhältnisse in Arabischen Ausnahmesätzen: Absolutakkusativ nach ʔillaa', *ZAL* 37: 25–31.
TROUPEAU, G. (1976). *Lexique-Index du Kitaab de Sibawayhi.* Paris: Klinckseick.
VANHOVE, M. (1993). *La Langue maltaise.* Wiesbaden: Harrassowitz.
VERSTEEGH, K. (1977). *Greek Elements in Arabic Linguistic Thinking.* Leiden: Brill.
—— (1983). 'A Dissenting Grammarian: Quṭrub on Declension', in K. Versteegh, K. Koerner, and H-J. Niederehe (eds.). *The History of Linguistics in the Near East.* Amsterdam: Benjamins, 167–93.
—— (1984a). *Pidginization and Creolization: The Case of Arabic.* Amsterdam: Benjamins.
—— (1984b). 'Word Order in Uzbekistan Arabic and Universal Grammar', *Orientalia Suecana* 33–5: 443–53.
—— (1989). 'A Sociological View of the Arabic Grammatical Tradition: Grammarians and their Professions', in P. Wexler, A. Borg, and S. Somekh, (eds.), *Studia Linguistica et Orientalia Memoriae Haim Blanc Dedicata,* 289–302.
—— (1993a). 'Leveling in the Sudan: From Arabic Creoles to Arabic Dialect', *International Journal of the Sociology of Language,* 99: 65–80.
—— (1993b). *Arabic Grammar and Qur'anic Exegesis in Early Islam.* Leiden: Brill.

VERSTEEGH, K. (1997). *The Arabic Language*. Edinburgh: Edinburgh University Press.
—— (1999). 'Zayd ibn Ali's Commentary on the Qur'aan', in Y. Suleiman (ed.), *Arabic Grammar and Linguistics*. Richmond, Surrey: Curzon, 9–29.
—— (2004). 'Pidginization and Creolization Revisited: The Case of Arabic', in M. Haak, R. de Jong, and K. Versteegh (eds.). *A Festschrift for Manfred Woidich*. Leiden: Brill, 343–58.
—— (2005). 'Breaking the Rules without Wanting To: Hypercorrection in Middle Arabic Texts', in A. Elgibali (ed.), 3–18.
—— and CARTER, M. (eds.) (1990). *Studies in the History of Arabic Grammar*, ii. Amsterdam: Benjamins.
VOIGT, R. (1987). 'The Two Prefix Conjugations in East Cushitic, East Semitic and Chadic', *BSOAS* 50: 330–45.
VOLLERS, K. (1892/1968) 'The System of Arabic Sounds, as Based upon Sibaweih and Ibn Yaïsh', in E. Morgan (ed.), *Transactions of the Ninth International Congress of Orientalists*, ii. Nendeln: Kraus, 130–54.
—— (1906/1981). *Volkssprache und Schriftsprache im alten Arabien*. Amsterdam: Oriental Press.
VON SODEN, W. (1969). *Grundriss der akkadischen Grammatik*. Rome: Pontificum Institutum Biblicum.
WALLIN, G. (1851). 'Probe aus einer Anthologie neuarabischer Gesänge, in der Wüste gesammelt', *ZDMG* 5: 1–24.
—— (1852). 'Probe aus einer Anthologie neuarabischer Gesänge, in der Wüste gesammelt', *ZDMG* 6: 190–218, 369–78.
—— (1855). 'Über die Laute des Arabischen und ihre Bezeichung', *ZDMG* 9: 1–68.
—— (1858). 'Bemerkungen über die Sprache der Beduinen', *ZDMG* 12: 666–75.
WANSBROUGH, J. (1977). *Quranic Studies*. Oxford: Oxford University Press.
WATSON, J. (1992). 'Kashkasha with Reference to Modern Yemeni Dialects', *ZAL* 24: 60–81.
WATSON, J. (2007). "Syllabification Patterns in Arabic Dialects: Long Segments and Mora Sharing". *Phonology* 24: 335–56.
WEHR, H (ed.) (1974). *A Dictionary of Modern Written Arabic*, trans. J Milton Cowan. Beirut: Libraire de Liban.
WEIL, G. (1915). 'Zum Verhältnis der Methode der moslemischen Grammatiker', in Weil (ed.), *Festschrift Eduard Sachau*. Berlin: Georg Reimer.
WELLENS, I. 2005. *The Nubi Language of Uganda: an Arabic Creole in Africa*. Leiden: Brill.
WENINGER, S. (1993). *Gəʕəz*. Munich: Lincom Europa
WERBECK, W. (2001). *Laut- und Formenlehre des Nordjeminitischen Dialekts von Manaaxa*. Münster: Rhema.
WILKINSON, J. (1987). *The Imamate Tradition of Oman*. Cambridge: Cambridge University Press.
WITTRICH, M. (2001). *Der arabische Dialekt von Azex*. Wiesbaden: Harrassowitz.
WOIDICH, M. (1993). 'Die Dialekte des Ägyptischen Oasen: westliches oder östliches Arabisch?', *ZAL* 25: 340–59.

—— (1997). 'Egyptian Arabic and Dialect Contact in Historical Perspective', in A. Afsaruddin and M. Zahniser (eds.), *Humanism, Culture and Language in the Near East*. Winona Lake, Ind.: Eisenbrauns, 185–97.

WRIGHT, W. (1896–98/1977). *A Grammar of the Arabic Language*. Cambridge: Cambridge University Press.

ZABORSKI, A. (1995). 'First Person Pronouns in Arabic in the Light of Arabic and Hamito-Semitic Dialectology', in Harviainen et al. (eds.), 289–94.

ZELTNER, J-C. and FOURNIER, J-C. (1971). 'Notice pour suivre un enregistrement en arabe salamat de la région du lac Tchad', Mimeograph. Fort-Lamy.

ZELTER, J-C., and TOURNEUX, H. (1986). *L'Arabe dans le bassin du Tchad*. Paris: Karthala.

ZIMMERMANN, G. (2002). 'Das arabische von Buchara zwischen alten Quellen und neuen Forschungsergebnissen', MA thesis (Magisterarbeit), Bayreuth University.

ZWETTLER, M. (1978). *The Oral Tradition of Classical Arabic Poetry*. Columbus: Ohio State University Press.

Original Arabic sources (definite article Al- is not used for alphabetizing):

AL-AhMAR, XALAF. *Muqaddima fi l-Nahw*, ed. ʕAzz al-Din al-Tanuxi. Damascus, 1961.

AL-DANI, ABU AMR. *Kitaab al-Taysiyr fiy al-QiraaʔAat al-Sabʕ*. Beirut: Dar al-Kutub al-Ilmiyya, 1996.

AL-FARRAʔ, ABU ZAKARIYYA. *Maʕaaniy al-Qurʔaan*, ed. Muhammad Al-Najjar and Ahmad Najati. Beirut: ʕAlam al-Kutub (no date).

—— *Al-Muðakkar wa l-Muʔannaθ*, ed. Ramaḍan ʕAbd al-Tawwab. Cairo: Maktab Dar Al-Turath, 1975.

AL-FARRUXI, MUHAMMAD. *Manḏuwmat al-Farruwxiy*, ed. Ibrahim Al-Zawi. Beirut: Dar al-Fath Li-l-Ṭibaʕa wa al-Nashr, 1984.

AL-JAZARI, MUHAMMAD. *Sharh Ṭayyibat al-Nashr*, ed. Ans Mahra. Beirut: Dar al-Kutub al-Ilmiyyah, 1997.

IBN MANḎUR, ABU FADL. *Lisaan al-ʕArab*. Beirut: Dar Ṣadir (no date).

AL-MUBARRAD, IBN YAZID. *Al-Muqtaḍab*, ed. ʕAbd l-Xaliq al-ʕUḍayma. Beirut: Alam al-Kutub (no date).

IBN MUJAHID, ABU BAKR. *Al-Sabʕ fiy al-QiraaʔAat*, ed. Shawqi Dayf. Cairo: Dar al-Maʕarif, 1972.

IBN AL-NADIM. MUhAMMAD. *Al-Fihrist*. Beirut: Dar al-Maʕrifa (no date).

AL-JAHIẒ, ABU ʕUTHMAN. *al-Bayaan wa al-Tabyiyn*. Beirut: Dar al-Kutub al-ʕAlamiyya (no date).

QUṬRUB, ABU ALI. *Muθallaθaat Quṭrub*, ed. Ibrahim Al-Zawi. Beirut: Dar al-Fath Li-l-Ṭibaʕa wa al-Nashr, 1984.

IBN AL-SARRAJ, ABU BAKR. *Al-ʔUṣuwl fiy l-Nahw*, ed. Abd al-Husayn al-Fatli. Beirut: Muʔassasat al-Risala (no date).

SIBAWAIH, UTHMAN. *Al-Kitaab*, ed. H. Derenbourg. Hildesheim: Olms, 1970.

AL-SUYUṬI, JALAL AD-DIN. *Kitaab al-Iqtiraah*, ed. Ahmad Qasim. Cairo: Maṭbaʕat al-Saʕada, 1976.

AL-ZAJJAJI, ABU AL-QAASIM. *Al-Iydaaĥ fiy ʕIlal al-Naĥw*, ed. Mazin Mubarak. Beirut: Dar al-NafaʔIs (no date).

AL-ZAMAXSHARI, ABU QASIM. *Al-Mufaṣṣal fiy ʕIlm al-ʕArabiyya*, ed. Muhammad al-Halabi. Beirut: Dar al-Jil (no date).

Index of Places

Aajiri 141, 145, 271, 276
Abbeche 141, 176, 271, 276–80, 283
Abu Dhabi 139, 240, 275, 283
Adamawa State 143, 271
Adana 274
Aden 161
Afghanistan 105–6, 139
Africa 36, 138, 245
Ajarma 139
Aleppo 6, 165, 244
Algeria 51, 140, 272–3, 283
Algiers 120
America 36
Am(m) Timan 141, 146, 271, 280
Andalusia 2, 28, 105–6, 140, 198, 212–13, 223–4, 241, 246, 273, 283
Anatolia 49, 143–4, 218, 274, 280
Antakya 283
Arabia 143
Arabian Peninsula 3, 14, 29, 31, 41, 68, 106, 150, 155, 161, 166, 168–9, 238, 244, 248, 250, 274–5
Armenia 139
Asia 36
Aswan 2, 141, 162, 272
Asyut 108–9
Atbara River 143, 146, 272
Atia 141, 146, 280
Awlad Eli *see* Wulaad Eeli
Azerbaijan 139

Baghdad 124, 139
Bagirmi 57, 141, 161, 170, 182, 240, 271, 276, 283
Bahariyya Oasis 17, 139, 283
Bahrain 139, 160, 165, 275
Balqa 284

Bangui 141
Banki 145
Baskinta 273, 283
Basra 3, 61, 68, 124, 139, 227, 240, 274, 283
Borno 15, 27, 141, 143, 271
Bukhara 146, 162, 275

Cairo 2, 39, 45, 109, 272, 283
Cameroon 27, 48, 141, 143, 145, 238, 244, 271, 276
Central African Republic 141
Central Arabia 68, 106, 275
Central Asia 106
Central Morocco 49–50, 272
Central Turkey 2
Central Yemen 74
Chad 27–8, 48, 138–9, 141, 143, 145–6, 162, 177, 238, 241, 244, 271, 276, 278
China 2
Cilicia 2, 139, 218, 274
Cyprus 217

Daaxila Oasis 173
Dala Axderi 57
Damascus 6, 18, 123–4, 139, 217, 248, 273, 283
Dambua Road 57
Darfur 271
Dathina 161
Dikkeceri 56
Djidjelli 140, 246, 273, 283

Eastern Arabia 61, 225, 282
Eastern Egyptian Desert 272
Eastern Iran 243
Eastern Libya 28, 50, 139, 192, 212, 220, 240, 283

Index of Places

Eastern Sudan 102, 143, 146, 153, 185
Eastern Syria 18
Egypt 28, 50, 105, 109, 141, 146–7, 156, 173, 190, 220, 243, 272, 283
El-Fasher 141
El-Obeid 141
Emirates 160
Euphrates River 14, 165
Europe 17

Fez 140, 253, 273, 283
Fusṭāṭ 2, 45, 162, 272

Gambaru 56–7
Germany 167
Gharyan 283
Gozo 217
Gwange 56–7

Hatay Province 217, 274
Hiit 274
Hijaz 3, 12, 74

Iran 139, 162, 282
Iraq 12, 27, 29, 49, 143–5, 224, 274–5
Israel 225, 273–4

Jerusalem 18
Jogari (Jugari, Djogari) 139, 146
Jordan 14, 225, 235, 246, 248, 273–5

Kanem 141
Kano 141
Khartoum 141, 240, 272, 283
Khaweetna 274
Khorasan 139, 160, 162, 240–1, 243, 275, 283
Kinyande 57
Kirenawa 141, 145, 147, 177–8, 183, 271
Kordofan 143, 271
Kormakiti 139, 218, 273–4
Kufa 3, 45, 61, 124, 162

Lagos 141
Lake Chad 2, 18, 141, 145, 162, 271

Lebanon 52, 198, 217, 273, 283
Levant 48
Libya 272

Mada 141, 145, 271
Mafa see Muba
Magonari 57
Maiduguri 54–7, 117, 141, 145–6, 171
Mali 140
Malta 139–40, 198, 212, 215, 217, 223, 226, 228, 246
Mariis 271
Mauritania 2, 15, 138, 140, 271–3, 283
Mecca/Mekka 12, 124, 275
Medina 3, 12, 124, 275
Mersin 274
Mesopotamia 50, 109, 138, 141, 143–4, 150, 153, 157, 159, 169–70, 175, 177, 219, 228, 243–4, 276–7, 280
Middle East 2, 18
Mississippi River 27
Mitene 57
Morocco 272–3
Muba 57
Mule Shuwari 57
Mzab 140, 253, 273, 283

Nabataea 86–7
Ndjamena 271, 283
Negev (Desert) 192, 273
Ngaoundere 141
Niger 140–1
Nigeria 15, 29, 99, 141, 143, 145, 148, 171, 176–7, 238, 240, 244, 271
Niger-Congo 79
Nile 169
Nile Delta 108–9
Nile Valley 15, 139, 272
Ndjamena 141
North Africa 2, 18–9, 28, 140, 149–50, 248, 272
Northeast Arabian Peninsular 252
Northeast Egypt 239
Northeastern Nigeria 27, 48, 117, 271

Northeast Saudi Arabia 235
Northern Arabian Region 73
Northern Bagirmi Area 145
Northern Cyprus 273–74
Northern Israel 240, 273, 283
Northern Iraq 138, 217
Northern Jordan 108
Northern Mesopotamia 217, 244
Northern Najd 275
Northern Sinai Littoral 192
Northern Syria 6, 217, 274
Northern Yemen 52, 165, 220
Northwest Saudi Arabia 273

Oman 139, 160, 240, 275, 283
Oxus River 146

Palestine 272
Petra 239
Port Sudan 141

Qatar 139

Red Sea 27

SaSiidi 283
SanSaʔ 139, 240
Saudi Arabia 102, 105, 244, 275
Saudi Arabia Coastal Area 149
Shia Baharna 160
Shukriyya Area 147, 272, 276, 283
Sicily 198
Sinai 14, 239, 272–3
Southern Bagirmi Area 145
Southern Egypt 138
Southern Iraq 3, 274
Southern Jordan 6, 86, 192, 239, 273
Southern Mesopotamia 219, 224, 276, 278
Southern Nigeria 145
Southern Sudan 17
Southern-central Turkey 113, 217, 274
Southern Turkey 18, 143
Spain 2, 140, 212–13, 228

Sudan 18, 31, 52, 108, 139, 141, 147, 162, 244, 271
Sudanic Region 105–6, 138, 147, 149–50, 192, 220, 272
Susa 140, 246, 273, 283
Syria 14, 49, 52, 150, 165, 177, 198, 224–5, 235, 241, 244–6, 250, 273
Syrian Desert 156
Syrio-Mesopotamian Area 244

Tamanrasset 141
Tarsus 274
Transoxiana 146, 156, 163
Tripoli (Lebanon) 139, 241, 273, 283
Tripoli (Libya) 139, 182, 253, 272, 283
Tunis 17, 140, 246, 253, 273, 283
Tunisia 18, 272–3
Turkey 139, 274, 279, 283
Turkmenistan 139, 146

Umm Hajar 141, 146, 271, 278, 280
Upper Egypt 18, 146–49, 156, 182, 185, 272
Uzbekistan 2, 105–6, 139, 146–8, 153, 155–7, 160, 162–3, 169, 175, 240–1, 275–6, 283

Wadi Halfa 141
Western Chad 117, 145
Western Egypt 28
Western Hadramaut 160
Western Libya 272
Western Nigeria 283
Western Sahara 2
Western Sudanic (Arabic) Region 2, 29, 138, 141, 143, 145–9, 153, 155–7, 159–60, 169–70, 172, 175, 177, 182, 239, 246, 271, 276
Wulaad Eeli 141, 280

Yaounde 141
Yemen 12, 50, 70, 102, 105, 109, 138, 149, 171, 237, 241, 243–5, 248, 275

Subject Index

Active participal + object suffix in historical reconstruction 159–62
Analytic vs. synthetic 27, 111–3
  Table of suggested differences 112
Arabic expansion 2, 3
Arabic grammars 6
Arabic inscriptions 20, 21
Aramaic substrate influence 244–5
Assimilation; see al-idgham al-kabiyr
Axfaa (xafiyy, xafaaʔ etc.) "hide, be transparent" 210–11, 211 n. 14, 242
Case endings 60, 72, 76, 79–118
  And object suffix pronouns 234
  And pausal forms 96–101
  Arguments against changing into epenthetic vowels 235–6, 256–8
  Caseless Nabataean Arabic 87
  Case epenthesis 92–3, 97–8
  Case traces 102–6
  Case variation in Sibawaih 87–96
  Case vs. caseless Arabic 114–8
  Coexistence of case and caseless varieties 117–8, 136, 233 n. 2
  Genitive variation 95
  In Cushitic 81–3
  In Semitic 83–5
  Lack of case traces 238, 253, 255–9
  Mixture of lexical and morpho-syntactic terminology 89–90
  Model development of 115
  Nominative, accusative, genitive 83, 104
  Nominative/accusative variation in topic position 91–7
  Stylistic, sociolinguistic, dialectal variation

Vs. assimilation 122
  See also functional yield
Classical Arabic 77, 80, 114–8, 206, 265
  As substitute for language history 9, 10
  Characterized 5
Comment (*xabar*) 91
Comparative method 9, 21–3, 28
  And cultural history 14, 15
  And language complexity 24–7
  And logical matrix 37
  Birkeland and object pronoun reconstruction 259–65
  Development in nineteenth century 34–5
  Future issues 267–9
  Illustrated 13
  Illustrated with reconstruction of imperfect verb 184–96
  In Hebrew tradition 35 n. 2
  Opposed to concepts of Old Arabic, Neo Arabic 47–74, 166–8
  Reconstruction and *imala* 220–8
  Reconstruction and suffix pronouns 230–65
  Status of minority forms 172–3
  Vs. contact 14
  the Arabic tradition 75–7
  see also object suffixes, short high vowels, stages in Arabic, statistical comparison of dialects, syllable structure
Creoles 16, 17, 23–4

Dialect, Arabic 80
  Characterized 5, 11
  Emerging information about 70–1
  Differences quantified 151–7

Holistic entity vs. individual
features 111–3
Homogeneity hypotheses 169–71
In Old Arabic-Neo Arabic
dichotomy 43–7
Inventory and summary of
dialects 271–5
Inventory of dialect features 276–80
Importance for Arabic history 8
Old Arabic dialects 11, 12, 27 n. 19,
69 n. 38
Need to reconstruct individual
histories 268
Reification of 137
Sociolinguistic status of 12
Types of dialects, pace
Kiparsky 189–90
See also short high vowels, stages in
Arabic; linker–n
Dialectology vs. historical linguistics 137
Drift 165 n. 17
Dual 71–2

Educated spoken Arabic 5
Emphasis (phonological) 25,
175–6, 200
Epenthesis 107–11, 175, 193–4
And extended sonority hierarchy 187
And sonority 109, 185, 191
And vowel deletion 188–90
As origin of 3MSG suffix 255
Blocked by stem constraint 194
Case vowels interpreted as epenthetic
vowels 235–6
Guttural 109, 185, 192
In 2FSG and 2MSG object suffix 247,
252–3
In Old Arabic 194–5
Linear 107, 184–5, 190–1, 237
Linear epenthesis in Najdi
Arabic 110
Mitchell's analysis 184–5
Simplification of representation 185

European attitude towards Arabic
linguistic tradition in 19th
century 35 n. 1

Fatħa, Damma, Kasra 89–90
Functional yield 86–7

Gahawa syndrome 25, 37, 46,
254–5, 277
Ghain [γ] reflex 165–6
Gilit and *qultu* dialects,
Mesopotamian 144

High vs. low vowels 58, 60, 100, 186
Deletion of high vowels 100; *see also*
short high vowels
Preformative vowel of verb 70
Holistic Arabic 34, 40–3, 77

al-idgham al-kabiyr, "major
assimilation" 119–36
as nominal declension 134–5
interpreted as inherently
vowelless 133–6
linear interpretation 129–34
major vs. minor 124–5
phonological attributes 125–9

imala 197–229
[ie] as basis of proto-form 199–201,
223
In the classical tradition 197–212
and pre-diasporic Arabic 162–4
as falling diphthong 199–201
characterized 197
conditioning factors 202–5
exceptional imala 209
in Koranic reading traditions 199
in Zamaxshari 281–2, 210 n. 13
Levin's distributional summary 202
medial variant (*bayna bayna*) 201,
223
of ʔalif maqṣuwra 97, 200

imala (*cont.*):
  of short /a/ 209–12
  phonetics and phonology
    of 197–206
    phonetic inhibiting factors 200–1
    phonetic quality of 198–201
    phonological variationist
      account 206–9
    Sibawaih vs. Zamaxshari 198–9
    Sociolinguistic variation 207–9
    type of assimilation 197
  In European tradition 228–9
  In modern dialects 212–20
    Allophonic and lexical 212, 218
    Andalusia 213
    And stress 215–6
    Eastern Libya 213–5
    Malta 215–7
    Mesopotamia 217–9
    Southern Mesopotamia, *imala*-
      like 219–220, 224
  Reconstruction and Sibawaih 226–8
  Reconstruction based on
    dialects 220–8
    Individual dialect regions 220–2
    Synthesis 222–6
Imperfect verb 140, 158
  And reconstruction 184–96
  Chronology of stem changes 190
  Mode endings 195–6
  See also sonority, epenthesis
ʔiʃbaaʕ "satiating, filling up" 232
ʔiʃmaam "rounding, fronting" 22, 133, 210–12
Internal passive 113, 158
Intrusive *-in* in active participle 160
Ixtilaas "furtiveness, short, centralized pronunciation of short high vowel" 60–1, 68 n. 37, 233, 260

/k/~ /c/variation 245, 250
Koine Arabic 8, 45, 58, 62

mushaf, Koranic text 120
Koranic reading tradition (Qiraaʔaat) 3, 6, 119–36
  10er version of al-Jazariy 123–5
  Imala 163, 199, 201
  Object pronouns 260–1, 264
  Summary of linguistic attributes 124
  Without cases 120
Koranic Arabic 7 n. 2, 58

Language transmission 15–19
  Inheritance and independent
    change 148–51
Linguists as spirits 269
Linker *-n* 102, 104–6, 158
  In various dialects 103–6
  Lack of correlation with other
    features 116 n. 40
  Opposed to case endings 103–6
  Reconstructed in pre-diasporic
    Arabic 105
Logical matrix 37
  Modern logical matrix 74–5

Mass comparison, morphology and
    phonology 138–9
  Features used in comparison
    276–80
  Statistical treatment 151–7
Mergers and near mergers 225
Mesopotamian dialect regions 144–5, 274
  And Imala 163–4, 217–20
  Compared to Western Sudanic Arabic,
    Uzbekistan Arabic,
    Shukriyya 151–7
  Innovations in 243
  Internal differentiation 154–5
Middle Arabic (Mittelarabisch)
  41, 46–7
Migration and dialect spread 156
Morphological differences
    quantified 151–7, 171,

Nabataea 20
Nunation (*tanwiyn*) 90; *see also* linker –*n*

Object suffixes 18, 106, 237–65; *see also* pausal forms
　Birkeland's reconstructions criticized 259–65
　In proto-Semitic 264–5
　Lack of evidence for case traces 255–9
　Loss of /h/ 241–3
　Reconstructions 239–55
　　1SG 239–40
　　1PL 240
　　2FPL 245–6
　　2FSG 246–50, 262–3
　　2MPL 246, 259, 261
　　2MSG 250–3, 263–4
　　3FPL 74, 240, 245, 261–2
　　3FSG 243–4, 259
　　3MPL 244, 259, 260
　　3MSG 253–5, 259–60
　Summary of dialect forms 283–4
Old Arabic (Altarabisch) and Neo-Arabic (Neuarabisch) 1, 2, 27, 37, 42–3, 69, 77–8, 80, *see also* Dialect, Arabic
　And analytic vs. synthetic distinction 113
　And dialects 43–7
　Continuity in Arabic 266–7
　Critical review of 47–74
　Early sources 6–8
　Epigraphic 4 n. 1
　Non-unitary character of Old Arabic 67–70
　Old Arabic characterized 4
　Old Arabic and pre-Islamic inscriptions 6

Pausal forms 22, 23, 85, 96–101
　And epenthesis 107–111
　Influence of foreign language learners 100
　Pausal position in text sample 99–100
　Problem for object pronoun reconstruction 261–3
　Terminology 232 n. 1
　Three types 231–4
Peripheral dialects 29
Person markers, pronouns 18, 80, 92, 158, 174, 177, *see also* object suffixes
Phonological differences
　quantified 151–7, 171
Pidginization of Arabic 23, 44–6
Pre-classical Arabic 39, 68
Pre-Diasporic Arabic 105, 137–83, 166–8, 266–7
　Characterized 2–4
　Derived via statistical comparison of dialects 155
　/h/deletion 243–4
　Reconstructed for intrusive –*in* on active participal 162
　Significance of *imala* 162–4
Pre-formative vowel of imperfect verb 69–70, 255
Proto-Arabic 2, 80
　And case endings 115
Proto Neo-Arabic 73

rawm "labialization" 22, 133
Reconstruction, general 3, 4
Roots 66
Rural vs. urban Arabic 27

Segolates and epenthesis 110
Short high vowels 51–67
　Elision of 131, 133, 188
　In old didactic manuals 61–63
　In lexicographical tradition 63–7
　In modern dialects 52–7
　In Nigerian Arabic 53–7

Short high vowels (*cont.*):
  In Old Arabic sources 57–67
  In Sibawaih and Farraʔ 59–61
  Non-contrastiveness in Classical Arabic 57–9, 132–3, 233
Shukriyya Arabic 146; *see also* Mesopotamian dialect regions
Social identities of speakers in *imala*, noun modifiers 207–9
Sonority 98
  In Nigerian Arabic 191
  Sonority hierarchy among consonants 186–9
Stages in Arabic 38–43
  Literary Arabic 38–40
  Old, Middle, New 40–3
Statistical comparison of dialects 142–59
  And hypothesis testing 168–71
  And innovations 172
  Coding problems 173–83
  Index of linguistic features used 276–80
  Of 2FSG object suffix 249 n. 11
Structural logic in Sibawaih 95
Syllable structure 48–50, 67–70, 237
  Final vowel length 104 n. 27
  Consonantal sequences 107–8
  Of 2FSG suffix –*ki* 248–9
  Sonority factors 109–10
  Syllable sequences 67–8, 130

Taxfiyf "weakening, lack of distinctive vowel quality" 128
Tamṭiyt "pulling, lengthening" 232
Topic (*mubtadaʔ*) 91, 93

Uzbekistan Arabic 146, 275; *see also* Mesopotamian dialect regions
  And 2MSG reconstruction 251–2
  And *imala* 163–4
  Compared to Mesopotamian, WSA, Shukriyya 157–9

Variation 179–81
  In /h/ deletion from pronouns 241–2
  In short vowels, dialects 52–7
  /k/ ~ /c/ 245
  Number of variants 181–2
  Of imala 206–9, 227
  Short vowels in Old Arabic sources 59–67
Verb paradigms 29, 74
Vowel deletion *see* epenthesis, short high vowels

waṣl 'connected speech' 99, 230
waqf 'pausal form' 230
Western Sudanic dialect region 145–6, 271; *see also* Mesopotamian dialect regions
  h-deletion quantified 241–2
  Innovations in 13, 164–5

Index of Personal Names

Abdel-Jawad 225, 245
Abu Amr/Abu ʿAmr/Abu ʕAmr Ibn
    ʕAlaaʔ 61, 120–2, 124–6, 128–34,
    163, 199
Abu Haidar 144
Abu Hanifa 65
Abu Jaʿfar 124
Abu ʔIsħaaq 208
Agha 156
Al-ʔAħmar 89
Al-ʔAʕmash 40, 260
Al-Anbari 1
Alcala de 213
Alhawary 281
Al-Kalbi 90
Al-Maliki 120
Al-Nassir 75
Al-Yazidi 128
Amara 28
Ambros 216–17, 228
Antilla 79
Aquilina 215–17, 224, 228
Arnold 274
ʿAṣim/ʕAaṣim/Aṣim 40, 124, 260
Asmaʕi 8
ʔAxfash 76
Azhari 64
Azzopardi-Alexander 216–17, 219,
    228, 246

Baalbaki 88–9, 93, 116
Banu Hassan 15 see also Beneesan
Banu Maʕqil 272
Barth 161
Barthold 146
Bazzar 124
Beck 122

Behnstedt 26, 28, 48, 52, 67, 70, 102,
    108–9, 117, 157–8, 165, 173, 177, 182,
    238–9, 244, 248, 250
Bell 134
Bellamy 6, 8, 20–1
Belnap 27
Beneesan see Banu Hassan
Birkeland 21–3, 71, 96, 106, 231, 233,
    235–6, 247, 256, 259, 261, 263–4
Blachère 8, 14
Blanc, Haim 97, 108, 144, 212, 218–19, 274
Blau, Joshua 46–7, 80, 86–7, 96, 100, 102,
    104, 106–7, 110–3, 167
Bohas 76
Borg 216–19, 228, 246, 273
Brockelmann 8, 11, 23, 43–4, 58, 62, 73,
    77, 96, 167, 244, 256, 259
Brugmann 34

Cantineau 201, 213, 235–6, 256–7
Caskel 275
Carbou 71, 106
Carter 88, 92, 204, 208, 281
Castellino 81
Caubet 49, 51
Chaudenson 17
Chouémi 58
Clements 187
Cohen 47
Corriente 5, 85–7, 100, 102, 104, 106, 109,
    114, 201, 213, 228, 233
Cuvalay 112

Dabbaʕ/Al-Dabbaaʕ 123–6, 129–30
Dani 199
Dereli 146
Diakonoff 81

Diem 86–7, 96, 104, 114–5, 117, 244
Ditters 88
Donner 14
Doss 46
Duri 125
Durie 14
Dussaud 20

Ehret 16
Eksell 113
El-Gibali 44

Farraʔ 5, 7, 11, 38, 40, 59, 61–3, 65–6, 70, 89–90, 135, 260, 269, 281
Farrukhi/Al-Farruxi 62
Ferguson 9, 24–5, 27, 45–7
Ferrando 102, 221, 273
Fischer, A. 259
Fischer, W. 11, 17, 29, 39–41, 43, 46–8, 50–2, 57, 67, 69–74, 77, 80, 85, 102, 107, 111, 146, 259
Fleisch 96, 198, 227, 229
Fleischer 34, 38, 40–3, 45–6, 77
Fournier 145
Fück 8–9, 23, 44–5, 62, 80

Gee 27
Gordon 83
Greenberg 14
Grünert 198–9
Guillaume 76
Guillot 70, 122
Guthrie 14

Hamza 124–5
Harrison 35
Hasselbach 264
Haywood 63
Heath 51
Hecker 35
Hetzron 79, 82, 106, 150, 171
Holes 17, 29, 68, 104, 160, 165, 245, 249

Ibn Al-Muqaffaʕ 38
Ibn Al-Nadim 168
Ibn Al-Sarraj 1, 88
Ibn Jinni 1, 281
Ibn Kathir 124, 260
Ibn Manḏur 58, 63, 65
Ibn Mujahid/Mujahid 6, 38, 59, 61, 120, 122–6, 128–9, 132–3, 163, 199, 201, 211, 223, 260
Ibn Muslim 156
Ibn Yaʕish 88
Ibn 'Amir/Ibn ʕAamir 124, 163, 260
Imr Al-Qays 231
Ingham 49, 102, 105, 108–10, 144, 220, 225, 247
Isserlin 217, 228
ʕIysaa 209

Jahiḏ 44–5
Jankowsky 34
Jastrow 47–8, 50–2, 57, 67, 69–72, 77, 107, 111, 144, 146, 158–9, 162–4, 167, 170, 179, 182, 198, 218–9, 228, 241, 277
Jawhari 64
Jazari/Ibn Al-Jazariy 6, 122–4, 126, 129–30, 133
Johnstone 245
Jong de 14, 192, 239, 272–3

Kahle 120, 134
Kaufman 15–16, 137
Kaye 71
Khan 90, 144, 180–1, 217, 274
Kiparsky 185, 189–90
Kisaʔi 58, 63–4, 121, 124–5, 133, 163, 199
Kofler 58
Koop 35
Kusters 268

Labov 225
Landberg de 161
Larcher 6–7, 21, 47, 62, 70, 76, 122
Lethem 71

Levin 91, 112, 198, 202, 205, 217, 228
Lewis 156

Macdonald 275
Mahdi 9, 46
Mahra 123
Malaika 144
Marçais 51, 246
Matisoff 16
May 221
Miller 28
Mitchell 5, 52, 184, 214, 225, 254
Molan 62
Moscati 10, 79, 83–5, 105
Mubarrad 282
Murray 187

Nafiʿ 124
Nassir 198
Nöldeke 39–40, 68, 96, 120–2, 129, 230

Osthoff 34
Owens 11, 14, 17–18, 28, 44, 51, 57, 75–6, 89, 94, 102, 105–6, 112, 117, 143, 145–7, 157, 170, 180, 184–5, 189, 204, 214, 225, 278

Pellat 62
Petrácek 84–5, 275
Pommerol 143
Prochazka, S. 113, 218, 274
Prochazka, T. 74, 173, 191, 193
Puin 6

Quṭrub 58, 61–3, 134–5

Rabin 5, 12, 84–5, 87, 118
Reckendorf 259
Reichmuth 52, 102, 105–6, 108, 146–7
Renfrew 16
Retsö 3, 14, 72, 112, 114, 161, 168, 275
Rosenhouse 108
Ross 14

Rössler 81
Roth/Roth-Laly 145, 241

Saeed 83
Sakkaki 1
Sarraj 11
Sasse 49, 81–3, 144, 182, 218–19, 277
Schaade 198
Schabert 217
Schleicher 34
Seeger 160, 275
Shafiʕi 269
Sibawaih 3, 5–8, 11, 21–3, 31, 38–9, 58–61, 63, 67–8, 74–5, 80, 86–100, 102, 105, 107, 109, 111–12, 115–16, 118, 121, 125, 130–3, 135, 163, 171, 174–5, 192, 194–5, 197–215, 217, 220, 222–4, 226–9, 231–3, 242, 244, 250, 253, 258, 260–3, 281–2
Singer 246
Smart 44
Soden von 85, 110
Spitaler 9, 114
Suleimann 75
Susi 125
Suyuṭi 7, 75–6
Swadesh 16

Taine-Cheikh 272
Talay 144, 180–82
Talmon 89, 199, 209
Talmoudi 246
Thomason 15–16, 45, 137
Tosco 81–3
Tourneux 145
Trimingham 71
Troupeau 211

Vanhove 216–17
Vennemann 187
Versteegh 17, 23, 28, 46–7, 70, 76, 89–90, 112, 135, 146

Voigt 81
Vollers 62, 77, 114, 119–22, 135–6, 265

Wallin 41–2
Wansbrough 119, 134
Wehr 210
Wellens 23
Weninger 110
Werbeck 48
Wilkinson 275
Woidich 28, 48, 108–9, 173, 182, 239
Wright 64

Xalil 208, 209, 242

Ya'qub 124
Yunus 209

Zaborski 114
Zamaxshari 198–9, 281–2
Zeltner 145
Zimmermann 52, 146, 251–2
Zwettler 8, 120, 233

Index of Arabic dialect names, languages and language families

Aajiri 276–7, 280
Aazex 139, 219, 241, 252–3, 274, 283
Abbeche Arabic 141, 145, 148, 150, 176–7, 179, 182, 241, 271, 276–80
Abu Dhabi 254
Afghanistan Arabic 102, 105, 106
Afroasiatic 72, 79–80, 83–5, 101, 115, 118
ʔAhl Al-ḥijaz 208
Ajarma 240, 273, 284
Akkadian 10, 30, 83–5, 110, 114, 150
Alawite 283
Alawite Turkey 248, 274
Algerian 220
Al-Mudawwar 139, 240–1, 243, 275, 284
Al-Nadhir 240 see also An-Nadhiir
Anatolian 18, 217
Anatolian Qiltu 278
Anatolian Qultu 144, 154–5, 170–1, 179, 218
ʕAnaza Dialect 236, 257
Ancient West Arabian 12
Andalusian Arabic 31, 163, 213, 221, 223
An-Nadhiir 139, 275, 284; see also Al-Nadhir
Arabian Peninsular Dialects 18, 41, 160, 190, 258
ʕArabiya 23
Arabkhona 52
Aramaic 83, 86, 110, 244, 273
Asiatic Arabic 28
As-Suwwadiyya 139, 240, 245, 250, 275, 284
Awngi 82

Bagirmi Arabic 145, 159–61, 170, 172, 177, 182, 240, 243–5, 247, 271, 276, 279

Bahariyya Arabic 48–50, 139, 190, 243, 248, 252, 254–5, 272
Bantu 14
Banu Assad 263
Baskinta 139, 248, 273
Bdul Dialect 139, 239–40, 246, 248, 273, 284
Benghazi Arabic 215, 225
Berber 80, 101

Cairene Arabic 13, 17–18, 24, 26, 108, 149, 160, 235, 247, 253, 272
Cameroonian Arabic 145
Central Cushitic 82
Central Morocco 49–50
Chadian Arabic 28, 106, 108–9, 112, 145, 148, 151, 239, 279
Chadic 80–1
Christian Baghdadi 144, 147, 149, 170, 218–19, 224, 241, 274, 276–7, 279–80, 283
Cilician Arabic 113, 218
Classical Arabic 5, 8, 9–12, 20, 23–5, 32, 39–43, 45, 47, 57, 68, 70–3, 80, 84–6, 90, 96, 98–100, 102, 104–7, 109–16, 119, 131, 134, 163, 167, 174, 190, 194–6, 206, 230, 233, 235, 238, 255–6, 260, 262, 264–5, 281, 284
Creole 13, 16–7, 23, 28
Cushitic 80–3
Cypriot Arabic 218–19, 241, 248, 252, 254, 273–4, 283

Daaxila 182
Damascene Arabic 48, 69

Daragözü 139, 144, 149, 182, 241, 252, 274, 276–80, 283; see also Kozluk Group
Djeinau 52
Djidjelli 17, 51, 246

East African Nubi 23–4
Eastern Arabian 245
Eastern Arabic 60
Eastern Libyan Arabic 52, 66, 107–11, 139, 160, 163, 184, 190–4, 201–2, 212–16, 219–21, 223–4, 229, 254–5, 257, 272
Eblaitic 84
Egyptian Arabic 26, 28, 81, 106, 109, 147, 185
English 151
Ethiopic Semitic Languages 84, 150

Faarisi 64
Fulfulde 19
Fushaa 11

Galilee 108, 139, 273
German 198
Germanic 36
Gəʕəz 84, 101, 110, 115
Ghaamid 74
Gharyan 139, 272
Gilit/Gələt, Qultu dialects 49, 109, 144–5, 147, 149–50, 154–5, 158–9, 162–64, 170–1, 181–2, 219–20, 223, 248, 250, 252–3, 274, 278, 280, 282
   Baghdad Qultu 154–5, 280
   Euphrates Qultu 144
   Iraqi Gilit 164, 192
   Iraqi Qultu 13, 164, 167, 171, 180
   Kurdistan Qultu 144
   Mesopotamian Gilit 149, 154, 254
   Mesopotamian Qultu 154, 162–4, 177, 212, 223–4, 228, 242, 248
   Non-Baghdadi Qultu Dialects 154–5, 280
   Northern Iraqi Qultu 170
   Tigris Qultu 144
Gozitan 217
Gulf Dialects 182
Gulf Pidgin Arabic 44

Hatay 139
Hebrew 83, 110, 115
Highland East Cushitic 82
Highland Yemeni 48–9, 67, 109, 111
Hiit 139, 144, 151, 178, 181, 217, 276–80
Hijazi Arabic 67, 109, 136, 190, 193, 207
Hofuf 18, 139, 240, 243, 250, 254, 275, 284
Holistic Arabic 34, 38, 40–1, 77
Horan 50, 108

Icelandic 36
Indo-European 34–5, 79
Iraqi 29, 108–9, 185
Israeli 245

Jewish Baghdadi 97, 144, 149, 170, 175, 178, 218–19, 223, 241, 274, 276–7, 283
Jewish Hiit 274
Jewish Middle Arabic 106
Jogari 52, 139, 275
Jordanian 225, 245

Khaweetna 139, 144, 178, 180–2, 274, 277–80
Khorasan Arabic 139, 237, 240, 243, 254, 275
Kirenawa 276–80
Koine 47, 171; see also poetic koine
Koranic Arabic 58
Kozluk Group 144; see also Daragözü

Levantine Arabic 48
Lingua Franca 17
Literary Arabic 38

Mada 280
Maltese 17–18, 139, 163, 201, 215–17, 219, 221–4, 226, 228–9, 273, 283
Mardin 49–50, 139, 144, 149, 175, 182, 218–19, 241, 243, 252–3, 274, 276–80, 283
Mauritanian Arabic 165
Maʕlula Aramaic 244
Mesopotamian 31, 140, 152–9, 164, 166, 169, 171, 175–7, 179, 212, 219, 221–3, 228, 241–2, 274–5
Middle Arabic 7–8, 41, 46–7, 87, 111, 115
Middle Egyptian 36
Middle English 36
Modern English 36
Modern Hebrew 150
Modern Standard Arabic 5, 9
Morrocan Arabic 51, 220
Morrocan Koine 51
Muslim Baghdadi 144, 147, 151, 224, 274, 276–80, 283

Nabataean Arabic 20, 87
Najdi Arabic 13, 41–2, 48–9, 60, 102, 105–6, 108–11, 113, 136, 139, 192–4, 220, 240, 248, 250, 254, 271, 275, 283
Neo-Arabic 2, 20, 24, 27, 30–2, 34, 37–8, 41–8, 50–2, 69–74, 77–8, 86, 107, 111–13, 156–7, 167, 185, 190, 257, 268
New Arabic 2, 23, 47, 78, 111, 113, 268; see also Neo-Arabic
New Egyptian 36
Nigerian Arabic 13, 17–19, 25–6, 29–30, 51, 53, 55–7, 59, 63–7, 103–5, 107–9, 111, 113, 145, 149–50, 157–9, 171, 176, 179–81, 184–5, 187, 189–96, 205, 239, 241–2, 258, 261, 267, 279
Non-Bagirmi Western Sudanic Arabic 150, 160
North African 17–18, 28, 49, 51, 185, 190, 192–3, 226, 253

Northeast Arabian Dialects 252–3
Northeastern Arabian Peninsular Dialects 247
Northern Arabian Dialects 249, 275
Northern Mesopotamian 273
Northern Rural Palestinian 245
Northern Sinaitic Littoral 185

Old Arabic 2, 4–6, 11–12, 14–15, 20, 22–4, 26–7, 30–2, 34, 37–8, 41–8, 50–3, 57, 59, 61, 63, 66–74, 77–8, 80, 86–7, 89, 97, 103–4, 107, 111–13, 115, 118–19, 129, 133, 135–6, 159, 161, 163, 167, 184, 192, 194–5, 197, 228–9, 231–2, 238, 252, 257, 259, 262, 264–8, 282
Old Egyptian 36
Old English 36
Old Semitic 114
Oman Arabic 50, 240, 250
Oromo 81–2

Palestinian 245
Peninsular Dialects 248, 250
Persian 65
Persian Gulf Dialects 173
Phoenecian 83
Pidgin Arabic 13
Poetic Arabic 21
Poetic Koine 2, 73; see also Koine
Post-Classical Arabic 41, 43, 46–7
Post-Diasporic Arabic 31, 137
Post-Old Arabic 226, 230
Pre-Classical Arabic 39–40, 68
Pre-Classical Literary Arabic 40
Pre-Diasporic Arabic 2–4, 14, 24, 29, 31–2, 69, 105, 114, 137, 139–40, 161–7, 169, 223, 238, 240, 242–3, 245, 255, 257, 266–7
Pre-Islamic Koine 32; see also poetic koine and Pre-Islamic Poetry
Pre-Islamic Old Arabic 111
Pre-Islamic Poetry 20, 38

316 Index of Arabic dialect names

Pre-Western Sudanic Arabic 149
Proto-Afroasiatic 114
Proto-Arabic 2, 4–5, 10, 14, 19, 31, 72, 77,
  80, 85, 87, 101, 111, 113–16, 118, 129,
  135, 151, 159, 165, 167–8, 223,
  238–40, 267–8
Proto-Cushitic 81
Proto-Neo-Arabic 2, 73–4
Proto-Nigerian Arabic 190
Proto-Peripheral Arabic 2
Proto-Semitic 72, 80, 83–4, 105, 110,
  114–15, 264–5, 267
Proto-Southern Hijazi 190
Proto-Yemeni 190

Qauz 139, 248, 275, 284
Qaysi 200–1, 208

Rwala 110, 240, 247, 250, 254–5, 275, 283

Saharan Dialect 51
SanSaaʔ 250, 254, 275, 284
Saudi Arabian 42
Saudi Arabian Tihama 74
Semitic 10, 30, 35, 43–4, 72, 79–85, 100–1,
  105, 110–11, 115, 118, 150, 264–5, 267
Shaṭṭ Al-Arab 278
Shukriyya Arabic 31, 52, 66, 102, 105, 108,
  141, 143, 146–7, 152–5, 161, 165–6,
  171, 179, 183, 185, 240, 244, 248,
  272, 280
Sidamo 82
Siirt 139, 144, 149, 179, 274, 276, 279–80
Sinai Dialects 192, 239
Somali 82
Soukhne 18, 139, 244–6, 250, 273, 283
South Arabian Languages 84, 275
Southern Borno Arabic 278
Southern Hijazi Dialects 190, 193–6
Southern Jordanian 192
Southern Mesopotamian (Dialects) 144,
  165, 224–5, 229, 245, 278, 280

Spanish Arabic 102, 104–5, 109, 111, 213,
  228
Standard Arabic 5, 12, 20–1, 24–5, 38,
  46–7, 74–5, 165, 171, 174–7, 239,
  241, 245–6, 263, 276
Standard Classical Arabic 39
Standard Maltese 217, 223
Sudanic Arabic Dialects 71, 102, 105, 108,
  161, 166
Susa 17–9, 246
Syrian Arabic 185, 245

Tamimi 60, 98–9, 207–8, 263
Teerib 139, 241, 273, 283
Tihama 149, 245
Tihama Yemeni 26, 50, 102, 104, 106, 109,
  111, 117
Tripolitanian 139, 173, 182
Tunisian 17, 220

Ugaritic 83–4
Upper Egypt Dialect 146
Urban Baghdadi 109, 111
Urban Neo-Arabic 42
Ur-Semitic 110
Uzbekistan Arabic 31, 50, 52, 102, 106,
  109, 142–4, 146–7, 149–50, 152–5,
  157–67, 169, 171–2, 175–6, 182, 243,
  248, 251–2, 267, 275, 280

Vulgar Arabic 265

Western Arabic 28
Western Libyan Arabic 26
Western Nigerian Arabic 271
Western Sudanic Arabic 13, 31, 48–50,
  108, 140, 145–50, 152–7, 159–60,
  164–6, 169–73, 175–6, 181, 191–2,
  234, 239, 241–3, 245–8, 254, 261,
  271, 280

Yemeni 109, 117, 190, 194, 244